THE MEN WHO LED UNITED

BY SIMON WADSWORTH

THE

CAPTAINS

CLUB

Sport Media

Sport Media

Copyright text: Simon Wadsworth

Produced by Sport Media, Trinity Mirror North West.
Executive Editor: Ken Rogers. Senior Editor: Steve Hanrahan
Editor: Paul Dove. Senior Art Editor: Rick Cooke
Production Journalist: James Cleary
Cover Design: James Kenyon

Published in Great Britain in 2011.
Published by: Trinity Mirror Sport Media.

ISBN: 9781906802752

Contents

Acknowledgements

Special thanks to Eamonn O'Neal for his constant support and advice; without him this book would never have been written.

Thanks to the club captains of Manchester United and in particular Willie Morgan and Martin Buchan, who generously offered their time and willingly shared their fabulous stories. Everyone's favourite 'Uncle' Wilf McGuinness, the nicest man in football, Brian Hughes, the best storyteller you will ever meet, Tommy Docherty and Jimmy Wagg for their advice and contacts.

Thanks to Tom Clare, who is the font of all knowledge when it comes to the Babes and who has been there for me all the way through, offering his help from across the pond. Stuart Matheson of the *Manchester Evening News*. Damien Keane of St Josephs and all the kind people of Cork who are so proud of their connections to Manchester United through the captains they have produced.

I must also mention Dave and Elaine Noar, Margaret Tullett, Jeff Lees, Pete Upton, Bernie White née O'Brien, Jim McSorley and John Hegarty for all their encouragement. My father-in-law Brian Burns; between us we have seen every player who ever played for the club since the war and we have never agreed on one! Mark Newsome, for all those great years following United.

Kieran, Ollic and the boys, who are now carrying the torch.

Thanks to Sir Alex for his best wishes with the book.

Finally to my girls Amanda, Georgia and Isobel who are love, life and happiness.

Simon Wadsworth

Introduction

It is hard to believe when you look at the global phenomenon that is Manchester United, that until the appointment of Matt Busby they were a mediocre team, spending periods in the First and Second Division. Formed in 1878 as Newton Heath LYR Football Club by railway workers from the Lancashire and Yorkshire Railway depot at Newton Heath, they wore the colours of the railway company – green and gold.

In January 1902, with debts of £2,670, the club was served with a winding up order. Fortunately four local businessmen, including local brewer John Henry Davies (who became club president), invested £500 each to save the club. Davies changed the club's colours from green and gold to red and white, and decided to hold a public meeting to determine a new name for the club. Manchester Celtic and Manchester Central were rejected for sounding too Scottish and too industrial but a man called Louis Rocca, who would go on to play a big part in the history of the club, suggested the name Manchester United.

Under the management of Ernest Magnall, the team won the First Division in 1908 and the following year the FA Cup. The chairman Mr Davies decided that their Bank Street ground in Clayton, where Manchester United played their home fixtures, was not fit for his team and so donated funds to have a new venue built. Davies looked around Manchester before buying a patch of land just off the north end of the Warwick Road in Old Trafford. With a new stadium, United won the First Division for the second time in 1911 – but the following season Magnall left to join Manchester City.

In 1921/22, three seasons after the resumption of football following World War I, the club was relegated to the Second Division. Promoted in 1925 and then relegated again in 1931, United became a yo-yo club that again found itself in financial difficulties. A proud Mancunian named James Gibson, who had made his money manufacturing army uniforms, stepped in and invested £2,000 in the club. One of the legacies of the Gibson administration would be the Manchester United Junior Athletic Club (MUJAC), set up at the behest of the supporters.

The MUJAC was charged with bringing the best young players in the local area to Manchester United, with the aim of eventually filling the first team with local talent. Rocca was appointed as the MUJAC's chief scout and, through his connections to the Manchester Catholic Sportsman's Club, he appointed a network of scouts.

Rocca's scouting system is best known for discovering Johnny Carey and Stan Pearson, demonstrating the breadth of the club's scouting network. Pearson was a local boy from Salford whereas Carey was discovered in Dublin. However, Rocca's most important signing was one that would change the club forever. It came at the end of the Second World War, when Manchester United were in desperate need of a manager. Rocca knew just the man.

Matt Busby served as a football coach in the Army Physical Training Corps, forging opinions about how football should be played and governed. He had been offered the job as assistant-manager at Liverpool but as soon as he received a letter from Rocca offering him the job of Manchester United manager, he knew that he had found the opportunity to put his dreams into reality.

Busby insisted that he should be directly involved in training, picking the team on matchdays and choosing the players to be bought and sold – without interference from the directors. Such a level of control was unprecedented in the English game, but the United chairman was in no position to argue. Busby was originally offered a three-year contract, but managed to secure himself a five-year deal after explaining that it would take at least that long for his revolution to have a tangible effect.

Busby's first signing was without doubt his greatest. Whilst in the army, he heard a man called Jimmy Murphy give a speech about football to some squaddies. Impressed by the Welshman's oratory skills, Busby engaged him in conversation and offered him the job of assistant-manager at Manchester United, which Murphy accepted there and then.

In the first few years after Busby's appointment as manager, the

Manchester United team was almost entirely composed of players discovered by Rocca and his scouting system. In 1948, Rocca had the ultimate honour bestowed upon him as his protégés won the FA Cup. In the team that day, Crompton, Aston, Anderson, Morris, Pearson and Mitten had all come through the youth system.

Busby and Murphy revolutionised the way football was played in this country, introducing young players at an early age. The team earned the nickname "The Busby Babes" and won admirers all over the country with their cavalier style of football. On 6th February 1958 the team, journalists and some supporters were returning home from a European game against Red Star Belgrade. The plane on which they were travelling stopped at Munich to re-fuel as a non-stop trip from Belgrade to Manchester was beyond the plane's capacity.

It was snowing and icy in Munich, and the plane struggled to take off. It had already made two failed attempts when, on the third, it ploughed through a fence past the end of the runway, before the port wing hit a nearby house and was torn off. Twenty of the 44 people on board the aircraft died in the crash, eight of them being members of the team. Eight journalists also died, one of them being my Great Uncle Don Davies, who was a reporter for the *Manchester Guardian* under the pen name 'Old International'. The famous cricket reporter John Arlott, who was also at the newspaper, was originally meant to take Davies's spot on the trip to Belgrade, as 'Old International' was unavailable. However, Davies expressed a desire to attend the trip at the last moment, and he replaced Arlott. He was age 65 at the time of his death, and was the oldest victim of the tragedy.

Most clubs count themselves lucky to have had one truly great manager – United has been blessed with two. Sir Matt Busby built the club into the institution it has become, overcoming tragedy and delivering European glory. Sir Alex Ferguson has taken Busby's vision and crafted a team that has dominated English football for the last 20 years.

For both men, the choice of club captain from amongst the players has been a critical decision. A great club captain is a valuable lieutenant and an indispensible leader of men, both on and off the field. What was it that these great managers looked for in their captains? What characteristics did a player have to possess to make an impression upon Busby and Ferguson? Also, and perhaps more interestingly, how did the managers know it was time to let them go?

Club captains, like mighty warriors of old, straddle the decades surrounded by stories and folklore that tell of their greatness and heroic feats. They are a breed apart, showing the same passion we would, given the opportunity to wear the red shirt for just one game. Will any Manchester United supporter ever forget Roy Keane's inspirational performance against Juventus in the second leg of the Champions League semi-final in Turin? When, as captain, he inspirationally hauled his team back from two goals down to win 3-2 – even though an early booking meant he would take no part in the final. As Sir Alex said: "It was the most emphatic display of selflessness I have seen on a football field. Pounding over every blade of grass, competing as if he would rather die of exhaustion than lose, he inspired all around him. I felt it was an honour to be associated with such a player."

An enigmatic French club captain of ours once said that he didn't want to be a prisoner of his past and his memories, that he preferred to be free and look forward. How ironic that a man such as Cantona, who brought us all such unforgettable moments, should want to forget them. Or is this just a sign of the mentality that Sir Alex developed in his players, to always look to the future and the next game?

For supporters it is a different matter: we can savour famous victories and spend hours reminiscing about great players and great games we have seen. Manchester United fans have been spoilt for longer than anyone can remember. We've had those beautiful bouncing Busby Babes, the Holy Trinity of Best, Law and Charlton and The Doc's Red Devils, who brought a brand of free-flowing exciting football that those lucky enough to have witnessed will always remember with a smile. In the Eighties, which I sometimes hear described as the wilderness, we had Captain Marvel and "Scousebustin'" Norman Whiteside. Anybody who was there the night we beat Barcelona 3-0 in 1984 will tell you there has never been a better atmosphere at Old Trafford, before or since. More recently we have had Fergie's Fledglings, the magnificent treble-winning team and that glorious night in Moscow.

If you are a Manchester United supporter these games, these teams and players are engraved in your memory. The first time you visited Old Trafford, standing like some giant cathedral, and the religious experience of thousands of people coming together with one belief, and one voice. You will always remember the first night game that you attended, the electric atmosphere, the sounds and the smells that emanated from the ground and, more importantly, the friends who shared your passion. For me, it was Marc Newsome, who went with me to home and away games at a time when winning was never guaranteed and trophies were scarce; but it was enough just to be there and be United.

You may have just started supporting Manchester United or you might have been watching them for 60 years, but I hope this book brings back memories to some, and educates others. We have such a rich and glorious history, this book is a tribute to those special few, that band of brothers who will always be able to look back with pride and say I was Manchester United's club captain.

Foreword

For me, being captain of Manchester United was an honour, not an onus, and it is with great pleasure that I write the foreword to this history of United's club captains. I consider myself fortunate that I will always be identified with Tommy Docherty's Red Devils who, for three exhilarating years after the disaster of relegation, thrilled supporters up and down the country with our attacking style of play. It was certainly the most exciting team that I ever played in. We felt that we could give anyone a two-goal start at Old Trafford, and still beat them.

When I joined Manchester United on 29th February 1972, I had already captained Aberdeen as a 21-year-old in an unexpected 1970 Scottish Cup final victory over Celtic, the youngest player ever to lift that famous trophy.

United, European Cup winners only four years previously, were a team in turmoil and the unthinkable happened – we found ourselves playing in the Second Division in season 1974/75. Despite plenty of interest from former First Division rivals, I never had any intention of leaving as I felt, as one of the squad who took the team down, that it was my duty to help them back to the top flight.

We took the Second Division by storm, playing some of the most thrilling football ever seen in this country. On Saturday 26th April 1975 we beat Blackpool 4-0 at a packed Old Trafford. I was presented with the Second Division championship trophy, parading it around the stadium with my team-mates for all the fans to see. United were back where they belonged after just one season.

I had my share of disappointments as well whilst captaining the Red Devils. When we played Southampton in the 1976 FA Cup final we were strong favourites, and I felt that some of the lads underestimated our very experienced opponents. It was a very painful lesson for us all as we went up those famous Wembley steps to collect our losers' medals. We were so low and deflated until we got back to Manchester Town Hall and saw the many thousands of supporters who had gathered in the square to welcome us home. That was the day I realised just what it meant to be a Manchester United player and, more so, how much it meant to me to be captain of Manchester United. I stood next to Tommy Docherty as he promised everyone that we would be back next year as winners, and not one person who was there that day doubted him.

Almost a year to the day later, it was a dream come true as I led the team up the 39 steps as winners after we beat mighty Liverpool in the Silver Jubilee final. Sadly, the joy was short-lived as revelations concerning Tommy Docherty's private life became too much for certain members of the club's board, and they dispensed with his services. We will never know how that team would have developed had The Doc stayed. I like to think that with the confidence of a major trophy behind us we could have gone on to greater things.

I never considered myself a 'yes' man and always tried to lead by example. I must confess that I had my differences with The Doc from time to time, but those two years back in the First Division were really special, as I'm sure my team-mates will agree. I was also privileged to continue as captain for a further four years under Dave Sexton, Doc's successor. I look down the distinguished list of United captains over the years and treasure my place among them.

I hope you enjoy the book and wish Simon every success with it. I know the love he has for the club and the time he has spent researching all the club captains of Manchester United, in order to give you readers a true picture of the individuals who have led the greatest football club in the world into the Theatre of Dreams.

Martin Buchan
Club captain Manchester United, 1975-1982

Gentleman John

JOHNNY CAREY

1945-1953

'J Carey, the captain, has been a model footballer – technically efficient, thanks to hard work; a fighter to the last, without ever fighting. He is a sportsman, a steadier of the younger and inexperienced, an inspirer of the older and tiring, and the most modest of men, though he has won every football honour open to him'

To van driver John Carey and his wife Sarah a son, John Joseph Carey (known as Jackie when he was in Ireland – only turning to Johnny when he came to England) was born on Sunday 23rd February 1919 in Dublin, a city of mass of contradictions. A second city of the British Empire, Dublin was also the first city of nationalist Ireland and, within its boundaries, the divisions of class and culture were extraordinary. This was a city of genuine diversity, its many complexities defying easy explanations. Rich and poor, nationalist and unionist, Catholic, Protestant, immigrant, native and many more, all bound together.

Dublin had been through a decade of incredible change – the 1913 lockout, the 1916 rising. The period 1919 to 1921 was to see the War of Independence and the ensuing civil war. But not all changes were caused by local events. World War I saw thousands of Dubliners go off and fight on the Somme, Gallipoli and Flanders, many not returning. Those who did were transformed partly by their war experience, and partly by what had happened to Dublin while they'd been away.

John's first taste of football came when, as a schoolboy, he joined Home Farm FC. The side was formed in 1928, in the Drumcondra and Whitehall areas of Dublin. Mr Leo Fitzmaurice arranged a street soccer league for boys that lived in the Home Farm Road, Drumcondra Road,

Hollybank Road and Ormonde Road areas. The league became the basis upon which a Dublin football institution was established. Home Farm FC came about from an amalgamation of the Richmond Road and Home Farm Road teams. In those early days, the club played home matches on the rhubarb patch behind the current Skylon Hotel.

Carey lived in Baggot Street on the south side of Dublin, a long way from the Whitehall grounds on the north side. Johnny was always confident that joining Home Farm, despite the journey, was worth the trouble due to the excellent training and coaching the club provided. Even though the club was in its first decade of existence, it was organised and progressive in its development of football skills and character of eager youngsters entrusted to its care. In his first year at Home Farm at Under-16 level, Carey won the Leinster Juvenile Cup. Two years later, in 1936, the club went on to gain their first All-Ireland Trophy when Carey's team won the National Youth (Under-18) Cup. Before Carey left he had been converted into a right-sided defender, the position in which his subsequent career was crowned with so many honours and success – and in which he won the All-Ireland title with Home Farm.

Home Farm gained temporary access to a pitch at Griffith Avenue, which required levelling and had to be cleared of stones. An initial fundraising effort garnered 28 shillings, which was used to acquire a set of black and gold football jerseys. In the next season the club switched to the current colours of blue and white hoops, playing home matches at Albert College and St Mobhi Road in Glasnevin, Dublin 9.

Johnny was a natural sportsman at school in Westland Row, and he helped them win the Dublin Colleges final at Croke Park in 1935. In the same year Johnny also helped his local Gaelic football team, Paeder Mackens, to victory in the Dublin minor final against St Vincent's. His final exploit on the Gaelic field was to play for Dublin in the Leinster minor final, when Louth defeated them. Unfortunately for Johnny he came up against the Gaelic Athletic Association, an amateur organisation focused on promoting Gaelic games including the Irish sports of hurling and Gaelic football. Until 1971, rule 27 of the GAA constitution stated that a member of the GAA could be banned from playing its games if found to be playing, or attending matches of other sports such as soccer, rugby or cricket, which were in conflict with the interests of the GAA. So Johnny found himself banned from Croke Park and from playing Gaelic football, leaving him free to concentrate on soccer.

Dublin is synonymous with many things, and probably its most famous export is Guinness. The St James Gate Brewery was leased for 9,000 years in 1759 by Arthur Guinness for £45 a year, and has been the home of Guinness ever since. In 1902, as part of the Guinness Sports and Social Club, a football side was formed. Taking their name from the brewery they were christened St James's Gate FC. When the League of Ireland was formed in 1921 containing eight teams, all from Dublin, St James's Gate was one of the founder members – and first champions.

At 17, whilst still at school studying to be a civil servant, Johnny joined the club in the summer of 1936, once again playing in the inside-forward position. It was a role he would play for the next six years, until Matt Busby took over and converted him into a defender. Carey's career at St James's Gate was destined to be short lived, as destiny was just around the corner. Watching was a Manchester United scout by the name of Billy Behan. Behan had played for United, making a solitary appearance in a 2-1 victory against Bury in March 1933, but had returned to Ireland after failing to make his mark. Behan continued to scout for United though, through his connections to Louis Rocca, and would regularly call him to update him on players.

In November 1936 Rocca was in Dublin to run his eye over a player by the name of Benny Gaughan, who played for Bohemians. Rocca liked what he saw and discussed buying the player – but was told that a £200 under-the-counter payment would be required to guarantee the signing. Rocca was happy with this and said he would return the follow-ing week with the money. He duly came back, only to be told that Celtic had beaten him to the signing by paying £300 for Gaughan. Rocca found himself in Dublin with time on his hands and money in his pocket so he contacted his friend Behan, to see if there was anyone else he should look at whilst he was there. Behan happily raved about an even better prospect, the best young footballer in Dublin by the name of Jackie Carey. Rocca went along with Behan to watch Carey play inside-left for St James's Gate against Cork Athletic.

This was only Carey's sixth game for Saints, but he scored in the first minute and by half-time Rocca had made his mind up about this elegant, commanding 17-year-old inside-forward, who glided around the pitch and never seemed flustered in possession. Louis Rocca was impressed and was not going to let this jewel escape him. That afternoon a deal was done to take Carey to United for £250.

Rocca still had to convince Johnny's father to let his son start a new life in Manchester. However, John Carey Snr was not going to stand in the way of his son's big opportunity, and happily gave his consent. Rocca and Carey Snr hit it off and though the deal was done, Rocca stayed long into the night to sample some Carey Irish hospitality. Rocca knew the potential he had seen and he was a happy man as he left for the journey back to Manchester with Johnny, knowing he had a bargain.

When Carey arrived in Manchester by train, accompanied by Rocca, he spied a newspaper hoarding proclaiming: 'United sign star'. He rushed over to the vendor to buy a copy of the paper, only to discover – much to his disappointment – that the star the newspaper was talking about was not the confident young Dubliner, but Blackburn Rovers' Ernie Thompson. The player had cost United £4,500 – although he would disappear into obscurity after three games. At the bottom of the article, two lines made mention of new Irish signing John Carey.

Carey settled quickly at Manchester United, and he was watched regularly playing for the United 'A' team. Charlie Mitten, who also played in the team with him, said of Carey:

"John was very cumbersome in those days – leggy, like a bloody big colt. He needed time to develop his strength. The further back in position John went the better he got. Rocca and Behan obviously knew how good he was going to be. He was also a good goalkeeper and a good centre-half. He made his name as a right-back of course, but he'd learned his skills further forward. You never saw John wildly kick a ball...he always did something sensible with his passes."

He was in direct competition for the inside-forward spot with Salford-born Stan Pearson, who was a month older than Johnny. It was often said that it depended on the state of the pitch as to which of the players United went with; if the ground was heavy, Carey would play and if it wasn't, Pearson would. On Saturday 25th September 1937, aged 18, he made his first-team debut playing as an inside-left in a Second Division game against Southampton at Old Trafford. The team that day was:

Breen, Griffiths, Roughton, Brown, Winterbottom, McKay, Bryant, Gladwyn, Thompson, Carey, Manley.

It was Manley who scored United's only goal that day in a disappointing 2-1 defeat. The *Manchester Guardian* described it as 'A Sorry Exhibition' by the team, and continued:

'Manchester United suffered a humiliating defeat at the hands of Southampton (2-1), and a long-suffering crowd at Old Trafford was driven to vivid profanity. It was not so much the defeat, as the startling ineptitude and futility of United's performance that made the faithful speak not so much in sorrow, as in wrath. The one bright feature of the game from Manchester's point of view was the play of Carey, a black-haired Irish youngster at inside-left. He was the one man on the side who used the ball thoughtfully and for 45 minutes he played so well that he created the illusion that United were winning. Carey did not deserve to have so disheartening an introduction to the Football League.'

His next game the following week was against Sheffield United, again at Old Trafford – with the visitors winning 1-0. After the first 14 games of the season, Scott Duncan resigned to take over at Ipswich, despite having four years of a five-year contract remaining. Walter Crickmer, the club secretary, again took over the managerial reins in November

1937. United were nothing more than a good Second Division side – though in his first game, United hammered Chesterfield 7-1 – beginning a run that would again gain them promotion up to the top flight.

Notably Crickmer had selected local lad Pearson, who played inside-forward in this game and would remain there until Tuesday 28th December, when United went to Nottingham Forest to play a return fixture. They had beaten Forest 4-3 the day before and the next day, as was tradition in those days, they went over to Nottingham to play them again. Pearson was rested and Johnny returned to the first team. He did not waste his opportunity, scoring his first United goal in a 3-2 victory.

Of the remaining 25 games that season Carey played in 16, scoring two more league goals – against Luton and Chesterfield – and netting his first FA Cup goal in a fourth-round round tie at Barnsley, which ended 2-2. United finished with 53 points, four behind Aston Villa – who ended up as champions. But United were back in the First Division, and Johnny Carey had made a considerable contribution.

At the time of Johnny's international debut in the late 1930s, there were two Irish teams to choose from. The Northern Ireland-based IFA and the Republic-based FAI, who claimed to represent the whole of Ireland – and picked players accordingly. Several Irish players, including Carey, played for both. In September 1946 Carey played for both against England, within three days of each other. But on 7th November 1937 he made his debut for the FAI XI against Norway in a qualifier for the 1938 World Cup finals, which ended in a 3-3 draw.

The 1938/39 season saw Manchester United again with a new manager. Jimmy Porter favoured Pearson at the start the campaign, with Carey not seeing any first-team action until five games into the season. That match saw United travel to Blundell Park to play Grimsby, a game they lost 1-0. Carey played well and held his position for the next six games, scoring in a 5-1 demolition of Chelsea at Old Trafford.

After a 5-1 defeat at Derby, Porter decided to make changes and Pearson was again brought back in. The next six games saw United win only once. Saturday 10th December saw Carey return in a 1-0 win over Arsenal at Old Trafford and of the remaining 26 games United played, Carey missed only three games and was now deemed a regular. In total he made 34 appearances, scoring six goals as United finished 14th. Internationally, 13th November 1938 saw Carey score his first goal for the FAI XI in a 3-2 win against Poland, and then net in his very next game, a 2-2 draw against Hungary on 19th March 1939.

Storm clouds hung over Europe as United began their second season back in the top division. On a sunny Saturday 26th August they kicked off the 1939/40 season with a home game against Grimsby Town. The season was notable for being the first in which teams wore numbers on the back of their shirts. The game was a stroll for United and Carey, with United winning 4-0 – with Carey scoring one of the goals – and the following Wednesday saw a 1-1 draw at Chelsea.

Nobody knew that the game on Saturday 2nd September 1939 against Charlton would be United's last official league game for six years. The players arrived at Euston station on Friday evening and found London blacked out, even though the papers they had read on the journey down had declared: 'Football will be as usual tomorrow.' It took an hour by Tube to get to the club's hotel in Marylebone. The United players were greeted with the sight of barrage balloons flying over The Valley as they turned up for the game. Normally the fixture would have attracted 40,000 supporters, but only 6,000 had the appetite to watch Charlton beat United 2-0. For once the result was unimportant. The previous day Hitler's Germany had invaded Poland and for the second time in a generation it seemed that a world war was inevitable.

At 11am on Sunday 3rd September 1939, as the United players gathered around the radio, they heard Prime Minister Neville Chamberlain announce that Britain was once again at war with Germany. The English and Scottish Associations immediately abandoned the Football League competitions, and cancelled all professional contracts.

In those first weeks after the declaration of war teams were urged to play friendlies until a league system could be organised. A series of regional leagues were formed, similar to those competed in during World War I. More than 3.5 million people had been evacuated from the major cities, and attendance in the early regional leagues was limited to 8,000 in more vulnerable areas. United's first friendly, a 3-1 victory over Oldham, was watched by 4,600. United also hosted Manchester City and played at Stoke and Blackpool before the regional competition, which started for United on 21st October 1939 against Manchester City.

When people talk about Johnny Carey, they talk about him as a true sportsman and gentleman – but as a 19-year-old he was about to darken his reputation in a League War Cup match at Old Trafford against Blackburn Rovers on 4th May 1940. In his report in the *Manchester Guardian*, 'Old International' wrote:

'This week "my cue is villainous melancholy with a sigh like Tom o'Bedlam". Carey, of Manchester United, our black-haired gentler version of the incomparable Doherty, was requested by the referee to accompany Guest of Blackburn Rovers to the dressing room, presumably for conduct unbecoming sportsmen and gentlemen. Three minutes only remained for play in a brilliant match. United were winning handsomely; then our eyes fell upon two of the gladiators mixed up in a private scuffle. Carey and Guest were soon identified and arraigned as the culprits. An Irishman coming away from the game described them as "Poor craythurs that couldn't do anybody any harm – a couple o' game cocks breastin, wan against the other" and he voiced the feelings of many. Carey and Guest had transgressed beyond doubt, but they were shocked as we were, when the blow fell!' Maybe 'Old International' and the referee were a little unjust as most other reports were full of praise for Carey's skills, having scored one of the goals in United's 2-1 win.

The League continued to encourage a multitude of cup and trophy competitions. The League North, in which United played, had its championship and cup, although the club never featured as winners at any time during the war. Blackpool, with its strong contingent of guest players who were also serving with the RAF at Squires Gate, won the North Regional Cup and League competition several times. United did at least manage to end the 1940/41 season by beating Burnley 1-0 in the final of the Lancashire Cup at Turf Moor, with Carey scoring the only goal.

Military service was made compulsory for fit young men between the ages of 18 and 41 – which, on the face of it, meant all professional footballers. However, Carey was left with an agonising decision. With his native Ireland neutral in the conflict, he had the right to go home if he wished and sit the war out. But that was never Johnny Carey's way. He declared that "a country that gives me a living is worth fighting for", and thus decided to stay in Manchester and look for work whilst waiting for his call-up. Carey duly went to Metrovicks, the aircraft factory in Trafford Park. He also got married – and then was called-up.

Carey enlisted to serve in The King's Own Hussars. He was given the job as sergeant, coaching and training all football-minded personnel in the unit. During the war Carey continued to play for Manchester United and between 1939 and 1943, when he was posted overseas, he played 112 games, scoring 47 goals in war-time regional leagues.

Due to the war-time commitments of players at other clubs, it was common for players to guest for other teams. This was the case for Johnny, who during the war guested for Cardiff City, Manchester City, Everton, Liverpool and Middlesbrough. Carey also played for Irish teams, and turned out for a League of Ireland XI against a Scottish League XI. Shamrock Rovers made use of him in their League of Ireland games, with whom he played and scored against Limerick, Shelbourne and in a League of Ireland Shield game against Waterford.

In 1943 Carey was posted overseas with his unit, travelling through North Africa and Italy. He spent two years abroad, firstly in Algiers, and then he was posted to Italy and stationed at Trieste. When local Italian teams found out he was there, he was invited to play for them as a guest. To give him an Italian feel they named him as "Cario" in the programme. Carey liked this, and used it for every Italian team he played for. Carey was popular with the locals and developed a cult following. When the war ended, Carey received attractive offers from Italian clubs – but Carey's heart was set on a return to England and United.

The Manchester United Johnny returned to on leave after the war was not the one he had left. For a start, Old Trafford was a bombed-out wreck and United were playing home games at Maine Road, home of Manchester City. The biggest change came in the shape of a tracksuited Scotsman. Company Sergeant-Major Matt Busby was in charge – and nothing would ever be the same again for Carey and the club.

Busby took over as manager of United in October 1945, his first game being against Bolton at Maine Road. One of Busby's first decisions was to make the soft-brogued Dubliner Johnny Carey club captain. Johnny was home on leave, and playing his first match for United for two years. He played brilliantly and scored the equaliser, justifying Busby's decision. Both men were wise, deep-thinking Catholics and took to each other immediately – but any thoughts Busby had about building his United team around Carey would have to wait because the popular Irishman had been told to return to Italy, leaving Busby only a faint hope that Carey might get early demobilisation. He managed one more game before he had to return – playing a major part in a 6-1 victory over Preston. The consistent, scheming inside-forward knitted the team together, and was an influence behind every goal.

On 5th January 1946 United found themselves in the first leg of a third round FA Cup tie against Accrington Stanley at Peel Park, Accrington's famous sloping pitch. Johnny Carey, now free from service responsibilities was back permanently and leading the side. United were leading 2-0 at half-time but had to settle for a 2-2 draw, after Accrington scored an equaliser two minutes from time. On the following Wednesday afternoon at Maine Road, United thrashed Accrington 5-1. The fourth round saw United matched with Preston but despite winning the first leg 1-0, they went down 3-1 at Deepdale and were out.

Six Victory internationals between the home countries were arranged that season, but United players had been absent from the sides until 2nd February 1946 when Carey played for Ireland against Scotland at Windsor Park, Belfast. Carey was picked as centre-forward – such was his versatility – but he actually played as inside-forward because of injuries to some of the selected players. Ireland lost 3-2 before a crowd of 53,000, but Carey was hailed as the best forward on the pitch.

Standing 5ft 11ins and weighing only 12 stone, many people were surprised when Busby moved Carey back into defence to play either as half-back or full-back. But Busby did not want a big bruiser; he admired Carey's positional play and efficient tackling, and especially his ability to organise. He was something different for the era, a constructive defender who could play the ball and make things happen.

Saturday 31st August 1946 – the day League football came back to England after the war. Matt Busby announced to his players that the fixtures would be identical to those of the abandoned 1939/40 season. The side named to take on Grimsby Town that day was:

Crompton, Carey, McGlen, Warner, Chilton, Cockburn, Delaney, Pearson, Hanlon, Rowley, Mitten.

Jack Warner, Allenby Chilton and Stan Pearson were the only United players who had appeared in the same fixture just before the war. United won 2-1, with Rowley and Mitten scoring for United. United made a fantastic start to the season, beating Chelsea 3-0 at Stamford Bridge and Liverpool 5-0 at Maine Road in the first few games. This was the start of something special, an attacking style built around flair and stylish wing play. This was football the Busby Way, as he said:

"Winning matches at all costs is not the test of true achievement; there is no dishonour in defeat as long as you play to the limit of your strength and skill. What matters above all things is that the game should be played in the right spirit, with fair play and no favour, with every man playing as a member of his team and the result accepted without bitterness and conceit. Played at its best between two first-class teams, football is a wonderful spectacle. I love its drama, its smooth playing skills, its carelessly laid rhythms and the added flavour of contrasting styles. Its great occasions are, for me at any rate, unequalled in the world of sport. I feel a sense of romance, wonder and mystery, a sense of beauty and a sense of poetry. On such occasions, the game has the timeless, magical qualities of legend." It was as if he was speaking about Johnny Carey, who epitomised all Busby values in a player.

The 1946/47 season saw United, who had spent the last 10 years before the war as a yo-yo club, finish second – a point behind champions Liverpool. In March 1947 there was a competition in the papers to pick a Great Britain team to play the Rest of Europe at Hampden Park on 10th May. Carey was voted into the side but when it came time to pick the team, it was found that Carey wasn't eligible – but he was qualified to play for the European team. He was still surprised to find himself selected for the Europe squad and he was notified that he should go to Amsterdam, then Rotterdam, where there was to be a trial against a Dutch team. There was little problem with the language in the team as most of the players could speak some English, and Carey could speak a little Italian because of the time he had spent there in the war.

Just before the practice game the president of FIFA asked him to be captain of the European team. The Rest of Europe team flew to Scotland and stayed at the Marine Hotel in Troon, to prepare for the game at Hampden Park. One of the waitresses at the hotel, who was looking after the team, complemented Carey on his excellent English; Carey, ever the perfect gentleman, smiled and thanked her. A crowd of 134,000 would see Great Britain win the game easily, 6-1.

The 1947/48 season was to be a dramatic and defining season for Manchester United and Johnny Carey. United had another successful league season, finishing second once again – this time to Arsenal. But in March 1948, almost seven years to the day after Old Trafford had been bombed, they were granted £17,478 to rebuild the ground.

The draw for the third round of the FA Cup is always one of the most anticipated dates for any football supporter, and United fans in those days would have had a good memory to recall the last time United had won the trophy – in fact, it was nearly 40 years before in 1909, when they beat Bristol City 1-0 in the final at Crystal Palace.

United faced a tricky tie at Aston Villa, the side that had finished as Second Division champions when United were also promoted in 1937/38. Villa scored early but then found themselves 5-1 down by half-time, with United eventually running out 6-4 winners. At the time, Carey thought Villa's early goal "was the worst thing they could have done…fancy taking the liberty of scoring like that so quickly! We settled down to it and set about them. The football we played was out of this world. You know, it was an extraordinary thing about this 1948 team – when the chips were down we could step up and destroy the opposition in 10 minutes. The passes flew – everybody played all out and we could transform a game where we found ourselves a goal down to one where not long later we were leading by several goals. It happened in the Villa Park game and it happened in many other matches as well."

The fourth-round draw interrupted a game of golf for the United players at Davyhulme Golf Course. As they gathered round a portable radio they duly discovered they would be playing Liverpool. It is estimated that 15,000 people were locked outside Goodison Park for the game, with over 74,000 packed inside. Liverpool made a good start but they were easily dispatched 3-0.

Next up was a home tie against Charlton Athletic – with Manchester City drawn out seconds later, also at home, to Preston North End. This caused a problem for the FA as they wanted all games played at the same time – but both United and City couldn't both use Maine Road. United were forced to find an alternative venue and finally settled on Leeds Road, Huddersfield Town's ground, as it had held semi-finals previously and had a capacity of 70,000. Charlton would prove no match for United and were flattered by the 2-0 scoreline – if it wasn't for the heroics of their goalkeeper, Sam Bartram, it could have been double figures.

United were drawn at home once again in the next round, this time against Preston – who had seen off City in the previous round. Saturday 28th February saw a capacity 74,000 crowd at Maine Road. United started well, and maintained a steady stream of pressure on the Preston goal. Carey, as usual, prompted United's attacks and steadied the defence – impressing with his strength and calmness. United ran out 4-2 winners and the papers reported that Preston had been 'out-run, out-witted and outgeneraled'.

The semi-final at Hillsborough on 13th March 1948 was between United and Derby. After an open first half-hour Stan Pearson scored United's first – and four minutes later he scored again. The Rams pushed on, trying to get themselves back in it but the United defence, yet again with Carey playing his usual immaculate game, held firm. But three minutes before half-time Allenby Chilton made the one mistake that let Derby back into the game, leaving the score 2-1 at the interval.

Derby started the second half as they had finished the first, with wave after wave of attacks – but on 55 minutes Pearson scored his third and decisive goal. Even though if had been a magnificent effort from the United team, the match reports singled out Pearson and Carey for their superb contribution to attack and defence respectively.

Huge excitement was generated by United reaching the final, with supporters trying every trick to get hold of tickets. The sports pages of the newspapers during the week before the final were full of facts and figures about United and their opponents, Blackpool, searching through the comparisons and contrasts for clues about who might win. As the train pulled out of London Road Station, Manchester, bound for London, the players finally got a chance to relax as they were away from the constant pressure in Manchester from being recognised and pestered for autographs and tickets.

There was only one issue bothering the United players – how little they were being paid for their efforts. Matt Busby and the directors were adamant the players would be paid their usual weekly wage plus a bonus of £20 each for reaching the final. Some of the players made a little from selling their spare tickets, but there would be no other financial reward except for a few pounds each from a players' brochure, which Carey put together and sold for 2s 6d a copy. The press had paid the players nothing for interviews and photographs so when the team pulled into Euston, they made a token of gesture by covering their faces as they left the station by coach for their Surrey hotel, refusing to be photographed unless they were paid £10 a photo.

The all-Lancashire final of 24th April 1948 has passed into history as one of the finest matches ever seen in the competition. Blackpool had the brilliant Stanley Matthews and Stan Mortenson in their side, while Manchester United were full of rising stars such as Rowley, Mitten and Pearson – and in Johnny Carey they had the ultimate footballing full-back. On the day United played in blue shirts with a white collar, white shorts and blue socks. Normally they didn't wear a badge on their shirts but for cup finals they wore the Manchester Coat of Arms.

Into the bright sunshine strode Busby's first great team, led by Carey – the man who had skippered them since Busby had taken over. He was as calm as always, and before the game he made a point of going round the changing room, wishing his team-mates good luck.

The game was a delight for the spectators, with both teams playing fluent, attractive football. But the hottest favourites in years were knocked back on their heels after just 15 minutes when Mortensen was tackled from behind inside the area by Chilton, and Blackpool were awarded a penalty – which Shimwell duly converted. Five minutes later Rowley had equalised from Delaney's pass, before Blackpool scored again with Mortensen's cross-shot. Half-time came and Blackpool were leading 2-1, on course to defeat the favourites to lift the trophy. Carey was having none of it and when he got his team-mates back in the changing room he gave them a rousing team talk. His message was clear: "If we keep playing football we must win it. If we start just kicking it around we've no chance." United had a motto in the team that 'the ball should never stop' – only the goalkeeper stopped the ball.

United came out for the second half fired up – but not much was changing in terms of the match. The game was ebbing away from United but the final quarter saw a complete turnaround in fortune that for sheer thrill and skill, mounted up in move after stirring move to a cup classic.

A quickly whispered midfield tactical talk between Carey and centre-half Allenby Chilton started the comeback. Throughout the team Carey's message spread: "Keep playing football. Fight – but play football. The goals will come." And they did, firstly from a quickly-taken free-kick, Rowley rising between two Blackpool defenders to head the equaliser. Blackpool hit back at the other end, with a fine Mortensen shot in the 80th minute bringing out the best from Jack Crompton.

Stan Pearson had listened to Carey's message, and minutes later he gave United the lead. It was typical of United's swashbuckling style of football and Carey's football mantra. Anderson intercepted a throw-in from Robinson then slipped the ball to Pearson, who impersonated Matthews with a serving run around Hayward before unleashing a 20-yard shot, that cannoned into the net off the post. The result was settled when, with five minutes to go, John Anderson's 35-yard shot took a deflection off Hugh Kelly's head, and flew in. United had won the cup!

Johnny climbed the steps to the Royal Box to collect the trophy, becoming the first Irishman to captain an FA Cup-winning team. He received the trophy from King George and in his excitement, dropped the cup's plinth and lid back on the table. When the players were back on the pitch Charlie Mitten and Jack Crompton hoisted Carey and the trophy onto their shoulders, and paraded him around the pitch.

That evening the United party attended a banquet at the Connaught Rooms and on the Sunday morning they travelled down with their wives and officials to Brighton for the day before returning back to London at night. The team journeyed back to Manchester on the Monday on the 1pm train from Euston. The team departed the train at Wilmslow, then travelled by road to meet the crowds gathering in the city centre to welcome them. On the way they stopped at the home of Mr James Gibson, the chairman, who had been too ill to travel. The players lined the lawn and Carey marched into the house carrying the trophy.

Manchester had not seen crowds like it since the end of the war. The team was in a single-decker coach with a hole in the roof, enabling the team to stand and be seen. The coach went along Princess Road in South Manchester, along Denmark Road and Oxford Road to Albert Square and the Town Hall through a sea of cheering faces. As they neared the Town Hall the crowd started chanting: "We want Carey, we want Carey". There was a massive roar as he appeared on the Town Hall balcony holding the cup, with the rest of the team gathered around him.

The FA Charity Shield match played on 6th October 1948 at Highbury saw Arsenal (winners of the First Division) host United (winners of the FA Cup). The Gunners, who had won the toss of a coin for home advantage, were three-up in the first five minutes in a match they eventually won 4-3. Despite the defeat, the season went well. United again progressed in the league while reaching the semi-final of the FA Cup, going out to Wolves 1-0 in a replay at Goodison Park. It was not all gloom though, as just before the replay it was announced that the Football Writers' Association had voted Carey as their Player of the Year, with Carey polling nearly 40% of the vote. Carey and Matt Busby headed to London on Friday 29th April, the eve of the FA Cup final, to collect the bronze statuette. United's captain gracefully accepted the award, stating disappointment at not leading United out at Wembley the following day.

The final game of the league season saw United host newly-crowned champions Portsmouth. United prevailed 3-2 in a thriller that included a penalty save by Jack Crompton. The result meant United would finish the season in second place again. It was also the last 'home' match for the club at Maine Road, as work had begun on rebuilding Old Trafford. Whilst United had been at Maine Road, they had played some of the finest football ever seen by United supporters. They had won the FA Cup and were semi-finalists the following season, whilst finishing as three-time runners-up in the league in successive seasons.

The 1949/50 season promised so much for United and their support-ers, who had tasted success and were now eager for more. At one point they were being talked about as certainties for the league and cup Double, but defeat to Chelsea in the cup and a poor end-of-season saw United finish without a trophy, down in fourth in the league.

Busby appeared to have his mind on other things, as he was disappear-ing from Manchester regularly on scouting missions. He also spent a lot of time watching the Central League reserve team, who were attracting a lot of attention and support because of the performances of players like Mark Jones, Roger Byrne, Dennis Viollet and Jackie Blanchflower.

People who believe that foreign tours by football teams are a new thing should remember that in the summer of 1950 United headed for a six-week tour of the USA. On 2nd May they boarded the Queen Mary in Southampton and set sail for New York. The *Evening Chronicle* com-missioned Carey to write articles, which were full of tit-bits about what was happening on the tour. Readers lapped it up. He reported that on the trip over the team entered the passenger's table-tennis competition and that he had reached the final, only to lose to Jack Crompton.

Upon arriving in the Big Apple, Carey regaled *Chronicle* readers with stories of parties they attended and people they met. Then, in a headline to a column headed '£3,500 a year does not tempt us', Carey told of a call he had received from an agent, offering a generous salary and expenses to go and play in Columbia for clubs like Santa FC and Millionarios. According to Carey, none of the United players would con-sider such an offer, as it would mean the end of their careers in Britain.

United moved on and the article seemed to have been forgotten, with the tour continuing across California, where they partied with film stars like Clark Gable. Then it was up to Canada, down to Chicago and back to New York to catch the boat home. One player who didn't catch the boat, but instead flew down to Bogotá, was Charlie Mitten. He had been invited by an agent from the Santa Fe Club to have an all-expenses no-obligation look around. Carey attempted to make him see sense in the bar on the night he left, but Charlie was his own man and wanted to go and see for himself. It didn't take Charlie long to make up his mind. He signed a year-long contract for £5,000 (compared to the £750 he was being paid by United).

Busby's programme notes for the first game of 1950/51 were positive, almost predicting subsequent glory: 'Is the championship trophy to find a resting place at Old Trafford this season? Well, it's United's turn – and if they do succeed it will be the reward of remarkable consistency.'

United started the season like a team possessed. Jack Rowley scored three hat-tricks in the first three weeks of the season, and after seven games he had scored 14 goals. But after a couple of surprising home defeats and losses at Chelsea and Portsmouth, United found themselves down in seventh. Busby decided it was time to make changes. For United's game at Liverpool on 24th November Busby not only brought Jack Crompton back, but more importantly gave a debut to two new players: Jackie Blanchflower, at right-half, and Roger Byrne at left-back. It was a 0-0 draw, but United's history had turned another page.

United raced on in the league but found themselves knocked out of the FA Cup at the third-round stage for the first time since 1939. Carey was now in his 30s and knew that time was running out for him and the other five members of the 1948 cup-winning side who remained. Busby was turning to youth and players who had been cleaning his boots were now challenging for positions in the first team. He was desperate to win a championship medal, to set a seal on his eventful career.

With three games to go it was between Arsenal and United for the title, with the teams due to play each other on the last day of the season. On Saturday 19th April United drew 2-2 with Blackpool, whilst Arsenal beat Stoke 4-1. Two days later United were back in pole position. Arsenal were beaten 3-1 at West Bromwich Albion on the Monday, with United beating Chelsea 3-0 – a game in which Carey scored a memorable goal. United were struggling, despite holding a one-goal advantage, until Carey struck. The Irishman accepted a square pass from full-back McNulty, went forward unopposed before unleashing a left-footed strike from outside the penalty area. The shot found the top corner of the net, before rolling back onto the penalty spot. The crowd were still applauding Carey's goal when the game had been restarted.

The results that Monday meant that Arsenal would now have to beat United 7-0 to prevent them from winning the league. Arsenal realised the magnitude of the task that lay ahead of them but they were determined to make a game of it, and tried to attack United. However, the Gunners were blown away by a magnificent United, who beat them 6-1.

After finishing as runners-up in '47, '48, '49 and '51 they were finally champions, and Carey was the first non-Englishman to captain a cup and league-winning side. The following Monday Don Davies, writing in the *Manchester Guardian*, captured the spirit of Carey and the club:

'After an interval of 41 years Manchester United have regained the championship of the Football League. The title has never been better earned. Not only has the team, in the five seasons before this one, finished second four times, fourth once and won the FA Cup; it has been captained, managed and directed in a way that is a lesson to many others. J Carey, the captain in this period, has been a model footballer – technically efficient, thanks to hard work; a fighter to the last, without ever fighting. He is a sportsman, a steadier of the younger and inexperienced, an inspirer of the older and tiring, and at all times the most modest of men, though he has won every football honour open to him.'

A poor start to the 1952/53 season found United fourth-from-bottom after six games, and Matt Busby explaining to shareholders at the annual meeting that United had a wealth of youngsters coming through that were worth hundreds of thousands of pounds. Through this season Carey got to captain teams that included David Pegg, Bill Foulkes, Tommy Taylor, Duncan Edwards and Dennis Viollet, as well as Roger Byrne. After a 4-2 win over Newcastle in the FA Charity Shield, the season petered out and they finished eighth, their lowest since the war.

The season did have a memorable moment for Carey, though. On

Wednesday 18th February United travelled up to Sunderland for a game and it became apparent that Jack Crompton had a bad bout of flu and would not be able to play. Busby looked at his ever-reliable captain and said: "You will have to go in goal John". The game ended 2-2, but Carey acquitted himself well. As a former Gaelic football player John had no problem with goalkeeping. Carey ended up playing in 10 different positions for United – the only position he didn't was at outside-right.

An article by Tom Jackson of the *Manchester Evening News* at the end of the season prepared United supporters for Carey's departure: 'There is an odds-on chance that this will be John Carey's last season as a player. Within the next few days the Manchester United captain, who has achieved every honour in football since he started his career as a junior at Old Trafford in 1936, is to decide whether or not to resign for next season. Carey, the most popular captain in United's history, has been offered terms for 1953/54, but he has told me today, "My future as a player hangs in the balance. I am not getting any younger (he is just 34), and I don't intend to become a has-been in the game which has been my life". United, anticipating that he might not be available as a player next season, have already offered him a job on their coaching staff. It is also known that several foreign clubs would value his services as a coach.'

Johnny Carey made his decision known in May that he was retiring. He was finishing after 17 seasons at United because he did not feel capable of playing the United brand of football for another year. John recalled: "I knew I could have played on for another two or three years. I was 34 when I finished but I was fit, and Matt would have liked me to continue. But I looked at the tremendous career I'd had…the six years of war had taken a lot away from it, but from 1946-53 I'd had seven years at the top and I'd set a standard. I felt the only way I was going was down. I also felt it wasn't fair for people who looked up to me and wanted to tell everybody what a good player I was. I didn't think I'd enjoy Second or Third Division football. I looked at Manchester United and thought, 'There's no way I can keep my place…or maybe only on reputation' and I didn't want to keep it on that."

He went on to explain: "In 1953 United were so well-equipped that you could see the club bulging with talent…Duncan Edwards, Roger Byrne, Dennis Viollet, David Pegg, Bill Whelan, Jeff Whitefoot…They were all there. The club was all geared up. Unfortunately there wasn't a position for me…Jimmy Murphy was doing a tremendous job, Walter Crickmer and Les Olive were there on the admin side. What Matt wanted was for me to stay on as a player and do a bit of coaching with the youngsters, gradually working my way into that side of the club's activities. But rightly or wrongly I decided that I would try my luck and see if I could make my name as a manager and, as it happened, I went to Blackburn where I had six tremendously happy and successful years."

And so ended the playing career of Busby's first great captain. A man who, with his Corinthian spirit, only brought honour to the game. He was a full-back with the skills of a ball-playing inside-forward, and the creative ability of a half-back. A mistake by Carey was so rare that it would bring gasps of disbelief from spectators. John Carey, a name that fits so easily into United's all-time greats, was capped 29 times by the Republic of Ireland and seven times for Northern Ireland. He also captained the Rest of Europe against Great Britain in 1947, was voted Player of the Year in 1949, and Sportsman of the Year in 1950.

Was he a great captain? He was the perfect captain for Busby's first great team. He personified the Busby ethos, on and off the pitch. Recognised by FIFA and asked to captain the Rest of Europe team, he was a natural leader of men, fiercely defensive of his team-mates and always a credit to the shirt. Captain of the first Manchester United championship team for 41 years, an inspiration to the Busby Babes. Humble to the end, and a gentleman captain.

Salford Boy

STAN PEARSON

1953-1954

'That [Aston Villa] game was when we played the best football I've seen from anybody. We pinged that ball around so quickly first time. We were shoving it around and darting here and there. The lads would be moving...taking somebody out of the way and another would slip into space...it was magic...everything seemed to click'

The start of the 1953/54 season left Matt Busby with a dilemma. In losing Johnny Carey, he had lost his captain, his confidant and mouthpiece on the pitch. Carey had been captain for as long as Busby had been manager, skipper of an FA Cup-winning team and the league champions. Busby looked around the dressing room and needed to find someone who could lead his team, someone who the other players would respect. Before handing the captaincy to Roger Byrne, Busby initially turned to a man who was born in the heartland of Manchester United supporters, a man who attended his first game at Old Trafford age seven – and who had supported United all his life. That man was Stan Pearson.

Stanley Clare Pearson was born in Salford on 11th January 1919, a month before Carey. As was the case with Busby and Carey, the man who must claim credit for bringing Stan to United was Louis Rocca. He spotted Stan playing for Adelphi Lads' club in the Manchester Amateur League, signing him to United as an amateur in December 1935.

Rocca was not the first person to spot Pearson's footballing talent. At Frederick Road Council School in Salford, under the tutorage of Scottish games teacher Jack Stuart, the school football and cricket teams, including Pearson, won every competition available. Stan soon went on to play for – and captain – Salford Boys for two seasons.

Set up at the behest of the supporters, the Manchester United Junior Athletic Club (MUJAC) was charged with bringing the best young players in the area to United, with the aim of eventually filling the first team with local talent. Louis Rocca was appointed chief scout, and he knew that he was fulfilling his remit when Pearson signed amateur forms, aged 16, in December 1935. Pearson also joined the ground staff, as well as playing in the 'A' team. He would spend days going across the pitch on his hands and knees, getting weeds out with a little dibber and a bucket. As he recalled: "They used to put string lanes about a yard wide across the pitch and four or five of the junior ground staff would do the weeding. Scott Duncan, the manager at the time, used to walk up behind the lads and if they missed a weed, he used to give them a kick and say: 'Hey lad, come on, there's one here.'"

Pearson was a graceful young inside-forward, who always had the knack of being in the right place at the right time. Everyone could see he was a special talent. A year-and-a-half later, in May 1937 at the age of 18 years and four months, he signed professional forms for the club he had dreamed of representing – not that this was the glamorous United we know today; the club was languishing in a poor Second Division.

Johnny Carey and Jack Rowley made their debuts that season, and had given fans hope. Sharper-eyed supporters may have noticed an article in the *Evening Chronicle* on 1st November 1937, which stated that Pearson, in his debut Central League game against Chesterfield, had been the outstanding forward. Later that week the paper reported that Pearson, after only two games, was to get an early chance of proving his worth in the first team. Pearson was picked against Chesterfield, the team he had made his Central League debut against only two weeks prior. Pearson made his bow at Saltergate on Saturday 13th November 1937. Monday's *Manchester Guardian* was gushing in its praise:

'Pearson played the chief part in United's 7-1 win at Chesterfield. For four years United have nursed him and the result is a young footballer with the self-possession of a veteran. He was the key man, for he dribbled and combined in such a delightful way that not only did he provide the passes to four goals, but he knitted the usually ragged United attack into a smooth working machine. His abilities have been known for a long time; only a belief that he might be too young for the hurly burly of Second Division football has kept him relegated to the 'A' Team.'

The following Saturday Pearson made his home debut against Aston Villa, which United won 3-1 – Pearson scoring the third. To prove this was no fluke, Pearson scored the next Saturday in a 3-2 win at Norwich. He stayed in the team for the next three games until a 4-0 defeat at Bradford Park Avenue, which saw the management make changes, including bringing Johnny Carey back.

Pearson did make a scoring appearance in a 3-0 third round FA Cup home win over Yeovil Town, but he had to watch on as Carey played most of the remaining games at inside-forward. Stan returned for the last four games that saw the team finish second to Aston Villa in the league to achieve promotion. It had been an amazing debut year for the Salford boy, who began it debuting in the Central League, and ended it as a member of the United first team promoted back to Division One.

The 1938/39 season began as the previous season had ended, with Carey and Pearson vying for the same position – the selection being decided on the state of the pitch. It was not until 31st December 1938 that Stan scored his first – and only – goal of the campaign, in a 3-3 draw against Birmingham.

Pearson played in all three games of the 1939/40 season, scoring in the opening game against Grimsby, a 4-0 win. But the onset of war meant the season was suspended, with the United players returning home to await the inevitable call-up. Jack Rowley, Pearson and Carey did manage to make regular appearances in regional league games. United didn't win any of these leagues, but they did manage to beat Burnley 1-0 in the final of the Lancashire Cup at Turf Moor, with a team that read:

Breedon; Topping, Roughton; Warner, Porter, Whalley; Smith, Carey (who scored the only goal), Rowley, Pearson, Mitten.

Don Davies, in his piece in the *Manchester Guardian*, offered hope in his match report: 'The new Pearson-Mitten wing is one of the treasures United are hoarding against the advent of a just peace.' This was at a time when newspapers carried blanket coverage about the war being fought all over the world, and the *Manchester Guardian* could often only spare a couple of lines to report on United's games. Sometimes they didn't even name the players, but that didn't matter to the United fans, who were now in uniform and fighting thousands of miles away.

Stan was called up and joined the 2nd/4th Battalion of the Lancashires, initially being stationed in Ireland, before a posting to India. The drill was that after the boat docked in Bombay, the troops went to a holding camp in Deolali for three weeks, then on to fight in Burma. Based there for 10 days, Stan was sent for and told about a football team being sent to Bombay, to take part in two tournaments. It was made clear that as long as the team kept winning, they would stay in Bombay – but if they got knocked out they would return to Deolali, and then to who knows where? Pearson travelled and having helped the team win both competitions, he was rewarded with a soft job in the stores.

A month after, the British turned the Japanese and started to drive them out of Burma. Then some months later different regiments were asked to recommend footballers to go for trials in Delhi, with a view to forming two touring teams. Stan found himself in the team that went north into Burma and ended up in Rangoon, playing matches for the troops in a team led by Dennis Compton.

The war ended and the world attempted to get back to normality. When new manager Busby looked at his team at the end of 1945 he saw a side 13th in a Northern Section table headed by Chesterfield. The good news was that Johnny Carey was home from duty, and back in the side. The defence looked solid – but the attack looked toothless. This didn't worry Busby, as most of his first-choice forwards had yet to return, and reports were reaching Old Trafford that Stan Pearson was the leading scorer in Compton's touring side. Things looked even better when, days later, the headlines in the *Manchester Evening News* announced: 'Stan's Back!'

At last, Pearson had returned after six-and-a-half years' military service. Stan enjoyed a couple of days' rest before visiting Old Trafford, where he re-signed his contract and began training. Busby didn't think Stan was ready for immediate inclusion, but he travelled as 12th man to Bury a fixture on 23rd February, and then played for the reserves on 2nd March – and scored. He looked fit and even though he had bulked up, he was desperate to get games under his belt, telling reporters that he would take a holiday when the season had ended.

Stan made his return on Saturday 9th March against Blackburn at Maine Road. This was the first game Pearson had played for United in two years, and it was a memorable one with United running out 6-2 victors – although Pearson failed to score. The best news Stan came back to was the decision by manager Matt Busby to convert Carey from an inside-forward to a full-back, thus leaving the position free for Pearson.

The prospects for United in the 1946/47 season looked good; Busby had found the right positions for his players and United were playing swift, attractive, flowing football. The fixtures were the same as the ones in the 1939/40 season that had been halted for the outbreak of the war. United duly opened on Saturday 31st August against Grimsby, with Pearson one of only three players who had played for United in the same fixture seven years earlier. After five games United found themselves top, and Don Davies for the *Manchester Guardian* wrote about the emerging brilliance of United in his report of the Liverpool game:

'The ever-popular Liverpool side (which on this occasion certainly took the palm for sartorial elegance) met Manchester United at Maine Road, and as a result of their meeting received a lesson in football craft which they are not likely to forget for many a long day. The first 20 minutes was an almost ceaseless bombardment of the Liverpool goal. Wave after wave of red shirts rolled over and round the Liverpool defenders at will; in the 12th minute Pearson converted a lob by Warner and soon afterwards, Pearson slammed a shot-cum-centre from Mitten high into the Liverpool net. This was progress indeed and soon a feast of football entertainment, which the 41,657 operatives who called in on the way home to tea seemed to find ample compensation for meals deferred.

'Still the attack went on and Delaney was floored by a charge heavy enough to buckle the plates of a submarine. Rowley collected the resulting free-kick and scored a handsome third. Four minutes after the interval a deflected ball put Mitten onside and his trusty boot did the rest.

'Even when United eased up, they still had the whip hand of Liverpool and treated the crowd to a taste of quality, which has taken Manchester by storm. In a team so strong and balanced there is little need to discriminate; but one cannot forgo the view that the acquisition of Delaney was one masterstroke, and the playing of Carey at right-back is another. One cannot recall an occasion when Liverpool's play was so undistinguished. Until the closing minutes, that is, when Paisley drove in a ball which forced Crompton, the Manchester goalkeeper, to reveal his whereabouts and prove that he had not gone home from sheer boredom.

'United's apt retort to Paisley's impudence was to walk the ball up field and invite Pearson to score the fifth, which Pearson most willingly did. Taken all in all this was a masterly performance and one even Manchester United will not easily repeat.'

United couldn't keep up the performances and at the end of the year they were in seventh – and soon out of the FA Cup, going out to Nottingham Forest. They did enjoy a strong final quarter of the season, winning 11 of the last 12 games. Unfortunately, the only match they lost was against Liverpool – who went on to win the title by one point.

After one of the shortest close seasons in football history, the first games of the 1947/48 season kicked off on 2nd August. United won the first two games, against Liverpool and Charlton Athletic respectively, but then found themselves near the foot of the table having failed to record a victory in nearly two months.

The tie of the FA Cup third round that season was Aston Villa v

Manchester United on 10th January 1948. The game kicked off at 2pm and the first United player to touch the ball was Jack Crompton, who picked the ball out of the net after 13.5 seconds. This didn't seem to rock United – in fact, quite the opposite. United played fluid football, getting the ball to their forwards quickly. Within half-an-hour they had scored three – Pearson scoring the third – and by half-time United were 5-1 up.

It looked like the game was over, but Villa came back strongly. With 10 minutes to go they had recovered to be within one goal of United. The deciding strike though came with two minutes to go, when Charlie Mitten took a corner that dropped to Stan Pearson, who hit it through a crowd of players to score what Matt Busby was later to describe as "one of the most valuable goals he ever scored for the club."

Straight after the game, Stan said: "In my opinion, and I don't care who hears it, that game was when we played the best football I've seen from anybody, anywhere, anytime. That's saying a lot, but we pinged that ball around so quickly first time – I've never seen anything like it, before or since. We were shoving it around and darting here and there. The lads would be moving…taking somebody out of the way and another would slip into space…it was magic…everything seemed to click."

The next rounds caused no major concern for United, and they found themselves in a Hillsborough semi-final against Derby on 13th March 1948. Much to team-mate Henry Cockburn's surprise and concern, he found Pearson being violently sick in the toilets before the game. When he asked what was the matter, he was told that Pearson felt sick with nerves – but was all the better for it. Pearson went out and destroyed the Rams, scoring a glorious hat-trick as United ran out 3-1 winners.

It was under blue skies at Wembley that Manchester United played Blackpool in the now famous Lancashire Cup final, a match that saw United come from 2-1 down to win 4-2 – with Pearson scoring the goal that took United back into the lead. He remembered his goal vividly:

"Stan Mortensen gets a scoring chance and Jack [Crompton] dives and grabs it, gets up and throws it to Johnny Anderson. He gets it and I start moving across and shouting my head off for the ball, I get away from Harry Johnston, collect a perfect pass from Johnny, take it in my stride and somebody is coming for me. I manage to slip him, and have a quick look at the goal. I'm about five or six yards outside the penalty area in the inside-right position and there's somebody coming…you have no time to see who it is…you just sense that they're there…another quick look at the goal and I hit a similar shot that Mortensen hit – across the goal – and I see it going a foot inside the post but swinging away. It hits the bloody post and goes back across the goal line and into the net!"

Nobody on the coach that drove into Albert Square carrying the team and the cup had a bigger grin on their face than Stan Pearson. The local boy, who had fulfilled his dream of playing for his beloved United, had now scored in a cup final. It seemed as if all of Salford had turned out to see Pearson and the team parade the trophy.

The next three seasons saw Pearson play virtually every game for United, only missing out when called away on international duty. The period saw United finish second, fourth and second again. But the team was getting older. The 1951/52 campaign began with a 3-3 draw against West Brom at The Hawthorns, and up until Christmas it looked like it might be another 'nearly' season, as United seemed to stutter through games without finding any form or rhythm.

However, after Christmas the team – and Pearson – clicked. United finished as champions, with Pearson hitting 22 goals, two coming in the final game when United thrashed Arsenal 6-1. United were worthy champions – no other team could rival their record of having topped 50 points in each of the six seasons since the war. But Busby had a dilemma: he had a belief in bringing youngsters in, and yet this team contained six who had won the FA Cup in 1948 – Johnny Carey, Allenby Chilton, Henry Cockburn, Stan Pearson, Jack Rowley and John Aston. Indeed, in the second half of the season, they played the kind of football that made United the most successful team in the league, and one of the most exciting to watch. Busby was reluctant to break up the side.

A poor start to the 1952/53 season saw United fourth-from-bottom after six games. Busby was under pressure to make something happen, to turn things around. What directors or supporters weren't aware of was the rich vein of talent that Busby had in his youth team. That season Busby introduced David Pegg, Bill Foulkes, Tommy Taylor, Duncan Edwards and Dennis Viollet into the first team, though the old guard still considered themselves first choice. This was a season of change, which saw United finish eighth – their lowest position since the war.

Supporters and team-mates alike greeted the news that Stan Pearson had been appointed as captain at the beginning of the 1953/54 season with a smile. Stan was a popular man, who got on with everybody. He was respected by all he played with, creating more goals than he scored, and the fact he won only eight England caps has much to do with the competition from Wilf Mannion and Raich Carter. Indeed, Carter would argue that Pearson was the equal of any player of that era.

Although never the quickest and without a powerful shot, what made Pearson stand out was his intelligence on the field, his masterful ball control and endless stamina, which enabled him to forage ceaselessly for possession. He was reliably consistent, and rarely missed a game.

One of new captain Pearson's jobs was to welcome two starry-eyed juniors called Bobby Charlton and Wilf McGuinness to the club. But on the field it was again an inauspicious start to the season, with three draws and three defeats coming from United's first six games, while Stan suffered a knee injury in the opening fixture with Chelsea.

Pearson returned for the derby against Manchester City at Maine Road, though United were easily beaten 2-0 by City. The club's first win came on Wednesday 16th September at Ayresome Park, United easing to a 4-1 victory over Middlesbrough. On Saturday 3rd October United went down 2-1 at home to Burnley, a match that will be remembered as the last time Pearson scored for United. His last game came three weeks later, a 1-0 win against Aston Villa at Old Trafford.

Stan was beginning to realise that his time at United was numbered.

He had been injured in the opening game, and had subsequently been unable to find the kind of form that had made him such a crowd favourite. He was never a great shouter and his captaincy relied on the respect that players had for him. Now he was struggling for form, and he had to suffer the indignity of playing reserve-team football whilst Dennis Viollet was making a name for himself wearing Stan's shirt.

Stan went for talks with Matt Busby. He felt that even though he was now 34, he was still good enough for first-team football, but both men were aware of the players coming through – and how difficult it would be for Stan to get back into the first team. In February 1954, to the regret of thousands of supporters who had seen him light up the red shirt of United at his brilliant best, Stan was transferred to Bury for £4,500.

Stan Pearson's tenancy as club captain was only a short one; it certainly wasn't a glorious or successful one. People say he was too quiet and nice to be a captain, and he didn't have the nasty streak that Allenby Chilton and Roger Byrne possessed in abundance. It was a period of change, when Busby was starting to create his second great team. Immensely popular, Stan will always be remembered as a classy footballer. Though not blessed with great pace, Stan seemed to glide through games gracefully. He scored goals with his head and both feet, and had marvellous awareness of the ever-changing picture around him. Those who saw him play will never forget his talent. Overall he played 345 games for United, scoring 128 league goals and 21 FA Cup goals, his most famous being the third goal in the 1948 final.

After retiring from football Stan became the sub-postmaster of Prestbury Post Office in Cheshire. Ever the gentleman, Stan always had time to stop and talk about the old days, and he never tired of describing his cup final goal. He was a season-ticket holder at Old Trafford, and followed his beloved United until the end. Stan died in Alderley Edge, Cheshire in February 1997. He was 78 years old.

Chilly

ALLENBY CHILTON
1954-1955

---

*'I don't feel enough credit was given to Allenby Chilton for
the change in the first-team's fortunes. With so many
immature, inexperienced players around him, he had to put
in a tremendous amount of work. He was a constant
inspiration to us and held the team together'*

Brian Hughes is a Collyhurst lad who went to St Patrick's, the school
that produced Nobby Stiles and Brian Kidd. Most days you will find
Brian down at Collyhurst and Moston Lads' Club gym, training another future boxing champion, as he has done so many times before. Brian's
life has been about training and being around fighters – he can spot a
real fighter a mile off. He has also watched Manchester United play and
train for over 60 years, and he remembers his favourite captain:

"Allenby Chilton, brilliant, a real gruff fella, hard as nails and I'm
telling you, he used to go on the speed ball – which all boxers do. They
didn't have The Cliff at first when Busby took over, they got that later
on. They used to have a little place round the back of the club; it's all
changed now. They used to have a speed ball in it and there was a little
bloke called Joe Travis who went to our school, he looked after the 'A'
team or 'B' team, he was there for years, until he died. He used to let me
come in and watch and let me tell you Allenby was brilliant. I train boxers now and I wish they could punch a speed ball like him. There's a
knack to it, hand and eye co-ordination, you can hear it 'rat tat tat tat
tat'. There was no messing with him. I once said to him, 'excuse me
Allenby'…he looked at me and said, 'Mr Chilton to you'.

"A great captain, everybody respected him, there was no taking liberties with him. Johnny Carey was a lovely man, he was like Matt Busby's clone, too nice, too quiet. Even though Carey was captain in name, it was Allenby Chilton who did all the shouting. I used to stand at the front near the pitch and it was always Chilton you could hear, never Carey."

Matt Busby attempted to replace Johnny Carey as captain with Stan Pearson, but a bad injury at the start of the 1953/54 season had never really given Pearson a chance to stamp his mark on the team. In February 1954, Pearson realised his opportunities for first-team football were becoming limited. There was a new dawn breaking at Old Trafford. Youngsters were coming through that Busby couldn't hold back any longer, prospects who would go on to change the history of Manchester United – and football – in this country. Pearson moved to Bury and once again Busby found himself looking for someone to lead the team, whilst he introduced his rich stream of youthful gold into the starting line-up.

Busby turned to one of the Class of '48, a man who never missed a game in his last three full seasons at United – Allenby Chilton. In Chilton, Busby had a captain who knew no fear, a man who had been to war, stared death in the face – and lived to tell the tale. Nothing on a pitch held any concern for this unyielding colossus of a man. Nobody appreciated Chilton more than Busby and when, in 1980, Matt was asked to select his all-time United XI, Allenby was given the No. 5 shirt.

Born in his parents' pub in South Hylton, a small village west of Sunderland on 16th September 1918, Chilton did not come into a world – and into a Britain – that was a "land fit for heroes", as Prime Minister David Lloyd George had promised during his General Election campaign earlier that year. After the Great War of 1914-18 ended, the country was plunged into massive unemployment, which caused hunger and despair to be prevalent facts of life. The North East of England was particularly hit with hardship.

Allenby began playing football for the school team, Ford School, in South Hylton. He stood out as a centre-half because of his size and ability, and was picked to play for Sunderland and Durham schoolboys – but not as a central defender! As Allenby recalled in an interview with *Charles Buchan's Football Monthly* magazine in April 1955: "The centre-half berth was more than adequately covered, but I was considered worthy of inclusion in another defensive position – full-back. In the Sunderland Boys' team at that time, about eight of us were actually centre-halves with our school teams. As displaced centre-halves, we were lucky to step into positions where there happened to be a shortage of talent. Even the goalkeeper for Sunderland Boys was a centre-half for his school at Boldon Colliery. He was Ray Middleton, who went on to be a star goalkeeper with Derby County and Chesterfield."

By the time Chilton was age 14, he joined Hylton Colliery Juniors, a team for boys aged between 14-16. However, the young Chilton was also an accomplished amateur boxer, and there was a period of some six months where he quit football to concentrate purely on his pugilistic ambitions. Fortunately Chilton decided that this wasn't the life for him and he returned to Hylton, before stepping up a level to play for Seaham Colliery FC on Seaham Recreation Ground in the Wearside League.

Being a mining team, the side was full of men who worked hard during the week – and played hard at the weekend. Even as a boy Chilton was big enough to handle himself in these surroundings. It was a league littered with ex-professional players and it was here that he gained invaluable experience – playing against and alongside – many of these players. His game improved immensely, and it wasn't long before he was the colliery's first-choice centre-half. Chilton caught the eye of a local man, who did a little scouting for Liverpool. So in August 1938, aged 19, Chilton found himself signing amateur forms for the Reds.

He spent a month there on trial, and did enough to convince then Liverpool manager George Kay to sign him on professional terms. Unfortunately for the Anfield club, the 20-year-old Geordie was young and homesick. Despite Kay attempting to sign him on several occasions, Allenby resisted. He duly went home to consider his future.

One Thursday night, Chilton was opening up the bar for his parents when in walked Louis Rocca – who asked if he would like to sign for Manchester United as a pro. Chilton explained that he had signed as an amateur for Liverpool, but Rocca insisted this would not be an issue – and that he could fix it if Chilton would be willing to sign professional forms, there and then. Within a fortnight he was down in Manchester, signing for United on 26th November 1938.

Chilton went straight into the reserve side, playing alongside Bert Whalley and Walter Winterbottom – and he helped the side win the Central League in his first year. He was understudy to the first-team centre-half George Vose who, after joining from Everton in 1932, had been first choice in the ensuing six years.

In the summer of 1939, Chilton tore his ligaments and returned to his parents' pub. Everyday he would go running, and swim in the sea to strengthen his leg. It worked, and by the start of the 1939/40 season, he was back training at United with the first team.

The season started well for United, with a 4-0 win over Grimsby Town followed by a 1-1 draw with Chelsea. On Friday 1st September Busby announced four changes to the team to play at Charlton the next day: McKay, Vose, and Carey were injured, and Johnny Hanlon was dropped. Allenby Chilton and Beau Asquith were selected to make their debuts. Chilton wasn't to know that his bow would be the last official game he played for United for six years. Chilton replaced Vose and though United went down to a 2-0 defeat, Chilton enjoyed a solid game and was confident of keeping his place.

However, the day after Chilton's debut, Britain declared war on Germany and the Football League competition was cancelled. Players were called up to regiments all over the country, where they would often play as guests for the team nearest their depot. Chilton joined the Durham Light Infantry, and went down to train in Thetford, Norfolk. Whilst there, Chilton contacted Charlton Athletic's manager Jimmy Seed, and asked if he could "guest" whenever his duties made him available. Chilton played for London club in the Southern Cup final against a Chelsea side containing a certain Charlie Mitten. Chelsea had reached the final by beating Reading – who listed Matt Busby in their line-up. Charlton won the final, with General Eisenhower, who was at his first-ever football game, presenting the trophy.

Chilton then went on Commando training in Scotland, which gave him the opportunity to play for Airdrie – playing against a Celtic side that contained future team-mate Jimmy Delaney. Chilton also played for Newcastle United, Hartlepool United and Middlesbrough, when he was stationed in the North East, before being posted to Iceland because of his training. There was no chance of playing football there, but he was given the opportunity to box again. On his return to England, he found himself in Hereford, where he was selected to compete for Western Command. Chilton put up a good fight, but was beaten on points.

Everything changed for Allenby on 5th June 1944, heading for the beaches on Normandy. D-Day was planned for the following morning; thousands of troops would hit the beaches in a combined assault in an attempt to push back the Germans. The 151st Infantry Brigade was made up of the 6th, 8th and 9th Battalion Durham Light Infantry, and they were one of the first to reach Gold beach. Chilton found himself crammed in the airless hold of the ship, feeling queasy due to the rough swell of the sea and the smell of hundreds of bodies. The temperature had been rising and he was tempted to rip off his oilskin and waders, as the heat was unbearable. The nausea was also caused by the apprehension of what was to come. But then the magic words were roared at them: "Move it, men". The smell of the fresh air rushed through his nostrils as he hit the open deck. Chilton no longer felt fear – only excitement. The lads were in good form, drinking in the cool, fresh air and joking as only Geordies can. The NCOs bellowed at them, and the men moved like a well-oiled machine, as they had practiced so often.

The skies that morning were misty and the seas were full of thousands of boats of all descriptions, ferrying men to the beach. From a distance they could see the shore and a few puffs of smoke, which were followed a few seconds later by a heavy shudder. They got closer and closer to the beach – and then all hell was let loose. The noise was deafening and Chilton found himself covering his ears as the shells from the battleships pounded enemy positions a couple of miles inland.

They were dropped a couple of hundred yards from the shore. Chilton scrambled over the side of his ship, down the ropeladders and packed shoulder to shoulder like a sardine into a LCI (Landing Craft for Infantry). He was near the front, with a good view of the beach. As they got closer he could see wrecked vehicles littering the shallow waters and the beach. To the left tanks, complete with flails, were clearing a path through the mines. Odd puffs of mortars erupted in the sand. Groups of men made their way, snakelike, off the beach. It seemed organised, but the noise was horrendous. The LCI hit the beach with a sudden jerk, and Chilton heard those words he had heard so many times in training: "Move it, men." They surged forward, into the icy cold water.

Scrambling ashore they got out of their waders and slowly made their way up the beach towards a small track and eventually into a narrow country road, claiming their first couple of hundred yards of enemy territory. But then a shell dropped nearby and they were showered with debris, and quickly dived into ditches. This brought Chilton back to earth with a crack and this is how his D-Day went; slow progress across difficult terrain – every time he got the chance to relax, a loud crack of sudden sniper fire would wake him. Occasional tanks passed through going forward, and a few German prisoners would walk the other way, hands above their heads or clasped behind their necks going backwards.

A few days after D-Day, on the road to Caen, Chilton and his battalion came under attack from mortar fire. Chilton dived into a hedge for cover, but could hear the shrapnel buzzing through the grass. He then felt a sudden burning pain as a piece hit him in the arm and side. He was taken to the nearest hospital, where they did their best to remove as many fragments as possible, before flying him home. He would say later that he considered himself lucky, "but not as lucky as some, who seemed to spend all the war in uniform but playing football every week, or being in the Home Guard looking after the Woodhead Tunnel."

Chilton spent the rest of the war in uniform – indeed, he was still in uniform when conflict ended, waiting to be demobbed. The FA had decided that the 1945/46 season would be one in which a regional programme would operate; all First and Second Division clubs would be grouped into two leagues: North and South. There would be no promotion or relegation, so the struggle for league positions would be missing – but it would give clubs a chance to re-group as preparation for the following season, when the league would officially start again.

Chilton, though still in the army and still in uniform, decided to go "absent without leave" to Burnden Park, to play for United against Bolton in the Northern Regional Cup in May. He stayed with his old landlady in Stretford and when he met Matt Busby, Busby asked: "Will you be coming back permanently, Allen?" Chilton responded in the affirmative: "If you want me back…I'm waiting to be demobbed in the '25' group." Within a fortnight of coming home, he was back in Manchester and playing again. This time though there would be changes, for as he had done with others such as Carey and Aston altering their positions, Busby decided to move Chilton from wing-half to centre-half. It was a position he would hold for the next seven seasons.

As the players turned up for pre-season training at Manchester University's playing fields in Fallowfield, they were met with a manager who told them that they didn't have enough training kit to go around. He informed the players of the need for a 'whip round' for clothing coupons to provide jerseys, socks and boots for training. He also had to make appeals in the programme and the paper.

On Saturday 31st August 1946, seven years after his first Football League game for United and two weeks short of his 28th birthday, Allenby Chilton played his second official league game in a 2-1 victory over Grimsby Town. It was one of five straight wins – and United's title prospects looked very positive. United were a disciplined team, initially as much as a result of the players' war-time experiences as Busby's man-management. They were also starting to play the kind of swift, flowing football they would become famous for.

The players were no 'Babes' that Busby would later be famous for bringing through. Very few of the team were under the age of 25 – and most had lost their best years to war. Maybe that is why they played as though they were making up for lost time, but they took a dip in form and United dropped down to seventh in the league. Though form may have been erratic, the one constant about the side was Chilton; he was the power at the heart of United's defence.

Busby's decision to move Chilton to the back had been taken in one of the pre-season practice games. Busby played centre-forward in the reserves and from that position, coached Chilton in the art of central defending. This is the way that Busby and Murphy would coach their teams in years to come. No jargon, no confusion, no shouting and screaming – at least not from Busby – rather a quiet word offering practical advice, leaving the rest up to the player who, if he had a football brain, would work the rest out for himself.

Britain came through one of the coldest winters on record that year, which saw many games cancelled. The disruption was thus that the FA gave special permission for games to be played on Wednesday afternoons, behind closed doors, so that industrial production would not be affected. Fixture congestion showed little sign of abating when the freeze ended, as it led to waterlogged pitches and more disruption.

The last quarter of the season saw United go on a strong run in a bid to win the First Division, winning all but one of their final 12 games. Unfortunately it wasn't enough as Liverpool clinched the title by a point. Chilton had only missed one game – a 4-0 win over Blackburn – due to injury, with only Stan Pearson made more appearances.

The 1947/48 season began well for United – a 2-0 win over the champions followed by a 6-2 crushing of Charlton, the FA Cup holders. However, following that initial burst of good form, United went without a win for nearly two months. But Busby knew he had some special players, and that they just needed to knit together. There were a lot of strong characters in the dressing room, and a steely resolve to rectify matters.

It turned out to be a struggle as by the start of 1948, United were lying fifth, some nine points behind Arsenal. Johnny Morris, the former United forward, used to tell a story about Allenby that relates to that part of that particular campaign. "Because of the poor start, Matt Busby called a special meeting with the players one Friday morning. He called us into the dressing room instead of training, and said: 'We can't go on like this. We've got to sort it out. What are we going to do about it?' So Allen Chilton says to Matt: 'You sit in the corner and be quiet and we'll sort it out.' In the team talk, Chilly got onto one or two players – I won't mention names – but he told them: 'If I was picking the team, I'd leave you in t'bath!' Allen was like that. Next day we were playing at Wolves, who were near the top of the league, and we beat them 6-2. That's when we knew we had a good side. Of course, Matt got all the credit."

The competition that gave them that opportunity was the FA Cup, starting with a classic against Aston Villa. United had taken a stunning 5-1 lead at half-time, and the game looked over. The second half, however, started with Villa scoring two quick goals. Trevor Ford, Villa's Welsh centre-forward, and Chilton were having a battle in more ways than one. Early in the game Ford had brought his foot up and caught Chilton in the stomach. Chilton waited for his chance – and it came to him in the second half. When the ball had been played up-field the ref followed the ball, giving ex-boxer Chilton the opportunity to let Ford feel the power of his punch, which the unfortunate forward did. He went straight down. It was a beautifully-timed punch, unseen by ref or Ford.

This did not mean that Chilton had won the battle, though. With 10 minutes left, he brought Ford down in the area and Villa scored from the resulting penalty to make the score 5-4. Fortunately, Pearson settled the United nerves by scoring from a Charlie Mitten corner.

Charlie remembered the game fondly and especially one moment, when Villa were given a free-kick within shooting distance, and United formed the customary wall. Dickie Dorset, a player known for a fearsome shot, ran up to take it. Mitten recalled: "Allenby Chilton, Henry Cockburn, Johnny Carey and all the boys were lining up as Dorset took a tremendous run up and hit one of his cannonballs – into the net. There was only Chilton left standing – everybody else had 'melted.'"

Liverpool were next up in the cup, and they found themselves up against a United defence – with Chilton at its heart – that dominated the forward line. The 3-0 scoreline flattered the Reds, such was United's dominance. Cup holders Charlton were the fifth-round opponents, the London side sporting their 'lucky' white shirts. There was only one team in the game though and United's defence enjoyed an easy afternoon. Sam Bartram, the Charlton goalkeeper, was in fine form and even though United beat them 2-0, the Charlton fans carried Bartram off on their shoulders at the end of the game, such had been his contribution.

United fans were hoping that Preston goalkeeper Hindle did not have the same kind of game when they met in the sixth round at Maine Road on 28th February. North End, containing Tom Finney and Bill Shankly, had beaten Manchester City in an earlier round and were confident about facing United. In Finney, they had a player who scared the opposition and who always needed close attention. However, the 4-2 scoreline does not tell the full story of the domination that United showed. It was a damp afternoon, with the United forwards taking charge and Preston getting no change out of Chilton, whose physical presence made it difficult for Willie McIntosh, the Preston forward, to get a kick.

The semi-final was against Derby at Hillsborough in front of a crowd of 60,000. It is a game best remembered for the hat-trick scored by Stan Pearson. United were 2-0 up in the first half – but then Chilton was punished for a rare error. Jackie Stramps' cross was allowed to bounce by Chilton, allowing Billy Steel to dart in and score.

The defence was rocked and Derby gained a psychological advantage. Even the relief of the half-time whistle did not settle United as the players trudged to the dressing rooms. Derby started the second half as they had finished the first, on the front foot – but Chilton and his team-mates did not crumble. If anything, Johnny Carey seemed to grow in stature. Chilton put his first-half mistake behind him and put in a towering defensive performance, which was made easier when Pearson scored his – and United's – third. Chilton lived on Ryecroft Road and walking home after training or the game with his mate Jimmy Delaney – they would subsequently be pestered for final tickets for weeks.

Six weeks later United and Blackpool met at Wembley in the FA Cup final. The build-up had seen Matt Busby take the squad to Davyhulme Golf Course, where they discussed how they would deal with Stanley Matthews and Stan Mortensen, plus the darting threats of left-winger Walter Rickett. Both teams were announced on the Tuesday and the only surprise for United was that Mortensen had been picked at centre-for-ward, and not his usual inside-right position. United took this news with a pinch of salt: they saw the change as a tactic that Blackpool would attempt to play the nippy Mortensen against the strong – but slow-turn-ing – Allenby Chilton. Chilton still had shrapnel in him and it made turning quickly painful and uneasy, which would often end in a clumsy attempt at a tackle that would give many free-kicks away. However, Busby and his team's defenders had been given plenty of notice to work out a plan to deal with this dangerous but likeable Tynesider.

As the teams lined up to be presented to King George VI, Chilton's thoughts went back to his comrades who would not be watching the game. Youth makes us feel invincible; war has a way of telling us we are wrong. Chilton's chest swelled with pride in the royal blue shirt that United were wearing for the first time in a Wembley final.

In attendance were the touring Australian cricket team led by Don Bradman, and seven survivors of United's 1909 FA Cup-winning side, including 63-year-old Billy Meredith. The country fell silent as people drew close to their radios to listen to the match commentary of Raymond Glendenning. League games were also being played that day.

A crowd of 20,000 attended a 0-0 draw between City and Arsenal at Maine Road, while 51,000 decided that a derby between Sunderland and Middlesbrough at Roker Park was more important than the final.

The game kicked off with Blackpool starting well. It seemed that their tactic of moving Mortensen into the centre might pay early dividends, with several chances falling to him. After 14 minutes, a through ball from centre-half Eric Hayward found Mortensen, who slipped past Chilton and raced towards the United goal with Carey and Chilton scrambling to get back. Chilton stretched to tackle Mortensen and brought down the forward in the 'D' outside the area. Mortensen's momentum carried him several yards into the box and referee Barrick, who was not up with play, pointed towards the penalty spot. Chilton went to complain but was silenced by Carey who, ever the sportsman, accepted the decision. The next day's papers and film of the game were to prove that Chilton's tackle was outside the area, and that he was unlucky to be punished by the penalty. Chilton commented:

"I never kicked anybody deliberately in my life and my foul on Morty was a genuine attempt to get the ball. John Carey was having a rough time against Walter Rickett – he was having to chase him, so I was having to keep an eye on Morty and watch the spaces, which were opening up around me. Eventually I was caught square and Morty was past me in a flash, I clipped him a yard out…penalty given…he wasn't hurt but jumped for joy. It annoyed me because we could see it wasn't a penalty. He stumbled then dived. They do it better today mind, swallow dives and everything. Anyway, I'm glad that goal didn't decide the match."

Being a goal behind in big games did not disturb United's composure and, if anything, seemed to focus them, making them more determined. On the half-hour Jack Rowley lobbed the ball over Robinson's head, rounded him and side-footed home. United had no time to enjoy the experience of being level though as, soon after, Stanley Matthews' free-kick was headed on to Mortensen, who darted past Chilton and on the half-turn struck the ball into the net wide of Jack Crompton's outstretched right hand. It was the kind of opportunist goal that only he could have scored. The attacking did not slacken, and Crompton had to make a brilliant save from Rickett to keep United in the game.

There are those who say that it was Carey's team-talk at half-time that changed the game for United – but there are also those who say it was Allenby Chilton who went in and put a rocket up his team-mates, ensuring that they came out for the second half firing.

Despite this, the half did not start well for United as Blackpool's tactics caused problems. Munro pushed deep into the United half, and Chilton had to make a desperate sliding tackle that resulted in the trainer being called on to administer a cold sponge. The resulting free-kick was cleared up-field to Johnny Morris, who himself was then fouled and United found themselves with a set-piece opportunity. Morris stood up and took the kick in one movement, and Rowley rose to head the equaliser with 20 minutes to go.

Blackpool weren't finished and once again Mortensen eluded Chilton, raced forward and fired an angled drive – but Crompton got down to it and held onto the ball, much to Chilton's relief. Stan Pearson's goal soon after allowed United to relax and play the kind of football they were famous for – and it was no surprise when Anderson added a fourth.

United had won the cup and Chilton had come out a victor in his personal battle with Mortensen. Both men had been injured in the war, with Mortensen serving as a wireless operator air gunner. One day he was flying in a Wellington bomber over Scotland when it caught fire and crash-landed in a fir plantation. The pilot and bomb-aimer were killed, the navigator lost a leg. Mortensen crawled out of the wreckage virtually unscathed apart from a head wound, which needed a dozen stitches. Chilton meanwhile played with shrapnel in his side. But he was a colossus of a man mentally, as well as physically. A man never willing to accept defeat – and never less than 100% committed.

The 1948/49 season was a case of so near, yet so far from the Double. Although they lost the FA Charity Shield to Arsenal 4-3, United began their FA Cup defence brilliantly, thrashing Bourncmouth 6-0, Bradford Park Avenue 5-0 and Yeovil Town 8-0 – with Rowley scoring five. The sixth round saw a 1-0 victory over Hull before a semi-final against Wolves, captained by superstar Billy Wright.

It was a typical semi-final, full of pace and incident. Chilton made his one blunder of the game when Johnny Hancocks – who passed to Sammy Smyth to score – pounced upon a poorly-directed back pass, although Charlie Mitten benefited from a similar mistake to score the equaliser. Wolves managed to hold on for a 1-1 draw, even though they finished the game with only nine men.

The replay, at Goodison Park, was drifting towards a goalless draw when Wolves centre-forward Jesse Pye, unmarked on the right-wing, collected a clearance and dashed forward. Carey, Ashton and Chilton hesitated, certain that Pye would be flagged offside – but the linesman kept his flag down. Before the back-tracking Chilton could make a tackle, Pye put in a cross which Crompton could only parry upwards, for Smyth to head into the net. There was not a word of complaint from United's disciplined defenders, who just looked at each other and shook their heads in an acceptance that they were about to fall short of the golden prize. This was the first time they had failed to score in 14 cup games, failing to put away several chances to win the game.

With the cup run over, United reverted to their league fixtures. They would end the campaign as runners-up, bringing to an end three post-war seasons at Maine Road where Manchester United – and Chilton – had played some of the finest football in their history. As well as winning the FA Cup they had been beaten semi-finalists the following season, and were runners-up in the First Division for three consecutive years. This wasn't enough for some United supporters though, who were starting to get on Chilton's back, blaming him for some of United's losses, and picking up on his obvious difficulty in turning. They were quite vocal on the terraces, and it was starting to affect Chilton's game.

During the summer Chilton visited Busby, to request that his name be put on the transfer list. His reason was that his wife's health was suffering because of the bad weather in Manchester and she had been unsettled, wanting to return home to the North East. Busby was not happy that his trusted centre-half wanted to leave but he also had a ready-made replacement waiting in the wings in the shape of Sammy Lynn. Lynn had signed pro forms in 1948 and was winning rave reviews for his performances in the reserves. So United started the 1949/50 season without the likeable Wearsider, and got off to a solid start.

Busby was delighted when he received another visitor at his home. It was Chilton again, asking for his name to be taken off the transfer list. Busby put the player straight back in as left-half against Liverpool at Anfield. Busby couldn't drop Lynn from the centre-half position as he had done nothing wrong, but a few weeks later Chilton was back in the No. 5 shirt, with Lynn being forced to move out to wing-half. Chilton had missed United's first league match at Old Trafford for eight years, a 3-0 victory over Bolton, as well as the first derby of the season there as well, watching United's 2-1 victory. This must have played a part in Chilton's decision, as there was a sense of excitement and expectation every time the players took to the Old Trafford pitch.

United impressed that season and hit a patch of consistent success. They were considered FA Cup favourites, and were only a point behind Liverpool with 12 games to go. The next match was a 2-2 draw at Sunderland, with Chilton heading the equaliser from a Rowley corner. It was his only goal of the season and his first since September 1946, yet it served to underline Chilton's renewed confidence which everyone, even his critics, were learning to appreciate. Chilton was a pillar of strength and everyone could see how many top-class centre-forwards had failed to score against United that season. But there was to be no cup success as Chelsea defeated United in the sixth round, and the charge for the title soon faltered. The First Division title, which they had not won since 1911, had eluded them for yet another season.

The 1950/51 season was not a great one for United – but a special one for Chilton. United had returned from America, where they had spent the summer touring and making friends – only to lose Charlie Mitten before they arrived back. The season had started well and Chilton was receiving positive plaudits, so it was no surprise when on 7th October, Chilton was picked to play for England against Northern Ireland in Belfast. His replacement for United while he was on international duty would be 17-year-old Mark Jones.

Chilton was enjoying one of the best periods of his career, and his selection had been just reward for a series of immaculate performances. Reports stated that Chilton started magnificently, and then settled into the usual determined stopper 'we see in most league games today.' It seems that the England selectors were not impressed though, as it was not until a year later that he would be given another chance. He would only receive two caps, scandalous for a player of his ability. Unfortunately the club season failed to live up to its potential. From the turn of the year United played 17, won 14, drew two and lost one. But they could not catch Tottenham, who had been at the top since January.

Some people will tell you that Johnny Carey was too nice to be a captain and the real leader of the team was Chilton. It was his steel that ran through the centre of the team and made the defence so hard for attackers to dominate. But this was a United team that had been to war, come back, won an FA Cup and come very close to winning the league. They were now another year older, very aware of the crop of young players that Busby was bringing through, and who would happily replace them.

The following campaign, 1951/52, started with the return of the prodigal son, Charlie Mitten. Mitten had returned home in June to rejoin his wife and children in Stretford, stating that he wished to play for United again, but having no regrets about the time spent in Bogotá and the money made. Mitten was still a big hit with the supporters, many of whom wrote to the papers and the club asking them to give Charlie another chance. But Charlie was to learn a lesson that Eric Cantona would find out many years later. The FA are rarely lenient with United players, and he was fined £250 and banned from receiving wages or training with any club until 1st November. The football establishment decided to make an example of Charlie – and United, despite their 'family' image, followed suit: Charlie had to go.

United started the season with a determination to make it 'their' season and they were soon top of the league. Chilton's impressive form was rewarded with a second England cap when he played against France at Highbury. The game ended in a 2-2 draw, and Chilton did not cover himself in glory. He was dropped for the next game against Wales, and was never picked again. Maybe Chilton, who was never shy, was just a little too opinionated for the England dressing room or selectors' liking. Whatever the reason, it was England's loss and United's gain that he was not called away more for international duty.

FA Cup third-round day came along and Matt Busby picked his strongest team to take on Hull, who were lying second-bottom of the Second Division. The game turned into a nightmare for United – Jack Rowley missed a penalty, and Hull won the game 2-0. This now left United in the unusual position of having only the league as the priority so early in the campaign. They duly went on to win it, beating Arsenal 6-1 in the last game of the season, with Chilton playing every game. This United team had achieved their aim; this was to be the last trophy for Busby's first great side. Busby was already planning for the future.

The 1952/53 season was played as if the job had been done; the determination that the whole team had shown in previous years now seemed to have waned as the team started to show their age. Knocked out of the FA Cup by Second Division Everton and finishing eighth in the league, it was United's lowest finishing position since the war. But the final placing and results do not tell the whole story of a season.

The game against Huddersfield on 31st October 1953 at Leeds Road marked the end of the old team. Busby selected Blanchflower, Viollet and Duncan Edwards. Only Chilton and Rowley were left of the old timers. The referee Bob Wood came up to Chilton after the game and said: "Hey, Allen, you've got some really good youngsters here." Chilton was still holding onto his place and Matt knew he could try a new defender or full-back, confident that Allen would cover for them. One of those defenders was Roger Byrne, who Chilton used to play hell with. If the ball came down the wing then Byrne, rather than getting up and heading the ball, would duck and let the ball go over his head, using his speed to deal with any problems. Chilton used to say to him: "One of these days, Roger, you'll meet someone faster than yourself!"

Chilton took over the captaincy from the departed Stan Pearson in 1954, and the responsibility came easily to a man who had always been a natural leader. Chilton was a strong character and strict disciplinarian, and this was a reason why Busby gave the big Geordie the captaincy. With so much youth and precociousness around the squad, he knew that Chilton would keep the young boys' feet on the ground. Chilton wasn't averse to using the back of his hand to make a point known! Out on the field, players like himself, Jack Rowley and Henry Cockburn (who could all look after themselves and mix it with the best) were able to 'mind' the younger players that were coming through. They made sure that opponents didn't take liberties with the kids in the team. These three players could see what the future of United was going to be like, and they did an invaluable job for the manager in that they were able to help school these youngsters the right way.

Chilton was a big presence in the defence, around whom attacks were started and the back line was organised. He was not all blood and thunder though, and was as much a fatherly figure to the young players coming through as Johnny Carey had been. Rowley was the only other player left from the 1948 team. Playing up front, he complimented Chilton's influence as a wise head amongst the young guns of United's attack.

Once again Chilton played every game, bringing the kind of stability Busby needed for this season of transition. The team finished a respectable fourth, and had shown the world a sign of things to come. Dennis Viollet said of Chilton: "I don't feel enough credit was given to

Allenby Chilton for the change in the first-team's fortunes. With so many immature, inexperienced players around him, he had to put in a tremendous amount of work. He was a constant inspiration to us and held the team together. He told us exactly what was wanted – he didn't mince his words – but never held off-field inquests."

The following 1954/55 season was to be Allenby Chilton's last as captain of United – and it started terribly with a 3-1 defeat at Old Trafford to Portsmouth. Then United went on a run of eight games undefeated, before losing to Manchester City at Maine Road on the 25th September. From then on it was a pattern of wins and losses. The third round FA Cup draw found United playing Reading, a hurdle they managed to pass at the second attempt. This brought a mouth-watering tie – a derby against Manchester City at Maine Road on Saturday 19th February 1955. The week before they had lost 5-0 to City at Old Trafford.

United started the game strongly and dominated, but were guilty of wasting chances. Frustrations were growing in the United ranks and Chilton was not happy with the refereeing that day, letting his feelings be known. Unusually for those days the referee blew his whistle and called Chilton over. The official told him to calm down – but Chilton was not happy and carried on. The referee duly pointed to the dressing room, sending Chilton off. City pair Don Revie and Ken Barnes rushed to the official and begged him not to send Chilton off, but it had no effect. He trudged off the pitch – and United went out of the cup.

This was the last game that Jack Rowley played for the club. Chilton played in the next game, a 4-2 defeat to Wolves at Old Trafford. Chilton was facing suspension due to his sending off, but he was still eligible to play against Cardiff the following week. He went to see Busby in the middle of the week and asked to be left out. Mark Jones, who was now aged 22, came in and took over the No. 5 shirt. It was inevitable that the Yorkshireman would keep his place from then on. There was a new era dawning at Old Trafford. Chilton was 37, and no longer felt that he was good enough to play at this level for a club he held so fondly in his heart.

He decided to hang up his boots and end a run of 175 consecutive games for United, which had begun on 10th March 1951.

It is amazing to look at Chilton's record with United. Notwithstanding the fact that he lost almost seven years of his career to the Second World War, he still managed to amass 391 appearances and in a period of nine years, he missed just 13 games. Chilton was so highly thought of not only by both Matt Busby and Jimmy Murphy, but also by team-mates and fans alike. Jimmy Murphy described Chilton as a "strong, fearless, hard-tackling, orthodox stopper." He paid him the ultimate compliment when picking his best United XI – choosing him at centre-half in preference to Bill Foulkes, with the comment "a shade taller than Foulkes and for that reason slightly more commanding in the air." Shortly afterwards Chilton moved to Grimsby, taking on the role as player-manager.

Busby had lost his Mr Dependable, his rock. This man had fought in the same war as Busby, and had never shown fear of any man on or off a pitch. He was the archetype stopper. No centre-forward ever relished playing against Chilly, as they knew he would stop them anyway he could. If they wanted to get physical he would show them what physical was. He was dominant in the air and better on the ball than he was ever given credit for. Mostly, though, he would go and get the ball and give it to one of the boys, who could weave some magic. He had the courage of a lion and would put his head where most would dare to tread. He was a players' player and someone you would literally want next to you in the trenches. But most of all he was a captain – our captain.

Allenby Chilton finally lost the ultimate fight on 15th June 1996 in Southwick, aged 77.

Captain of the Busby Babes

ROGER BYRNE

1955-1958

*'Following in the footsteps of such eminent leaders as
Johnny Carey, Stan Pearson and Allenby Chilton was certainly
an honour. Playing under the captaincy of such players
you cannot fail to learn and improve your football'*

No team has taken up so much of the written page as the Busby Babes; they have cast a shadow that still hangs over Manchester United today. They are men of legend and folklore; anyone who saw them play will tell you they were the greatest club team ever. Who, in that case then, would captain the greatest club side of all time? The answer is easy, and never in doubt to those who knew him: Roger William Byrne.

Bill and Jessie Byrne lived at 13 Beech Street, Gorton. Bill worked in the furniture department of Lewis's department store in Manchester. The date of 8th February 1929 was a momentous day for their family, as Roger William came into the world, kicking and screaming. I say kicking, as Roger was kicking from the day he could walk. At every opportunity he would be out in the streets or at nearby Debdale Park, playing football. Roger attended Abbey Hey Infant and Junior School. As well as football he also played cricket, and was a good gymnast. Unlike his footballing peers, Roger didn't let sport get in the way of his education and he won a scholarship to Burnage Grammar School.

Things could have been so different for young Roger. When he first went to Burnage Grammar, he concentrated more on cricket than football and later, along with his friend Brian Statham – who went to Manchester Central High School – he joined Denton West Cricket Club.

Brian was a natural and made the first team easily, whereas Roger played for the second XI. They would both go on to find themselves as a captain at Old Trafford – Roger at United, Brian at Lancashire CCC.

It was whilst both were at Ryder Brow Boys Club that they came to the attention of United. Roger had played for Burnage Old Boys at 16, though he was very slight. Even though he had talent he was not deemed big enough, so Burnage dropped him with Roger moving to Ryder Brow. Brian played left-wing with Roger inside-left. Both came through trials with United, and Brian also went to Liverpool and was offered a junior contract. Brian's father, though, wasn't sure about football as a career and so United's loss was Lancashire and England's gain.

Roger began his United career on 18th August 1948. He started life as an amateur playing in the Lancashire League, and signed pro forms on 4th March 1949. The following day the *Manchester Evening News* was more interested in the possibility of Johnny Morris moving to Liverpool for £25,000, and could only spare a couple of lines: 'Manchester United have signed on professional forms 19-year-old Roger Byrne, a left half-back, who has been playing as an amateur in the "A" team.'

A month later Roger made his debut for the reserves at Everton. This was no *Roy of the Rovers* debut though, with United beaten 3-0. But at least Roger had his first taste of football at a higher level, and had taken to it like a duck to water. He managed three further games for the reserves before the season ended.

The first time most United fans got to see Roger was on 13th August 1949 in a pre-season curtain-raiser, first team versus reserves. Roger was left-half for 'the Blues', and the team he lined up against was:

Crompton; Carey, Aston, Warner, Lynn, Cockburn, Delaney, Pearson, Rowley, Birch, Mitten.

Roger only played the first 45 minutes, but he made a good impression. The rest of the 1949/50 season saw Roger make 28 appearances for the reserves, playing mostly as left-half or on the left-wing. Much to Roger's annoyance Matt moved him to left-back for five games, which

Roger hated as he wanted to play further forward and show off his pace.

The following season he was a regular in the Central League team, making 31 appearances – 18 at left-back, one at left-half and 12 as left-wing – and scoring two goals. He also played in the side that defeated Bury 2-1 to win the Lancashire Senior Cup, alongside future stars Jack Crompton, Mark Jones, Jackie Blanchflower and Dennis Viollet.

On 25th April 1951 Roger made his debut for the first team in a friendly at Reading's Elm Park. The game was a testimonial for two Reading players and was played in a spirit befitting the match, the game ending in an exciting 4-4 draw. The line-up for Byrne's first game read:

Allen; Carey, Byrne; Gibson, Chilton, McGlen, Viollet, Pearson, Aston, Downie, Rowley.

The game had been a big success, with gate receipts of £1,255 and Matt Busby had been impressed with Byrne – so much so that at the end of the season Roger found himself on a first-team tour of Denmark.

The tour began against a local amateur XI, with Roger starting at left-back. United had just finished a tough season, and players were treating the trip as a holiday – a notion reflected in the 2-2 score. Two days later they faced a Copenhagen XI and Roger was once again included. The team again lacked motivation, although they scraped a 2-1 win. For the remaining games Roger sat out as Busby weighed up his other options.

Roger may have felt confident about the 1951/52 season, but he found himself back in the reserves. Their season started against Bolton on 18th August, and Roger played like a man with a point to prove, scoring a hat-trick in a 5-1 win. He remained in the second string, playing a number of left-sided roles and hit two further goals, against Blackburn.

On 23rd November, Roger checked the team sheet for the reserves and was shocked to see that he had been left out. Fortunately he had a quick look to see who was playing for the first team. There in the left-back position was the name Roger Byrne. The United line-up read:

Crompton; Carey, Byrne, Blanchflower, Chilton, Cockburn; Berry, Pearson, Rowley, Downie, Bond.

Roger, at the age of 21 was not the only one making his debut – 18-year-old Jackie Blanchflower, brother of Danny, was also making his bow. The game ended 0-0, but praise flowed for the debutants, especially Byrne. Alf Clarke reported that: 'In his first big match, Byrne kicked admirably with both feet, positioned himself well against Jackson and in at least one instance showed the coolness of Carey himself.'

This was high praise indeed, but more importantly was the fact that Matt had been happy with his performance. He wore No. 3 the following week against Blackpool, and impressed in a 3-1 win. He had waited a long time to get his chance, and doubted whether he would make it. But with Busby's encouragement, his patience had been rewarded.

United had not started the season well – of the 18 games played before the Liverpool game, they had won only nine. Byrne's debut was to see United go on an unbeaten league run that would last until 22nd March when Huddersfield, who were bottom, beat them 3-2 with Roger giving away a penalty. United didn't fare well in the FA Cup, as an upset occurred on 12th January when Hull knocked United out 2-0.

United were still top but the Huddersfield defeat meant Arsenal had narrowed the gap. Being out of the cup and with a free weekend in March, Matt arranged a home friendly with Hibernian. For the 20,000 who battled against a snowstorm, Matt had a surprise – moving Roger to left-wing. It was the first time he had played the position for the first team. Both sides found the weather tougher opposition than each other, and the game ended 1-1. Roger's forward foray lasted 45 minutes as he had to fall back due to an injury to Henry Cockburn.

The following Saturday saw Roger back in his familiar position for a 1-0 defeat at Portsmouth. United were now only top on goal average. Busby had much to mull over – and he shaked things up. The next game was at Burnley and Busby made six changes, with Roger moved to left-wing – and it proved to be an inspired move as he opened the scoring with a header. Unfortunately, the Clarets hit back to grab an equaliser.

Liverpool were next up at Old Trafford. Roger again wore No. 11 and again he was the first scorer, this time from the penalty spot. Downie made it 2-0, Roger followed up a Johnny Carey shot to make it three before Rowley hit a fourth. Easter Monday saw Burnley at Old Trafford, hoping for a repeat of the draw they had managed three days earlier. But United were in clinical mood and in Roger, they had a man in a rich seam of form. The game ended 6-1 to United, with Roger scoring twice.

A trip to Blackpool on 19th April saw United draw 2-2. Roger was again on the scoresheet with a tap-in before the home side hit back, leaving United level with Arsenal – but ahead on goal average. They still had Chelsea and the Gunners to play, and everything to play for.

Chelsea came to a cold and muddy Old Trafford on 21st April and were brushed aside, although Roger received criticism from the crowd for wasting possession, as well as holding on to the ball too long. He had the opportunity to make amends when he got a late penalty – with United leading 3-0. As if to sum up his poor afternoon he missed.

There was better news at the final whistle. You could hear the cheer down the Warwick Road as the United players discovered that the Gunners had lost 3-1 to West Brom. United would now have to lose heavily at home to Arsenal to prevent league championship success.

The crowds meant that the Old Trafford gates were shut an hour before kick-off. Those lucky enough to be there saw a football exhibition, as United swept the Gunners aside 6-1. Roger scored one and could have scored another as United got a penalty. Whether he passed up the chance having missed recent spot-kicks, or allowed Jack Rowley to complete his hat-trick, is open to debate. What did matter when the final whistle blew was that United were crowned champions. A band came onto the pitch and attempted to play, but were brushed aside by invading supporters. Fans rushed for the tunnel hoping to get a glimpse of the players, demanding that Johnny Carey return with his heroes – but they were in the changing room celebrating a win they had waited so long to achieve.

United had been crowned champions and the newspapers were full of praise. Alan Hoby in the *Sunday Express* commented on Busby's masterful tactical change by pushing Roger up on the wing when he wrote: 'This 21-year-old kid is goal hungry – and doesn't Matt Busby know it? It was Matt who, a few weeks ago, moved Byrne from left-back to out-side-left at the time when Manchester United lacked goal punch. What happened? Roger has repaid his faith by scoring seven goals in six games, once again proving that Busby is soccer's "Master switcher".'

It had been 41 years since United's last championship. Since the war and Busby taking over, Manchester United had achieved an undisputed level of consistency in the league that no other team could compete with, and you would be hard-pressed to find any football supporter in the land at that time who would deny United their title glory.

The period had also seen the club buy The Cliff training ground at Lower Broughton in Salford, where they had installed floodlighting. Roger would watch the youngsters, players who in the future he would captain to glory. One game in the FA Youth Cup, United beat Nantwich 23-0. Albert Scanlon was on target, David Pegg scored five while there were another five from a lad from Dudley called Duncan Edwards.

United set off for a 12-game tour of the USA and Canada, a trip that would see Roger again make headlines. The party were in great spirits on the Queen Elizabeth. Carey was presented with a 'championship cake' from the ships' head baker. Iced in red and white and made to represent a pitch, the cake had a sugar sign behind one of the goals, which read 'United 6 Arsenal 1'. The team made friends, integrating with crew and passengers, playing in competitions and entertaining with songs.

The team arrived in New York and stayed at the Paramount Hotel on 46th Street, where they had stayed on their first trip. They were still relative unknowns and maybe Tom Connell, the Newark correspondent who penned United's welcome, should have done more homework before writing his squad intro. Of Johnny Carey, he wrote: '...two other sons of Erin in the Manchester line-up are Tom McNulty and Roger Byrne, a pair of 21-year-olds who rate as the most promising stars in the game'. Roger's surname was clearly not English enough for the reporter.

The first game was against a New Jersey XI in Kearney. Johnny Carey fired in a free-kick, and Roger scored twice to give United a three-goal advantage by half-time before Johnny Berry claimed a late fourth. Roger also scored in the second game against Philadelphia All-Stars in which United again ran out 4-0 winners. The games came thick and fast and saw United score plenty, with Roger getting his fair share.

The tour took a dramatic turn for United and Roger when United played a double header against the Atlas Club of Mexico in Los Angeles on 1st and 8th June. Both teams had played each other on United's last tour of America, playing out an enjoyable 6-6 draw. What was to follow shocked everyone who had come to watch an entertaining game.

The Mexicans started well but were getting little change out of Johnny Carey and Reg Allen before Stan Pearson scored the first on the half-hour mark. After the break United were the better side. Roger, playing on the left-wing, beat a man and drove into the box, when he was brought down. The referee blew for a penalty – signalling chaotic scenes. An Atlas player attempted to punch the referee, and the right-half Varrillo charged the official and knocked him over. The referee had no choice but to send Varillo off – cue more unrest. The Atlas coaches and subs ran on, charging towards the official, which seemed to encourage the crowd to join in. Sheriffs had to come on to protect the referee, having to drag one spectator off the man in black.

When peace finally returned to the game, Byrne stepped up and gave the keeper no chance. The game ended 2-0 to United, although the final whistle signalled another pitch invasion from some Mexican fans.

The return game seven days later would not have taken place if Matt Busby had his way, as he had no wish for United to be involved in another game with the scenes that he had previously witnessed. However, the game went ahead and saw United win 4-3 – but Roger did not cover himself in glory. Matt wrote in his book *Soccer At The Top*:

'Atlas were a rough lot. Seeing how things were going, I told Johnny Carey to instruct the team to keep their heads. He did this, but Roger defied him and was sent off. I did not like my players to be sent off abroad, where club and national reputations suffer more. Nor did I like mine or my captain's instructions to be forgotten, even allowing for provocation. So I had to make my point once more – we would do it my way. I told Roger he must apologise to Johnny Carey, or I would send him home the next day. I would give him two hours to do it in. No more than 15 minutes later Johnny came to see me to say, "Roger has been to apologise." So Roger rose in my estimation, high in it though he already was. I knew it was only a lapse into a headstrong state that had caused his dismissal. Now he'd shown he was big enough to apologise.'

Johnny Carey, ever protective of his players and his club, painted a different picture in his 'Letter from America' column that appeared in the *Manchester Evening Chronicle*. His version of events read:

'There is no truth in the report that the referee sent Jack Rowley or Roger Byrne off. "The Gunner" never left the field and he gave no cause for anyone to suggest such a step be taken. I brought on Harry McShane for Roger midway through the second half, because the Mexicans didn't like the way Roger was skating past them, and Roger didn't like the methods they were using to stop him. As we had the game in hand I decided to prevent trouble before it started and made the change, which later Mr Busby and Roger himself agreed was the best thing to do.'

Roger played in two of the remaining three games, so it was obvious that Busby had been impressed with the way Roger had dealt with the situation – perhaps seeing the makings of a future captain?

The 1952/53 season began at home to Chelsea, the crowd having been treated to the championship trophy being paraded by two ball boys beforehand. United ran out 2-0 winners, but it was not a good game for Roger, who missed a penalty. 'Old International' was critical in his *Manchester Guardian* column: 'Byrne came under the lash for his overelaboration and selfishness, chiefly though to those sins he must add a missed penalty to fill his cup to overflowing.' The criticism continued the following Wednesday when United lost 2-1 to Arsenal at Highbury.

The next Saturday saw United beaten 2-1 in the Manchester derby, and Busby knew changes were needed. Arsenal were next up and Roger found himself back in a defence that were solid in a 0-0 draw – but this was followed by a 2-1 defeat to Portsmouth. This was hardly the start of champions, and Busby was left in a quandary as to Byrne's loss of form, as well as where his best position lay. Once again he found himself at left-wing and thanks to a Stan Pearson hat-trick, United beat Derby 3-2.

United were huffing and puffing, unable to find any rhythm. Busby was struggling to find a fixed position for Roger, playing him at left-back, left-wing and even centre-forward. Roger struggled to find the form he had shown in the championship season. His goals, which had come so naturally, had now dried up and he was missing simple chances.

There was some respite for Roger though in late September, such as adding the FA Charity Shield plaque to his collection after scoring in the 4-2 victory over Newcastle. But the happiness was short-lived as three days later, Sunderland earned a 1-0 victory at Old Trafford.

Roger could not hide his disappointment as he looked at the teamsheet to play Wolves the following week: his place had been taken by 18-year-old John Scott. Roger had been brooding about his form, and was not happy with the positions he was being asked to play. Being left out was the final straw and he went to Matt Busby's office and handed in a transfer request. The cause of his discontent was the fact that he didn't like playing at outside-left. He pointed out to Matt that he was more at home playing in a defensive role, at left-back. Busby unhesitatingly told him that he would play in whatever position he was selected for.

Fans stared at their back pages in disbelief when they read 'United Place Byrne On The Transfer List'. Alf Clarke told his readers: 'Byrne's complaint is that he wants to play at left-back and not in the attack. He was experimented with at outside-left last season, scoring many goals. This season, however, he does not seem to have taken kindly to outside-left and was recently dropped. He cannot get the left-back position from John Aston and feels he would have a better chance elsewhere.'

Johnny Carey took Roger to task about the situation, as did Allenby Chilton and Jack Rowley. They pointed out that something exciting was about to be unleashed on English football from within Old Trafford. The three elder statesmen explained that they were nearing the end of their careers and that a defensive position would be his for cementing, if he buckled down. Youngsters were emerging, who would make United the team of the future. Fortunately, Roger eventually withdrew his request.

On Saturday 18th October 1952 Roger returned against Preston, playing in his preferred left-back position. Many supporters saw Roger as having an inflated ego, and for a few months they made their feelings known. For a while he was known as 'Mr Big'. He couldn't have picked a harder test to make his comeback, as he would be facing the majestic Tom Finney. Anyone who had any doubts were soon reassured as United ran out emphatic 5-0 winners, with Finney having a quiet game.

Roger started to find the form that had made him a favourite. It was not long before Alf Clarke was banging the drum for Byrne. He wrote: 'This is a message for the England selectors: there is a long time yet to the Scotland international and I don't suppose England would be inclined to change the side which has done well. But if England wants a left full-back with possibilities of being there for many years then I advise them to see Roger Byrne. Byrne is 23, which gives him a long time to remain in football. He ought to be considered by England and should be an automatic choice for any "B" side which may be chosen.

'Byrne is the fastest left full-back in the country! I rate him England standard and I am sure Nat Lofthouse will agree. How ironic that Byrne has stepped in so confidently, probably to keep John Aston out of an England team at left-back anyway, though England could do worse than select the two. And there is Henry Cockburn, now back to his best. He overshadowed England's left-half, Dickinson, in the recent game against Portsmouth. Is it too much to ask the FA selectors to see those three United players? They know how Aston and Cockburn can play, but they have never had the reason to contemplate the future of Roger Byrne.'

Clarke and Byrne both got the news they had been waiting for when Roger was selected for the first 'B' international between Scotland and England. Roger impressed in a 2-2 draw and received many plaudits, pushing for him to be included in the summer party to tour South America. Unfortunately Roger was overlooked; instead he returned to Scotland with United, to compete in the Coronation Cup where they were beaten by Celtic. Roger did show his golfing prowess at Troon though, where he recorded a hole-in-one at the 125-yard eighth hole.

United had finished eighth in the league while Johnny Carey announced his retirement, a player who had been the biggest influence on Roger in terms of leadership and how to behave on and off the field.

The 1953/54 season saw Busby introduce more youngsters, while Roger earned rave reviews. Don Davies of the *Manchester Guardian*, reporting on the Huddersfield home game, wrote: 'Byrne gave a faultless rendering of modern full-back play. So much so, that his opposite number Burrell was goaded into a few peppery exchanges, which did little more than obtain the gentlest of rebukes from the referee.'

Davies was not the only one casting admiring glances in Byrne's direction. Roger received his full England call-up to face Scotland at Hampden Park on 3rd April 1954. Even though Roger had a mix up with goalkeeper Gil Merrick, which led to Scotland scoring a second goal, Roger had an impressive debut as England ran out 4-2 victors.

Roger's next two games saw England lose 1-0 in Yugoslavia and then suffer a 7-1 humbling by Hungary in Budapest. Desmond Hackett, writing in the *Daily Express*, noted: 'Only Roger Byrne came through with any pride. Somehow he found the heart, courage and endurance to go goal seeking when the Hungarians were six-up. It was a brand of fighting football that the rest of England had not been able to produce.'

Roger went away with England to Switzerland for the 1954 World Cup, but the current world champions Uruguay cut their route to the final short at the quarter-final stage. This was a great experience for Roger though, as was the chance to play alongside England captain

Billy Wright, who was always there to offer Roger encouragement.

Roger was now an established international and first-teamer, and with this came commercial opportunities such as a column in the *Manchester Evening News*. His first offering looked back on the World Cup, in which Roger noted the need for improvement in the technical ability of English players. Roger also believed teams should make themselves fitter and faster. This is ironic coming from a smoker though so were most of his team-mates, as were Busby and Jimmy Murphy.

Roger was quick, and never one for diving into a tackle. He was slightly built but had a good tactical brain. It was unusual that he played as left-back as his stronger foot was his right, but it never seemed to deter him. He would jockey wingers, and then nick the ball. He was masterful at reading the game and had an uncanny sense of anticipating danger, which was often seen when he covered behind the centre-halves.

Roger didn't enjoy much of a break, and the 1954/55 season started with a home defeat to Portsmouth. However, this proved a blip as United then went on a run of undefeated games, which only ended at Maine Road. Roger gave the ball away to Don Revie, who set up Manchester City's winner. Henry Rose in the *Daily Express* wrote: 'Byrne was often petulant, lacking the deportment expected from an international.'

A footballer's wage did not guarantee him the luxury of never needing to work again when his career ended. Roger was aware of this at the age of 25, even though it was only his third full season as a First Division player. The thought of management or coaching did not appeal, but Roger did have an interest in physiotherapy and he enrolled at Salford Royal Hospital. The course was for three years, but because of Roger's playing commitments he was allowed to do it over six years.

It must have been thrilling for boys on the ward when Roger did his rounds. He was happy to sign autographs, though he did not speak about football. Not that it was all work for Roger; whilst there he met student Joy Cooper. Joy was not a football fan and unimpressed by his status. She did enjoy his company though, and they were soon dating.

As 1955 began United endured some poor form, including a 5-0 home battering by City and then a week later, a 2-0 defeat in the cup at Maine Road. Wolves then visited Old Trafford and won 4-2, before Cardiff inflicted a 3-0 defeat, ending any realistic title hopes. The Cardiff game was notable for the end of an era – and the beginning of another. Allenby Chilton had been sent off in the cup against City and was due to begin a ban. He asked Matt Busby to leave him out for the Cardiff game and after much soul searching, Chilton decided to hang up his boots.

Busby had no problem in appointing Roger as the new club captain. It was a role that suited Roger, and was a popular decision with players and fans. Busby knew from his past run-ins with Roger that here was a man who could think for himself, who was not afraid to have his say. If any player had a problem they would approach Roger, and he would go and see Matt. That didn't mean he always got the better of Matt, though. He would go and ask for more money for a certain player and Matt would listen – and then Roger would return empty-handed.

Roger said of being asked to be captain: "Following in the footsteps of Johnny Carey, Stan Pearson and Allenby Chilton was an honour. Playing under the captaincy of such players, you cannot fail to learn and improve. Obviously the captaincy is not just a case of running out and spinning a coin. I remember on my first tour with United in Denmark, we were playing a combined Copenhagen XI, which included five of the Denmark side. They were awarded a free-kick two yards in front of our goal and being so inexperienced I did not have a clue what was expected. Johnny Carey calmly walked to the ball and directed the rest of us onto the line – and we prevented a goal from the resulting kick.

"After the game I made a point of asking quite a few of the team what they would have done if they had been captain and they surprised me by answering that they did not know. From then on I paid special attention to the captain's role just in case the honour ever came my way."

Roger was seen by younger players as aloof – he didn't mix with them socially. Even though he was only a couple of years older, he seemed more mature and took his role seriously, as Wilf McGuinness remembers: "When breaking into the first team, you didn't automatically get dressed with them after training, you still got changed in the away dressing room with the reserve players. The only problem was that to save money, United only used to run one bath and that was in the first team or home dressing room. In order to have a bath, reserve players would have to walk up to the first team dressing room, knock on the door and wait. If nobody answered you waited. You'd knock again and eventually someone would answer, 'what do you want?' You would ask if you could have a bath, but if Roger hadn't finished talking, the answer would be 'no' and you would be left until Roger decided it was okay to let you in. It was his way of building respect from the youngsters."

The 1954/55 season ended with a 2-1 victory over Chelsea – but it wasn't enough to stop the Stamford Bridge side from winning their first ever league championship. United ended the season in fifth position, five points behind the champions.

The following campaign saw the team that would be christened the "Busby Babes" start with draws against Birmingham and Tottenham, but Busby had faith. He believed that in Roger, he had the man who could captain them to glory. The first eight games saw a return of only eight points which, considering the ability in the team, was a disappointment. United soon responded and by Christmas it was a competition between Blackpool and United for top spot. Roger netted on Boxing Day when United thrashed Charlton 5-1. You can imagine the raised eyebrows when, the day after, the Addicks beat United 3-0 in the return.

It was in 1955 that Roger bought himself a Morris Minor, and would drive to training. This was a time when most players travelled on public transport, while Matt was not happy at the thought of players driving and risking an accident. January 1956 was particularly cold, and the roads were hazardous. Roger was driving along Wilberham Road in Chorlton-cum-Hardy when a van pulled out in front of him, forcing him to swerve. Resultantly his car went through a garden wall. This wasn't just any wall though, for it belonged to one of Matt Busby's neighbours. You can imagine Matt's shock when he heard the commotion, went out to see what was happening and saw the captain of his side, parked in his neighbour's front lawn. Fortunately the only thing hurt was Roger's pride and Matt gave him a lift to training, where he spent the day fending off offers of cement and bricks so he could repair the wall.

A shock 4-0 defeat at Bristol Rovers in the FA Cup third round left United with only the league to concentrate on. Though at some points of the season United had held a seven-point lead over Blackpool, it all came down to Saturday 7th April when United hosted the Tangerines at Old Trafford in a game that would decide who would be champions.

The ground was full to capacity, and after Roger lost the toss United found themselves a goal down after only 90 seconds. United went in search of an equaliser, a fruitless task even after laying siege to the Blackpool goal for most of the first half. The half-time whistle blew and Blackpool were a goal-up, with United's title dreams floating away.

The second half began as the first had ended with Blackpool's goal under threat, but an injury to Tommy Taylor left the team effectively chasing the game with 10 men, with Taylor remaining on the field. On the hour fortune smiled upon United with the award of a penalty. Roger had been the penalty taker, but had missed a couple that season, yet the crowd were still surprised when Johnny Berry stepped up. The ground fell silent, half out of expectation, half out of trepidation. Berry calmly took a few steps backwards, ran up and converted.

Both teams had everything to play for, but it fell to the injured "Silent Assassin" Tommy Taylor to score 10 minutes from time. Blackpool threw everything they had at United, but Roger and the defence stood firm – United were champions. The crowd went crazy, running onto the pitch. The players made a getaway to the dressing room, where champagne was waiting. Roger said: "To say I am a proud captain is to put it mildly. I can hardly realise the championship trophy is really ours and the months of tension since we took the lead last December are over."

The final game was on 21st April at Old Trafford against Portsmouth. Beforehand, Roger led his team-mates to the centre circle to acknowledge the fans. The game was a dull 1-0 win for United, but it was a proud Roger who received the trophy after the game, as the crowd swarmed on. Tom Clare, who writes so eloquently about the Busby Babes, remembers the day: "I raced across the pitch from the 'Glover's side' to see them presented with that wonderful trophy. The crowd was huge in front of the old main stand and player's tunnel as Roger led his team up a makeshift stairway and podium to be handed the trophy by Joe Richards, the Football League chairman. Those young boys mounted the platform at the top of the stairway and their smiles and exuberance told a story. As Byrne brought the trophy and his team down, they were happy to talk to the fans, show their medals and allow fans to touch the trophy before they disappeared up that tunnel and into the sanctity of the dressing room. There was no lap of honour in those days!"

A civic reception was held at Manchester Town Hall, with the team travelling in an open-topped coach led by police motorcyclists. Thousands lined the streets to cheer the players, as they took it in turn to raise the trophy. They then made their way onto a platform on the Town Hall steps. Roger stepped forward, holding the trophy above his head. The crowd fell silent as Roger spoke: "We could not have won this championship without your support. During my brief stay at Old Trafford, never has this club been more United."

When an invitation arrived on Matt Busby's desk to take part in the European Cup, he and the board were determined that this was the way ahead, despite expected opposition from the Football League. The FA were keen for United to enter, but the League refused to support United's bid to become European champions. Busby had no intention of giving up the opportunity – and Manchester United went into the draw.

United started 1956/57 playing like the unstoppable force they had become, winning 10 of their first 12 games. The date of 12th September 1956 saw Roger captain the first United team to enter the European

Cup. The opposition was Anderlecht; the venue, Park Astrid in Brussels. United were too strong, running out 2-0 winners, though not without a scare – goalkeeper Ray Wood saving a penalty with the score only 1-0.

It seemed that United were unstoppable at the time. They returned from Europe and dispatched Sheffield Wednesday 4-1 at Old Trafford. Frank Taylor, writing for the *News Chronicle & Daily Dispatch,* said:

'It was a triumph of top-class teamwork. If I must single out anyone, then I name Roger Byrne as man-of-the-match. Roger has his critics, but his was a streamlined display out of the top drawer. He had Finney – who can be one of the most dangerous wingers in the game – a prisoner on the touchline. Byrne not only kept the Wednesday match-winner out, but also zoomed into attack to start the moves which led to the first three goals. There was England class written all over his display.'

A derby victory over City followed before the return European tie at Maine Road, the game being played there because of the absence of floodlights at Old Trafford. A massacre is the only word to describe what happened to Anderlecht. United thrashed the Belgians 10-0, as the Busby Babes announced themselves to Europe. Arsenal, Charlton and Sunderland were then all defeated by this group of gifted youngsters.

It appeared that Borussia Dortmund would go the same way as Anderlecht as they found themselves 3-0 down after 35 minutes, but they rallied and the game ended 3-2, leaving a lot of United fans convinced that the one-goal lead would not be enough. Frank Taylor, who had praised Roger weeks ago, was in a different mood when he wrote: 'I blame Byrne for the slip which started the avalanche of Borussia attacks. In the 70th minute, instead of kicking the ball away, Byrne breasted it nonchalantly down for Ray Wood. Alas, Kapitulski was there first and Byrne held his head in disgust as the ball rocketed into the net.'

Things did not get any better the following Saturday when Everton came to Old Trafford and emphatically ended United's undefeated run. The Toffees overcame United 5-2, and Roger again received criticism, many reporters saying it was his worst game of the season. Days later the FA Charity Shield at least provided some respite. United should have won more comfortably at Maine Road, but to Manchester City's credit, they kept the score down to 1-0. The victory also saw Roger lift his second trophy as captain.

The return to European football and the Dortmund clash at the Rolfe Erde Stadium gave Roger the chance to make up for previous mistakes. Roger was in commanding form as he marshalled the defence in a 0-0 draw, a result that saw United through. The media hailed the defence, but Roger had more pressing problems. Due to the successes that United were having, the players felt they should be receiving financial reward for their efforts and after a meeting between the players, it was decided that Roger would approach Matt and put the players' requests to him.

Roger went to see Matt and came away with the news that the Football League would be approached regarding bonus payments. Later it was announced that bonuses were increased and if United won the European Cup, each player would receive the princely sum of an extra £5.

United were challenging on all fronts, chasing an unprecedented treble, but it looked a distant target when United were 3-0 down at half-time to Athletic Bilbao in the quarter-final of the European Cup. The San Mames was not the sun-drenched Spain Roger and his team-mates had expected. As Roger had led the team out, it had been snowing and the pitch was a mixture of mud and slush. United got themselves back into it in the second half, but eventually went down 5-3.

Before the second leg, United faced a tricky derby at Maine Road. Roger was booed throughout, though United came out 4-2 victors. Derek Wallis in the *Daily Mirror* told of an inspired display: 'Say what you like about Roger Byrne. Maybe he does fuss like a maiden aunt. Maybe he does throw out the occasional flash of temperament, but Byrne bullied his men out of a second-half slumber and saved a point for United at Maine Road. Here was the captain courageous – a strong man who listened to the crowd's boos and heard a call to action. Here was a captain courageous who listened to two stern lectures from the referee and charged back into the game as if they had been pep talks.'

Four days later on 6th February, Bilbao made the trip to face United under the floodlights of Maine Road. The ground had never seen a night like it as 65,000 people packed in to cheer on United, who had only one intention – to score goals as quickly as possible. It looked as though it wasn't going to be United's night as the minutes ticked away, but just before half-time Dennis Viollet scored an opener to give United hope.

The second half saw wave after wave of United attacks and in the 72nd minute, Tommy Taylor levelled the tie on aggregate. United pressed for the winner, seeing 'goals' by Viollet and Whelan disallowed for offside. But with five minutes to go Johnny Berry gave United the goal that would see them through to the semi-final, to the joy of players and fans.

Arsenal stood no chance as they turned up at Old Trafford for the league game on the Saturday; they were playing against a team that felt invincible, and they were dispatched 6-2 as United looked unstoppable.

April saw United travel to Spain again to face Real Madrid in the semi-final of the European Cup. The weather was kinder, and the players took the opportunity to make the most of the hotel swimming pool. A young Wilf McGuinness was with the party as cover. McGuinness was never short of confidence, and he remembered with a rueful smile how this outlook got him more than he'd bargained for from his captain:

"There was a garden at the back with a few chairs spread about. I was looking for a chair and I came across one and thought, 'I'll have that.' I sat and then Roger came in and said: 'Out of there.' I thought to myself, 'beggar off; I don't care if you are captain.' I told Roger it was mine and that I'd been sat here for 10 minutes. 'I went to the toilet and that is my chair' was Roger's reply. With that he gave me a crack round the head, much to the amusement of my team-mates, who knew that it was Roger's chair – they had kept quiet to wait for his return."

Wilf still talks about Roger in a way that people speak of their favourite school teacher, with respect and fondness. His admiration shines through whenever he is given the chance to talk about him: "He was more intelligent than us. He went to Burnage Grammar School and was taking a course in physiotherapy – anybody who did that was above our educational background. Roger lost his temper sometimes, but I never saw him lose it. Everything he said, he said as if in control. On the pitch he was class, with tremendous pace – a great reader of the game. He wasn't a kicker like a [Tommy] Banks or [Roy] Hartle. His pace, interceptions and reading of the game made him a fabulous player. He got 33 England caps and would have gone on to be England captain."

United were used to playing in front of big crowds, but this was something different as they ran out at the Bernabeu Stadium to 125,000 screaming Spaniards. The game was close, with Roger giving a commanding display at left-back – so much so that Madrid's French winger, Raymond Kopa, took to moving inside in an attempt to get more of the ball, and to escape Roger's attention.

Madrid took the lead on the hour and added a second 15 minutes later. When Tommy Taylor pulled one back with eight minutes to go it looked like United might be in a great position for the second leg, but with the players tiring, Madrid broke and nicked a third. However, Roger was upbeat in his appraisal: "Madrid are a good team, but the bounce of the ball did not go our way. We can win the return as we did against Bilbao. We should have had a penalty when Johnny Berry was brought down, but I do not think we played well until we went two goals behind. We have a chance of turning the deficit into success. Real Madrid are the best side we have played, the best we have faced in any competition."

Roger and the United team celebrated a second championship in the dressing rooms at Old Trafford on Saturday 20th April as they beat Sunderland 4-0 and discovered that their nearest rivals, Preston, had been held to a goalless draw by Blackpool. The first part of the 'treble' was in the bag and now came the second leg of the European semi against Madrid. This would be the first European Cup tie to be played at Old Trafford, and the *Daily Herald* carried a picture of Roger playing bowls in reference to Francis Drake and his attempt to beat the Spanish.

Unfortunately, history did not repeat itself and United could only draw 2-2 in an ill-tempered game. The supporters were furious at the Spanish players' gamesmanship, and booed them throughout. But ultimately United had not done enough. Roger reflected: "We have learnt every ingenious device ever invented to prevent a team from winning, but with Madrid winning 5-3 over the two games, it was a fair result. We scored some of our best goals, swinging suddenly from defence to attack. This was also how Madrid's goals came. They are a great side. As for the reaction of the crowd, they are entitled to their opinion."

The final game of the season was a 1-1 home draw with West Brom, but as Roger received the gleaming trophy, he told the crowd that he could see no reason why they would not win it for a third time. To go along with Roger's title medal, he was also voted *Charles Buchan's Football Monthly* Player of the Season. Buchan wrote of Byrne:

'At the end of each season *Football Monthly* selects a "Player of the Year." I have no hesitation in awarding the honour to Roger Byrne. Not only has he played in every England international, but he has led his side to victory in the league championship for the second year running, to the final of the FA Cup and to the semi-final of the European Cup.

'Though the fame of John Charles – the Wales and Leeds centre-half transferred to Juventus – and the exploits of Tom Finney – Preston's centre-forward discovery – have commanded attention, there can be no denying the wonderful stimulus given by Byrne to England and Manchester United. His cool, calculated work either when his men are in winning mood, or fighting to avoid defeat, have been an inspiration.

'Byrne has his detractors, who assert that he is too inclined to take risks...But one of the reasons why Byrne is the best full-back in the country is his confidence. What appear to be risks – and would be risks to the ordinary player – are part of Byrne's style. The square pass-back from the byline to his goalkeeper and the dash forward to assist attacks comes naturally to Byrne, who has complete command of the ball.

'If Byrne resents the attention paid to him or his colleagues, it is because he is so immersed in the game. That he is captain proves that these moments are insignificant. The longer he plays, the better he will become. He has the brains to make the best use of his great skill.

'Born in Manchester, he has been a United man first and foremost. He has played a conspicuous part in their success. Byrne is not only a quick thinker but very fast on the run. He has the speed to cope with the fastest of wing forwards, and the positional sense to limit their activities.

'Most important of all, Byrne always uses the ball to advantage. His well-timed clearances have started many attacks from within their own quarters. With either foot, Byrne places the ball from his full-back position, straight to the feet of his forwards. It is a relic of his youthful days when he put across many accurate centres from outside-left.

'Byrne is busy, too, planning for the future. He is training hard to qualify as a physiotherapist and I have no doubt he will become as skilled in this art as he is on the soccer field.'

United relocated to Blackpool for the FA Cup final, in a bid to escape the pressure in the city. Roger had a lot on his mind for not only did he have an ankle injury that might keep him out, but he was also due to marry a month later. Taking the opportunity to make extra money, Roger did an interview for *Picture Post* magazine. Not quite what United fans wanted to read before a cup final, Roger stated that he would be prepared to play abroad if the right offer came along. Roger was thinking about life after football, and he knew that a few years playing on the continent would set him up financially. There is also the belief that Matt was seeing Roger as a potential successor to him as manager.

On Saturday 4th May 1957, Roger awoke at Hendon Hall, United's FA Cup headquarters, and had his pre-match lunch of steak, toast and tea. Matt was keeping the team away from Wembley for as long as possible to keep their nerves down, but this was United – they feared nobody.

Roger led his team-mates out dressed in their all-white cup final strip. He introduced the team to the Duke of Edinburgh, and there was a feeling that this side was the future of English football. They would surely be adding the FA Cup to their league win, making a historic Double.

After six minutes Peter McParland, the Aston Villa centre-forward, charged United keeper Ray Wood, who at the time was in possession of the ball. McParland's shoulder crashed straight into Wood's cheek. Wood fell clutching his face, and a stretcher was called for as the unfortunate keeper was carried off. Roger acted quickly and gave the blood-soaked green jumper to Jackie Blanchflower. United were now down to 10 men, and so Roger had to re-organise to protect his stand-in keeper.

Wood reappeared on the touchline five minutes before half-time and was quickly ushered out onto the wing where, although of not much use due to the concussion he was suffering from, he still made it necessary for Villa to employ a man to mark him. United held out until the 68th minute when the villain of the day, McParland, beat Blanchflower with a header. Minutes later it was 2-0 and United looked out of it.

Roger, in one of his most heroic performances in a United shirt, urged his men on and with seven minutes to go Tommy Taylor pulled one back. Wood was put back in goal as United threw everything at Villa to try and get an equaliser. Unfortunately, it was not United's day.

It is a mark of Roger Byrne as a man that after the final whistle, despite the disappointment and despite the nature that alluded to that loss, Byrne gathered his team-mates around him. As Johnny Dixon, the Villa captain, arrived at the top of the Royal Box, Byrne led his charges in applause for the victors as they received the famous old trophy.

The headline in the morning paper the day after declared: 'Villa Get The Cup But United Get The Glory.' Not all newspapers agreed though, and Joe Hulme of *The People* blamed Roger for not putting Wood back in goal sooner. Roger had believed that Wood wasn't even fit enough to be on the pitch, never mind in goal. Ironically McParland complained after the game about the rough treatment he had received after his collision with Wood. It was only strong captaincy from Byrne that had prevented Duncan Edwards from settling the score with McParland.

If Roger and the players thought that they had let anybody down, their fears were soon dismissed as they arrived at a packed Albert Square to the sight of thousands of United fans. The roar could not have been any louder if Roger had been lifting the trophy above his head.

Saturday 5th June 1957 was Roger's biggest day of the year – when he married Joy at St Mary's Church in Droylsden. These were the days before *OK* weddings and Roger was surprised when he turned up to find a large number of fans, many wearing United colours. By the time the couple emerged from the church, the crowd had swelled to a couple of hundred and required a dozen policemen to keep matters under control.

Roger returned in pre-season determined that United were going to improve. The squad went on tour to West Germany, starting off in Berlin against Berliner Stadtelf – a team made up of players from the city's five senior clubs. The game was played in the Olympic Stadium, built by Hitler for the Berlin Olympics. There was noisy home support and the only backing United received was from 1400 British servicemen who were stationed there, who had been given tickets to attend. The home crowd had little to celebrate though as United brushed them aside 3-0.

For the second of the two fixtures they were to play, United travelled to Hanover, where they dispatched a Lower Saxony XI 4-2. The journalists who had followed United on the tour were unanimous in their belief that Manchester United would equal Huddersfield and Arsenal's feat of winning three First Division titles in a row.

Not everything was going as smoothly as the tour, though. Just before the season began, the team was approached by the BBC to make a film about football training. Each player was offered £10 but Roger, acting as team spokesman, turned the figure down. Suddenly United, who had been media darlings, were now being criticised. Roger, never the shrinking violet, went in front of the cameras to defend the decision: "If anyone is interested enough to make a film of us for commercial purposes, they should be prepared to make a reasonable offer. We did not want the money just for ourselves. We had agreed that if the offer had been stepped up, the cash would have gone to the footballers' benevolent fund. So please lay off the 'too big for their boots' tag."

United began 1957/58 with a sense of invincibility, sweeping aside all who came before them, scoring 22 goals in their first six games. It was only when they visited Bolton that they proved they were human. United were thumped 4-0 by a side that cared little for reputation, and who possessed two full-backs, in Banks and Hartle, who would happily introduce you to the cinder track that ran around the outside of the pitch.

Tuesday 22nd October saw United meet Aston Villa in the FA Charity Shield, giving them a chance to get some revenge for the cup final defeat. There was ill-feeling around the game after the McParland incident, but this was forgotten as Roger gave up his captain's role for the game and allowed Ray Wood to lead United out – whilst McParland led Villa. The game was completely one-sided, as a hat-trick from Tommy Taylor and a goal from Johnny Berry saw United win 4-0.

Despite this victory, United's league form had dipped and they were now down in fifth due to a defence that was shipping more goals than normal. This bothered Matt enough to see him pay Doncaster Rovers £23,500 for the services of their Northern Ireland keeper, Harry Gregg. Gregg moved over to Manchester immediately and found himself with nowhere to stay. Roger came to his aid and he moved in with Roger and Joy for a couple of months, until he found a place for himself.

Gregg's addition saw results improve. On 14th January they welcomed Red Star Belgrade for the first leg of the European Cup quarter-final, though a thick Manchester fog made it difficult for most of the crowd to see the action. United won 2-1, but many thought the lead too slender to take over to Belgrade for the second leg. Inbetween the European games, United would gain revenge on Bolton, winning 7-2 in the league while also knocking Ipswich out of the FA Cup. The last fixture to be played before the trip to Belgrade was against Arsenal at Highbury.

Preparations took a back seat as on the morning of the game, director of the club for 22 years, Mr Whittaker, was found dead in his room. Roger led the team out wearing black armbands, but the performance they put in was anything but subdued. By half-time United were 3-0 up, and were applauded off by the home fans. The second half saw a complete turnaround though as Arsenal hit back to level. The momentum was with the Gunners – but this was the United of the Busby Babes, led by the original 'Captain Marvel'. United held firm, despite Roger picking up an injury making a desperate clearance, spending the rest of the game as a virtual passenger. United hit a further two goals and though Arsenal clawed one back, they held to win one of the most thrilling games ever. It would be the last time English fans would see the Babes.

Roger was now a doubt for the trip to Yugoslavia. The injury required intensive heat treatment, and reserve full-back Geoff Bent travelled as back-up. Even when they got to their Belgrade hotel, Roger had more treatment on his thigh, until he was finally declared fit to play.

United got off to the perfect start, with Dennis Viollet scoring after 90 seconds before Bobby Charlton added a further two, to give United a comfortable 3-0 lead, 5-1 on aggregate. The game was not over though and Red Star fought back and drew level in the game, but time was against them and when the final whistle went United were through to the semi-final for a second successive season. Roger was relieved when he spoke after the game: "Football is a funny game, isn't it? I thought we were going to walk it after taking a three-goal lead, but it just shows you that you cannot give these continental sides an inch. Once they get a goal they play like demons. Never mind, we are through."

There was plenty of partying to celebrate, with Matt Busby extending the player curfew by an hour. The players were at the British Embassy Staff Club, which saw drinking and dancing taking place. This meant the normally exuberant United party were subdued when they arrived at Zemun Airport, due to sore heads. But the flight took off on time, before the Elizabethan AS57 airliner G-ALZU reached Munich's Riem Airport for a 40-minute scheduled refuelling stop.

The skies had turned to dark grey and the ground was covered in snow. Soon the plane was ready and everyone settled in their seats, preparing themselves to get back into their card schools. To everyone's surprise, the plane came to a sudden stop after 450 yards. A couple of minutes later the plane set off again to make a second attempt, but once again the take-off was abandoned. The passengers sat for about 20 minutes, before they were allowed to unfasten their safety belts and disembark. Both the players and the press had good reason to want the plane to take off: United had a tough league fixture against Wolves coming up, while the journalists had the Press Ball to attend in Manchester that evening.

The call went up and everyone trooped back out of the warmth and onto the plane. With everybody on board, the Elizabethan made its way down the slushy runway to make a third attempt at take-off. The plane never left the ground as it span off the runway, crashing through the perimeter fence and into a nearby house. The time was 3.04pm. Roger and many others on board died instantly.

It was Monday 10th February when the Babes finally came home. Flags flew at half-mast and the crowds that had gathered lowered their heads as the coffins of Roger and 16 others were taken off the plane at Ringway Airport. Manchester fell silent that night as the procession made its way from the airport to Old Trafford. The cold wind and falling rain made no difference to the thousands who lined the streets. Men, women and children, weeping in disbelief and grief as the coffins passed. It was after midnight when the horses reached Old Trafford, but the police struggled to hold back the crowds that had gathered.

On the afternoon of Wednesday 12th February, at St Michael's in Flixton, a service was held for Roger Byrne – captain of the Busby Babes – before a procession of 30 cars moved on to Manchester Crematorium. Roger died not knowing his wife Joy was pregnant and that he would have a son, Roger Byrne Jnr, to carry the famous name.

United lost not only a great captain, but also a man of great integrity, a born leader. It was also a big loss for the England team. With Billy Wright's imminent retirement on the horizon, there was only one man left to fulfil the role of national captain – and that was Roger Byrne. He was a man that exuded class and was full of charisma, whose sense of fair play and leadership gained him the respect of not only his teammates, but also everybody who came into contact with him. His tongue could be sharp at times, but those young kids accepted him and his discipline. He was simply their captain. Those who saw him can still see him now leading the Babes out, tapping the ball up twice into his hands, and then kicking it up into the air towards the Scoreboard End goal.

Perhaps the sheer class and quality of Byrne as a captain and leader can be summed up by a story told by Ken Rogers, former sports editor and chief soccer writer of the *Liverpool Echo*, who has worked at the heart of the Merseyside football scene for 40 years. Ken explains: "These days, the rivalry between Manchester and Liverpool is red hot, a tribal clash of cultures inflamed by many different things down the years. But in the 1950s, when I was a kid, it was possible to have super heroes at different clubs. One of mine was the supremely gifted Roger Byrne, who looked a class act – as well as being one.

"I would get the *Big Book Of Football* every Christmas. One edition featured a full page image of the United captain, colourised for special effect – there were no natural colour images then. I began to read about Matt Busby's European dreams and I knew of his powerful links with Liverpool, where he had been captain. I remember going to school one rainy day and spotting a white badge floating down the gutter, which I picked up. In bold red letters, it declared: 'Roger Byrne Fan Club'.

"I wore that badge to school with pride, and it made me follow Roger's career with a new focus. I was devastated by the Munich Air Disaster, the loss of that great team, and the death of captain Roger Byrne. I can't imagine any Scouse kid going to school now wearing a 'Wayne Rooney Fan Club' badge, for instance, without the potential for a playground fight. It encapsulates how the culture of football has changed.

"Of course, my real heroes all wore Merseyside football shirts but I, for one, will never forget Roger Byrne. I'm still a member of that particular fan club, even if that little white badge has long since gone."

PB

BILL FOULKES

1958-1959

'Foulkes was as tough as granite...as hard as anybody that played the game. Nobody took liberties with him. He was almost never out of the team through injury, and there was a solid consistency in his play. He was a rock, the minder for ball-playing colleagues of a more delicate disposition'

Thirteen days after the Munich Air Crash and 30 hours before they were to lose Duncan Edwards, Manchester United had to play an FA Cup fifth-round tie against Sheffield Wednesday at Old Trafford. United were staggering like a wounded fighter, trying to stay on his feet. Matt Busby was in a hospital bed in Munich and the cream of English football, the flowers of Manchester, had died or, in Duncan's case, were about to. Someone had to take charge, steady the ship. Fortunately United had such a man – and not just any man – but Jimmy Murphy. Murphy had been Busby's assistant; he had nurtured, cajoled and cared for these boys. He had made them feel invincible every time they put on a red shirt. Jimmy's heart was broken by the tragedy and it never really mended, but he had to carry on for those boys – for Matt's sake.

Jimmy had flown out to Munich, and travelled back with Bill Foulkes and Harry Gregg on the train. The airline had offered to fly them home but Bill told them in no uncertain terms that nothing, or no person, would ever get him on a plane again. The train journey had been no easier for Foulkes and Gregg; every time the train stopped suddenly or shuddered, they would sweat and shake as the memories of that horrific crash came back. It was on the train journey back that Jimmy told Bill he would be taking over as club captain. He didn't ask him if he would like to be captain, he just told him that he was. Jimmy needed someone on the pitch he could rely on, who he could trust to lead whatever side he manage to put out on the pitch. He chose Bill Foulkes.

Bill was born in the Lancashire coal-mining village of Thatto Heath near St Helens on 5th January 1932. He was born into a staunch rugby league family; his grandfather had captained St Helens, and played for England. His father had played in goal for New Brighton before the war in the old Third Division North. But it was the oval ball that ruled the Foulkes household, and no thought was given to football – that is, until the family moved house, a couple of miles down the road to Rainhill. Though only a couple of miles apart, they couldn't have been more different in their sporting preferences. Thatto Heath was a rugby league village through and through whereas Rainhill was a football stronghold.

Bill attended Whiston Secondary Modern School, where a man named Mr Churchward noticed Bill's athleticism and got him playing football. At the time Bill was playing rugby league as a full-back, and had even been offered a trial by St Helens. The school football team entered the Daily Dispatch Cup, a competition for sides from all over Merseyside. Even though they were not a big school, they found themselves in the final, where they lost 2-1 to St Sylvester's. However, their performances attracted appreciative glances from scouts. Bill knew he was a decent player, but it was still a pleasant surprise when he was informed that he had been selected to play for St Helens Schoolboys.

It may be hard for some younger readers to believe, but when Bill was a boy you were allowed to leave school at 14 and become an apprentice. This was the route that Bill took. Although he came from a mining family, his father was adamant that Bill would not follow the same path. Bill's father knew only too well about the risks and hardships that faced a miner every day, and didn't want that for his son. So Bill became an apprentice carpenter at Pilkington Glass. The job suited him – he worked during the week and on Saturday mornings, which left him free to play football for Prescot Celtic in the local league. The only problem with the job was the relatively poor wage. Like all young men of that age, Bill wanted to have money to spend on a Friday night. So Bill tried a few different trades, while also holding the hope that one day he could make it as a professional sportsman. Whilst still at Prescot Celtic he got an invite, along with his friend Derek Hennin, to go for a trial with Bolton Wanderers. Unfortunately for Bill, Derek's father ran Prescot Celtic and the trial coincided with a big cup game – he decided that he did not want to spare two players. Unsurprisingly it was Derek who was sent for the trial, whilst Bill turned out for Celtic.

Bill felt deflated and let down, and he soon left Prescot Celtic to join Whiston Youth Club, playing centre-forward for the open age team and centre-half for the Under-18s. Bill was enjoying his football, unaware that someone who would change his life was watching him. In 1949, after a local cup final in which the team with Bill at the centre of defence lost 5-1, a gentleman approached Bill by the name of George Davies. George was a scout for Manchester United, who covered the Liverpool area. He had liked what he had seen and asked Bill if he would like to go for a trial. The club weren't Bill's team – all he knew about them was that they had won the FA Cup the year before.

The trial took place at St Bede's College, Manchester, at the time the headquarters of the Lancashire County Football Association. Bill went to the trial on his own – his dad had been invited but decided to leave it to Bill. As Bill walked in, George was waiting for him and introduced him to Matt Busby, who was there with Jimmy Murphy and coach Bert Whalley. Bill couldn't fail but be impressed by this trio of great men, who as well as running the famous Manchester United, took the time to come down to a trial and watch the boys.

Bill was asked to play wing-half. It wasn't his natural position, but he didn't complain. Bill's first thought was the high standard of the boys at the trial so as the game ended, he felt happy with his performance – but didn't expect to hear from United again. After the game the boys got changed and were about to leave, after being thanked for coming. Bill's name was called out along with some other boys and he was told to go and see Jimmy and Bert, who were standing at the back of the room. Bill was surprised to be offered amateur forms immediately. This was more than he had dared to dream, and it now seemed that he had a chance to make a career for himself playing football.

Bill went back to Whiston, expecting a call – but it didn't come. After three months, Bill was starting to doubt that United really wanted him, though George Davies reassured him that their interest was genuine. St Helens Town, a semi-professional club playing in the Lancashire Combination League, then approached Bill. Although Bill had signed forms with United and was unsure about turning out for St Helens, he was assured that this would be fine and he was not doing anything illegal. He was paid £6 per win, and £5 for a loss. By this time, Bill was working as a miner at Lea Green colliery. He had joined the mine without his family's knowledge and though his father was disappointed when he found out, he respected his son's show of independence.

Bill was playing as a right-back for St Helens alongside an experienced ex-pro called Bill Twist, who was at centre-half. Bill was playing at a good standard and getting paid well for it, and had almost put the disappointment of not hearing from United behind him. They played a game against Bolton Wanderers' 'B' team and beat them comfortably, with Bill giving a strong performance. Bolton's 'B' coach was so impressed that he asked him to come for a trial at Bolton. Bill explained that he had signed forms with United, and the coach said he would write to United to see what the position was. Within four days Bill received a letter from Manchester United, asking him to turn up at their training ground to play for the 'A' team.

Helped by his work down the pit, Bill had become a fine physical specimen, weighing thirteen-and-a-half stone and standing six feet tall. Turning out for the 'A' team held no fears – Bill was physically strong enough to play against men, and was already playing at a good standard for St Helens. Bill looked around at the other young players who were with him at United, and knew that technically they were more gifted than he was; his only chance was to listen to what Jimmy Murphy told him to do, to try his hardest to carry out what he was being told. Jimmy obviously liked what he saw in Bill and he especially liked his attitude; you never had to tell Bill twice, he was a willing listener and a very determined student. Bill was playing at right-back for the reserves, not his position of choice, he was always happier in the centre of defence. But he was in the team, happy to play wherever he was picked.

In the 1950/51 season Bert Whalley decided to change things around, pushing Bill upfield to play centre-forward for the reserves. Bill had played in attack for Whiston, and also a couple of times for the 'A' team. He had always been comfortable in that position, and found the net a couple of times. Bill impressed further forward, scoring the only goal in the final of the Gilchryst Cup against Leek Town in front of 10,000 supporters. Foulkes impressed so much that he found himself playing as centre-forward in a trial game for the reserves against the first team. He was up against Allenby Chilton, who was centre-half for the first team and gave him a hard time, scoring both goals in a 2-0 win for the reserves. Bill's work down the pit had helped build him up, toughening him. He needed it when playing against Chilton, who tried everything to intimidate Bill, knocking him from pillar to post – but Bill just bounced off him and took everything Chilton could throw at him. As well as the physical marks Chilton left on Bill, he also left a massive impression on the young Foulkes due to his commitment and desire.

Matt Busby was impressed with the raw young forward and called him up for his first-team debut against West Bromwich Albion. On the Thursday before the game, the first team was practicing at The Cliff. Bill, trying to impress the watching Busby and his fellow first-teamers, went up for a header against Mark Jones. Bill landed awkwardly and tore ligaments in his ankle, putting him out of action for several months. Bill's chance to be United's first-team centre-forward had come and gone, for in the time that he was injured United went out and bought

Tommy Taylor from Barnsley. Such is footballing fate – if Bill had made his debut and got on the scoresheet, who knows whether Matt Busby would have gone out and bought one of the finest players ever to grace the Manchester United No. 9 shirt?

This was a massive setback for Bill who because of his two jobs – one with the National Coal Board, and one with Manchester United – found himself a bit of a loner at the club. He worked everyday at the pit and only trained at United two nights a week. He didn't know any of the other players well, and he didn't socialise with them. Bill had to be up at 5.30am for work, so he didn't have time to hang around after training, as there would be a train to catch from Manchester to Rainhill. On the nights that Bill wasn't training at United, you could find him down at Charlie Fox's gym in St Helens. He was a fitness freak and would push himself to the limits, desperate to squeeze that extra 10% out. If Bill was ever going to make it as a professional footballer then it would be through hard work and determination. He hadn't been born with silky skills or great technical ability; Bill's only chance was to impose himself physically on the game.

In December 1952, Bill had been training with the reserves, though only lightly as he had picked up an ankle injury. One day he received the nod from Jimmy Murphy to go and see Matt in his office. He thought it was to discuss his injury, but in fact the first thing Mr Busby did when Bill walked in was to ask him how he was. He replied that he was fine, but Matt was not easily convinced and asked him to jump as high as he could. Bill jumped and felt a shooting pain in his ankle, but told the boss that he was just fine. Matt smiled and said he was pleased, as he was playing on Saturday against Liverpool. He told Bill that as he lived in St Helens he could make his own way to the ground, and the team would meet him there. Bill pointed out that it was the first team, not the reserves who were playing at Anfield, at which point Matt informed him that he knew what team was playing where and that he would be playing for the first team. Any pain that Bill had felt in his ankle was now gone – all he could think about was making his first-team debut for Manchester United against Liverpool. A flu epidemic had swept through the club, taking out right-back Tommy McNulty and leaving a vacant spot for Bill. He couldn't have asked for a trickier opponent against which to make his debut, for playing against him for Liverpool would be the legendary Billy Liddell.

Saturday 13th December 1952 saw Bill Foulkes make his first-team bow. Liddell wished him luck before kick-off, and then did his best to take Foulkes to the cleaners. Liddell got away from Foulkes in the first 10 minutes and put Liverpool ahead. Fortunately for Bill, he had Johnny Carey playing alongside him to calm him down, encouraging him to do the simple things well. Carey showed why he was such a great captain, shielding Foulkes from Liddell as much as possible by his excellent positional play. After the game, which United won 2-1, Carey asked Foulkes his age and then told him that he thought he would do well. It was compliment indeed from a master like Carey.

Bill's ankle was in agony, but he did not mention it as Matt Busby had told him he would be playing the following week against Chelsea. Bill took a taxi to his fiancée's house in Liverpool, although he soon ended up in hospital as the ankle swelled and turned black. The hospital packed it with ice and sent him home, unaware that they were treating a professional footballer – a fact that Bill had kept to himself. Bill made it through the first half of the game against Chelsea, but when he hobbled in at half-time, Matt could see that he could hardly walk. With no substitutes permitted, Bill was moved up to centre-forward, with John Aston filling in at right-back. His contribution in attack was minimal, except for a shot that crashed off the bar and fell to John Doherty, who scored as United won the game 3-2. Bill's ankle was in a bad way and he needed plenty of rest, which brought an end to his season.

The 1953/54 season saw Bill back in the first team, displacing Tommy McNulty at right-back on 19th September for a home game against Preston – and he stayed in the side for the rest of the season. The team never looked like winning the league, but they did find some consistency to finish the season in fourth spot, nine points behind Wolves. The season was a memorable one for Bill, and he also scored his first goal in top-flight football, at Newcastle United's St James' Park on Saturday 2nd January 1954. Bill pumped a long ball from his own half towards Tommy Taylor, who had made a run into the box. Instead, the wind caught hold of the ball and took it over Taylor and Ronnie Simpson in the Newcastle goal, straight into the net.

Another first for Bill that campaign was receiving the only booking of his career, against Cardiff City on 14th November 1953 at Ninian Park. United dominated the game and won 6-1, but it should have been an even bigger stroll for Bill and the United defence. Cardiff left-winger George Edwards was taking pleasure in trying to humiliate Bill. He duly lost his head and hit Edwards with a tackle that sent him sprawling over the fence, into the spectators. Nowadays a straight red card would have been brandished, but a booking was deemed as sufficient punishment. It was the least of Bill's worries for when he got into the changing room, Matt Busby tore a strip off him, telling him in no uncertain terms that if he couldn't control himself – or his temper – then he was no use to the team. Bill heeded this warning for the rest of his career, and it was the last time that the red mist descended during a game.

The following campaign saw Bill cement his place in the United team as the regular right-back, with the majestic Roger Byrne at left-back. The team would finish fifth, but it was obvious to anybody who watched Busby's team that something special was happening at United. The young players that Matt was bringing through were gathering plaudits from everybody who saw them. The season also saw Bill receive his one and only full England cap, against Northern Ireland in Belfast.

The 1955/56 season saw Matt Busby's plans come to fruition as the team ran away with the First Division title, 11 points ahead of runners-up Blackpool. Bill was also now a full-time footballer. Up to this point, he had been part-time at United and an assistant under-manager at the colliery. He was receiving £15 a week from his job, compared to the £7 he was receiving from United. Bill knew he could go far with the Coal Board, and was not sure how much long-term security football could offer him, with the FA having enforced a maximum wage. It was only the England call-up that convinced Bill that he had future in the game – while Matt convinced him that if he were to pen a full-time contract, he would probably be able to avoid National Service.

Unfortunately for Bill, two weeks after giving his job up at the Coal Board and turning to football full-time, he received his call-up papers for the Army. Bill was not a happy man; Matt had managed to get Mark Jones out of National Service due to his so-called flat feet as well as David Pegg, who apparently walked in his sleep. There was no escape for Bill though, so he and Duncan Edwards were ordered to report to Piccadilly Station. Bill was posted to Blandford Forum in Dorset, whilst Duncan was off to Woolwich Barracks.

The call-up had a big effect on the finances of the Foulkes household – they had gone from having two wages coming in from the Coal Board and Manchester United to having a basic Army wage of 15 shillings and six old pence per week. Matt spoke to Bill before he left for the start of his service stating that if he wanted to keep his first-team place, he would have to make his own arrangements for getting to games. He promised Foulkes that if he arrived at the various grounds United were playing at, in good time, then he would play. Despite this seemingly unfair demand Foulkes turned up at Birmingham City's St Andrew's on 20th August 1955 for the opening game of the 1955/56 season. The story goes that Ian Greaves, the young reserve full-back, was already in the dressing room getting ready to play at right-back. Foulkes' arrival put Busby in a predicament, given his statement to Foulkes just before he departed for military service. True to his promise, he told Foulkes to get changed and Greaves had to hand over the No. 2 shirt.

Bill felt unwanted by United, with his wife Teresa forced to work in order for them to have enough money for Bill to be able to travel. The

Army were also unsympathetic to Bill's plight and many times he had to go AWOL just to make a game. Things got easier when Bill was drafted to Buller Barracks. There he was under the command of a CO who was a keen football supporter, and who enjoyed the kudos which came his way from having the Army football team captain under his command. This meant that he was billeted to a civilian hut just off the canteen, while he also had no inspections and minimal duties – a blind eye was turned to Bill's extra footballing activities which included skippering a side including Bobby Charlton and Duncan Edwards.

Bill was becoming stressed by the travelling he had to do, which affected his form. He soon received a phone call from Bert Whalley, explaining that Matt was giving him a rest and that Ian Greaves would be stepping in. Greaves played well, and kept his place for the rest of the season. Bill had played 26 games that season, so he at least qualified for a championship medal. As well as winning the league with United he had also played himself into the hearts of the fans, earning the nickname of "Cowboy" because of his bandy legs.

For the Busby Babes, the 1956/57 season looked like it would be the most exciting season any football team had ever experienced. They looked unstoppable in the league, were favourites for the FA Cup and they were also entering the uncharted waters of European football for the first time, as the first English team to enter the European Cup. Chelsea had been invited to participate in 1955, but had declined after taking advice from the football authorities. But Matt Busby had his eyes set firmly on the future – and that lay in European football. You can only imagine the excitement amongst the United players at the beginning of the season. Not only would they pit themselves against the best that the English league could offer, but they would also be going up against the best in Europe. Bill was embarking on his second year of National Service, but there was no way he was going to miss out on this adventure. To this end he made sure that he was supremely fit by training full-time over the summer in order to get himself in the best shape possible to win his place back from his replacement, Ian Greaves.

The extra training paid off and as the season began, the No. 2 shirt again belonged to Bill Foulkes. United progressed to the semi-final of the European Cup, before being knocked out by Real Madrid over two legs. Bill, like the other players, had enjoyed a taste of the competition, and they were determined that nothing would stand in the way of them winning the league again, in order to enter again.

The league was won comfortably, but there was to be no dream Double. The cup final against Aston Villa was not decided by a piece of sublime skill or by a momentous mistake by a defender, but by an act of aggression which is still shocking when viewed today over 50 years later. Peter McParland's deliberate charge on Ray Wood shattered his cheekbone, and left United without a recognised goalkeeper. Jackie Blanchflower went between the sticks for part of the game, but left United with a challenge that unfortunately proved a little too steep. Bill and Duncan Edwards came close to taking retribution on McParland, but they both remembered how Matt had reacted the last time the red mist had descended on Bill, and got on with the game.

In the aftermath of the 2-1 defeat everyone believed Roger Byrne when he stood on the steps of Manchester Town Hall, promising the crowds that they would be back at Wembley the following year aiming to win it. Who wouldn't believe him? This was the Babes – anything was possible. Nobody then knew what tragedy lay ahead.

Bill finished his National Service by the time the 1957/58 season had begun, and rejoined a team possessing the belief that any competition Manchester United entered, they would win. The side was near enough unchanged from the one that had enjoyed the previous two successful seasons. The only major change had been the purchase of goalkeeper Harry Gregg in December 1957. Everything seemed to be going right for United and by February 1958 they were just a few points behind the leaders. They thrashed Bolton 7-2 at Old Trafford, and then went to Highbury and beat Arsenal 5-4. The team was still in the FA Cup and going well in Europe – how could anyone imagine that everything was about to change, and that nothing would be the same again?

United flew out to play Red Star Belgrade for the quarter-final, second leg of the European Cup with an advantage – and secured a 3-3 draw to go through to the semi-finals. The players and officials, accompanied by journalists, couldn't wait to get on the plane home. There had been a slight problem at the airport in Yugoslavia with Johnny Berry's papers, but this was soon sorted and the party was ready to leave.

The plane refuelled in Munich and then made two aborted attempts to take off in blizzard-like conditions. The players disembarked whilst the crew had a look at any potential problems – and then got back on to make a third attempt. The atmosphere had changed from the carefree banter that was normal on European flights. Something was wrong – and everybody could feel it. Some prayed, some sat there with their eyes closed and Roger Byrne stated, prophetically: "It's all or nothing this time." The plane began to taxi forward. Bill just had a feeling that they weren't going to make it, that the plane was not going to leave the ground. He crouched right down, jamming his head tight into his chest so that his head was well below the top of the seat. He couldn't have fastened his safety belt any tighter; it was hard for him to breathe. Bill took one more glance out of the window at the snow rushing past. He listened to the engines, which never seemed to reach full power. Then came the three bumps; the first as the plane went through the perimeter fence; the second as the pilot pulled up the wheels; the third – and loudest – when the plane crashed into a house. Then silence – and darkness.

There is a period of time when you are involved in a major accident when time stands still – you could be there for hours or just a matter of seconds, it's impossible to tell. Suddenly a knock at the window next to him brought Bill to his senses. A man was yelling at him to get out of the cabin. Bill looked around – half the plane was missing, the whole of the right-hand side of the plane had gone. He unfastened himself from the seat and scrambled out through a hole in the side of the plane.

Looking around he could see the pilot, Captain Thain, attempting to fight fires with a little extinguisher. Bill set off running, continuing through the sleet and snow until he was out of breath – only then did he turn around to look at what he had left. The aircraft was cut in half, a mess of jagged, burning metal. Bodies were lying on the runway in the slush and snow, lit up by the flames coming from the plane.

Bill made his way back towards the plane. He could see Matt Busby trying to sit up, so he knelt beside Matt to comfort him and wrap him in something warm. Bill noticed Harry Gregg coming out of the wreckage carrying a bundle – a baby – shouting for help. A man in a Volkswagen minibus drove up, acting as a makeshift ambulance. They managed to get Matt in and also Bill, Bobby Charlton, Dennis Viollet, Harry Gregg and Jackie Blanchflower. It was only when they reached the hospital that reality set in. Bill looked down and realised that he had no shoes on – he must have taken them off before the plane had set off, but it was only now that he was aware of it. He was shown into a ward and asked to identify a body lying on a bed. Bill recognised team-mate Johnny Berry immediately. They were walking around in a daze and though hospital staff tried to sedate them, Bill and Harry were having none of it. Insisting they were fine and had no need to be there, they were taken to a hotel where they sat together all night, in a dumb state of shock.

Time stood still for those first few days; life seemed to have lost all importance to Bill and Harry. They were both suffering from shock, but in those days it was not a recognised condition and so the two of them were left alone in their room. One afternoon Bill went to the hospital to see the lads, but when he got there he found himself not allowed into any of the wards. Bill was getting angry and frustrated; he wanted to know where his team-mates were, and where they had been taken. He found a female doctor and started going through names. It was only then that the true scale of the tragedy hit home – friends, colleagues, team-mates, all gone. Bill realised just how lucky he had been to survive.

Bill, Harry and Jimmy Murphy arrived back in England to be greeted by hundreds of photographers and journalists. After a tearful meeting with their wives, they were driven up to Manchester. Bill constantly told the driver to slow down, unaware that he was being driven at a leisurely pace and that the problem was in his head. For a long time he had a problem with speed and especially braking. The doctors informed Bill and Harry that they both needed a long rest, to get away from everything and to just spend time with their families. But Manchester United were on their knees and needed all the players they could muster. Jimmy was somehow managing to keep things going. He had been to the hospital, seen the players and then sat for hours weeping for the young boys he had lost. What made Murphy such a special man and probably what Busby had always seen in him was his personal strength, a strength that seemed to be holding Manchester United up on it's own.

Jimmy knew that with the hysteria surrounding the funerals and the tragedy, that it would be impossible for the players to concentrate. So he took his available squad to Blackpool to stay at the Norbreck Hotel. He kept them there until Wednesday 19th February, just 13 days after the air crash, when United played Sheffield Wednesday in an FA Cup tie at Old Trafford. Tom Curry, the trainer and Jimmy's close friend, had died in the crash so Jack Crompton was recruited to help out.

Bill Foulkes led a makeshift Manchester United team out at Old Trafford to face Wednesday. He had a haunted look on a gaunt face; he had not eaten properly, or enjoyed decent rest since the disaster. It is a mark of Bill's fitness and determination that he was even able to run out that night, for inside he was screaming and should have been anywhere, rather than running out on a football pitch. Albert Quixall, who captained the opposition that evening and who would later join United, was a friend of several of the United players who had died. He would also rather have been elsewhere that night. He too was in shock, and did not have the heart to put this makeshift United team to the sword.

Wednesday were a decent team, who should have beaten the inexperienced United side easily. However, like the rest of the country, they were filled with an overwhelming sense of sympathy and grief. United won 3-0, but there were no celebrations afterwards – players just sat in silence with their heads bowed. West Bromwich Albion were next up in the quarter-final, and it seemed as if the whole country was willing the club on to FA Cup victory. United duly defeated the Baggies 1-0, but were then thrashed by the same opposition 4-0 in the league; it was as if all United's efforts were going towards the FA Cup. Fulham were beaten in the semi-finals, and United somehow found themselves in the final for the second successive season, facing Bolton Wanderers.

The week leading up to the cup final found Bill suffering from depression, at a time when there should have been great excitement and rejoicing. All Bill could think about were the people who were gone, unable to run out onto the Wembley pitch in that famous red shirt. Matt Busby, who was now back home, came to the game but as he walked out onto the pitch with the aid of his walking stick, he looked like an old man, a shadow of his former self. Bill sat in the dressing room before the game; he could hear the band playing *Abide With Me* and he struggled to find the strength to walk out onto the pitch. This should have been his proudest moment, leading Manchester United out at an FA Cup final as captain – and yet it was one of his darkest hours.

Bill took several large breaths of fresh Wembley air while leading United out for the 1958 FA Cup final. The team he led out consisted of:

Harry Gregg, Bill Foulkes, Ian Greaves, Freddie Goodwin, Ronnie Cope, Stan Crowther, Alex Dawson, Ernie Taylor, Bobby Charlton, Dennis Viollet, Colin Webster.

It was not a vintage final, and Bolton were always the stronger team. But once again in consecutive years, United suffered at the hands of an outrageous challenge on their goalkeeper. Nat Lofthouse barged into the back of Harry Gregg as he was collecting a loose ball, pushing Gregg and the ball into the net. The goal was allowed to stand, and Bolton eventually ran out 2-0 winners. Manchester United and the country – except for Bolton – did not get a fairytale result, and Wanderers were an unpopular side for not playing along with the country's wishes. Upon arriving at the station in Manchester, Bolton's players boarded an open-top bus to make a victorious trip back home. Travelling through parts of Salford they were pelted with rotten fruit and roundly jeered.

Five days after the disappointment of Wembley, United played AC Milan in the semi-final of the European Cup. Though United put out a side that, on paper, looked like it had no chance against the Milanese giants, they managed a 2-1 home victory. It was a different story in the return though. There was no sympathy here for United, no compassion for what some of the players had been through. Instead, as the United players took to the pitch, they were pelted with rotten vegetables and Bill was caught on the back of the head by a large bunch of carrots, which had the required unnerving effect. Most of the team had never played in such a hostile environment, and were not ready for the flares and fireworks that were being set off. United collapsed to a 4-0 defeat, with Bill and his team-mates running out of steam. He was not disappointed though, just relieved that the season was finally over and he could now rest, spend time with his family and get away from it all.

The 1958/59 season saw Matt back at the helm. Jimmy Murphy returned from a successful World Cup in charge of Wales and Harry Gregg returned, having been named the goalkeeper of the tournament for Northern Ireland. United did well, considering they were still a largely makeshift side. Matt did bring in Albert Quixall from Sheffield Wednesday in September, but he did not enjoy the best of starts for United as they lost his first six games in the side. United eventually got themselves back on track, and made a charge for the top of the table.

Things may have been going well for United but the same could not be said for Bill, as he was not happy and suffering from a lack of confidence. Nowadays he would be identified as suffering from post-traumatic shock and he would receive counselling; in those days, he was simply left alone. He became introverted and moody, keeping himself to himself. The younger players christened him 'Popular Bill' or 'PB' for short, a sarcastic reference to his moodiness and solitary personality.

As club captain he carried an enormous responsibility on his shoulders. It was difficult to put a red shirt on and not think of the Babes without feeling guilty, that he had survived when so many had perished. The pressure was always likely to eventually tell, and so it was at the start of 1959, when Bill's form became erratic. The burden was proving too much. He might have been the senior professional, but he did not want to be captain. It was after a 4-4 draw with Newcastle that Matt called him into his room. He told Bill that he thought he needed a rest, that he was going to leave him out and give the club captaincy to Dennis Viollet. Bill was devastated, fearing that his days at United may be over, but Matt convinced him that he needed the rest so that he could get fit and put on some of the weight that had dropped off him since the crash.

Bill rushed back into the side due to an injury to Ronnie Cope, in his favoured centre-half position although it wasn't until the middle of the 1960/61 season that Matt made it Foulkes' permanent position. For the next eight years he was a virtual ever present. He was a member of the victorious FA Cup-winning team of 1963, secured another two First Division championship medals in 1965 and 1967 and, of course, was in the team that triumphed against Benfica in the European Cup final at Wembley in May 1968. It was also a fitting script that Foulkes should score the goal against Real Madrid in the Bernabeu, which took United into the final. At this stage of his career he was 38 years of age.

Tom Clare, historian of the Busby Babes, said of him: "Bill Foulkes had played his part in the club's history. No player plays 679 games for Manchester United, and for a manager like Sir Matt Busby, without being a half decent player. Foulkes was as tough as granite and in my opinion was as hard as anybody that ever played the game. Nobody took any kind of liberties with him. Even in training he neither gave, nor asked, any quarter. As a full-back he played against some of the greatest wingers in the game; as a centre-half he also mixed it with the toughest and best of centre-forwards of his era. In both cases, the number of times that he came off second best could be counted on one hand.

"He was almost never out of the team through injury, and there was a solid consistency in his play. He was a rock at the heart of the defence, the minder for ball-playing colleagues who were of a more delicate disposition than he was. Foulkes was very destructive in the tackle and relentless in pursuit of a man he had been assigned to mark. In his 'minders' role, I recall that sunny afternoon in Madrid in April 1957 when the great Alfredo Di Stefano had kicked young Eddie Colman to the ground in his frustration of being man-marked so effectively. It was both a cruel, cowardly act, and one that should have brought the great man an early bath. Foulkes was onto Di Stefano in an instant, grabbing him by the front of the shirt. The great Alfredo paled visibly, and uttered the words, 'Okay Foulksy – no more!' as he feared for his own well-being!

"On another occasion, in a league game at Preston's Deepdale, I saw Tommy Docherty cynically kick him off the ball. He'd picked the wrong guy to be cynical with – Foulkes was onto him like lightning and picked him up with one hand, hurling him into the mud like a rag doll! Unpretentious, unassuming, solid and dependable, that was Bill. Never one to court the limelight, nor be in the news for the wrong reasons."

Age did finally catch up with him just a year after that wonderful European Cup success. At the start of the 1969/70 season, after just three games, United suffered a 4-1 home defeat to Southampton. Ron Davies, the Welsh centre-forward, scored all four goals and it was to be Bill Foulkes' last game for United – a sad end for a fine servant.

When we look at Bill as a club captain we look at someone who never wanted the job but, as through his entire playing career, he was ready to serve the club in any way he could. A tough man, only his closest family probably ever saw the true scars from that dreadful night in Munich. He led the team to Wembley, but never got to lift the trophy. What he did do, along with Jimmy Murphy, Bobby Charlton, Harry Gregg and all the young boys who came in, was hold the club up on his shoulders when it was down on its knees. Jimmy Murphy made the right choice.

Tricky

DENNIS VIOLLET

1959-1960

'Dennis was fast of foot, quick-thinking and a great goalscorer – the records prove that. But there was so much more to his game. As a defender it was great when you knew you could knock a ball to a team-mate and you knew where to find him, and what he would do once he had it'

"We were rough diamonds and he was the jewel in the crown" – the words of Wilf McGuinness, when talking about Dennis Viollet. "A wonderful player to play with, brilliant technique. I used to play balls through and sometimes the ball would be higher than it should have been. Dennis would pull it down with one touch and move it. He was like playing with a dream player on a computer, he did everything that should have been done. He was always in the right place, and when he went through one-on-one, you would nearly always back him to score."

I could fill this chapter with quotes from former United players, who will tell you that Dennis Viollet was one of the greatest players ever to wear the red shirt. Then there are those who played against him who will tell you of his awareness on the field, his balance and his tremendous burst of speed from a standing position. Most people who saw him play would find room for him in their all-time Manchester United XI.

Dennis Sydney Viollet was born at 7 Clinton Avenue in Fallowfield, Manchester on 20th September 1933. He lived and went to school in close proximity to Manchester City's old Maine Road stadium. As a young boy he was an ardent City supporter, and dreamed one day of playing for them. The youngest of three, Dennis had two elder sisters Vera and Audrey, who doted on their younger brother. Born into a typical Manchester working-class family, Dennis' father Charles was a telephone fitter for the post office while his mother Hannah was a small, friendly woman, who brought her children up to be courteous and polite. From the day he could walk, Dennis was kicking a ball, either on the fields with the bigger boys, or on his own with a tennis ball outside Maine Road. These were different times, and Moss Side was a different area than today. Young boys would play out all day until it got too dark to see the ball, or until they heard their mother calling them in. Physique was not a problem to Dennis for although he was very small and slight, he would make up for it with natural ability and instant ball control.

There were usually organised games on wasteland near Dennis's house; the lads would split into two teams – one United, one City. They would play for hours, no quarter asked or given. Dennis had the ability to control a ball and stop it dead on any surface. He would often use walls to play one-twos, in order to get around opponents.

Dennis attended St Margaret's Church of England School in Whalley Range and was the star of their football team, far too good for the local opposition. He soon came to the attention of the Manchester Boys selectors, who picked him to play aged 13, going on to captain them for two years. Alf Clarke reported on a game at Belle Vue in June 1946 between Manchester Boys and Glasgow Boys. Manchester won 6-2, with Dennis scoring two and contributing to the other four goals. Clarke noted: 'In the full bloom of youthful soccer craftsmanship, Viollet promises to blossom into one of the game's stars.'

Every time he played for and captained Manchester and Lancashire Boys, Dennis was the star. At the age of 14 he received a call-up for England Schoolboys that included soon-to-be team-mate Mark Jones. A proud moment came on Saturday 15th May 1948 when he captained England Schoolboys against Ireland Schoolboys in the Victory Shield at Old Trafford, in front of 45,000 people. Dennis scored twice, as England won 4-0. When presented with his cap, 300 of his fellow pupils at St Margaret's formed a guard of honour as he went to receive it.

It seemed to Manchester City that this prodigiously-talented teenager, who lived in their back yard and who supported them, was destined to become a City player. This assumption could have been realised had it not been for a soldier, home on leave, who decided to kick a ball in the street with some kids. The soldier was Matt Busby, at the time still a City player. He was visiting his friend Alex Herd, whose son played football with Dennis and who invited Matt to join in one of their games.

Frank Swift, the legendary Manchester City goalkeeper, had spoken to City about them signing Viollet. He organised for Dennis and his father Charles to meet with a scout to see about a trial. Unable to get time off work, they went in Charles' lunch hour. They were kept waiting with his son for nearly an hour outside an office. Charles became annoyed to the point that he stormed off with his son. When Frank came to find out how the trial had gone, he was told what had happened – and was furious. Swift promised to put things right and return with a definite date.

The next day there was a knock on the door of the Viollet household – it was Matt Busby, and the Manchester United charm offensive began. Jimmy Murphy, Bert Whalley and chief scout Joe Armstrong all called in an attempt to convince this house full of City supporters that Dennis' future lay with United. Jimmy waxed lyrically about their son, and how United was going to become the greatest club in the world. Dennis duly signed and City, who never did call back, would let a golden nugget slip through their fingers – into the welcoming arms of their neighbour.

August 1949 was a momentous month for Manchester United – they returned to Old Trafford, after a 10-year absence due to Luftwaffe bombs. Besides Bolton, the other visitors that day were three members of the England Schoolboys team: Cliff Birkett, Jeff Whitefoot and Dennis. Mark Jones had signed the year before as United, under Busby's leadership, attempted to sign the best youngsters available.

Dennis fitted in immediately. United was a happy club, where talent was encouraged to prosper under the tutelage of Bert Whalley and Jimmy Murphy. He was soon turning out for the 'A' and Colts teams, playing in the Manchester League, and the Eccles & District League respectively. Dennis signed his first pro contract on his 18th birthday, in 1950. Everybody was noticing Dennis as he impressed in the 'A' team and the reserves. He was as fast as lightning, and scoring goals for fun.

Dennis was popular with the lads in the club, and with the girls around town. Some of the other players gave him the nickname "Tricky", because he was always wearing the latest fashion in clothes or jewellery. The younger players fancied themselves as ladies men, but none could hold a candle to Dennis. He had the same magic way with women as he did with a ball – both being bewitched by him. Other players would talk to a girl and arrange to meet for a date in the pictures, but not Dennis. With Dennis it would be a meal and champagne, then the cinema.

Albert Scanlon, another local lad at the club, remembered Dennis as being suave and debonair whereas Albert was a scruffy scallywag. A little bit older than Albert, they soon became friends. Sadly, whilst writing this book, Albert passed away and most of the stories he told me I couldn't repeat. But his overriding memory of him was as a lovely man, who loved a laugh and a joke – and on the pitch he was exceptional.

On 25th April 1951 Matt Busby took a team to play Reading in a joint-testimonial for Freddie Fisher and Jeff Gulliver. It was a United side blending youth with experience. Alongside players like Johnny Carey, Allenby Chilton and Jack Rowley were two youngsters making their debuts. Lining up at left-back was Roger Byrne, whilst Dennis was at outside-right. The home side took an early lead before John Aston levelled. Ten minutes later Dennis made a run down the wing before crossing for Aston, who controlled and then scored with a low drive. Soon after the home side hit back, with the sides going in level at the break.

Dennis had played well in the first half, if a little within himself. Jimmy Murphy spoke to him at half-time and told him to express himself more, as he had the beating of this Reading defence. He took this on board and ran at the defenders every time he got the ball. Within five minutes he was brought down in the area. Carey stepped up to take the penalty, and restored United's lead. Stan Pearson gave United a two-goal advantage, but two late goals gave the home side a deserved 4-4 draw.

Dennis really enjoyed playing in the first team, and had proved that he could fit into the side. His biggest thrill had been playing alongside his hero, Stan Pearson, who helped Dennis and made a point of congratulating him afterwards. It had been a good season for Dennis, who won the Manchester League with the 'A' team and the Lancashire Senior Cup with the reserves; he had also made an appearance for the first team.

When Dennis was called up for National Service in the Army, he could have appealed against his call-up on the grounds that he had recently married, and had a baby to support. Dennis had wed his girlfriend, Barbara Southern, in August 1951. Both were still teenagers, and had needed their parents' permission to marry. Soon daughter Stephanie was born, and three other children would follow: Roger, named after Roger Byrne, Deborah and Malcolm. Dennis didn't want preferential treatment and so did not appeal, joining the 17/21 Lancers – who were a tank regiment. Like all other United players doing National Service, he was told he would have to make his own way to play in games.

On Saturday 24th November 1951, as Roger Byrne and Jackie Blanchflower were making their first-team debuts, Dennis was back on leave, playing for the 'A' team in a 4-0 win at Bury. Army life wasn't helping Dennis progress as quickly as he would have liked, and he also picked up niggling injuries, one of which stopped him being posted to the Middle East with his regiment. Dennis was playing regularly for the reserves and getting rave reviews as an outside-right, with journalists commenting that it wouldn't be long before he got a first-team chance.

Dennis made his league debut on Saturday 11th April 1953. On a weekend pass from his Army camp at Catterick, he made his way up to Newcastle. Dennis replaced an injured Johnny Berry on the right-wing whilst Les Olive, who after Munich would go on to become club secretary and a director, replaced Jack Crompton in goal. More importantly for Dennis, he got his first chance to play alongside Tommy Taylor.

Taylor had joined in March 1953 and become an instant success, hitting two goals on his debut. Tommy guaranteed that Dennis got off to a winning start, scoring twice as United won 2-1. Dennis later reflected:

"I was on cloud nine. There were so many gifted players that every player in the club's teams had to perform every week – if you didn't, there were three others waiting to take your place. What made it doubly difficult for me was that I was also doing my National Service. When Matt told me I was playing I was pleased as punch – this was what I had been dreaming of since I first joined. I wasn't unduly nervous, just anxious to play well and let Matt see what I could do in top-class company. I cannot thank those experienced players enough for helping me.

"I played with Jeff Whitefoot as a schoolboy and he was a good player. Johnny Carey was polite and kind – they all were. They shook my hand and wished me well. Tommy eased me through and was available when I had possession, in case I wanted an easy option. I couldn't have hoped for such great players to make my debut with. My idol Stan Pearson talked to me throughout, telling me what to do."

The following week, the home crowd got its first view of Dennis, against West Brom. The Baggies took an early lead, only for Pearson to equalise. In the 29th minute Dennis beat two men and as he looked up, he saw the goal in front of him. His legs suddenly felt like jelly and as he shot, he miskicked the ball – but fortunately it ended up in the corner. For a second the world stood still and all was calm, and then a roar rang out as Dennis was congratulated by his team-mates. Albion did hit back, but that did nothing to take the gloss off what had been a wonderful day for Dennis. United finished that season in eighth which, though disappointing for Matt and Jimmy Murphy, they were looking at the bigger picture, having introduced a number of young players into the side.

The start of the 1953/54 season saw Dennis back in the reserves – but not for long. He scored four in a 6-2 win at Newcastle, this despite Albert Scanlon having been taken off early due to injury, and United being forced to play the remainder of the match with 10 men. This performance made Busby act, and be brought Dennis back into the first team to play West Brom. Unfortunately United lost 2-0, as they did the next game against Manchester City. This defeat was particularly hard for Dennis to take as he always tried that bit harder whenever he played City. The only thing Dennis had to celebrate was the fact that he had been demobbed from the Army, free to concentrate full-time on his football. Dennis was again left out and found himself finishing the month scoring for the 'A' team against Miles Platting Swifts and Droylsden.

Everything was about to change, for Dennis and for Manchester United. The team were struggling in the league, and were not playing attractive football. Matt took the team up to Scotland for a friendly against Kilmarnock at Rugby Park on 28th October 1953. Stan Pearson and Jack Rowley were rested from the under-performing first team, with Dennis taking up a central position playing off Tommy Taylor.

Henry Cockburn opened the scoring after three minutes when a speculative punt towards the goal saw the goalkeeper slip, and the ball end up in the net. Soon after Cockburn was injured and Matt introduced a sub at left-half, a certain Duncan Edwards. Tommy Taylor walked the ball into an open net to make it 2-0, and it seemed that United would swamp the home team. However, they wasted opportunities and had to produce some last-gasp defending to keep the advantage. With five minutes remaining Dennis scored a third goal against the run of play.

The first team were back in competitive action on Saturday 31st October at Huddersfield Town. Matt Busby had decided it was time to unleash his youngsters, with the teamsheet that day reading:

Wood, Foulkes, Byrne, Whitefoot, Chilton, Edwards, Berry, Blanchflower, Taylor, Viollet, Rowley.

This was the birth of the Babes. Dennis kept his place and made 29 appearances that season. He hit two at Cardiff in a 6-1 rout, and would finish with 11 goals. Dennis had stood five feet six inches and weighed just over eight stone when he joined. This season, he'd grown two inches and weighed 10st 10lbs, as he would remain throughout his career.

This was a season of great change for United: Johnny Carey had retired, and Stan Pearson went to Bury. A year later Allenby Chilton moved to Grimsby Town and Jack Rowley went to Plymouth Argyle. They had been the backbone of Matt Busby's first great side and now they were gone – it was time to build an even better one.

The 1954/55 season saw United starting without the injured Tommy Taylor, so Dennis played in attack with Colin Webster. He was a hit, scoring five in the first four games as he stepped up to the responsibility. On 16th October, United met Chelsea in a game that would remain long in spectators' memories. It was an 11-goal thriller, with United running out 6-5 winners against a side who would go on to win the title. Jackie Blanchflower struck, Taylor got two and Dennis scored his first senior hat-trick – three goals in a total of 20 from 34 starts that term.

The following season started similarly to the last, with Taylor picking up an injury in the opener against Birmingham City. Once again the goalscoring responsibility fell to Dennis and he rose to the occasion, netting both goals in a 2-2 draw. Dennis was injured in the fourth match of the season at Tottenham, and this just emphasised his importance: in the next four games without him or Taylor, they won one and lost three.

It was a relief to supporters on 17th September when both players returned against Preston. The game ended 3-2 in United's favour, with Taylor and Viollet on target. Dennis would end up missing eight games up to Christmas, when in a rush of fixtures played over a week (against West Brom, Charlton twice and Manchester City) he scored six goals. United began 1956 four points clear at the top of the table, so there was shock when Bristol Rovers knocked them out of the FA Cup 4-0. Some fans claimed United had thrown the game to concentrate on the league, and it seemed plausible when United then went on another good run.

The only team who had any chance of stopping United winning the title was Blackpool and as they came to Old Trafford on Saturday 7th April, the gates were locked half-an-hour before kick-off. Mounted police were called in to control most of the 62,277 expectant United supporters, desperate to see their heroes clinch the championship. Matt Busby had suffered a family bereavement so Jimmy Murphy was in charge. He had known most of the team since they were boys, and none of them were about to let him down. As was expected it was a close game, with Blackpool taking an early lead and then frustrating the United frontline, including Dennis, for long periods. United's will to win kept them attacking though, and Johnny Berry equalised with a penalty. United could have settled for a draw, but this approach was not in Murphy's nature. He was on the touchline screaming at his boys to go for the win, and somehow Tommy Taylor scrambled the ball in. Busby and Murphy's faith in youth had paid off – United were champions!

The final game was at Old Trafford against Portsmouth, with Dennis claiming the only goal in a 1-0 victory. Dennis' return of 20 in 34 league appearances proved exactly the same statistics as the season before – only this time they came with a championship medal.

United began the defence of their title with a 2-2 draw against Birmingham in torrential rain – but with Dennis on fire. He was playing with confidence, feeling he would score every time he played. In the first five league games he scored seven goals, and soon it was time for Dennis and United to test themselves against Europe's finest.

Against the wishes of the Football League, Matt Busby entered United into the European Cup, and they travelled to Belgium to take on Anderlecht for their first game. United were weakened by the loss of Duncan Edwards through injury, but Jackie Blanchflower was a fitting replacement. The Belgians started well, with captain Jeff Mermans a threat. But midway through the first half Dennis set off on a run, taking on opposition defenders before firing home, a goal which meant he became the first Englishman to score in the European Cup. It took a Ray Wood penalty save to preserve United's lead, before Tommy Taylor doubled the advantage to give Busby's side a two-goal lead for the home leg.

United now had to come home to play a league game against Sheffield Wednesday on the Saturday, with the FA watching to see if they slipped up. Murphy was aware of this and got into his boys, reminding them of the importance of a positive result. He had nothing to worry about as United brushed aside the Owls 4-1, with Dennis again on target.

Prior to the home game against Anderlecht, there was the matter of a derby game against Dennis's boyhood team to take care of. Many supporters, and some of the press, thought that United might take it easy and save themselves for Europe – but they couldn't have been further from the truth. United, and especially Dennis, turned on the style in a 2-0 victory with the name Viollet again appearing on the scoresheet.

Wednesday 26th September 1956 saw United's first European home game, played at Maine Road. It felt like the whole of the city was trying to get to the game, as everyone rushed home from work with a sense of expectation. However excited the fans were, nobody could have predicted what was about to happen. United put on one of the finest performances in their history, beating the Belgian champions 10-0. It was as if everything that Busby had been preaching came to fruition that night. Not only was it a perfect evening for United, but for Dennis too, as he scored four on a wet greasy pitch – which suited his electric pace.

The factory floors and public houses of Manchester were buzzing with pride and excitement after the victory. People couldn't wait for the next European game, and the continent's biggest clubs suddenly sat up and took notice. The Anderlecht captain even suggested that England should play the United team as the national team, they were that good.

The next opposition for Busby's team came in the shape of West German champions Borussia Dortmund. Some people thought that the Germans would face the same result as the Belgians, and that all United had to do was turn up and the game was won. People picked up on the fact that Dortmund were a lot older than Busby's team, but forgot that they were also a lot more experienced in European football.

United set about the Germans like a young fighter sets about an old timer. They were all pace and power, catching Dortmund off guard and it looked like they would overrun them. Dennis had scored twice within the first 27 minutes, and it looked like he was going to make the tie safe on his own. When David Pegg scored the third, it seemed like it might be another landslide result. However, the German side pulled two back – and could easily have drawn. The tie was now in the balance.

United were doing well in the league, building a gap at the top of the table. They had gone on a 26-match unbeaten run and were due to face Everton at home. Dennis missed out due to injury, but Bobby Charlton stepped in – and when the Toffees announced a debutant in goal, the outcome seemed like a formality – but United went down 5-2.

The next game was the FA Charity Shield against Manchester City at Maine Road, so Matt took the team away to Blackpool for some clear sea air and light training. It did the job, and United looked a lot fresher as the game began. Dennis was back in the team, and scored the only goal. He later claimed that the goal gave him more pleasure than any other during his career. It was mixed emotions for his proud parents though, who were at the game watching as City supporters.

Due to a groin injury that Dennis picked up, he had to miss the game in West Germany, so Duncan Edwards played further forward with Wilf McGuinness coming in at left-half. United withstood the home side's pressure to secure a 0-0 draw, and qualification to the quarter-final.

Dennis was back for the last-eight tie after an injury lay-off, and was looking forward to playing in the Spanish sunshine against Athletic Bilbao. Instead, the plane touched down in freezing conditions, and it looked like the game might be off. The referee was happy enough, however, but as the United players examined the pitch they could not believe how bad it was. United did not settle and found themselves 3-0 down before half-time. Matt and Jimmy got the team in at half-time and told them to play to their strengths, to get the ball to Dennis and Tommy up front, and they would make something happen. United got themselves back in it, with Tommy Taylor scoring from Dennis' pass, and then Dennis got a second goal to silence the crowd. Some strange refereeing decisions helped the home side extend their lead – but Billy Whelan grabbed a late goal with the game ending 5-3 in Bilbao's favour.

A crowd of 65,000 turned up for the second leg to experience a European night that people who were there still talk of in hushed tones. United needed to score three to go through, but they were struggling to get a breakthrough. Then, just before half-time, Duncan Edwards shot at goal, only to see it blocked by a defender. Fortunately it fell to Dennis, who knocked the ball into the net and United were up and running. Dennis had a goal disallowed due to a questionable offside decision, but United were now playing like a team possessed and in Tommy Taylor, they had a constant threat. Soon he scored the second goal to level the tie, and then with six minutes to go he crossed for Johnny Berry, who smashed home the crucial, tie-winning third goal.

Dennis was still having a problem with his groin injury, which meant he missed defeats against Blackpool and Bolton. Matt decided to bring Dennis back for the FA Cup semi-final against Birmingham, as Tommy Taylor was missing. He wore the No. 9 shirt and led the line brilliantly, and Berry and Charlton scored the goals that saw United reach the final. The game had taken its toll on Dennis' injury though, and he was looking doubtful for the away tie against Real Madrid. Dennis and Tommy Taylor were declared fit, but were not 100%. The Spanish were physical with Dennis, who received little protection from the officials, and Real won 3-1. Matt was so desperate for Dennis to be fully fit for the second leg that he rested him in the league, nursing him through the Easter period. Before United played the return they had already confirmed themselves as First Division champions for a second successive year. Having also reached the final of the FA Cup, they were on for a unique treble.

The second leg came too soon for Dennis, with Bobby Charlton taking his place. The crowd were treated to a footballing spectacular by Real Madrid, who were soon leading by two goals, but United fought back to draw 2-2. Alas United were out of Europe, and the dreams of a treble were gone. Dennis was gutted at seeing United knocked out of Europe – and even more upset when he failed a fitness test for the FA

Cup final against Aston Villa. As he walked into Matt Busby's office, Dennis knew what the outcome would be. Matt asked him how he was feeling and how his leg was. Dennis knew he was not fit, and did not want to let his team-mates down. He duly told the boss to count him out.

We will never know if Dennis would have made a difference to a final that was all but decided when United's goalkeeper Ray Wood saw his cheek shattered by Peter McParland. Only the players who played in the 2-1 defeat received medals, but Matt appealed to the FA, as Dennis had played in every round. They reluctantly agreed to the request.

Prior to the 1957/58 season Matt took his team to West Germany for a pre-season tour. He was determined that his team would make their mark in the European Cup, and saw German opposition as a good test for his squad. The first game on 14th August 1957 took place at the Olympic Stadium in Berlin. Berliner Stadtelf were the opposition, a team made up of the city's five senior clubs. The impressive stadium, built by Adolf Hitler for the Olympics, was full with a vociferous crowd apart from 1,400 British servicemen who had been given free tickets.

The troops had plenty to cheer as United set about the home team. After 16 minutes, Billy Whelan picked out Dennis with a defence-splitting pass. Like a flash, Dennis was away and he slammed the ball home. Tommy Taylor made it two just before half-time, with United in complete control. The second half was a repeat of the first, with United on top. Duncan Edwards and Taylor went close before the final goal came, Johnny Berry's pass being converted from a tight angle by Dennis.

Dennis was again on the scoresheet when United beat a Lower Saxony XI at Hanover. Anybody watching would have been confident that United were sure to win the league again, they seemed unbeatable. Fate though had other plans, and other endings, to the fairytale.

United started the season as if they were in a rush to seal the league as early as possible, winning five of the first six games while drawing the other. Dennis scored in five of those matches, including one in the 4-1 demolition of Manchester City. Shamrock Rovers were also outclassed in the European Cup, with Dennis scoring two in the home leg.

He picked up a nasty ankle injury against Portsmouth in which a United team missing Byrne, Edwards and Taylor – due to international commitments – lost 3-0. The injury put Dennis out for six weeks, meaning he missed the European games against Dukla Prague. United were never the same when Dennis was out and of the six league games he missed they won three, lost two and drew the other. In Europe they beat Prague 3-0 at home, but lost 1-0 away. Matt was keen to get Dennis back as United were falling short in the title race. Matt was sure that with Dennis' return, they could make a charge for the top of the table.

Saturday 4th January 1958 saw United taking on Workington at Borough Park in the third round of the FA Cup. The pitch was a mess of frozen mud, perfect for Workington to pull off a giant-killing act. The home side played to the conditions and at half-time were 1-0 up, looking the stronger team. It was a different United that came out in the second half though. In a pulsating six-minute spell Dennis scored a hat-trick, which put the tie beyond doubt. Frank Swift, writing in the *News of the World,* stated: 'Dennis Viollet, Manchester United's goal-poaching inside-left, will remember this game for the rest of his life. His brilliantly-taken hat-trick in a dramatic six minutes saved his team. Dennis was superb. His balance and majestic control of the ball, in such severe circumstances, stamped him as a craftsman of the highest order.'

Back in the league Dennis scored in a 1-1 draw at Leeds, before it was back to European action and the European Cup quarter-final, first leg against Red Star Belgrade at Old Trafford. United made a quick start, with Dennis and Bobby Charlton going close, but it was Belgrade who took an early lead. Bobby equalised and then with 10 minutes left Dennis produced a piece of breathtaking genius. On the right-wing, he tricked his way past three defenders as if they were glued to the ground. He crossed, and Eddie Colman met the ball to score the winner.

Four days after beating Red Star, United faced bogey team, Bolton, at Old Trafford. Wanderers had earlier put an end to United's impressive start, beating them 4-0 at Burnden Park. This time United were determined to gain revenge and they did so, with a 7-2 win – Bobby Charlton scoring a hat-trick, and Dennis hitting two. The final game before the team flew to the former Yugoslavia was the 5-4 victory at Arsenal.

The weather in Belgrade for the second leg was atrocious – cold and icy. Nowadays the game would be abandoned, but by kick-off the sun was up. Parts of the pitch were rock hard with ice, and some were like a swamp. Up to an hour before kick-off Roger Byrne had been a doubt, but had made it; this was such a crucial game. If Matt Busby could have scripted the start, this is how he would have written it. The game kicked-off and within seconds the ball fell to Tommy Taylor, who ran from his own half, holding off some physical challenges. He broke into the box and everyone expected him to shoot – but instead he passed the ball to Dennis, who fired home. Bobby Charlton scored two more and the Red Devils were 3-0 up in the game, 5-1 on aggregate. The match became physical and the Austrian referee seemingly did everything he could to help Belgrade get back into the game. The home side pulled three goals back and in the end United were hanging on, but hang on they did to reach the European Cup semi-final for a second consecutive year.

After landing in Munich to re-fuel on the flight home, the aircraft made two failed attempts to take off for Manchester. The weather was poor, it was snowing and everyone on-board was nervous – though trying not to show it. Dennis had originally been sat at the back, but had moved to the front with Bobby Charlton when Tommy Taylor and David Pegg had asked them to swap seats, as they felt it was safer at the back. Up at the front now were Albert Scanlon, Bill Foulkes, Dennis and Bobby Charlton, all ready for a card game Albert was organising.

The passengers fell silent, collectively holding their breathes as they waited for the moment the plane leaves the runway and takes to the air – but it never came. The aircraft was ripped in half, with passengers crudely thrown onto the runway. Dennis and Bobby were left in their seats next to each other, with Dennis unconscious with a nasty gash on his head. Those who could walk got away from the wreckage and searched for survivors. Harry Gregg ignored shouts to leave the area and, forgetting thoughts for his own safety, went back into the burning plane several times to help survivors – including a 22-month-old baby.

Dennis later recalled: "Looking out through the snow-flecked window I could see the wheels. I watched them on the final attempt to take off and felt a terrific surge – then a loss of power. Even then, I don't think anyone was too worried; it was just a question of waiting for the plane to leave the ground. The first I knew that things were not right was that we had come off the end of the runway and were ploughing through a fence across a road. I turned to Bob [Charlton] and told him to relax; he too had seen what was happening. The next thing, I heard a terrible grinding, a tearing noise and looking in horror through the window I saw the wing of the plane being torn away. There was an almighty bang and the side of the plane had a huge hole in it. I felt myself falling into pitch darkness. Then, in what seemed like seconds, it was all over.

"Bob and I, still in our seats, were 70 yards away from the plane. I had no socks or shoes on my feet. I was freezing, and my head was aching. It was then that I saw the full horror of what had happened, the twisted wreckage of the aircraft with steam or smoke rising from the tangle of metal. My head was split wide open and I was covered in blood, but Bob seemed to have received only a slight knock to the back of his head. It's strange what people do in certain circumstances. Bob just got up and walked away. I was not really conscious and didn't know what had happened. I remember walking back to the plane, and Bob was there with Bill Foulkes and Harry Gregg. Bob put his arm around me and I asked him a stupid question: 'Have we crashed Bob?' It was then I understood what had happened, for I could see the carnage all around me. It was a nightmare, a scene of utter destruction, with mangled wreckage and bodies lying in the snow. I felt angry at what had happened. I just wanted to dash into that wrecked plane, find the pilot and attack him."

Dennis was rushed to hospital in a makeshift ambulance, drifting in and out of consciousness. At one point he saw Bill Foulkes, his hands around the neck of the ambulance driver, trying to strangle him for going too fast. Dennis was put in a ward with some of the other players; he was kept in bed for two weeks and not allowed to take a bath or shower due to his head injuries. On 4th March Dennis was allowed to return to England, refusing to fly back, instead taking the train to Holland and then the ferry to Harwich. On the morning the ferry berthed in England, he received the news that United had beaten West Brom in the FA Cup sixth-round replay – just the tonic that Dennis needed.

Dennis returned to the club, and the enormity of it all hit him. He recalled: "I remember going back to Old Trafford for the first time since Munich. There was a strange feeling about the place for me. I walked into the dressing room and then out onto the pitch; there was a strange silence, I cannot really describe the strange feeling that came over me. I knew then that Old Trafford would never be the same. But I realised life had to go on and I wanted to get back training and helping the club."

It was a beautiful evening on Monday 21st April 1958 when Dennis ran out at Old Trafford against Wolves. It was the first competitive game he had played since Munich and though the doctors had warned him that any knock on the head could have serious consequences, Dennis was desperate to start. He played brilliantly, and did everything but score – though champions-elect Wolves were in no mood to make this a joyful homecoming for Dennis, outclassing United 4-0. Dennis managed to play again against Chelsea, in a bid to prove to Jimmy Murphy that he was fit to play in the FA Cup final against Bolton. However, the match proved one step too far for a makeshift side, and the Trotters came out on top. Chances did fall to Dennis that, before the crash, he would probably have tucked away – but he was rusty and lacking match sharpness.

Five days later, on 8th May, United faced AC Milan in the semi-final, first leg of the European Cup at Old Trafford. The Italians made a dream start, opening the scoring but five minutes before the break, Dennis latched onto a weak back-pass from Milan centre-half Cesare Maldini, and slipped the ball into the net. The second half saw chances for either side until, with 11 minutes remaining, Dennis was brought down in the area and Ernie Taylor scored the winner from the resulting penalty.

Unfortunately, the second leg proved a disappointment as Milan eased to a 4-0 victory to secure a 5-2 aggregate success. Despite Munich and his injuries, Dennis finished with 23 goals from 31 first-team games. Now what was needed was a rest and a complete break from football.

The 1958/59 season saw United finish a commendable second in the league to Wolves, though Norwich had knocked them out of the FA Cup with a 3-0 third-round victory. The club was invited by UEFA to compete in the European Cup as a tribute to the club's services to football and United accepted – but the joint-Football Association and Football League committee met and decided that United could not enter.

The big change for Dennis that campaign came after a game against Newcastle in January 1959. Bill Foulkes had been struggling, and Matt Busby decided that he needed a rest from the first team – and especially the captaincy. Bill had been skipper since Munich and had not missed a game for two seasons. Matt told Dennis he was making him captain, and that he should lead by example. Dennis celebrated by giving a near perfect display of forward play as United beat Tottenham 3-1.

Dennis never got the international recognition he deserved, but on 18th March 1959 he was selected to play for the Football League against the League of Ireland at Dalymouth Park, Dublin. Unfortunately for Dennis, this turned out to be a woeful game that ended in a goalless draw. Dennis was criticised for his performance, and it seemed that half the pressmen who had been campaigning for him to be selected were now condemning him as a complete failure.

The following Saturday United faced Leeds and the new captain gave an exemplary display of finishing, scoring a hat-trick in a 4-0 victory. The team pushed Wolves all the way, but they just ran out of legs. The season did end on a high though as United beat City 4-0 in the Manchester Senior Cup, with Dennis lifting his first trophy as captain.

As he had done two years previous, Matt decided to take his squad to West Germany for some pre-season games ahead of the 1959/60 campaign. It was the first time United had flown since the crash, and it was a quiet and sombre flight over. The first game proved eventful, as United beat Bayern Munich 2-1. The result only told part of the story, as did Albert Quixall's goal scored straight from the kick-off. Unfortunately for Matt, the game got physical and United had two players sent off. The other two games on the tour also ended in victories for United but now Dennis, as club captain, was desperate to get the new season started.

Dennis might not have been so keen if he had known that they would lose the first two games – 3-2 to West Brom, with Dennis scoring both goals – and then 1-0 to Chelsea. Dennis also scored another brace in the next game, a 3-2 victory over Newcastle at Old Trafford. Though United had not started well, Dennis was leading from the front.

United next found themselves in the capital, playing the return against Chelsea at Stamford Bridge and as had become the pattern for the season, Dennis hit two in a 6-3 victory. Dennis remembered the game as one of his best, saying: "This was United's greatest game, at least in my time. What a wonderful experience! I rate the victory as the finest exhibition of football by a Manchester United team in which I have played. I always considered the 10-0 licking of Anderlecht in the European Cup as our best display, but I've changed my mind because that match was too one-sided to be a real test. Chelsea played well but we played better, and we touched the high spots in a way I have never experienced before. I feel proud to be captain of a team that played such excellent football."

The team's results were up and down – one week beating Leeds 6-0, the next week getting thrashed 5-1 by Tottenham. The only constant was the form of Dennis, who seemed to score in every game. Though United were struggling in the league, Dennis's goalscoring was getting noticed by the press. He was having his best season in a United shirt; not only was he scoring at a phenomenal rate, he was also assisting. Those who had doubted Matt's decision to make Dennis captain were now eating their words as they saw the confidence he was giving other players.

November 1959 saw Dennis make himself unpopular with the League and Wolverhampton Wanderers when he gave an interview to the *Manchester Evening News,* in which he criticised the Wolves team after they reached the quarter-final of the European Cup. Talking about their cup chances, he commented: 'Their power football may get them through another round, but I cannot see it taking them to the final. Even if they do bring the trophy to England, I wonder whether their style would enhance our reputation in the arts and graces of the game.'

Dennis was critical of their physical style, comparing them to Bolton – who were also a super-fit team who had big, strong, powerful players, and who could grind their opponents down. In the end Dennis was called into Matt's office, and made to apologise to Stan Cullis, the Wolves manager, over the phone. As for Wolves, they came up against a Barcelona side that defeated them 9-2 over two legs in what remains their last appearance in the competition.

Dennis was forced to attend a meeting in London with the Football League management committee and the Professional Players' Union, to discuss what he had written. Dennis defended the article well, and was backed by the Players' Union. After the meeting he was informed that neither the League nor the FA would be pressing charges. Dennis had apologised to Wolves, and the whole matter would be quickly forgotten.

All this off-field activity had no adverse effect on Dennis's goalscoring abilities. Dennis realised how lucky he was, when he found out that his friend, Wilf McGuinness, had broken two bones in his right leg, in a game against Stoke City reserves. Wilf was buoyant and confident that he would be back playing before the end of the season, but people around the club were rightly worried as it was such a bad break. The press got a whiff of this fear and started to speculate that the robust, rough-tackling wing-half Maurice Setters would be joining United.

United started the 1960s in mid-table, a disappointment after the previous season's runners-up spot. On-field fortunes didn't get any better in the first game of the new decade as United conceded seven for the first time in a competitive game under Matt Busby, beaten 7-3 by Newcastle. It was obvious the team needed steel at the back and Matt acted quickly, signing the 23-year-old Setters from West Brom.

On 26th March Dennis broke Jack Rowley's record of 30 league goals in a season set in 1951/52. Dennis scored two goals that day at Fulham to take his total to 31. When the game ended, the team toasted their captain with champagne, his tally from 34 games a record that still stands. Dennis hit one more that season, in a 4-2 defeat to Sheffield Wednesday. Picking up a knee injury against the Owls, he made only one other appearance that term. Who knows how many goals he would have ended up with if he had not missed six of the last seven games?

At last Dennis was recognised with an England cap, playing against the mighty Hungarians in Budapest. Although Dennis gave a good account of himself, the team lost 2-0. Afterwards, Dennis and Bobby Charlton flew to America to join their touring United team-mates. It had been a great season for Dennis – if not for United. He had broken Rowley's goalscoring record, and been recognised by his country.

There was no doubt, as United kicked off the 1960/61 season, that the team were in decline – a notion reflected in falling attendances. Dennis played in 17 of the opening 18 games, scoring 10 goals, but United only managed two wins in the first 10 games, losing six. It was a disastrous start and nowhere near the form needed if a title challenge was to be made. The crowd were getting restless, demanding to see United challenging at the top. A great team can take years to build and after Munich, nobody was sure that they would be able to do it again. The crowds reflected this; the season after Munich, the average attendance had been 53,238. Now, two seasons later, it was less than 40,000. United also suffered further disappointment when they went out of the FA Cup to Bradford City, bizarrely on a Wednesday afternoon in front of a crowd of 4,670. Even though Dennis had given United an early lead, the Bantams shocked the small crowd by coming back to win 2-1.

Matt knew that he couldn't afford to wait for youngsters to come through, so he paid £29,500 for West Ham full-back Noel Cantwell. Noel was an impressive player on and off the pitch, and quickly struck up a bond with Dennis. "I first saw Dennis play in the Busby Babes team against Charlton when Bobby Charlton made his debut and scored two cracking goals," Noel recalled. "What a team they were, so fluent and majestic. Dennis made that team run like clockwork. When I signed, Dennis was club captain and he kindly let me stay at his home for a few months. In those times, when a player arrived from another club, he went into digs, not in top-class hotels like today. We went training together and he was fast of foot, quick-thinking and a great goalscorer. But there was so much more to his game. As a defender it was great when you knew you could knock a ball to a team-mate and you knew where to find him, and what he would do with the ball once he had it!

"I remember sitting with Denis Law and Matt Busby in a restaurant. Dennis had moved to Stoke and we were discussing the merits of certain great players to have graced Old Trafford, and Matt turned to us and said: 'I would have Dennis Viollet in my best team that has ever played for Manchester United!' That was some tribute, wasn't it? Matt loved Dennis, he thought the world of him. I agreed with him because he was so easy to play with. He wasn't an individualist like Bobby. Although Bobby was a brilliant, world-class player, he would drop his shoulder and go off on one of those surging, electrifying runs, beating man after man. You never knew what he was likely to do – but you knew what Dennis would do, which is a great advantage when you're playing."

On 26th November Dennis made his last appearance as captain. The game was at Cardiff City's Ninian Park, and United were aiming for their first away win of the season. In the 18th minute Dennis was involved in a collision with Cardiff goalkeeper Graham Vearncombe, which broke his collarbone. Dennis went down in agony and was carried off; it would be four months before he would return. With Dennis sidelined, Matt needed a captain and he turned to Maurice Setters.

On 8th January Dennis decided to resign as club captain. This was not a rush decision or one taken lightly. Dennis loved the role, but decided it was only right that Maurice should be installed as the permanent club captain. The team's results had picked up since Maurice had taken over, and Dennis felt it was best for the team. Dennis returned to the side after injury, and his presence seemed to rejuvenate the whole team.

It was clear United were a better team with Dennis in it and they went unbeaten until the end of the season. In spite of being injured for four months, Dennis scored 15 in 24 games. It had not been his best season, having also given up the club captaincy, but as he set off for the club tour of Italy and Malta he felt that the problems were behind him. David Herd had just signed from Arsenal, and he would go straight into the first team for the start of the season – partnering Dennis up front.

Dennis began 1961/62 in form, scoring four in the first nine games – with United losing only once. Dennis received his second England call as a replacement for Johnny Haynes, playing against lowly Luxemburg. However, the team – and Dennis – failed to impress. Although he hit the second in a 4-1 win, the biggest cheer came when Luxemburg scored. The press were critical of some of the fringe players – and Dennis.

Things got no better when Dennis returned to United as the team were hammered by Arsenal and Bolton. On 11th November United hosted Leicester in front of a crowd of just 21,567. Dennis scored in a 2-2 draw, but the following days' papers made for unpleasant reading. They described Dennis as being slow, and were critical of him for missing chances. Dennis was dropped to the reserves, playing in the Manchester Senior Cup final at Old Trafford that United lost 1-0.

It was not unusual for Matt to put players in the second team if they suffered a loss of form. Bill Foulkes had played 11 times before forcing his way back, and Dennis was confident he'd return. Saturday 13th January saw Dennis in the dressing room pulling on the red shirt. He was set to play for the reserves against Blackpool, a game they lost 2-1, not a finale a great should have to mark the end of his career.

The following week, Dennis was sat at home watching television, when the phone rang; it was Tony Waddington, the Stoke City manager. He told Dennis that he had spoken to Matt Busby and that he had been given permission to speak to him. Dennis was dumbstruck. Tony realised that Dennis was in shock, and asked if he could call round to see Dennis. When Tony came round he explained that he had negotiated a fee with Matt and as long as Dennis had no objections, the deal was done. The terms were good, but Dennis's mind was in turmoil. He shrugged his shoulders, turned to Tony and said: "Right, this sounds great, where are the forms? I'll sign." Tony left and Dennis experienced a sudden feeling of emptiness. He called Matt, who answered and apologised for not mentioning the fact that Stoke were interested, but he had been busy. Dennis was hurt, and felt unwanted. Dennis was duly transferred for a fee of just over £25,000 and even though he was stepping down a league, he doubled his wages to £70 a week before bonuses.

That was that – Dennis was no longer a United player. He had joined in 1949, won two First Division titles, played in an FA Cup final and two European Cup semi-finals, became an England international and record goalscorer for the club – but now it was over. No mention of Viollet's departure appeared in the match programme, there were no public messages of good luck from the manager; it was as if Dennis had never been at United. Was Dennis after more money? Was Dennis's private life causing embarrassment? Was he raising the question of a testimonial, which the club didn't like? Or, quite simply, was Matt Busby making one of those tough decisions that good managers have to make when they break up a successful team and start to build the next? Matt was able to build that side; he knew there was no place for sentiment.

On Saturday 6th March 1999, just before the usual kick-off time, Dennis Viollet passed away from a brain tumour. The tumour was located just under the scar he received at Munich. His wife Helen brought his ashes back to Manchester from America, where he now lived, and they were scattered in the Stretford End goalmouth. Dennis was back home.

West Country Enforcer

MAURICE SETTERS

1960-1962

*'He wasn't overawed by his surroundings or his team-mates
– if anything, he thrived. He was a natural leader and earned
the respect of the other senior players. Maurice played every
game after his debut that season, bringing the necessary steel
to the defence that Matt had been looking for'*

When Matt Busby went into the transfer market in the second week of January 1960 he knew exactly what he was doing. Paying around £30,000 to West Bromwich Albion for Maurice Setters was the shot of steel his team desperately needed. In November 1958 United played at Everton and lost 2-1. It was not a massive defeat, but Matt Busby saw something in certain players' performances that he thought was dropping below United's high standards. Matt acted, not by dropping any of the younger players, but three of his more senior players in Harry Gregg, Wilf McGuinness and Bobby Charlton. This was Matt's way of telling them to not only have a rest – but to pull their socks up, too.

This decision was meant to be a short-term measure for McGuinness, but it turned out to be catastrophic. Two weeks later, he broke his leg playing in a Central League game, an injury that ultimately ended his active playing career. Losing a player of McGuinness's calibre was a huge blow to United. Seamus Brennan had replaced Wilf in the first team, but he wasn't the swashbuckling, ball-winning half-back that United really needed in midfield. Freddie Goodwin was the other wing-half, but he was more of a forager, a ball player. There was no real aggression in the team, and when Matt looked at his reserve and youth sides, he could not see a player to fit the bill.

In Maurice Setters, Busby bought a tough, no-nonsense, uncompromising player who gave no quarter – nor looked for any in return. It was a strange signing in the eyes of many supporters, as he was not a 'Manchester United' type of player. They found it even more surprising as Stan Crowther, a similar type of player to Setters and who Jimmy Murphy had signed from Aston Villa after Munich, had been shown the door once Busby returned to the helm.

Maurice Edgar Setters came into this world on 16th December 1936, born in Honiton, Devon – not exactly a hot-bed of footballing talent. Maurice was always a tough, competitive player even at school and after leaving at 15, he played local amateur league football. Even though he was young, Maurice had no problems with the physical aspect of the local leagues, and quickly picked up a reputation as a hard nut. It was whilst playing amateur football that Maurice caught the eye of his local Football League club Exeter City. City brought Maurice down for a trial and liked what they saw. In June 1952 Maurice signed amateur forms and in January 1954 he signed his first pro contract with the club.

Like most young men of the time, Maurice found himself being called up for National Service just after his 18th birthday. He was conscripted into the King's Troop, Royal Horse Artillery in London, where he spent the next two years. The unit was set up in 1945 when King George wanted a troop for displays at state occasions. It wasn't all spit, polish and drill for young gunner Setters though. The commanding officer was Colonel Spencer and when professional footballers came in for National Service, he would give them the chance to play for the King's Troop as they would get a better deal under him – like more freedom at weekends, for example. The RHA had a redoubtable football team and service football was of a very high calibre, mainly because of the number of young professional footballers who had to serve their mandatory two years in military uniform. Setters played in an Army team that included several First Division and international players, including the brilliant Scottish inside-right John White, who was to play for the famous

Tottenham Hotspur Double-winning team of 1960/61, and who tragically lost his life a year or so later.

Whenever Army games were played, scouts would be watching and Maurice soon caught the eye of a West Bromwich Albion representative, who saw potential in this raw-boned youngster. During the 1954/1955 season, Maurice had returned to Exeter as many times as possible and made 10 first-team appearances, but it was obvious even then that he was destined for better things. As soon as he was demobbed and had returned to Exeter, West Brom acted quickly and obtained Setters' signature, paying City £3,000. His new club had won the FA Cup the previous season, and Maurice found himself training with quality players like Don Howe, Bobby Robson and Ronnie Allen. With players like that around him, Maurice could only improve. Initially he played in the reserves' Central League team but it wasn't too long before he was drafted into the first team, holding down the wing-half position.

Maurice wasn't very tall, standing at only 5ft 7ins, but he weighed 13 stone and was as tough as teak. He was a natural ball-winner, could pass and read the game well, and would never give his opponent a moment's peace. To say he was intimidating is an understatement. With his GI flat top hairstyle and his ferocious appetite for a physical game, he had won many battles before the game began.

Maurice soon gained England Under-23 caps playing alongside Wilf McGuinness, who was also a performer who could mix it with anyone. Wilf remembers him as a "ferocious little pit-bull of a player". During a game against France, Wilf kicked one of the opposition, and Maurice was booked for arguing that a foul had been given. In 1958 he was named in the initial 30-man squad for the World Cup finals in Sweden, but was left bitterly disappointed to be one of the unlucky ones to be trimmed from the squad when the final selections were made.

Setters was a larger than life character, strong-willed and opinionated – maybe that is what Busby saw in him and what he felt the team needed. He had the drive and energy to be a good leader both on and off the field, just what Manchester United were crying out for. Bill Foulkes had been unable to carry the mantle of club captain – the responsibility had weighed down on him, and his playing performance had suffered because of it. Dennis Viollet was much admired by the players and fans alike, but his off-field activities were not always to Matt's approval. Both Foulkes and Viollet had grown up in the club and had been there since they were young men. In effect, they were too close to the club and the tragedy that had befallen it. Maurice Setters was an outsider, and would not have the burden of Munich to carry on his shoulders.

Setters made his United debut against Birmingham City at Old Trafford on 16th January 1960, a game that United won 2-1 with a goal each from Albert Quixall and Dennis Viollet. The man Maurice replaced was Freddie Goodwin, a 6ft 2ins lanky half-back who had also played cricket for Lancashire. Sadly for Goodwin, who played such an integral part in United's survival after Munich, he never again regained his place in the first team. In early March he was sold to Leeds for £10,000.

Maurice settled into the first team and his tough, combative style soon made him a crowd favourite. He wasn't overawed by his surroundings or his team-mates – if anything, he thrived in the atmosphere. It became a regular occurrence at matches to see Maurice barking out orders from the middle of the park, rollicking, urging, cajoling and minding the young players around him. He was like a Regimental Sergeant Major, in complete control of the troops on parade ground. He was a natural leader and earned the respect of the other senior players in the first team. Maurice played every game after his debut that season, bringing the necessary steel to the defence that Matt had been looking for.

On 26th November 1960 United were playing at Cardiff City when club captain Dennis Viollet was involved in a collision with the Cardiff goalkeeper Graham Vearncombe, which broke his collarbone. Dennis went down in agony and was carried off – it would be four months before he would return. Matt had no doubt whom he needed to appoint as his new captain. Maurice was already the natural leader on the pitch, and these were the qualities Busby saw in him when he gave him the job. With United going through the transition that they were, with players coming and going frequently, it needed somebody with Setters' capabilities to lead the team. Even when Dennis recovered, he was happy to let Maurice take over the mantle of club captain, as he was more concerned with getting back amongst the goals.

Maurice Setters' stint as captain was a period of much change. Munich had ravaged the club, and meant that United had to start again on the playing side. To ensure the team wasn't relegated, both Murphy and Busby had to buy experienced players who could steady the ship. Unfortunately, some of the youngsters had been brought in too early, failing to impress and being quickly moved on.

It seemed as if the suffering from Munich continued. Johnny Berry had been horrifically injured in the air crash – it was a miracle he survived at all. His injuries included a broken jaw, elbow, pelvis, leg and fractured skull. He remained in a coma for nearly two months and when he finally returned to Manchester, he still had no idea what had happened, initially thinking he had been in a car crash. He was admitted into a Manchester hospital when he returned to England and his first clue as to the tragedy came when he picked up a newspaper and read a match report on the back page. Johnny read the team line-up and couldn't understand why these players had been picked. He badgered one of the doctors, who finally explained to him exactly what had happened. Johnny sat there and wept as he was told the names of his team-mates that hadn't made it. He had been in the crash and yet seemed to be the last person in the world to know about it. His injuries meant that he could never play football again, so he had to leave United and take a job with Massey Ferguson in Trafford Park. He was living in a clubhouse in Daveyhulme but when Maurice Setters joined United in 1960, the club asked Johnny and his family to vacate the property so Maurice could move in. The Berry family were left feeling let down by United and moved back to Aldershot, Johnny's hometown.

Matt Busby and Jimmy Murphy were trying to rebuild a team and get some consistency within the side – but this could not be done overnight. In the 1959/60 and 1960/61 seasons, United finished a very creditable seventh, which enabled Matt to make his future plans without the fear of fighting relegation. Maurice was part of this consistency, but his performances weren't without controversy. Being the type of player he was, he fell on the wrong side of a number of referees and was sent off on a couple of occasions. Even back then, it seemed that there was one rule for Manchester United players and another for players from other clubs.

The 1961/62 season saw United struggle, finishing 15th in the league. This was understandable given the chopping and changing that went on in the side, as Busby and Murphy struggled to re-build a team from players who did not have the natural talent of the Babes. The United supporters had been spoilt by watching the likes of Edwards, Byrne and Taylor play the kind of football that was to be the benchmark of every United team that would follow. Some of the players found it difficult to cope with the shadow that the Babes team cast over them, but Maurice was still his fierce, ebullient self, never one to shirk a challenge, always at the forefront of the action. Maurice needed to be on form as coming through the ranks were a couple of youngsters who played in his position – a young player from Belfast called Jimmy Nicholson and local lad, Nobby Stiles.

At the beginning of the 1962/63 season Maurice's form dipped and he lost his place to Nobby Lawton, a young Mancunian player. Busby felt the captaincy was starting to affect Maurice as the team now had some equally big personalities. This was a side that now contained the likes of Pat Crerand, Nobby Stiles, Denis Law, Johnny Giles and Noel Cantwell. Maurice's Sergeant Major-style of leadership had worked for a while, but these were players that needed a different type of leadership. Busby recognised this, and reluctantly took the club captaincy off Maurice. His next choice of skipper would be a football man who liked to think about the game: Noel Cantwell. It says a lot about Maurice's character and temperament that he was back in the team after only five more games, and he was then ever-present until the end of that season.

The campaign was an enigma as far as Manchester United were concerned. Despite having a team that was now brimming with the talent of Gregg, Cantwell, Dunne, Crerand, Stiles, Foulkes, Setters, Giles, Quixall, Herd, Law and Charlton, they were almost relegated from the First Division – finishing in 19th. Survival was only guaranteed after a 1-1 draw with neighbours Manchester City at Maine Road on 15th May 1963. It was a result that saw United all but safe – and City relegated.

The FA Cup, however, proved a different proposition, the catalyst that sparked the revival of the club in the mid-1960s. The previous season United had reached the semi-final of the same competition, but been defeated 3-1 by Tottenham on a glue pot of a pitch at Hillsborough. The following year, they went a step further to reach the final.

United's line-up was by far the most expensive ever to take to the field for a Wembley final – six of the players had cost a total of over £300,000. Despite this, it was Leicester City, their opponents, who were strong favourites. They were a side that relied on defending deep and hitting hard on the break. However, on the pristine wide-open spaces of Wembley Stadium, United put in a magnificent team performance to secure the trophy by winning 3-1. Maurice played a significant part in the victory, acting as a holding midfielder. Protecting the defence, he allowed Pat Crerand to roam around and use his wonderful passing ability to make opportunities for the likes of Law, Charlton and Herd.

The day after the final, Maurice and the rest of the team arrived back at Manchester's Central Station to be greeted by 300,000 fans. It was the first major trophy won since Munich, and the outpouring of emotion as the team passed under a speedily erected red-and-white triumphal arch was immense. It took the coach carrying the team 45 minutes to travel the one mile from the station to Albert Square, and 400 people had to be treated for injuries caused by pushing. The victory would prove a springboard to the glorious period the club would enter for the next five years; unfortunately for Maurice, he was not part of that golden period.

The supporters obviously believed that good times were just around the corner and this was reflected at the first home game of the 1963/64 season when 62,965 turned out at Old Trafford to see United play champions Everton. Two weeks earlier, in the FA Charity Shield match at Goodison Park, the champions had made United look like no-hopers as they thrashed them 4-0. In front of the Old Trafford faithful though, it was a different story as United handed out a 5-1 thrashing that had supporters talking about the team as possible champions.

In the end United finished as runners-up to Liverpool, and went out to West Ham in the semi-final of the FA Cup. The team also reached the last eight of the European Cup-Winners' Cup. Despite a terrific 4-1 win in the home leg against Sporting Lisbon, a disastrous collective team performance three weeks later saw them annihilated by the Portuguese team 5-0. In all competitions United had been second only to the winners, but the football they were playing had been far from second best.

Maurice's influence on the team was decreasing, as Busby took the team in a new direction. He managed only two games in the 1964/65 season before he lost his place to Nobby Stiles, and he was never able to regain his spot again. His last game was on 24th October 1964 when he played in a United team that drubbed Aston Villa 7-0 at Old Trafford.

Just two weeks later, Busby sold him to Stoke City for a similar £30,000 fee than what he had paid West Bromwich Albion. He spent almost five years at Old Trafford, and more than played his part in the rebuilding of the club after Munich. He is remembered with fondness by the United fans that watched him during that period, and his team-mates of the era will undoubtedly testify to his commitment and determination in helping make United a force in both domestic and European football once again.

Son of Cork

NOEL CANTWELL

1962-1967

*'Noel was a student of the game...Noel would question
certain things, in a sensible way, not in a nasty way; he was a
true gentleman and a class player with loads of experience.
He was respected for what he knew, he was a good talker on
the game and gave you a different point of view'*

There can't be many more elegantly named footballers than Noel
Euchuria Cornelius Cantwell. Such was the title bestowed upon this
'Son of Cork' when he entered the world on 28th February 1932.
Cantwell was educated by the Roman Catholic Presentation Brothers at
St Joseph's National School, Mardyke, and at the Presentation Brothers
College in the Irish Free State of Cork. He was the son of a master tai-
lor, who wanted him to go to college and become a banker.

Noel developed into an all-round athlete whilst at the college,
excelling at football, rugby union, cricket and athletics. Football was his
first love and his favourite team was Manchester United, mainly
because of Johnny Carey, who was Noel's favourite player and who he
modelled himself on. For this reason, whilst most of his young contem-
poraries would talk of one day playing for Cork City, Noel always
dreamed of pulling on the red shirt and playing for United.

Cantwell's football career began at local league side Western Rovers,
before he moved up a level to play full-back for Cork Athletic in the
League of Ireland. At the time, Noel didn't think that he had the skill or
the right attributes to be considered as a player who was good enough to
play in the English leagues – but how wrong he was.

Two Cork men who played for West Ham United, Tommy Moroney

(who also played rugby for Ireland) and Frank O'Farrell, were regular visitors back to their hometown and quite often they would guest for the local club – and in so doing, boost the attendance. One such game was against Birmingham City, in which the young Cantwell played along-side the two West Ham players. When they got back to London they went to see manager Ted Fenton and told him about a big, tall gangly full-back playing for Cork, who was worth having a look at. Fenton heeded their advice and liked what he saw. He went to see Noel's father and told him that he would like to take Noel back to London with him, to see if he could make the grade in the English league.

Noel didn't immediately agree to the invite, as he was not completely sure what he wanted to do as a career – while he also had eyes on a potential rugby career playing for Cork Constitution. However, the West Ham offer made him just a little more ambitious and so he agreed that he would join the Hammers, to try and make a go of professional foot-ball in England. Fenton paid Cork Athletic £750 for his signature – with Noel receiving £150 of the fee.

Noel was an outstanding sportsman; as well as playing football and rugby union to a high level, he also played cricket for Cork Bohemians Cricket Club, as a left-handed batsman and a right-arm medium bowler. He played five times for Ireland, including the annual first-class match against Scotland in 1956, when he made 31 and 17 not out, in a drawn game in Edinburgh. Two years later he top-scored with 40 in a two-day game against New Zealand, earning praise from *Wisden* for both his sound defence and bold hitting. Whilst at West Ham he also received an invitation to play for Essex but he turned them down, as he didn't want to spend the whole year in England.

Upon arriving at Upton Park and training for the first time with his team-mates, Noel had something of an inferiority complex. He told his parents that he thought he might struggle, and that within a year he would be on the boat back to his native Ireland. Noel's father spoke to Fenton about his son's doubt, and the West Ham boss put him in digs with Tommy Moroney, who became his mentor. The Cork man helped him settle, and was able to guide him through that first formative year as a West Ham United player – a period when he broke into the first team. Another person who was a big influence upon his early career was Malcolm Allison, whom Cantwell thought was an exceptional coach.

Noel loved playing for West Ham, who at the time were in the Second Division. He was playing football the right way with a very talented group that included Frank O'Farrell, Dave Sexton, Malcolm Musgrove and John Bond. At West Ham players were taught to play football in the proper way, with the coaching staff trying to teach players the good principles of the game – namely passing the ball. The violence of the sport was non-existent in their make-up. Whatever the coaching staff were teaching them obviously had an affect as this group of players all went on to have successful careers as managers at the top level.

In the 1952/53 season, Cantwell made his initial debut against Colchester in a 3-2 victory on 13th November, before making his league bow five months later against Fulham at Craven Cottage (also in a 3-2 victory) on 6th April. The following season saw him become an established member of the first team and on 28th October 1953 he made his debut for the Republic of Ireland, against Luxemburg.

Cantwell was as intelligent off the field as he was on it. In November 1957 he suspected something amiss with West Ham captain Malcolm Allison, and urged him to see a doctor. Allison subsequently had tuberculosis diagnosed, and underwent treatment that saved his life.

West Ham needed a new captain – and looked no further than Cantwell. His first season as skipper, 1957/58, saw West Ham win the Second Division. Their first term in the top flight saw them finish in a creditable sixth place, but the following campaign they slipped to 14th.

During the period Manchester United had to rebuild after suffering the ravages of the Munich Air Disaster. Matt Busby had returned to manage the club, and was trying to find the right blend of youth and experience to stabilise the side. Busby felt the team needed time to strengthen so it would be able to challenge for honours, both domestically and in Europe, once again. Between 1960 and 1962 there were a lot of comings and goings as Busby strived to get the blend right.

In November 1960 Matt made West Ham an offer of £29,500 for Cantwell, which at the time was a record transfer for a defender. He subsequently joined new signings David Herd and Maurice Setters at Old Trafford. Noel remembered the shock he got when he joined United:

"Matt had to do a big rebuilding job at United. Although there were some exceptional kids there, they were still kids, and Matt must have thought: 'I've got to get some experience in there.' It was a really difficult period because the memories of those great young players were still so prevalent – Duncan Edwards, Eddie Colman, Tommy Taylor, David Pegg and their great captain, Roger Byrne. My first 18 months were difficult, and we weren't a good team. Things were a little disorganised."

Eamon Dunphy, who was an apprentice at Old Trafford at that time, remembers Cantwell's incredulous fury in his first few weeks in Manchester. "'Doesn't anybody actually talk, or even think about the game here?' he'd fume. 'Why isn't it organised? Why don't we ever see Busby? Just a bit of running, head tennis, then around the back for a free-for-all kick about…Then pre-match, Busby's simplistic 'enjoy it all lads and just give it to a red shirt. Give it to a f***ing red shirt! You don't need to be a manager for that. How do you find a red shirt to pass to if you haven't planned it, worked on it, thought about it and talked about it?'" Busby's answer was to make the radical Irishman captain!

Noel went on to say that United were a "bitty team", a "fits and starts" outfit who relied on individual players to carry them. There were some good kids coming through, but the club needed time.

Cantwell's debut for United was one to forget as the team went down to a 3-0 defeat at Cardiff City. United then went eight games undefeated, until an injury to Harry Gregg saw the team go with the inexperienced Ronnie Briggs in goal. They were subsequently thrashed 6-0 at Leicester, and then humiliatingly knocked out of the FA Cup by

Sheffield Wednesday 7-2 at Old Trafford. The hapless Briggs was blamed for the defeat, and only managed a couple of other games for the club. Gregg came back for a few games, with Dave Gaskell playing in goal for the rest of the season as an unsettled backline saw United finish a distant seventh in the league.

Matt knew what kind of man he was buying in Cantwell; he reminded him of Johnny Carey, and saw him as a father figure to the younger players – as Carey had been. They were both elegant, vastly experienced top-class international full-backs, completely respected by the players. Wilf McGuinness remembered when Noel joined United: "Noel was a student of the game, coming from the West Ham academy. But sometimes football's a simple game, and that's the way that Jimmy Murphy would have it – and so would Matt. Noel would sometimes look beyond that, coming from West Ham, and maybe the training didn't suit him. Sometimes he'd say, 'What are we training like this for?' or 'Why are we doing that?' Noel would question certain things, in a sensible way, not in a nasty way; he was a true gentleman and a class player with loads of experience. He was respected for what he knew, he was a good talker on the game and gave you a different point of view."

The 1961/62 season was a poor one for United, with the team finishing in 15th. Noel never got a run in the team due to injury, playing only 17 games in the league and two in the FA Cup. Such were United's problems that season that Noel even found himself playing as a striker in quite a few games, even finding the back of the net in games against Burnley and Arsenal. Crowds were down and the fans were getting restless – any sympathy and sentiment left over from Munich was quickly running out. Busby needed to act – and act quickly.

Over in Italy a fiery young Scot by the name of Denis Law had been suspended and fined by Torino for allegedly not trying. Torino were looking to offload Law, and it didn't take Busby long to hear about it. Negotiations began in May 1962, but it wasn't until July that the transfer was completed. Law became a United player for the record fee of

£115,000 and, once again, the club became Britain's most talked about team with Britain's most talked about player. Lots of people said it was a big risk to pay so much money for one player, but it wasn't a risk – it was a bargain, the spark that ignited the fire.

Manchester United were now a team full of expensive players costing more than £300,000 in transfer fees, as Busby had spent to rebuild. It was a fact they would often be reminded of in defeat. The league campaign did not go well, even though Law scored 29 league and cup goals in his first season. Indeed, there was a serious chance that Manchester United could have been relegated under Matt Busby. Busby acted again by spending more money and in February 1963 he bought Celtic's Scottish international wing-half Pat Crerand. Youth had not been completely stifled by all the spending at the club though and with Nobby Lawton, Nobby Stiles and Johnny Giles forcing their way into the side, Maurice Setters was finding it harder to keep his place: the club captaincy was duly passed to Noel Cantwell.

Noel was not only now the captain of United, he was the captain of his country as well. Like another Cork man who would captain Manchester United later, Noel wasn't impressed with the set-up when he went away with the national side, as he remembered fondly: "Irish football was ridiculed for it's unprofessionalism, but we still enjoyed it. Joe Wickham was the Irish secretary and you would get a phone call from him, or a letter, to say that you had been selected. I could show you an itinerary now, that told you to bring your own soap, towel – in fact, your own everything, and it would tell you what time to report and that was it, you made your own way. Then you got your expenses at the table after the game. We used to get £50 a game and they would give you a cheque for £45, and £5 in cash. That was the deal! Then you'd make your expenses and if you were lucky, they'd pay for a taxi. There was many a time that they would query your expenses and tell you that you were claiming too much, and you wouldn't get what you had laid out! So that was the scene as far as the financial side of things.

"The strip that we used was made by Elverys and the shirt was like a rugby jersey. The shorts were something else – I don't know who they thought played for Ireland! But if you put Johnny Giles and Joe Haverty together in a size 44' pair – and they used to do this sometimes in the dressing room – they could pull them over their heads and tie them, just like a sack! We got to the stage where people like Charlie Hurley and myself felt better in our own gear and we'd bring our own shorts, we wouldn't accept it. You would often see Gilesy in a rolled-up pair of shorts, tucked in. How he could ever play in them I just don't know. Little Joe Haverty was a tiny man and he looked like a slapstick comedian when he put on the Irish strip, it was the funniest thing to see. We put up with it for a while. Johnny Carey was the Irish manager and he was a smashing fellow, but he just didn't want any problems – just peace and quiet. He didn't want to upset anybody at all. He just loved the game and just wanted to sit there and smoke his pipe. All he ever told us was, 'Just fizz it about, fizz it about.' He loved us just to pass the ball.

"So we used to assemble at the Gresham Hotel at 12 noon on a matchday. Charley Hurley, Pat Saward and myself would travel overnight before on the boat. In those days, they couldn't afford flights. If the crossing was rough, well, you didn't get much sleep. We'd arrive in Dublin early morning and check into the hotel – The Forecourt – and we'd try and grab a few hours' sleep before going down to the Gresham, and assemble there. We'd have a so-called teamtalk and Johnny would tell us about fizzing the ball about, but he would also tell us to get the ball up in the air, to get at them and charge into them, to 'make yourself known'. That's how it was playing for Ireland in those early days."

Whilst in 1963 United showed no improvement in their league results, they moved comfortably towards Wembley in the FA Cup. Huddersfield Town, Aston Villa, Chelsea and Coventry City were overcome, before Denis Law's goal against Southampton put United in the final for the first time in five years. Before Wembley, they had a relegation battle to fight. Thanks to Law's goalscoring exploits though, they managed to steer clear by three points – and in so doing condemned Manchester City to relegation, a fact many City supporters overlook when they talk about goals that Denis scored which sent teams down.

United's opponents on Saturday 25th May 1963 were Leicester City, who had finished fourth in the league and who – according to the press and most neutrals – were the definite favourites. But on this sunny afternoon Manchester United gelled and played football the Busby way, with thrilling, attacking football. That isn't to say that Leicester didn't have their chances; United nearly gifted them a goal when Noel deflected Mike Stringfellow's goal-bound shot just past the post. But after half-an-hour Law pounced, driving Crerand's pass past Gordon Banks with demonic speed and accuracy.

Once they were ahead, United grew in confidence. David Herd added a second goal 13 minutes into the second half, and it looked like the game was won – but with 10 minutes to go Leicester pulled a goal back. It could have made for a nervy final 10 minutes, but Herd made it 3-1 with five minutes to go and there was no way back for Leicester.

Noel was happy to recall the victory. "Leicester were favourites, and I think they had been going for the 'Double'. But we always played in flashes, and we thought that Wembley would suit us. It would also be a day that Law, Charlton and Crerand would play very well. We'd beaten Southampton in the semi-final, and Wembley then was a guaranteed 100,000. It was a lovely day and things went well. We played well, Pat Crerand was a star in midfield, Johnny Giles played, as did Albert Quixall, Herdy and Denis. Denis played exceptionally well, and everything just seemed to come together and we won the cup.

"I was fortunate enough to be captain. I think I'd only taken over the captaincy earlier that season because Maurice Setters had been captain and before him Dennis Viollet. Again I think that it reflected the turmoil within the club in how many times we'd had to change captains."

This was Manchester United's first FA Cup win for 15 years, and it was five years since Munich, but United were now finally looking like a team. It was a proud Noel Cantwell that led his team up those famous 39 steps to receive the FA Cup from Her Majesty the Queen. After collecting his medal and leading the side back down on to the pitch, his team-mates looked on in astonishment as Noel hurled the famous old trophy 15 feet into the air. Cantwell was never sure what possessed him to do it. As he explained: "It was a spur-of-the-moment thing, an impulse. We were very, very happy. It had been such a wonderful day." Soon a Wembley commissionaire, whose task it was to look after the old trophy, walked across to him and said: "Excuse me, sir, but the FA Cup is not to be thrown into the air." Cantwell's response was, "Don't worry – I knew that I would be able to catch it because I play cricket for Ireland!" The celebrations continued at the Savoy Hotel before the team travelled back to Manchester by train with the cup, and then went on an open-topped bus to the Town Hall, where hundreds of thousands turned out to greet the victorious team.

Winning the FA Cup meant that the following season, United would appear in European competition for the first time since the Munich Disaster, entering the European Cup-Winners' Cup. Everybody at the club was looking forward to it, and once again European fever hit Manchester. It was also the season that George Best emerged from the junior teams and became a first-team regular.

The 1963/64 season did not get off to the best of starts at Goodison Park, as Everton hammered United 4-0 in the FA Charity Shield. Yet only three games into the league season, United gained revenge with a 5-1 thrashing at Old Trafford, as the team and Denis Law got off to a tremendous start. Unfortunately for Noel, it would prove a campaign when he would eventually see him lose his first-team place.

United's first European opponents since 1958 turned out to be Dutch team Willem II. After a 1-1 draw away at the Feyenoord Stadien in Rotterdam, the Dutchmen were dismantled 6-1 at Old Trafford with Law claiming a hat-trick. The next round saw United draw the holders of the trophy, Tottenham Hotspur.

The first leg was played at White Hart Lane on 3rd December in front of a crowd of 57,000 people, who saw Tottenham win 2-0. United performed poorly, and the press didn't give them any chance of recovering the deficit in the second leg a week later. Normally, a European evening would have seen Old Trafford full to capacity and the gates locked early, but with a two-goal deficit to make up it seemed as though some of the supporters thought that the tie was already over – reflected in the official attendance of only 50,000.

After just eight minutes there was an incident which changed the whole course of the game. Noel Cantwell went for a 50-50 tackle with the Tottenham half-back Dave Mackay. Both players hurled themselves into the challenge, before the crowd went silent as they could hear the crack of bone. The result of the tackle ended with Mackay breaking both the tibia and fibula in his leg. It was a horrific injury and as they carried him from the field, his toe was actually touching his knee. There were no substitutes allowed in those days and United went on to win the game 4-1, going through 4-3 on aggregate.

Whether the tackle on Mackay affected Noel's performance is a matter of opinion, but it does seem to have some relevance as just a few weeks later, he was to lose his first-team place at Old Trafford. Busby moved Tony Dunne to left-back and brought Shay Brennan into the team, and they cemented a partnership that would last another five years. Noel was philosophical when he looked back on the move:

"Well, I was in the reserves and Tony Dunne had taken my place at left-back. I was playing at centre-half, but only getting the occasional first-team game. I'd passed all my coaching badges, and was chairman of the PFA. I was thinking ahead, thinking it was time to move on and I remembered Matt telling me that he wanted me to be a coach at Manchester United – I was very excited at the prospect. There had been numerous times when I had taken the training, when somebody wasn't available, and I'd always had it in my mind that the training could have been much better, more entertaining and exciting for the players.

"Unfortunately, things never materialised. The reason being, I think, that although Matt appreciated me, thought that I knew something about the game and that I could lead men, I don't think he wanted to upset the balance of the club – the Jack Cromptons, Jimmy Murphys and the rest of them. I think that he may have thought, by bringing in this young upstart, that it might just upset the rest of them and the whole balance of the club. He used to have long conversations with me in his office. He would call me in and it would be friendly but secret, and we'd talk about the club and the game – but it would never go any further. He did say to me: 'Noel, you can stay at Old Trafford.' He wanted me there, but I was ambitious and I didn't want to play in the reserves for too long."

With his movement becoming distinctly ponderous in his early 30s, Noel was out of the side during the title-winning campaign that followed, returning to offer cover for the full-backs Shay Brennan and Tony Dunne and the centre-half Bill Foulkes in 1965/66, then falling once more to the periphery, missing out on another championship triumph in 1966/67. At that point, however, it spoke volumes for his stature at Old Trafford that, although Denis Law skippered the team, Cantwell remained club captain, fuelling speculation that he was being groomed as the club's next boss.

At the end of the 1966/67 season Noel decided to retire as a player and move into management. Many thought Matt was grooming him to take over at United when he retired, but it was not to be and instead he went to take over as manager at Coventry City.

Noel Cantwell was a major chapter in the story of Manchester United in the 1960s. He was brought to United by Matt to pass on his experience and knowledge to the young players coming through, a committed and intelligent thinker about the game. He was a strong header of the ball, an excellent positional player who was always eager to move upfield and have a crack at goal, scoring 19 goals in all for United. He will always be remembered as the first captain to lift a trophy after Munich.

Was he a good club captain? Yes, he was a great club captain, a notion reflected in the way that Matt kept him as club captain when he could no longer find a place for him in his first-team plans. A great thinker about the game, Busby saw Cantwell as a good influence on young play-ers and would have been more than happy to see him join his coaching staff. Maybe if he had stayed it would have been Cantwell taking over the reigns at Old Trafford, rather than Wilf McGuinness. What we do know is that like a Cork man who would follow him as club captain, he set himself – and his team-mates – the highest of standards, which drove them on to victory.

The King Becomes Captain

DENIS LAW

1967-1968

'Denis led by example...Brave beyond belief, he often turned out when he was far from 100% fit...For opposing teams, just seeing the name Law on the Manchester United teamsheet had a big psychological effect'

Early in 1964, it was obvious to Matt Busby that due to the emergence of his Republic of Ireland team-mate, Tony Dunne, Noel Cantwell could no longer command a regular place. Busby had so much admiration for Cantwell that he did not take the club captaincy off him, but he needed a skipper on the pitch. Matt surprised many when he gave the role to a player who was the opposite of the calm-thinking Cantwell. He gave it to an impetuous, fiery genius – Denis Law. Between 1964 and 1967, Cantwell and Law shared the duties. Whereas Cantwell was from the West Ham school of football, who liked to analyse and work on tactics, Denis relied on his ability and the fact that if you got the ball to him in the box, he would score. Idolised by United fans, to whom he was "The King", his roots were anything but royal – and certainly not palatial.

The youngest of seven, Denis was born on 24th February 1940 in a council flat, 6 Printfield Terrace – a tenement block that also housed another 29 families – in Woodside, Aberdeen. His father was a trawler man, who went to work on Monday and didn't return until Saturday. So it was down to Denis's mother to bring the children up. She was a hard-working housewife who made sure her children were well fed, well mannered and lived in a spotless house. A proud woman, she refused the free school meals and boots offered to families with low incomes, preferring to face the hardships with family and friends. Denis was 14 before he received his first pair of shoes – before that he had gone to school in pumps – which was fine in summer, but no fun in winter.

Denis got his first taste of organised football at Hilton Primary School, where his talent shone. At the age of nine he was picked to play for the Under-11s, though Denis didn't possess a pair of boots. Fortunately a neighbour had just bought a new pair and was throwing his old ones out, but instead he gave them to Denis.

Denis was bright and passed his exams for Grammar School, much to his families' pride, as he was the first to pass the 11-Plus exam and achieve a place. You can only imagine their horror when Denis informed them that he had no intention of taking a place at the Grammar School as they only played cricket and rugby union, and Denis wanted to play football. Luckily for Denis and the rest of us, his parents wanted to see their son happy and so Denis went to Powis Secondary Modern School.

During his first year there, Denis was selected to play for Aberdeen Schools' U12s, reaching the final of a cup competition – only to lose to Motherwell and Wishaw on aggregate. Denis also started playing for Aberdeen Lads' Club, which meant his weekend was taken up playing football. Anyone reading this would assume that Denis was always going to be a footballer. If you had suggested that to anybody when Denis was young they would have looked at this little skinny kid with a squint and laughed. Denis was tormented for his squint, which probably toughened him up and certainly made him more determined to prove his worth. He only had one pair of glasses, and couldn't afford to break them so he didn't wear them – instead he played with one eye closed.

Aberdeen had a talented schoolboy team, which also included Alex Dawson. Even as a boy Alex was a bull of a centre-forward, who would attack every ball that came into the area. It was no surprise when United snapped him up and had it not been for the Munich tragedy and the need for Alex to be rushed into the team along with other juniors, his career at Old Trafford might have lasted a lot longer.

Denis never played for Scotland Schoolboys, although he did get picked for one squad against Northern Ireland. That didn't mean that Denis wasn't getting noticed though and just before Easter 1955 the Law household received a visit from Archie Beattie whose brother, Andy, was manager of Huddersfield Town. Archie offered Denis a trial and assured Mrs Law that he wouldn't be sending her son to Yorkshire if he wasn't confident he would be offered a contract. Denis was overjoyed – he couldn't believe an English First Division club would be interested in him, a scrawny kid with a squint and owl-round glasses.

Denis went to Huddersfield expecting to be back within days, but after a few weeks he was offered a job on the ground staff, being paid £4.14s a week while playing as an amateur. His week consisted of cleaning the boots of senior players and laying out their kit for training, cleaning dressing rooms and sweeping terraces. Tuesday nights and Saturday mornings were his highlights, when he would get to play in a match.

It was whilst at Huddersfield that Denis's life changed completely when he had corrective surgery on his eye. The effect was immediate; Denis had always been so self-conscious about his eyes and how it made him look, even to the extent of playing football with one eye closed. Now he was full of confidence, ready to play with both eyes wide open.

Playing for the youth team, Denis came up against United. Huddersfield raced into a 2-0 lead, but class told and United hit back to win 4-2. As Denis trudged off, an elderly Scottish gentleman congratulated him on his game and introduced himself as Matt Busby. Denis didn't have a clue who he was, but it was obvious he was keen on Denis joining United and becoming part of the Busby Babes. It was only on that February night in 1958, as Denis listened to the radio and heard about the Munich tragedy, that a chill ran through him as he thought how he might have been on that plane with the others who perished.

At the end of the 1955/56 season Huddersfield were relegated to the Second Division. This turned out to be a bonus for Denis, as it would now be easier to break into the first team. On Christmas Eve 1956, still only 16, Denis ran out at Meadow Lane to make his debut against Notts County. Town won 2-0 and as was the tradition, they played a return on Boxing Day. Huddersfield won 3-0 but, more importantly, Denis got on the scoresheet – his first goal for the club – on his home debut.

Soon after, Matt Busby made his first attempt to sign Denis. Matt offered £10,000, a record for a 16-year-old – but it was rejected. Things were changing at Leeds Road, as Beattie had gone to manage Nottingham Forest, with his assistant taking over. Luckily for Denis, the No. 2 was a Scotsman named Bill Shankly. Shankly had monitored Denis's progress, and knew he was looking at 100% gold. If he could only get him to stop running all over the pitch and concentrate on the penalty area, he knew he would have a world-beater. Shankly believed in youth and his team reflected it, as he blooded youngsters in an attempt to build an exciting side. He looked after his players – and put Denis on a regime of steaks and milk in an attempt to build him up.

In October 1958 Busby selected Denis for the Scotland team to play against a Welsh side managed by Jimmy Murphy. Busby received criticism from the Scottish press for picking a five-man forward line made up of players from English sides and especially for picking Denis, who was 18-years-old and played for an English Second Division side. He would be the youngest player in the 20th century to represent Scotland.

Shankly broke the news to Denis, and congratulated him on his selection. Shankly told him to express gratitude to Matt Busby, who had showed belief in his ability. Scotland went on to win 3-0, with Denis scoring the first of his 30 goals for his country, athough how much he knew about it is another matter. Welsh defender Dave Bowen's clearance hit Denis on the back of his head, before flying into the Welsh net.

When Shankly left in 1959 to join Liverpool, Denis assumed he would be going with him. He would have been happy to follow Shankly anywhere, but Liverpool did not have sufficient funds. After Matt's offer of £10,000, Huddersfield knew they had a valuable commodity, and weren't going to part with it cheaply. Eddie Boot took over as manager at Huddersfield, but the chemistry wasn't there. When Denis found out that clubs were showing interest, he knew it was time to move. He was told Town had received bids from Arsenal, Chelsea, Manchester City, West Brom and Rangers. Denis was keen on Arsenal and a move to the capital and when he was told to attend Highbury on a Tuesday night on 15th March 1960, he assumed that George Swindin, the Gunners' manager, would be there to discuss terms. However, when he arrived he was met not by Swindin but his assistant Ron Greenwood, who had no power of negotiation. Swindin's apparent snub upset Denis.

A delegation from Manchester City, including the manager Les McDowell and chairman Alan Douglas, plus some of the club's directors, met Denis. He was young and had little advice; he was insulted by Arsenal and so signed for City for a British record fee of £55,000.

The *Manchester Evening News* carried the headline 'Golden Boy Arrives – All Smiles' as Denis swept into the city that would define his career. The press made a fuss regarding the amount City had paid for the youngster, as it was £10,000 more than the previous record. Bill Shankly jumped to Law's defence, saying: "There is only one player in Britain who can carry such a price tag and that's Denis Law. He'll play his heart out because he wants to prove he is the best. He'll be worth £100,000 in a year's time. He is the greatest thing in football."

A few weeks after signing, he was coming out of the Midland Hotel when he bumped into Matt Busby. They greeted each other warmly, and Matt told Denis that he had considered putting in a bid. However, with Dennis Viollet scoring for fun and Albert Quixall and Alex Dawson starting to blossom, he'd decided not to move for him. As he left, Matt gave a wink and said: "You never know what will happen in the future."

The Manchester City who had spent big to bring in Denis were not flying high in the table; they were at the other end, trying to fight off relegation. On 19th March Denis ran out in a City shirt for the first time, at Leeds. They lost 4-3, but Denis showed the supporters what City had paid the money for by scoring. The defeat left City fourth-from-bottom and, in the opinion of most experts, heading in only one direction. The next game saw Denis make his home debut against West Ham and once again he found the net as City won 3-1, inching away from the drop zone in the process. Denis played in the last seven games of the 1959/60 season, helping City avoid the drop – but he began to think he might have been a bit hasty joining a team that looked destined to struggle.

The following season Denis made 37 appearances, scoring 19 goals. He was even picked to captain the side when Ken Barnes was out injured, but Denis was getting itchy feet. He told a journalist that if City went down, he wouldn't be staying. Unfortunately, this news got out and Denis received flack from fans – even though on the pitch he was giving everything to help them stave off relegation. City stayed up – just – but Denis knew it was time to leave. He was first approached by Inter Milan, who were keen to sign him, but a deal broke down. Instead Denis joined Torino, despite warnings from friends and team-mates. Yes, he would be earning a relative fortune, but he would be a stranger in a foreign land – was he ready for that? However, Denis's mind was made up.

Maybe if Denis had looked at the path trodden by fellow goal poacher Jimmy Greaves, who lasted only a couple of months in Italy, then he may have acted differently. But Denis was young and cocky, arriving in Turin like a film star – the blond hair, a smart suit and a big grin on his face – although the smile did not last long. Denis had moved for the money, but he also wanted to improve as a footballer. However, all he seemed to come up against were hatchet men. The press were on his back, following him wherever he went. The sports paper *Tutto Sport* gave him a symbolic lemon as the most uncooperative player in Serie A, as he refused to give them the interviews they constantly demanded.

Denis's brother came to visit and along with Denis and England forward Joe Baker, who also played for Torino, they went for a meal. Joe decided he would drive them in his Alfa Romeo, but he forgot that he should be driving on the right-hand side of the road. As he jerked back to the correct side, he clipped the curb and flipped the car over. All three survived, but Joe was badly injured and spent seven weeks in hospital. It was a lonely period for Denis, and it made his mind up that he wanted out. He put in a transfer request, but this was rejected.

Things changed on 25th April when in a game against Napoli, Denis was sent off. The manager and captain screamed at him, blaming him for the side losing. Denis then had a row with the club president, and was banned from the stadium for two weeks. Denis was eventually instructed to travel to Switzerland, where Torino were playing Lausanne in a friendly. Denis had not been forgiven and he wasn't selected – but what was about to happen couldn't have made him happier.

Matt Busby was in Switzerland and he met with the Torino president. Denis was not allowed in the room but when Matt came out, the grin on his face told Denis all he needed to know. He was going home – and he was going to be a United player. The deal did not go through immediately, as at one point Denis was told he had been sold to Juventus, but on 12th July 1962 Denis Law became a United player for the record fee of £115,000. Denis signed a two-year deal for £100 a week, and was about to begin a love affair with the club that would never end.

The press went crazy about the news, though not all of it was positive. Some suggested Denis was arrogant and cocky, and would be a bad influence. They were also quick to point out how frail and injury-prone he was, and how he wouldn't make it in the rough and tumble of the English league. They couldn't have been more wrong on both accounts.

Denis moved back into the old digs he had stayed in when he was at City. He had to get a lift to Old Trafford on his first day, as he didn't know how to get there. The Manchester United supporters couldn't wait for the season to begin though, wishing the days away just to get a look at their new hero – but they would not be the first to see Denis in red.

A crowd of 80,000 crammed into Hampden Park to see Caledonia's favourite son make his debut. It was 8th August 1962, with United playing a pre-season game against a Glasgow Select side. The team was virtually the Scotland side, made up of predominantly Rangers and Celtic

Clockwise from top left: Johnny Carey, United's first post-war skipper; Allenby Chilton gets the chance to improve his grip; Roger Byrne – Busby Babes skipper; Stan Pearson, leader from the front

Bill Foulkes leads United's makeshift side out at Old Trafford for their first game since Munich, 19th February 1958. Below left: Dennis Viollet, goalscoring hero and one-season captain; (below right) Maurice Setters running out at Everton's Goodison Park

Noel Cantwell strides out at Villa Park, and (below right) responds to BBC presenter David Coleman's questions after captaining the side to FA Cup success in 1963

Left: Unlikely skipper Denis Law is followed by his United team-mates at Hillsborough ahead of the 1965 FA Cup semi-final with Leeds United

United legend: Bobby Charlton runs out at Old Trafford, followed by Nobby Stiles, while (below) he takes charge of the European Cup after victory over Benfica in '68

Left: Fans' favourite Willie Morgan, skipper from the flank, and (below) Martin Buchan – 1970s United hero in an era of relegation, promotion and FA Cup success

(Below left) George Graham: Much derided for his short spell at United; (below right) Ray Wilkins, who preceded Robson's reign, in FA Cup final action in 1983

Two ages of Bryan Robson: The bubble perm upon signing for the club in 1981, and (below) being 'welcomed to hell' by Galatasaray, 11 years later

Lifting silverware: Steve Bruce holds aloft the European Cup-Winners' Cup in 1991, and (above right) the Premier League trophy, alongside Mark Hughes, in 1994

Captain's example: Match-winner Eric Cantona lifts the FA Cup to complete a second Double in three seasons following the 1-0 victory over Liverpool, May 1996

Signing for Norwich: Eric Cantona stops for fans; (left and below) Roy Keane celebrates Paul Scholes' late goal at Inter Milan, March 1999; cut eyebrow and all, tasting FA Cup success in 2004

Gary Neville dons the captain's armband against Roma in the Champions League quarter-final second leg at Old Trafford, April 2008

players – and it was they who took the lead. United pulled a goal back through Herd just before half-time, and the game was evenly poised.

The second half began and the home team regained their lead after Paddy Crerand, who was playing for Glasgow and giving a performance that convinced Busby he was a must for United, played in Ian McMillan, who beat David Gaskell. It seemed that time was running out for United – and then the crowd got to see what Busby had paid the money for. Denis beat three men, cut inside and then passed to Maurice Setters, who fired home from 25 yards. United added two more in the last 10 minutes to leave the Scottish team and fans stunned. It was as if United had switched into a higher gear – and Glasgow couldn't live with.

United kicked off the 1962/63 season against West Bromwich Albion. Hoping to catch an early glimpse of the new star and maybe an autograph, some of the supporters had gone down to Davyhulme Golf Club, where the team met up before home games for lunch. As Denis got out of his car, young fans trying to get an autograph from the new hero surrounded him – but Denis looked nervous and didn't hang around, he just wanted to get to Old Trafford and onto the pitch.

The team arrived at Old Trafford to be greeted by photographers snapping away as soon as Denis stepped off the coach. Denis made his way to the dressing room and paced about nervously, like a caged animal wanting to run free. The game couldn't have started better for United and Denis though, as David Herd put them into an early lead. Denis had not yet got into the game and was aware of the pressure on his shoulders, but he could also feel the crowd willing him on – and then it happened! The ball came out to Johnny Giles on the wing and he crossed into the area. He had over-hit the ball and it seemed too high for anyone to get their head to. However, out of a crowd Denis rose, seeming to hang for an eternity until his head connected with the ball – and sent it crashing into the goal. Denis Law had announced himself to the United faithful, and they went wild. The fact that West Brom fought back and earned a 2-2 draw didn't matter to the supporters as they left Old

Trafford. All they could talk about was 'that' header.

Denis will never forget the reception he received at Old Trafford. Maybe the special relationship he has with United fans was sealed that day, a relationship that would never wane. Today there are still men who get misty-eyed when they tell you how they saw Denis's first game for United, and the goal he scored. Denis seemed to understand the crowd straight away and the more they gave him, the harder he tried for them.

After his initial success, it was seven games until Denis got on the scoresheet again – and that was two goals against Manchester City in a 3-2 defeat. The team was not playing well; in the first 10 games United had won only three times. This was no reflection on Denis, who was giving his all. In fact, Matt had to explain that he didn't want him tearing all over the field – he wanted him in the box, concentrating on scoring.

United were in trouble at the wrong end of the table, even though there was talent throughout the team. The press had a field day, claiming United weren't getting the best out of Denis Law and that he wasn't getting the best out of United. This wasn't the Law who had been unplayable for his national side. Denis was never one to hide though, and when asked about his poor start, he commented: "What the man in the crowd and the press have to say about me never causes me a moment's worry. The only place I can prove myself is on the field and there, I have my good days and bad days. It's not possible to play like a £250,000 footballer every week. If I worried about it I would only play worse. Once I've done my best, I can accept praise or adverse criticism with indifference. I see no call to complain or explain."

Denis listened to Busby and started to put his demands into practice. Against West Ham at home, rather than tearing around trying to do everybody else's job, he stayed in or around the box. United won 3-1, with Denis scoring the third. The next game was at champions Ipswich Town, with the press claiming that this classy Ipswich team would thrash United. The weather was terrible and nearly caused the game to be abandoned, but the referee decided that the game would go ahead.

The game set off at a frenetic pace. United took the lead after only two minutes through Denis, netting from a tight angle. Ipswich equalised seven minutes later and the United fans feared that the game would now slip away. They needn't have worried, as on 15 minutes Denis made it 2-1 and then on 21 minutes he completed his hat-trick. David Herd made it four, before Ipswich pulled two back. With either side going for the win, both sets of supporters went crazy. Ipswich were pressing when United broke. The Ipswich keeper parried a shot from Nobby Stiles but it fell to Denis, who scored his fourth – and United's fifth.

United were now a different team – and with Denis playing up front anything was possible. This was never more evident than on 17th November when United were at Wolves, and found themselves 2-0 down at half-time. However, in the space of 30 second-half minutes United turned the game on its head to claim a 3-2 victory. Herd scored the first and then Denis took over, first tapping in the equaliser. Then in the 73rd minute Denis beat three men before scoring the winner.

In December 1962 Denis married Glasgow-born Diana Thomson, who worked in a solicitors in Aberdeen. Denis had met Diana at a dancehall in the city during the summer, just before joining United. Matt Busby liked his players to get married and settle down, so he was only too happy to give his blessing to the couple. This was also good for United. Denis had been travelling back to Aberdeen from Manchester on Saturdays after games. Maybe not such a long trip nowadays, but back in 1962 it was three flights there – and three flights back.

Denis was settled in Manchester and the team had just been strengthened, with the influential Paddy Crerand signed from Celtic for £56,000. Busby told the press he had bought the best wing-half in Britain – and possibly Europe. Now it was time that United got back to the business of winning trophies, five years after Munich.

The FA Cup was the only chance of glory that season, and for Denis it would be a game against his old club Huddersfield in the third round. The tie had been postponed seven times due to the terrible weather that brought havoc to the league for several weeks in the winter of 1963. As the teams ran out, the loudest cheer was for ex-United goalkeeper Ray Wood, who was now between the sticks for Huddersfield. It proved an easy game for United as they won 5-0, with Denis completing his hat-trick two minutes from time with a trademark header.

Aston Villa and Chelsea were the next sides defeated, before a quarter-final at Third Division Coventry City. Noel Cantwell was out injured, with Tony Dunne replacing him at full-back. Matt had no hesitation in handing the captain's armband to Denis. His first game as skipper could have turned into a nightmare as Coventry took a shock lead. For a spell it looked like they may cause an upset, but Bobby Charlton single-handedly dragged United back into it by scoring the equaliser, and then giving them the lead. Albert Quixall added a third in a 3-1 win.

United wore all-white as they faced Second Division Southampton in the semi-final. It was a game dominated by defences, separated by a moment of opportunism from Denis in the 22nd minute. David Herd's cross found Denis, whose header looped into the air. Denis fell, but managed to stick out a foot and prod the ball into the net.

Before the Wembley final, the team had a relegation battle on their hands. Manchester City were also struggling, and were below United when the teams met on 15th May 1963. City were within a point of United, knowing a victory would take them above their rivals. The atmosphere at the cup final would be nothing compared to the noise generated by the 52,424 packed into Maine Road to witness the most important Manchester derby ever. Whoever won would probably be safe while the draw would suit United – so City desperately needed to win.

The atmosphere was electric and when City's Alex Harley scored after nine minutes, you could hear the cheer over the other side of town. City scored again after 30 minutes, but the goal was ruled offside – and United were still in with a chance. Denis had been quiet, but things were about to change. With only six minutes to go City's David Wagstaffe made a suicidal back-pass towards his keeper, that Denis latched onto.

Denis was heading towards the corner flag, though he was still in the area. Harry Dowd, the City goalkeeper, charged out and pulled Denis to the ground. The referee had no choice but to point to the spot, and Albert Quixall calmly stepped up and slotted the ball home to level. The match finished 1-1, a result that saw City heading for the drop.

United won their final game 3-1 against Orient, while City lost 6-1 to West Ham. People are quick to remember the goal the Denis scored with the last kick of his Football League career for Manchester City against Manchester United to help relegate his old club, but how many of them remember him helping to send City down in his first year at United?

The date of 25th May 1963 proved a red-hot day in the capital as 100,000 spectators packed into Wembley. Record gate receipts yielded £89,000, while it seemed that 80 per cent of the crowd were sporting red. It had been five years since United had appeared in a Wembley final, which had been a matter of months after the Munich Air Crash. That occasion had proved a sombre affair, as the team lost 2-0 to Bolton.

The atmosphere could not have been more different this time – there was a sense of joy about the United supporters, who were out to enjoy the day. The band of the Royal Marines played, and Frank Rex led the community singing. Matt Busby, followed by Noel Cantwell, led the team out into the bright Wembley sunshine and a wall of sound.

David Herd kicked off for United, who were in their usual red, with Leicester in white. United looked confident from the start, with Paddy Crerand masterminding attacks. City goalkeeper Gordon Banks was tested early on, saving from Bobby Charlton. Banks attempted to throw the ball out, but Paddy anticipated the throw and took the ball, beat three players and squared to Denis. Law shielded the ball and then spun, putting the ball to Banks' right and into the corner of the goal.

Denis looked like he was going to win the final on his own, as soon after he went on a brilliant dribbling run, played a one-two with Herd and beat Banks – only for a young Frank McLintock to clear off the line.

The half-time whistle went with United leading 1-0, disappointed that they hadn't added to that lead. The second half began with Leicester improving, but just as they thought they might be getting back into the game, the ball fell to Charlton on the left; he went forward, and shot at goal. Banks managed to parry the ball away, but only towards the oncoming Herd, who knocked the ball into the empty net.

Leicester pulled a goal back when United failed to clear a free-kick, and suddenly looked like a team revitalised. United were determined to maintain their grip on the cup though, and they soon went close. Denis rose with a gravity-defying leap to head past a static Banks – only to see the ball strike the post and as the goalkeeper turned, the ball rebounded into his hands. Denis duly fell on the ground and beat it with his fist, in disbelief. Banks later looked back on that header:

"That effort of Law's was the most staggering header I have seen from any player. I was concentrating fully as United sent over a cross from the right. I decided against going for it as I could not sense any danger and, although Denis was in the penalty area, it seemed to be far too high for him to get to. Yet he made contact. With amazing reflex action and power of take-off he lifted himself what appeared to be at least three yards from the turf. I stood transfixed. I was staggered that anyone could possibly leap so high. But he wasn't finished. He flashed in a header that I had no chance of saving, and I could only sigh with genuine relief as the ball bounced off the post and flew straight into my waiting arms. I doubt if he had ever risen as high as he did for that cross. And, of course, the ironic twist about it from his point of view is that he failed to score. He was one of the game's greatest headers of the ball."

Back on his feet again, Denis initiated another attack. The ball found Johnny Giles on the wing, who crossed into the area. Banks came for the ball but fumbled, and it fell to Herd, who lashed it into the goal to win the game – and the cup – for United.

Both sets of fans applauded as the team took to the steps up to the Royal Box, led by Noel Cantwell. Denis was fourth in line behind Noel, David Herd and Bobby Charlton. They began their lap of honour, but one player was missing – Denis. He had headed for the dressing room for a cup of tea. Harry Gregg, who hadn't played, was with him and he came over and gave him a cigarette. Soon the rest of the team, led by Albert Quixall, returned. They drank bottles of milk and poured quite a few into the empty cup. It wasn't long before Harry Gregg poured the contents over Paddy Crerand's head, much to the amusement of Matt Busby. Matt then went round the team with a bottle of Moet and Chandon champagne, pouring each of them a drink into empty teacups.

There was plenty of praise for Denis. Sam Leitch, in his *Sunday Mirror* report, wrote: 'I rate the Law performance almost as glittering as the historic Stanley Matthews Final of 1953. Law was a probing puma in a number 10 shirt, scorer of the vital opening goal, the master man of soccer whom Leicester manager Matt Gillies admitted had wrecked his final dreams.' That triumph was the spark that ignited the drive towards two championships and a European Cup over the next five years.

The team finally came together. The signing of Crerand played a major part, plus that of David Herd, and then the emergence of Nobby Stiles, Tony Dunne, Shay Brennan and George Best. Bobby Charlton moved into a more central role and the side became a full unit, one that could compete with the best. When Denis first signed, Noel Cantwell was club captain and a big influence at the club. Unfortunately for Noel, he lost his place to Brennan during 1963/64, and never really competed for it again. The man who took over as skipper was Denis Law.

The decision was a surprise. There were former captains in the team in Bill Foulkes and Maurice Setters, plus Bobby Charlton was at his peak. So why Denis? Well, I believe Busby gave him the responsibility to calm him down. Denis was a 'firebrand' and quick to anger, and had been sent off a few times. It was always for the same thing...retaliation.

Denis took on the role, but did he really captain the team and the club? He was a single-minded person and had tunnel vision when it came to playing. He admitted that he dreaded Busby's team talks, and preferred them to be on a Friday before a game – come 3pm on the Saturday he had forgotten all about them! He was to say that he never worried about who was playing for the opposition. The games when United played in London, Denis dreaded because the team talk would be held in the hotel on the Saturday morning! Going to the game he would have all sorts of things that Busby had said ringing inside his head, and it wasn't until he walked onto the pitch that he could disperse with them.

Denis wasn't a good trainer, and only liked training with the ball. He detested stamina training, especially in pre-season. Jack Crompton and his staff used to take the players to Heaton Park and run them around the hills and valleys of the area, and then the players would be required to run back to The Cliff in Lower Broughton. Denis was to recall that "Crompo" could never understand how so many would get back before he did – but once the trainer was out of sight, they would catch a bus!

The next season began poorly, as United travelled to Goodison Park to face champions Everton in the FA Charity Shield. This was United's chance to show that they were serious title contenders. Busby was in confident mood, telling the press that if his team played as they had done in the cup final, they would be a match for any side. However, United looked out of their depth, and were thrashed 4-0. Busby was furious and dropped Albert Quixall, Johnny Giles and David Herd. Quixall and Giles both put in transfer requests, but Herd decided to fight for his place. Two weeks later, United played Everton again, in the league, and won 5-1 with Denis scoring two goals. This was to be an astonishing season for a team that had just avoided relegation the season before, and an incredible season for Denis, who scored 46 goals: 30 in the league, 10 in the FA Cup and six in the European Cup-Winners' Cup.

On 23rd October 1963 Denis played for the Rest Of The World against England at Wembley in what was billed as "The Match of the Century". It was a game to mark the 100th anniversary of the FA, and the Rest Of The World team was littered with world-class stars like Ferenc Puskas, Raymond Kopa and Alfredo Di Stefano. The game was taken seriously, with England winning 2-1 – though Denis was on target.

From the high of a Wembley goal to a red card at Aston Villa, as Denis was dismissed for the first time in his United career, on 16th November. Denis was given a 28-day ban, a punishment unheard of, and it seemed that the FA were out to make an example of Denis. In those days a player under suspension did not get paid, and was not allowed anywhere near his club. This makes his goal tally for the season even more amazing.

The season ended in disappointment for United. They finished as runners-up to Liverpool, were knocked out of the FA Cup by West Ham in the semi-final, and lost to Sporting Lisbon in the European Cup-Winners' Cup quarter-final. But it was clear that United were a team on the rise. The money Busby paid Torino for Denis now seemed like a steal. It must be said that the introduction of a boy from Belfast by the name of George Best didn't do the team's chances any harm, either.

Denis became a father for the first time when son Gary was born in June 1964 – and as soon as the 1964/65 season began it was obvious that Denis had no distractions other than leading United to success. Club captain Noel Cantwell played only two games late in the campaign: scoring at Birmingham in a 4-2 victory, and playing against Liverpool.

The season began with Denis leading the team out against West Brom, scoring in a 2-2 draw. Despite dropping a point, Denis remained confident United could go all the way and win the league. It was a period when the United crowd were divided in their admiration for the club's star players. Older supporters cheered loudest for Bobby, as he was their link to the Babes who never gave less than 100%, plus he had a rocket shot on him. Younger fans idolised George Best for his genius and pop star looks. The one thing that was guaranteed was that everybody loved Denis – he was "The King", their representative on the pitch. Boys in schoolyards stood with one hand in the air, clutching their sleeve in homage to their hero; it was recognisable then, and still is today.

They were the perfect trio on the pitch, the Holy Trinity, but off the pitch it was rumoured that Denis and Bobby didn't get on, and that Bobby and George wouldn't pass to each other. Noel Cantwell, talking about relationships in the team, said: "It was a strange dressing room. You'd be standing, stripping and talking to people every day, maybe five days a week, and half of them did not get on very well together."

Whatever was happening off the field certainly wasn't affecting the results on the pitch as United charged towards the title, as well as challenging in the FA Cup and the Inter-Cities Fairs Cup. Both United and Leeds were chasing a Double when they met in the FA Cup semi-final. The first game was at Hillsborough on Saturday 27th March. Leeds were a tough, cynical, streetwise team. Jack Charlton tore the shirt from Denis's back, and it wasn't long before the pair were trading blows. Soon their team-mates joined in, and the game turned into a shambles. The match ended goalless, and went to a replay four days later at Nottingham Forest's City Ground. Billy Bremner scored with barely two minutes left to put Leeds into the final and end United's Double hopes.

There may have been disappointment for Denis in the FA Cup but there was a massive personal honour when he was voted the European Footballer of the Year for 1964, becoming only the second British player to win the award. The honour was voted for by journalists from 21 European countries, and showed just how highly Denis was thought of all over Europe. The 'Golden Football' was presented to him the same night that United were presented with the league championship trophy.

Seven years after Munich had robbed the world of the beloved Busby Babes, Matt Busby had re-built a team that had now won the First Division. What a season it had been: champions of England, FA Cup semi-finalists and still in the quarter-finals of the Inter-Cities Fairs Cup. They had already beaten Strasbourg 5-0 in the first leg but on 19th May there was a party atmosphere at Old Trafford as Denis was presented with the league trophy. The team did a lap of honour and, then came a special moment when Denis was presented with the Golden Ball by Max Urbini, the editor of *France Football*. The match ended in a 0-0 draw, but who cared? United would eventually bow out in the semi-final to Ferencvaros in a season that saw Denis hit 39 goals, as well as being the first United captain since Roger Byrne to lift the league trophy.

The 1965/66 season saw United return to the European Cup – while it was also the campaign that George Best announced himself to the world with his performance against Benfica. The press christened him "El Beatle", and the first pop star footballer was born. However, the campaign as a whole did not go as well as Matt Busby had hoped, as United finished fourth and went out in the semi-final to Partizan Belgrade. The FA Cup also saw semi-final defeat at the hands of Everton.

Denis only managed 24 goals, his lowest tally since joining the club, and he was also frustrated with the team's lack of success. At the end of the season he travelled back to Aberdeen with his family for the summer. Before he left though he lit the touch-paper on a firework that very nearly blew up in his face. Denis's contract was up for renewal so he wrote a personal letter to Matt Busby, who was on holiday in Ireland, setting out what he required in his new contract. He asked for a signing on fee and an increase in his wages, but he stated that if he didn't get what he wanted, he would be prepared to leave.

He didn't have to wait long for Busby's response as Matt called a press conference to inform shocked reporters in attendance that he was placing Denis on the transfer list. Matt was annoyed when he spoke to the press, stating that "Manchester United are bigger than any player, no matter how famous they might be." The news was not only a shock to the reporters, it shook Manchester to its core – how could The King be on the list? What was Matt thinking of? In Aberdeen, the news reached the Law family, who were holidaying and enjoying the quiet life as Diana was expecting their second child. But newspaper reporters and photographers converged on the city, hoping to get a scoop.

Once Denis flew back into Manchester and met with Matt, everything was resolved. Matt handed out a press release in which Denis publicly apologised to Matt and the club, whilst privately he received what he had wanted. It was a master class in PR by Busby, who had sent a message to his star players that nobody was bigger than the club. Anyone who thought they were, would soon be shown the door. It was obvious who was boss, a lesson not lost on Sir Alex Ferguson years later.

With Law settled, the team could look forward to regaining the championship. Before the campaign began there was the small matter of a World Cup final being played at Wembley. Whilst the country was glued to its TV sets, Denis was on the golf course with a pal. It was a great afternoon for them as they had the Chorlton-cum-Hardy course to themselves – the only thing that spoiled the day was when someone came to tell him that the 'Auld Enemy' were now world champions.

The sun was shining as Denis led United out at the start of 1966/67. The crowd were treated to a first-day feast as United beat West Brom 5-3, with Denis scoring twice. The team had no problems scoring; the trouble was stopping them, an issue addressed when Matt bought Alex Stepney from Chelsea. With Law, Best and Charlton on form United seemed unstoppable – though some thought George held the ball too long, and prevented Denis from scoring more. Denis would pass to George and look for a quick return, only to see the Irishman tormenting defenders for amusement. Denis wasn't shy about chiding George for his showboating, when a quick pass would have been profitable.

A surprise exit to Norwich in the FA Cup meant the team could concentrate on the league – which is what they did, not losing another game. They needed just a point as they arrived at West Ham for the second-to-last game of the season. A crowd of 38,424 packed into Upton Park, the ground's biggest crowd since the War. If ever a game summed up that United team in their pomp it was this. They swept the Hammers aside, and were leading 4-0 by half-time with goals from Charlton, Crerand, Foulkes and Best. West Ham pulled one back in the second half, but two goals from Denis made the score 6-1 – securing the championship again. Denis didn't play in the last game at Old Trafford, but came out with the team before the game and afterwards, to receive the trophy.

The 1967/68 season will go down as one of the greatest in the history of Manchester United. Everything that Matt Busby and Jimmy Murphy had dreamed of, and worked so hard to achieve, was about to come to fruition. Even though it was the only season he was officially club captain, the season turned out to be a disaster for Denis.

The campaign started with a trip to a packed Goodison Park. Fortune did not shine on United that day though as a rejuvenated Everton side won 3-1. Things never really got going for Denis as injuries wreaked havoc, as well as run-ins with referees and the authorities. On 7th October Denis was given his marching orders for fighting with Ian Ure of Arsenal, with both receiving six-week bans. The press questioned Busby's attitude to discipline, with many saying he was being too soft with Denis, as this was Law's fourth sending off in four years. Would United take disciplinary action? Would Denis remain captain?

During Law's enforced absence, United produced title-winning form, suffering only three defeats before Christmas. Denis still believed that he could play a big part, but it was not to be and the season would prove to be Denis's worst at United. He only played 23 league matches, scoring seven goals, and only appeared once in the FA Cup. Denis did play in the first two European Cup games against Hibernians of Malta, scoring twice in a 4-0 victory at Old Trafford, but he had a quiet game in the away leg due to an injury and a rock-hard pitch. Denis was suffering with a knee injury, and was unfit to play. He went to see Harley Street specialist Mr Osmond-Clarke. He wrote to the club, stating that Denis's knee was in such a bad state that it would only last a couple more seasons – although the letter was never shown to Denis.

Denis did make a return towards the end of the season, and on a warm April evening he led United out at Old Trafford in the semi-final of the European Cup against Real Madrid. A crowd of 63,000 packed in, hopeful of seeing Law inspire the side to victory. Unfortunately Denis looked out of sorts and failed to impress, although a piece of magic from George Best gave United a 1-0 lead to take to the second leg. Though Denis travelled for the return, he played no part in the miracle comeback, which saw United come from 3-1 down to reach the final.

Denis had been playing through the pain barrier all season and it was recommended that he would need surgery as soon as possible. Matt was willing to give Denis an opportunity to be fit for the Wembley final and delay the surgery, but Denis wanted the operation as soon as possible, so that he could get back for pre-season training. Rather than prepare for and play in United's biggest-ever game, he entered St Joseph's hospital in Whalley Range for what was supposed to be an exploratory operation. Instead, when he came round, he was greeted by the sight of a piece of floating cartilage an inch-and-a-half long in a jar.

On the morning of 29th May 1968 Denis was woken by the nurses, wearing red rosettes and buzzing with excitement. Though Denis wasn't the greatest of spectators, this was different: this was the European Cup final. Though traumatised at missing the biggest game of his life, he was going to be United's most enthusiastic supporter. He watched on TV with some pals and the on-duty nurses. Ever the private man, he turned down David Coleman's request to bring a BBC camera crew to watch the game and get Denis's reaction to the result.

The night ended in triumph for United as they beat Benfica 4-1 after extra time. The crowds cheered Matt Busby and Bobby Charlton wept while everybody spared a thought for Denis. Would he ever get a chance to play in a European Cup final? Denis celebrated with his friends and staff but there must have been massive feelings of regret and disappointment as he watched his team-mates celebrate with the trophy. The following day the whole team and Matt called into the hospital with the trophy to let him know that he was an important part of the victorious team. Although he did get a winner's medal, he admitted that the gloss was taken off it because he never actually played in the game.

Matt decided that Denis needed to get back to full fitness and concentrate on his own game so he gave the club captaincy to Bobby Charlton, who had captained the European Cup-winning side. Times were changing – things would never be the same again. Players were getting older, as was Matt, and he had achieved his dream. The ghosts of Munich still haunted him, but he slept a little easier knowing that the dream his Babes had begun had now been achieved, captained by a Babe in the form of Bobby Charlton. The great team of the mid-to-late 1960s was a wonderful side to watch and in essence, it didn't really need a captain. There were so many commanding figures within it who played with a freedom and attractiveness that few clubs could ever match. Their "off-the-cuff' style packed opposing team's stadiums, the fans attracted by the silky skills of Law, Charlton and Best. Effervescent, fiery, ebullient, resilient, all those words aptly describe Denis Law.

As a captain I am certain he commanded both Matt Busby's and the players' respect. Certainly in the fans' eyes he was "The King" and even now, almost 40 years after he hung up his boots, he is revered. It says much for his qualities that today, at Old Trafford, there are two statues bearing his image. One in the Stretford End, and of course the statue of the Trinity opposite the stadium forecourt.

Denis led by example, and never failed to give United any less than 100%. It says much that he captained a team to two First Division championships, and was club captain when they won the European Cup. Denis was an effervescent character, although he never courted the limelight. He was popular amongst the players, and they all had great respect for him. However, once a match or training was over, he was quickly off home to his wife Diana and the children.

Brave beyond belief, he often turned out for the club when he was far from 100% fit, and he was to suffer because of this towards the end of his career and in later life. He had so much respect for Busby that whenever he asked him to play, even knowing that Denis was less than fit, he did so. For opposing teams, just seeing the name Law on the Manchester United teamsheet had a big psychological effect. For me, and thousands of others, he will simply always be "The King".

There Is A Light That Never Goes Out

BOBBY CHARLTON

1968-1973

'Bobby captained United for five seasons at probably one of the most turbulent times in the club's history...he handled it as he always did, with great dignity and with one thing on his mind — the wellbeing and reputation of the club'

"His story is the best in English football. After Munich he was the hope of both Manchester United and England, and he carried the burden brilliantly." The words of Johnny Giles, a team-mate of Bobby's in the 1963 FA Cup-winning team – the club's first major trophy since Munich.

On 24th April 1948 United played Blackpool in the all-Lancashire Wembley final. In Manchester people huddled around their wireless sets to listen to the game. Further north in the Northumbrian mining village of Ashington, a 10-year-old boy remembers that afternoon.

"We played for East Northumberland Boys in the morning, and were invited to go to one of the lads' houses to listen to the final on the radio – we had no television in those days. After a while we went out to play football – we couldn't get enough in one day – and every so often we would come in to ask the score. I remember United equalising, and the next we heard they'd won. They said it was the greatest cup final of all time. I think it was from that day that I wanted to be a footballer and join Manchester United." The name of that boy was Bobby Charlton.

It is almost 40 years since Bobby Charlton hung up his boots, and finished playing for Manchester United. Even now, after all those years have passed, he is still instantly recognisable, still such a high-profile football figure who commands the respect of everybody in the game worldwide. Travel anywhere in the world and mention the name Bobby Charlton and there is no doubt that it will bring smiles, warmth and much affection into any conversation. Today, in this new century, he is still very much as big an icon in the game of football as he was during those glorious halcyon years of the late 1950s and 1960s, when he was driving both Manchester United and England on to glory.

Nobody symbolises English football – or a nation's sporting aspirations and achievements – more than Bobby Charlton. During the 1960s he was the most famous, and most popular Englishman in the world, a byword for sportsmanship and fair play, whose fame and universal esteem were based upon phenomenal footballing ability and a quintessentially Corinthian spirit. He was, and remains, English football's ultimate ambassador, with an unsurpassed record of achievement. That record is impressive enough: Charlton won three Football League championships, the FA Cup, European Cup and World Cup; he was Footballer of the Year in England and Europe, and scored more goals for Manchester United and England than anyone else. But it is also the context of his career that made it so unique, poignant and globally admired.

Bobby was born in Ashington, a mining village situated deep in the heart of the Northumberland coalfield. His father was a miner while his mother, Cissie, came from the famous north-eastern footballing family known as "the Milburn's." The Milburn's were the most famous football family during the period, synonymous with the north east of England.

The very first Milburn was named Jack. He played for Shankhouse, and also Northumberland during the early pioneering days of the game. After him came a real feisty character who went under the name of "Warhorse" Milburn, famous in local football. He fathered 13 children, several of whom went on to play to a decent level. "Tanner" Milburn was one of these children, and he appeared for Ashington during their Football League days. The Milburn family tree grew further branches when this particular Milburn had four sons and three daughters. Inevitably, the boys played football. One of Tanner's brothers was named

Alec and he also played for Ashington, after turning down the chance to travel south and play for Tottenham. It was Alec who produced the son who would later become famous throughout the football world, idolised on Tyneside, a player known as "Wor Jackie." Tanner's four male offspring also turned out for teams in the Football League. Sons George, Jim and Jack played for Leeds United, whilst the other one, Stan, made his name as a tough-tackling full-back with Chesterfield and Leicester City, and also appeared for the Football League. Cissie Milburn was one of Tanner's daughters. She married a miner named Bob Charlton, and they too had four sons. Of these four sons, two were to become famous in the football world in their own right, and appear in the only England team to win a World Cup – namely Jackie and Bobby Charlton.

The development of his football skills came naturally to Bobby. He became star of his school, county and North of England sides, and then the England schoolboy team. Wilf McGuinness remembered the first time he saw Bobby. "I first met him when Manchester Boys played against East Northumberland Boys at Maine Road in a cup competition – we were both 15. I was captain of the Manchester team and remember we beat them easily, 3-0. This young lad came up to me after the game and said: 'We could both be going to Manchester United, I'm Bobby Charlton.' I remember thinking, 'Who the hell is Bobby Charlton?' He was a little skinny kid who had made no impression on the game, even though I could tell he was not a bad little player. Manchester United scout Joe Armstrong had told him to make himself known to me."

Joe had been to watch Bobby play for East Northumberland Boys, and knew that he was looking at something special. He approached Bobby and his father after the game and told them that he would like Bobby to come and play for United. There were no shortage of scouts from other clubs queuing up at the Charlton's front door, promising 'the world' if only they could obtain the young schoolboy's signature. They came from Wolves, they came from Arsenal – but Armstrong needn't have worried, as Bobby's heart was set on playing for Manchester United.

Joining United on 6th June 1953 was like going back to school for young Bobby, such was the youth around the club. Star schoolboy players had joined from all over the country. The competition was fierce, but in the eyes of Jimmy Murphy, Bert Whalley and Tom Curry, there was no doubt that Bobby Charlton would go on to become a world-class footballer. But as Bobby remembered, he needed a bit of coaching. "The difficulty in turning from being an amateur player, who only worried about himself and his own position, to becoming a team player was apparent to me when I first came. There was a problem there, because I did crazy things. I used to try and do the most difficult things, when all I needed was someone to tell me what was the right way to do it.

"When I arrived, Jimmy Murphy did that. He'd take me after training on a Sunday morning or after a match on a Saturday, he'd bring me down to the pitch. We'd talk, and he'd tell me all the wrong things I was doing. He turned my world around as far as football was concerned."

Jimmy took him to his digs at Birch Avenue, where he met his fellow borders Duncan Edwards, Jackie Blanchflower, Mark Jones, Tommy Taylor, David Pegg, Billy Whelan and Gordon Clayton. Bobby was instantly accepted, and they all became great friends, going to the pictures together or just out walking. Bobby saw a lot of David Pegg and Tommy Taylor as, like himself, they were from mining communities. Eddie Colman and Wilf McGuinness were local boys who looked after Bobby, and would invite him to their houses – especially at holiday times. The team would play on Christmas Day so Bobby couldn't get home to be with his family. They would invite him on Christmas Eve, which was important to Bobby, who had begun to feel homesick. It didn't last long, but those friends were the ones who helped him through it.

Bobby promised his mother that when he went to Manchester he would not go on to the ground staff, but instead learn a trade in case things didn't work out. Joe Armstrong got Bobby a job with an electrical engineering company called Switchgear and Collins, where he earned 50 shillings a week for making tea, filing and packing equipment. Bobby enjoyed his time there, but his heart wasn't in the job – and why should it have been? His friends on the ground staff were getting an extra hour in bed in the morning, 30 shillings a week more pay and spent everyday practicing football, whilst Bobby only got to practice two nights a week. Money was tight, and the other lads in the lodgings could see this. Duncan Edwards even gave Bobby a new shirt, claiming it was too small for him. It is a perfect example of how close the boys were – and it was also a welcome addition to Bobby's sparse wardrobe.

Bobby contacted his mother and explained that football and a part-time job could not mix. His argument worked, and she agreed he could join the ground staff – although soon after he was called up into the Army. Number 23312133, Lance-Corporal Charlton, 17th Company, R.A.O.C, was stationed at Nescliffe barracks near Shrewsbury. He was put in charge of the ammunition store, but spent most of his time playing sport. Most people might have expected Bobby to be the star of the football team and he would have been, if it hadn't been for the fact that his friend, Duncan Edwards, was also serving with him and playing in the same side. Duncan cast a shadow over Bobby's life; he was the only player he ever felt inferior to. There was no star distinction amongst the Babes, but from the beginning everybody recognised that Duncan was the outstanding player in United's youth side. It wasn't long before he was gracing the first team, and playing for England.

During the 1955/56 season, most of Bobby's pals, including Wilf McGuinness, Eddie Colman, David Pegg, Albert Scanlon and Billy Whelan had played in some of the games that helped United to win the league championship that year whilst Bobby, who had been scoring lots of goals in the reserves, was champing at the bit to get his chance.

Saturday 6th October 1956, five days before his 19th birthday, Bobby made his first-team debut at Old Trafford against Charlton Athletic. A fortnight earlier, playing against Manchester City reserves at Maine Road, he had injured his right foot – but had told Matt Busby he was fit to play. When he got out onto the pitch, he found that he couldn't use his right foot as much as he would have liked so when the ball came to him in a shooting position he used his left foot – and scored. Five minutes later, he scored another with his left foot. From that day it was always impossible to say which was Bobby's strongest side. Martin Buchan works for the PFA, trying to help players without a club back into the game. When he talks to them, he always asks them which is their strongest foot. Many of them say they are two-footed and equally as good with both feet, so he asks: "If you had to take a penalty to save your life, which foot would you use?" Their reply is what he puts down as their strongest foot. Whilst writing this book, I spoke to him about different players he had played with and the only truly two-footed player he had ever seen was Bobby.

That championship-winning season he made 14 appearances, scoring 10 goals, including a hat-trick against Charlton in February 1957. He also managed to score in the FA Cup semi-final against Birmingham, booking himself a place in the starting line-up for the final against Aston Villa. The game did not go as Bobby had hoped, and the 2-1 defeat owed much to the physical impact of Peter McParland, the Aston Villa centre-forward, who collided with Ray Wood's cheek, making the goalkeeper a virtual spectator for the rest of the game.

Bobby was convinced that United had a good chance of winning a third consecutive league crown at the start of the 1957/58 season, as well as challenging for the FA Cup and European Cup. Though Bobby didn't play in the early European ties, he did play – and score – in the quarter-final against Red Star Belgrade. In the league, United were going well and gaining plaudits for their performances. On 2nd February 1958, wearing their all-white Wembley strip, United ran out at Highbury to play Arsenal. The team wore black armbands as a mark of respect for Mr G. E. Whittaker, a club director who had died in the team hotel that morning. What the crowd saw that day was one of the greatest games an English league ground has ever hosted. United dominated, and went in at half-time leading 3-0 – only for Arsenal to come out in the second half with all guns blazing. The home side clawed themselves level, only for United to regain the lead. Arsenal hit back again, only for United to score an eventual winner to leave the crowd breathless. This would be the last league match Bobby Charlton would ever play with the most famous Manchester United team.

There has been much written about what happened on that Munich airfield on 6th February 1958. The effect it had on Manchester United as a club and Manchester as a city, as the "Flowers of Manchester" were lost on that icy runway, never to grace the football grounds of England again. There were survivors, one of them Bobby. But it was not the same Bobby who had got on the plane, not the same Bobby who had messed around with his pals, had gone dancing with his pals, had gone to the cinema with his pals, had lived, eaten, slept and played with his pals. For they were now gone, and Bobby had never felt so alone and guilty. Why had he survived when all his friends had perished? There was no grief counselling for Bobby and the other survivors – they were just expected to come home and get on with it.

Bobby missed the fabulous FA Cup fifth-round tie against Sheffield Wednesday, when an emotional crowd roared a makeshift United team to victory. He was back for the sixth round and for the remaining games of that unforgettable season. On 3rd May 1958 Bobby returned to Wembley to play centre-forward for United in the FA Cup final against Bolton Wanderers. In January of that year United had beaten the Trotters 7-2, with Bobby scoring a hat-trick, but this was a completely different United and a Bobby Charlton who needed to rest. Bolton won the game 2-0, but it might have been a different story. Just before Bolton scored their second controversial goal, Bobby hit one of his trademark screamers, which looked to be heading into the corner of the net – only to curl at the final split-second and hit the inside of the far post, before rebounding into the hands of the Bolton goalkeeper.

Bobby did at least earn selection for England's World Cup campaign that summer in Sweden, but remained on the bench as his team-mates drew all three group matches, failing to qualify for the quarter-finals by losing 1-0 to Russia in a play-off. In 1962 he went to his second World Cup, this time in Chile – and as a first-choice player. England qualified for the last eight thanks to a 3-1 defeat of Argentina, in which Charlton scored. But the Brazil of Garrincha, Didi and Amarildo were too good for England, and they were knocked out 3-1.

Back at Old Trafford, United's rebuilding was taking shape. The team included Albert Quixall, a British record signing at £45,000 from Sheffield Wednesday, Maurice Setters from West Brom and Johnny Giles, who had been discovered in Ireland. By 1960/61 Nobby Stiles had made his debut, and Bobby was United's leading scorer that season with 20 goals. David Herd from Arsenal, Noel Cantwell from West Ham, Denis Law – a record £115,000 signing from Torino – and Celtic's Pat Crerand were soon brought in. It took Matt five years to get his team back to Wembley, and this time he hadn't done it by bringing through prodigious young talent, but by dipping into the transfer market. They beat Leicester City in the 1963 FA Cup final with the then most expensive team ever to play in a final, although they were not the favourites. The reason for the underdog tag was United's wayward league form, having finished that season 19th out of 22 teams in the First Division – but in the FA Cup they had scored 12, conceding only one. It would prove to be a one-sided final, with United winning 3-1. Charlton had a hand in the second goal, his shot proving too hot to handle for goalkeeper Gordon Banks – with Herd scoring the rebound.

Two years prior to this, in 1961, Bobby married Norma Ball at St Gabriel's Church in Middleton, with captain Maurice Setters acting as best man. Many people believed he would have his good pal Wilf McGuinness in the role, but in those days it was not the done thing for a catholic like Wilf to be the best man at a protestant's wedding. I asked Wilf about this, and he insisted that the real reason was that he was far too good looking, and would have overshadowed the groom! Marrying Norma was the greatest day in Bobby's life, but it brought many problems with his family, as his mother and Norma did not get along. This factor would lead to Bobby and his brother Jackie falling out publicly. Jack, in his autobiography, blamed Norma for the ill-feeling with their mother, accusing her of being 'hoity-toity' and having airs and graces.

Back on the pitch, the 1963/64 season was memorable for two reasons. First, against West Brom, the Holy Trinity of Law-Charlton-Best played together for the first time. Significantly, they all scored in a 4-1 victory. The second factor was that United and Bobby were back in Europe for the first time since Munich, this time in the European Cup-Winners' Cup. Charlton, now coming inside more often, had scored a spectacular acrobatic goal in the 7-2 aggregate demolition of Dutch part-timers Willem II Tilburg in the preliminary round.

The next round pitted them against holders Tottenham Hotspur. United lost the first leg 2-0 at White Hart Lane, and faced a seemingly uphill task. They were 2-1 up in the second leg – but trailing on aggregate – when Charlton scored twice to put United through to a quarter-final against Sporting Lisbon. The first match was at home, and Bobby scored again in an impressive 4-1 victory. However, the away tie proved a nightmare, with United suffering their worst defeat in Europe, 5-0.

The league form that campaign could be described as erratic. For example, they lost 6-1 at Burnley and yet won the return fixture a couple of days later 5-1. These were the days of attacking football, however, and big scores were not unusual. Despite the inconsistency, they finished as runners-up to Liverpool in the championship.

The turning point came in the 1964/65 season. United won the league and reached the semi-finals of the FA Cup and the Inter-Cities' Fairs Cup. Bobby Charlton was in top form as United inflicted heavy defeats on some decent teams. They beat Liverpool 3-0, Aston Villa 7-0 and Blackburn 5-0 at Ewood Park. Charlton claimed a hat-trick against Rovers and, as Nobby Stiles admitted, he "played them on his own."

The most impressive performance was a 6-1 hammering of Borussia Dortmund in West Germany in the second round of the Fairs Cup.

Charlton hit three, one of them a rocket which crashed in off the cross-bar, and added two more – one from 20 yards – in the 4-0 victory at Old Trafford. It is worth remembering that Dortmund won the West German cup that season and the European Cup-Winners' Cup the following year.

Manchester United were back in the European Cup, chasing Matt Busby's elusive dream. It proved an impressive run. A 9-2 aggregate humbling of HJK Helsinki was followed by a 7-1 aggregate defeat of ASK Vorwaerts of Berlin. Benfica were next up, Eusebio and all. United shaded the first leg at Old Trafford 3-2 and travelled to Lisbon, knowing that Benfica had never lost in 19 European Cup ties at home. There's a first time for everything though – and that night United turned on the magic with a stunning 5-1 victory. Charlton scored, but the night belonged to George Best – and nothing would ever be the same again as they returned home with "El Beatle". Almost overnight the entire world wanted to know about the boy from Belfast. Young ladies, who did not have the slightest care for football, suddenly took an interest in United and started to hang around the ground, hoping for a glimpse of George.

Manchester United were on top of the world – but success was not to be that season. The semi-final took them back to Belgrade for the first time since Munich. They went down 2-0, and a 1-0 victory at home was not enough to prevent them going out on aggregate to Partizan. They had played some breathtaking football that season, but had inexplicably missed out on honours, their FA Cup run having also been ended in the semi-finals, while they finished fourth in the league.

At the end of a long, hard season Bobby joined his brother Jack for the World Cup in England. They began dismally with a 0-0 draw against Uruguay, but then Bobby lit up England's hopes with a stunning goal in the 2-0 defeat of Mexico. He ran 30 yards with the ball before letting fly – and it thundered into the net. That was the goal that convinced a cynical nation that England could win the World Cup. Before then, there was a feeling that they just weren't good enough, an impression confirmed by the sterile performance against the Uruguayans. Charlton changed the national mood in seconds, yet to hear his version made it seem nothing more than good fortune: "I picked up the ball quite deep and I had no intention of shooting at goal," he said. "I didn't really expect them to allow me to keep going. I just banged it and it came off so sweetly. When it went on its way I thought, 'well, that's a goal.'"

A 2-0 victory over France put England on course for a quarter-final showdown with Argentina. It was a nasty game; the Argentine defender Antonio Rattin was sent off and England manager Alf Ramsey sent a chill through FIFA by calling the Argentinians "animals." But a 1-0 victory meant a semi-final against Portugal. It was against the Portuguese, according to Brian Glanville in his book *The Story of the World Cup*, that 'Charlton had much his best game of the World Cup, perhaps the best he ever played for England.' His passing was crisp, his running made gaps in Portugal's defence and he scored both goals in a 2-1 win. Charlton had put England into the World Cup final.

Geoff Hurst, the hat-trick hero of the final, grabbed the headlines as England beat West Germany 4-2 after extra time. But perhaps the crucial factor in the game was the German manager Helmut Schoen's decision to tie-up the great Franz Beckenbauer in a policing role on Charlton. It was a battle of wits. Charlton was the player the Germans feared most, and as Beckenbauer himself said years later: "England beat us because Bobby Charlton was a bit better than me." Sir Alf Ramsey had no doubts how crucial Charlton had been. "He was one of the greatest players I have seen," he said: "He was the linchpin of the 1966 team. Early in my management I knew I had to find a role suitable to Bobby's unique talents. He wasn't just a great goalscorer, with a blistering shot using either foot. Bobby was a player who could also do his share of hard work." The reward for Charlton was not only a World Cup winners' medal. He was named as Player of the Tournament and the Footballer of the Year, as well as the European Footballer of the Year.

It came as no surprise that in the 1966/67 season, after 18 months of non-stop football, Bobby suffered a loss of form. He went three months without scoring, before getting two in a 4-0 defeat of Blackpool at the end of February. Even with Bobby looking tired and losing form United were too strong for the rest of the league, retaining their title in style with a 6-1 win at West Ham. The next season, 1967/68, would be the one that defined the Busby era. United were champions and going for the elusive prize of the European Cup. They beat Hibernians Valletta of Malta and FC Sarajevo of Yugoslavia in the first two rounds, before meeting Gornik Zabrze of Poland in the quarter-finals.

United took a 2-0 lead from the first leg to Poland, where they had to play on a snow-covered pitch in treacherous conditions. Matt Busby didn't want the game played. Apart from the risk of serious injury to his players, Busby did not want to chance the hard-fought lead to a lottery, which included ice skating! However, referee Concetto Lo Bello decided the pitch was fit to play on. United defended like demons on that treacherous surface. The snow fell and after 10 minutes or so, it was almost impossible to see the red line markings. It was a bitterly cold March evening and even the Polish fans, hardy miners from the local region, were given to lighting bonfires on the terraces in an effort to keep out the chill. Late in the game Lubanski, the Gornik star player, did get free to score, but United held out to advance to the semi-final on a 2-1 aggregate, where they would face the mighty Real Madrid.

A George Best goal at Old Trafford meant that Manchester United held only a fragile 1-0 lead as they went to the Bernabeau for the second leg against Real. Denis Law was out with an injury and by half-time United were 3-1 down. The dream was dying again. However, somehow United stuck to the task and, through David Sadler and Bill Foulkes, came away with a 3-3 draw. Charlton has no hesitation in naming it the greatest match he played in – his favourite above World and European Cup final glory. "Real were murdering us" said Charlton, "but we came out after the break, battled away and they collapsed."

The night of 29th May 1968 at Wembley was to be the fulfilment of Bobby Charlton's long and heartbreaking journey. The Red Devils of

Manchester against the Red Devils of Lisbon...the old foes, Eusebio's Benfica. The Portuguese champions were vastly experienced. They had played 52 European Cup ties, winning 29. United had played 32 and won 20. Benfica, who had won the trophy twice, were appearing in their fifth European Cup final in eight years – while it was United's first. In Eusebio, Benfica had the competition's second-highest goalscorer of all time with 36, topped only by the peerless Di Stefano of Real Madrid with 49. Bobby Charlton had played in all four of United's European Cup campaigns, but this was the first in which he had not scored. A week before the final, in an international against Sweden, he had broken Jimmy Greaves's record of 44 goals for England. Now, on this historic night as captain of United, he was determined to put matters right.

The first half passed without much incident, but just after half-time Sadler crossed and Bobby rose to score a rare headed goal. United held the lead but with only nine minutes Graca was left unmarked and he stunned the crowd with an equaliser. United were tiring, with Benfica coming on strong. With time running out, Eusebio twice had good chances to grab the glory – but each time goalkeeper Alex Stepney foiled him. Benfica were dominating – but United were saved by the whistle. They now had the chance to regroup before extra time.

It was a hot night, and Benfica suddenly looked dead on their feet. Matt noticed the Benfica players lying down and insisted that his United players stood on their feet, ensuring they didn't run the risk of stiffening up by lying down. As the first period of extra time kicked off, United took the game by the scruff of the neck. Best weaved his magic, beating a defender and rounding the keeper before side-footing the ball into the net. Brian Kidd, celebrating his 19th birthday, headed the third. As if written by scriptwriters in a Hollywood epic, Charlton, the Busby Babe, the spirit of Munich, scored the last to secure a crushing 4-1 triumph.

The game ended and all Bobby could think about was Matt. In Bobby's mind, Matt was an old man and not in the best of health. As the final whistle went, everybody seemed to be heading for Matt. Bobby raced over and started to pull people off him, shouting to "Give him room." The pair embraced, and the usually reserved Charlton wept tears of joy and regret as he thought of all his pals who never got the chance to fulfil their potential. Manager Matt Busby said: "They've done us proud. They came back with all their hearts to show everyone what Manchester United are made of. This is the most wonderful thing that has happened in my life and I am the proudest man in England tonight."

The team was staying at the Russell Hotel, and as soon as they returned the party began. Bobby and Norma went up to their room to freshen up and while Norma came down to join in the celebrations, Bobby stayed in his room with his thoughts and memories of boyhood friends with whom he made those first steps into Europe. Norma came back up to the room and told him what was happening downstairs, about all the old United players who were there and asking to see him. But the night and the emotion had taken its toll and Bobby never did go downstairs to celebrate with his team-mates. It was a fact he was later to regret, as he never got the chance to celebrate a big cup win with United again. He even missed the homecoming to Manchester's Albert Square, as he had to report for duty with England. This was more of a relief than a hindrance to Bobby, who had done all the celebrating he needed to do.

Bobby never really had the chance to take time off during the summer as England played in the European Championship in Italy, where they finished third. In June Matt Busby, having achieved his life's ambition, became Sir Matt. He said of Charlton: "There's never been a more popular footballer. He was as near perfection as it is possible to be."

Bobby, then aged 31, was rewarded with an eight-year contract, the longest in Football League history. Matt also decided to make him club captain, allowing Denis Law to concentrate on his return to fitness and playing career. For Bobby, the 1968/69 season was to be an exciting, though disappointing one. United began the season with the team that had won the European Cup, but injuries and loss of form began to take their toll. Names like Frank Kopel, Alan Gowling, Carlo Sartori, Steve

James and Jimmy Rimmer began to appear on the teamsheet. They reached the quarter-final in the FA Cup, losing narrowly to Everton and, contentiously, to AC Milan in the semi-final of the European Cup. In the league they were disappointing, finishing in 11th position.

The big shock came on 14th January when Sir Matt announced he would retire as manager at the end of the season – FA Cup final day on 26th April. Sir Matt, who was 59, told a news conference at Old Trafford: "It's time to make way for a younger man...a track-suited manager." He added that the pressures of managing a top-class team were becoming too great for a man of his age, and he would now take on the role of general manager. "United is no longer just a football club", he said, "it is an institution. The demands are beyond one human being."

As club captain, it must have been a difficult period for Bobby. Little did he know that the club was about to embark on a period of great unrest and turbulence. Wilf McGuinness was appointed as first-team coach, a decision which did not sit too well with many of the senior players. Bobby had played as a team-mate of Wilf's from schoolboy through to first team and international level. They were very close friends – they still are today. Professionally, it was going to be a difficult relationship, no matter how much they felt towards each other, and initially it was a very uneasy period. As Bobby has said often before: "There were times when I had to sort out in my head whether it was Wilf my mate talking to me or Wilf the manager."

The infamous 'press-ups' incident occurred after a training session. Bobby had gone to get changed as he was going to an engagement. Wilf called the players, including Bobby, to the middle of the training pitch for a chat. Wilf had a rule that any player with his hands in the pockets of his tracksuit had to do 10 press-ups. When Bobby arrived in his suit he had his hands in his pockets. Behind him he had Nobby Stiles and Shay Brennan up to mischief, mouthing to Wilf: "Look, he's got his hands in his pockets." Wilf was in an impossible position; he could not be seen to have one rule for Bobby and one rule for the rest of the team.

So he ordered Bobby to give him 10 press-ups, there and then, in his suit. Bobby understood the position Wilf was in, but he wasn't happy about it. Wilf had big shoes to fill, and some felt this was his way of showing that he was big enough to do so. It didn't win him any friends in a dressing room that was already becoming fragmented as cliques began to appear. Bill Foulkes had retired, and Ian Ure was brought in from Arsenal to replace him. Shay Brennan left for Waterford, Stiles and Law were out for long periods with injury. The first signs of George Best's disenchantment with the game – and the club – began to emerge.

Yet in Wilf's first season and under Bobby's captaincy, the team did reasonably well, reaching the semi-finals of the two domestic cup competitions. Unfortunately Manchester City won the League Cup tie, and after three acrimonious games against a cynical Leeds United team, the Yorkshire club triumphed in the FA Cup. In the league the side finished in eighth position, three places better that the previous season. So for a while it did at least look as if progress was being made.

The 1970/71 season saw the end of Wilf as manager and Matt came back to take charge. The big problem for Wilf was even though Matt had stepped upstairs, he was always in the background, having the final word on players he wanted to bring in. Colin Todd, Mick Mills and Malcolm MacDonald would all have strengthened the team, but Wilf was not allowed to bring them in. The side began to age and the quality coming through the reserve team was not good enough. There was also distrust of Bobby by some of the players, as they looked upon him as "Matt's Man." By Christmas 1970 the team was in 18th, and had been knocked out of the League Cup semi-finals by Third Division Aston Villa. Two days before Christmas, Wilf was relieved of his duties.

The question is: were all the players 'pulling' for Wilf as manager and Bobby as captain? Obviously Brian Kidd did not think so, as the day following Wilf's sacking he was critical of the senior players, saying: "It's you that got Wilf the sack. I hope you're proud of yourselves." With Matt back, the team rallied and finished eighth, though they did not make it past the FA Cup third round, being knocked out by Middlesbrough – the team Nobby Stiles joined at the end of the season. Matt stepped down and Irishman Frank O'Farrell was appointed manager, after impressing with his stint as Leicester City boss.

It seemed that United had found the perfect solution as the team began the 1971/72 season on fire. The forward line of Willie Morgan, Kidd, Charlton, Law and Best were terrorising defences and scoring goals for fun – by Christmas they were top of the league by five points. Pat Crerand, knowing he was not in O'Farrell's plans for the future, retired that December. Unfortunately, form went downhill rapidly, with the team eventually finishing in eighth once again. O'Farrell found it difficult to deal with the big personalities in the dressing room. George Best's off-field problems manifested themselves more, and the fallouts in the dressing room became more frequent and fierier. Both George and Denis would not speak to Bobby and as for O'Farrell, he was a virtual stranger to all the players as they only really saw him on matchdays.

Despite spending big on players like Martin Buchan, Ted MacDougall, Ian Storey-Moore and Wyn Davies, the start to the 1972/73 season was a disaster. George would regularly go missing; the new players didn't trust the older players, and the club was hurtling towards the Second Division. Relations between George and Bobby were strained and there appeared to be an underlying mistrust of the manager's judgement by Bobby as he brought in players like MacDougall and Davies, who were not "Manchester United" players. The final act for O'Farrell came on 16th December 1972 when an ordinary Crystal Palace team destroyed United 5-0 at Selhurst Park. The result left the team in 21st position; the next day O'Farrell was fired.

The club was in a crisis: it was only five years since the team had conquered Europe, with a side containing three European Players of the Year playing free-flowing attractive football. Now it was a team floundering, hurtling towards relegation. The club needed a radical overhaul on the playing side and someone big enough to manage in Busby's shadow. The board had the perfect man. On Monday morning the ebullient Tommy Docherty was installed as boss at Old Trafford and the wheeling and dealing in the transfer market began. Docherty knew that the club need a radical overhaul on the playing side, but how do you tell players like Bobby Charlton and Denis Law that their time is up?

Fortunately for Docherty, in Bobby's case, he wouldn't need to. Bobby was beginning to lose interest, the excitement felt every morning prior to a game was no longer there. Games were passing him by, he was not making the impact he used to. Bobby went to see Tommy and told him that he intended to retire at the end of the season. Tommy didn't openly give a big sigh of relief, but he made no attempt to talk Bobby out of his decision. As with all things that concerned Docherty, it didn't take long for the press to find out about Bobby's decision, and tributes flowed at every ground he appeared at until the end of the season. The final time Bobby led the team out at Old Trafford was 23rd April 1973 against Sheffield United. Old Trafford was a cauldron of emotion as the United faithful bid farewell to one of their greatest-ever players.

On Saturday 28th April 1973 Bobby captained United for the last time. He walked out at Chelsea's Stamford Bridge to a guard of honour formed by both teams, and a tremendous reception from the crowd. The game ended in a 1-0 defeat for United and when the final whistle went, Bobby raised his hands above his head, clapped all sides of the stadium and then left with great dignity. Twenty years of playing service to United had ended and with it, the last of those bouncing Busby Babes.

Bobby captained United for five seasons at one of the most turbulent times in the club's history. It wasn't an easy captaincy; there were many trials and upheavals along the way. He served as captain under four different managers, each of whom saw things differently. He had to handle dressing room rancour and cliques, and also more than a hint of jealousy. But Charlton coped as he always did, with dignity and with one thing on his mind – the wellbeing and reputation of the club with which he has had a love affair for the whole of his adult life.

The Scottish Gunter Netzer

GEORGE GRAHAM

1973-1974

'Not only did Docherty want George to come and play for United, he wanted him to captain the team...Docherty was convinced he had brought real quality into the United side...a little bit different from the Docherty who had told George [at Chelsea] that he had seen a carthorse run faster than him'

Many people forget, or didn't even realise that George Graham played for Manchester United – let alone became club captain. The Scot took over from the retiring Bobby Charlton, although he did not last long before the mantle was handed to Willie Morgan. Graham was a luxury player, nicknamed "Gorgeous George" or "Stroller", having made his name at Chelsea and Arsenal before answering the call from "The Doc".

Docherty had taken over at United; it was the only position he would leave the Scotland job for. Now he was coming to terms with the size and seriousness of the job that lay ahead. United were in turmoil: players were getting too old, and some were not good enough. The first player he brought in was George Graham. The Doc had managed George at Chelsea, but they had fallen out. George and some of his team-mates, including Terry Venables, were sent home for breaking a pre-match curfew in 1965. But that was in the past – and Tommy was now in need of players to bolster his side. He made the call and offered George the chance to play a lead role on one of the world's greatest football stages.

George was born on St Andrew's Day, 30th November 1944 in a village eight miles outside Glasgow called Bargeddie. George's father, Robert, died soon after, on Christmas Day, and so his mother Janet was left a widow with seven mouths to feed. The world was still at war and all Janet had was a widow's pension. The family had to scrimp and save to get by. George was aged 13 before he got a new coat for the first time, as his other clothes had been hand-me-downs, though his mother did somehow manage to find money to buy him a pair of football boots when George was nine. It was maybe the best money she ever spent.

Playing as an inside-forward for school teams and sailing through district and county sides, George found himself playing for the Scotland Under-15 side; it wasn't long before professional scouts started to take an interest. Long before he got the nickname "Stroller", George was also quite an athlete, winning sprint races at school and holding the school record for the high jump at both junior and senior level. Rangers were interested in signing George, as were Aston Villa, Newcastle and Chelsea. George visited all four clubs and spent a month at each, deciding which suited him best. Bill Shankly also expressed an interest, but at the time he had just joined Liverpool, then in the Second Division. His future was decided when Joe Mercer visited the family home and convinced George's mum that the best place for her boy was Aston Villa, as well as promising that they would take good care of her son.

George signed as an Aston Villa professional on his 17th birthday, even though his brothers were desperate for him to pull on the famous Rangers blue shirt. He also played for Scotland in the 'Little World Cup', the tournament for Under-18 international teams. Though George scored on his first-team debut for Villa against Liverpool, he could never cement a regular place and was soon transfer-listed. Southampton made a serious offer, and he would probably have accepted if it wasn't for the persuasive powers of Chelsea's young boss, Tommy Docherty.

George arrived at Chelsea in 1964, and his game suddenly fell into place. The Doc was putting together a team that mirrored his personality, playing with swagger and flair. As at Villa, George made a scoring start, netting against Sunderland. Everything was going smoothly at Chelsea for George and his team-mates. On their day they were a match for any team, and respected football judges were predicting the team would be champions within three years. But one of those events that have paved The Doc's career occurred and became known as 'The Blackpool Affair'. The Doc sent eight Chelsea players home, including George, after they had broken an 11pm curfew. He put a reserve team out against Willie Morgan's Burnley, who duly thrashed them 6-2. The players lost confidence in The Doc, and he in them. After turning down two transfer requests from George, The Doc suddenly changed his mind and accepted £50,000 plus Tommy Baldwin from Arsenal.

It is with Arsenal that George will always remembered. Like the beautiful tailored suits that he wore, Arsenal fitted George perfectly. Joining in 1966, he instantly became a first-team regular and for the next two years he was the club's leading goalscorer. He was part of the famous 'Double Team' of 1970/71 season, but halfway through the following campaign Arsenal bought Alan Ball from Everton for a British record fee, and George knew that his time at Arsenal was coming to an end.

When Tommy Docherty called, he was as enthusiastic as George had ever heard him. Even though United were in a relegation battle, The Doc gushed to George, telling him United were the greatest club in the world, and the only one he would have given up the Scotland job for. George was initially hesitant about uprooting his family, but this was an offer he couldn't turn down. He rented out the family house and bought a place in Sale, so that he could fully concentrate on making a success of his United career. Within days of buying George, Docherty continued to recruit Scottish-born players, bringing in Alex Forsyth from Partick Thistle, Jim Houlton from Shrewsbury Town and Lou Macari from Celtic, adding to the Scottish contingent at United which included Denis Law, Willie Morgan, Martin Buchan, John Fitzpatrick and Ted MacDougall. This became known as the era of MacChester United.

George's debut was on 6th January 1973 against, of all teams, Arsenal. United were beaten 3-1, and George got a big wake-up call as to what kind of team he had joined. Once great players were now tired and the most gifted these isles have ever produced, George Best, was in one of his disappearing moods. Busby's pure football teams were a thing of the past and United were now involved in a battle for survival. Docherty decided that United were going to have to get physical. This suited warriors like Houlton, who would go into every tackle as if his life depended on it, but to a ball-player like Graham it came as a culture shock to suddenly be asked to put his foot in. Now it was about stopping teams, rather than outplaying them. Bobby Charlton would finish as top scorer with six goals – and two of those were penalties.

Time has no respect for ability and reputation and as United successfully battled to avoid relegation by finishing 18th, Bobby Charlton realised his time at United was over, as he had no wish to play in a team that was playing the kind of football that was the antithesis of everything he had become famous for. On the last day of the season, 28th April 1973, Bobby played his last game against Chelsea at Stamford Bridge. To a man, the 45,000 crowd stood to applaud a living legend.

Not only did Docherty want George to come and play for United, he wanted him to captain the team. There were raised eyebrows when Tommy announced that George was taking over as club captain. Most assumed that he would hand it to the assured Martin Buchan, but Tommy did not consider Martin experienced enough in the English First Division, even though he had previously captained the cup-winning Aberdeen side. Docherty was convinced that he had brought real quality into the United side and described George to the press as "Britain's Gunter Netzer", who at the time was one of the world's most accomplished midfield playmakers. This was a little bit different from the Docherty who had told George when he was playing for Chelsea that he had seen a carthorse run faster than him.

Bobby Charlton was not the only one to leave the club that summer as Docherty set out to completely rebuild a crumbling side. Denis Law was also released, which saddened George as the pair only got to line up together three times in the league. One of Graham's regrets was that they played more times together for Scotland than United.

George's form suffered as he struggled to come to terms with the tension and upheaval around the club. The Old Trafford faithful didn't take to George, as they sensed that he was past his best. He never showed them the "Stroller Graham" who had graced Highbury so elegantly. This was a thoroughbred being asked to be a workhorse; it was never going to work. George's loss of form cost him his place in the Scotland team, now managed by Willie Ormond. He made his final appearance in a Scottish jersey at Hampden on 30th June 1973, when he came on as a substitute against a Brazilian side including Jairzinho and Rivelino.

The fateful 1973/74 season got off to a terrible start for United as they visited Highbury for the opening game. Arsenal were in no mood to do their old player any favours, and hammered United 3-0. It was as if the relegation battle began that day, and continued for the rest of the season. Even the return of the mercurial genius Best did not alter the team's fortunes. This was highlighted by the fact that for a period Alex Stepney, who was the penalty taker, was the leading goalscorer with two goals.

On New Year's Day 1974 United were beaten 3-0 at QPR. The players sat dejected in the dressing room, except for Best – who wasn't going to waste an opportunity in London, going off to a party. He then skipped training and The Doc suspended him, fined him two weeks' wages and put him on the transfer list. George reacted by going to the media, telling them he was quitting football, adding: "If I am not good enough to get into a struggling team as bad as United, then it's time I retired."

Things were going from bad to worse for Graham: he was captaining a struggling side that just weren't responding, and his form was the worst of his career. On 16th March 1974 United lost 1-0 at Birmingham City, a defeat that saw them go bottom of the league. Docherty knew George's confidence had gone and the supporters were getting on his back. Docherty decided it was time for a change. He took the captaincy off Graham, handing it to fellow Scot Willie Morgan. This was bound to please the supporters, as Willie was a crowd favourite whereas George had turned into a pantomime villain.

George Graham's United career was over after just 43 league games. He now got to see the other side of Tommy Docherty. No longer needed, he was given the cold shoulder treatment, demoted to the reserves and forced to train with the youth team. The Doc's attempt to ostracize him did not force George into submitting a transfer demand that would have cost him a lot of money. Instead, he kept his head down and played in the reserves until Docherty called him into his office, and asked him if he fancied a move to Portsmouth. Stroller's days at United were over.

There can be no doubt that George's best days were over when he joined United. He could pass the ball and was good in the air, but United were a struggling side that could not afford to carry a luxury player like Graham. His relaxed style probably gave the false impression that he didn't care, when in fact he never gave less than 100%. He was singled out for abuse from certain sections of the crowd, even when he played well. For many supporters at Old Trafford he could do nothing right.

There have been far greater, and more deserving players who never got to be club captain. That was not George's fault, and Docherty obviously thought that he would bring quality and stability to the side. Unfortunately, this was not the case. He captained a team that was falling to pieces and he wasn't up to the job. Maybe he was unlucky; maybe in a better side we would have seen a different George Graham.

As it was, we rarely got to see the real George Graham. It's difficult to assess his period of captaincy as the reality is, it only really spanned just over half a season. He may have been unfortunate in that United were in free-fall, and the turbulence in turnover of players was immense.

George Graham's impact seems to have been minimal, and there may well have been underlying reasons for that. He was a very strong character, an experienced player. Was there a coincidence that his demise under Docherty happened at the same time as the demise of George Best? I suppose we'll never know. But certainly, from that moment on until he left for Portsmouth, he never played any significant part at all.

Willie Morgan on the wing

WILLIE MORGAN

1974-1975

*'Willie took the responsibility of being captain very seriously.
He loved Manchester United – and he loved the fans...he did
everything he physically could to try and help, but the team
was on an irreversible slide towards relegation'*

Situated on high ground between Alloa and Tillicoultu in central
Clackmannanshire is the village of Sauhcie. It was a small community,
whose men folk were miners. The Morgan family lived at 29 Sprotwell
Terrace, and had no television or telephone – just a coal fire for warmth.
On 2nd October 1944 in Glasgow, Annie Morgan produced a son,
named William. Coming from a small mining village, expectations
weren't high for a boy: you either went down the pit or into the priest-
hood. But if God did have plans for young Willie, they certainly didn't
involve a dog collar or the coalface. Willie was blessed with an exceptional talent, an ability that would take him to the biggest club in the
world, and to the World Cup with his country.

Willie first attended St Mungo's RC School in Alloa. Even at primary
school age, his footballing abilities made him stand out. In his village
everyone played football, as he remembers: "Everyone could play, the
whole village could play. We used to throw shirts down, or a couple of
tin cans as goalposts. There were very few balls in the village, occasionally you got an old leather footie with laces, and we used to fill it with
old papers, because no one had a bladder. The criteria in the school and
in the village was, if you had five minutes, you played football. It was
always who was picked first [who was the best player]. I was always

200

picked first, it was that simple. I still maintain if you want to find a good player just go and ask a group of kids, 'who is the first pick?' They'll tell you the best player." By the time Willie had moved to the secondary department of the school, he was a player of outstanding ability.

Willie earned a county trial, although he was two years younger than the normal age for selection. He was the star of the school team, and was picked for Clackmannanshire in the Schools' Cup, playing against the other counties in Scotland. He also turned out for Fishcross Boys, meaning he would play for the school on a Saturday morning and Fishcross in the afternoon. But he had no aspirations to become a professional footballer – it was beyond his imagination.

"Your vocation was down the pits or to be a priest, that was the choice that you had, it was a tiny village" he said. "It wasn't bad; people say it must have been dreadful; you slept five in a bed. It was a mining community so we didn't have any ambitions to be footballers, we just played football. My ambition was to play for Sauchie, I didn't believe you could get better than that; they used to call them Sauchie Juveniles, who eventually became Sauchie Juniors, a long, long time later. Sauchie Juveniles were just the guys from the pit, they were all miners and you played against other miner's teams, it was very rough. So my ambition was to play for Sauchie and work down the pit."

In those days you left school at 15 and became a 'Bevan Boy' – an apprentice in the pits. Even though he was bright, what he did academically was irrelevant. His career choice was simple: become a priest, or go down the pits. Willie was 14 and playing for Clackmannanshire, the smallest county in Scotland. They had progressed through the first two rounds of the Scottish Schools Cup. Willie was due to leave school in December, as he was 15 in October. The next round of the cup was due to be played in January, so the headmaster went to see Willie's dad to see if he could stay on and play in the competition. Willie's father told him that Willie would be leaving school, and earning a wage down the pit. Times were always hard and every penny counted – another wage coming into the house would be a godsend.

The following night, the local priest came knocking at the door and explained to Mr Morgan that it would be very helpful if Willie stayed on at school. Mr Morgan was never one to go against the wishes of the church, and Willie duly found himself staying on at school. This meant he was still eligible to play for the county, which he did, helping them beat Dundee and the all-conquering Glasgow. The press was raving about young Morgan, who was the star of the Clackmannanshire team.

All of a sudden scouts started to appear from Celtic and Rangers, St Mirren and Stirling Albion. They approached Willie's father, and informed him that they would like his son to come and play for them. Then the scouts started to appear from England – representatives from Chelsea, Manchester United, Blackpool, Arsenal and Burnley. Willie remembered the latter club's scout coming to his house: "The Burnley scout, a guy called Jimmy Stein, came from Whitburn and he had a car, because you have to remember there were no cars in the village. He brought a paper with him and showed me the table. Burnley were at the top of the league, and he said: 'That's Burnley, the best team in England.' I had never heard of them, I had only really heard of Stanley Matthews and, of course, that's what Blackpool's scout told me. 'Come to Blackpool and you'll be with Stanley Matthews.'"

Willie received offers from all these teams. They would pay him to come on trial with them, and he recalled the plan that he and his dad came up with: "I was going to go to Burnley, then Arsenal, Chelsea, Blackpool and then back home, where I would sign for Celtic. I was going to do two weeks at each of them, as everywhere you went they paid you £8 a week, which is what they paid the apprentices. My dad at the time worked 60 hours on the pit face for 3 pounds, 10 shillings a week. So we worked it all out. We'd get £16 at one club and £16 at another – then I would go back and play for Celtic."

Things never work out as planned, though. Willie went to the first club on his list, Burnley, and in his first practice match he chipped a bone in his toe. He was ruled out for six weeks with his foot in plaster. Burnley were helpful, putting Willie up in digs with other players, continuing to pay him while he was there. Manager Harry Potts made a point of going to see Willie, telling him that they liked what they had seen and that they would like him to sign for the club. Willie, of course, said he would have to speak to his father before he made any decisions, so they brought his father down to the club. This was the first time that Mr Morgan had been in a car, the first time he had been out of the village and it was the first time he had ever stayed in a hotel – as it was for Willie.

Willie told his father that Burnley had been good to him, and that they had looked after him. He said that he didn't want to go to the other clubs, and that he had made his mind up. Mr Morgan was disappointed that his boy wasn't going to be wearing the green and white hoops, but he could see he was happy. So at 15 years of age Willie Morgan signed apprentice forms with Burnley. Willie had no regrets about signing for Burnley, and not going up to Celtic:

"I had a great time at Burnley, the lads that I played with, all the ground staff lads, we had some great players. I don't have any regrets over what I did. Would I like to have played for Celtic? Yes, I would. Jock Stein came back to try and sign me when I was 18 before I signed professional forms with Burnley. He took me round Celtic Park and I was close to going there, but I didn't – I decided to go back to Burnley."

However, things didn't all go smoothly. When Willie was 16, he was living in digs with other players. There was an 11 o'clock curfew at the digs, and Willie was 20 minutes late getting in one night. He was warned that the next time it happened he would be in real trouble, and reported to the club. Of course, being a young man, it happened again and Willie found himself locked out of his digs, even though he was only 20 minutes late. He tried to sleep in the coal cellar around the back of the house, but it was far too cold. It got to about two in the morning and Willie could take the cold no more, so he went round to the front of the house and banged on the door until they let him in. The next day he was reported to the club. Willie tried to explain himself, while his land-lady at the digs had told the club that he hadn't got in until 2am. The club sent Willie home immediately.

Willie's father was less than pleased to see his son sent home in such embarrassing circumstances, but consoled himself with the fact that his son could now play for Celtic. However, it didn't take Burnley long to realise that this was a possibility, and they sent someone up to see Willie, who apologised on the club's behalf for not believing his story.

Upon returning to Burnley Willie quickly impressed, but such was the talent around Turf Moor at the time that he couldn't always win a regu-lar place in the reserve team. John Connelly was the regular outside-right in the first team, whilst there was plenty of cover, notably from Trevor Meredith. You couldn't hold back talent like Willie for long though and he soon earnede himself a regular spot in the Central League side for the 1962/63 season.

In 1963, just before he turned 18, he made his debut for the first team against Sheffield Wednesday. He was up against a full-back called Don Megson, who was a fearsome character, but Willie destroyed him and made the game look easy. In those days, playing for the first team at such a young age was a big story, but Willie took it all in his stride. He would tell his mates on the ground staff and in the younger teams to stand in the corner of the ground where staff were allowed, and when he got to that corner he would do tricks on the ball or a pirouette just for their amusement. Long before Cristiano Ronaldo was a twinkle in his father's eye, Willie Morgan was tormenting and torturing defenders with step overs and tricks, leaving many with twisted blood.

Like Ronaldo, Willie was popular with the ladies. He was young, good looking and his hair was considered to be long, although it just about touched his collar. Two girls approached Willie and asked if they could start the 'Willie Morgan Fan Club'. They produced a monthly magazine, and sent out photos of Willie. This was 1963 and no footballer had ever had a fan club before – and it would be years until another one would.

On Boxing Day 1963 Willie scored his first goals for Burnley when he hit two in a 6-1 thrashing of a certain Manchester United. Two days later United played Burnley again, this time at Old Trafford, and won 5-1. Making only his second appearance for the first team that day was a young Irish boy, with whom Willie would be compared to during his entire career. His name? George Best. George's light was yet to rise; Willie was already a star, and a big crowd idol at Turf Moor. He was treated the same as any other player inside the club but outside, things were completely different, as he was getting contracts and doing articles that no other player was being offered. The papers loved him because he was different; he had pop star looks and was brilliant at what he did.

Morgan established himself as one of the best wingers in the league; he had great close control, could beat defenders almost at will and was a superb crosser of the ball. He was selected for his country and made his debut against Northern Ireland at Windsor Park in 1967.

Towards the end of the 1967/68 season it was time for Willie to sign a new contract at Burnley so he went to see Harry Potts, the Burnley manager, and wrote down what deal he wanted. He left this with the club and travelled to Majorca for a short holiday. When he returned he found out from the press that Bob Lord, the Burnley chairman, had been slaughtering him, stating that no player would tell him what to do, and that he would make him tow the line. Willie went in to see Potts, who made him an offer. The figure was nowhere near what Willie wanted, so he refused to sign a new contract. Lord was furious and determined to make an example out of Morgan. He banned him from training, and told him that he would never kick a ball in football again.

It wasn't long before top clubs heard about the fall-out, and if Burnley weren't prepared to pay him what he wanted then they certainly were. Willie remembers getting a visit from Don Revie, the Leeds United manager: "He came round to the house for a cup of tea, and said: 'Would you like to come to Leeds?' Of course I did. 'Well,' he said, 'Burnley are asking £100,000 for you. We're going to make an offer of

£75,000, but there's £15,000 for you.' Now 15 grand in those days was a fortune, and it was going to be in readies. So he said: 'Would you join us? You'd be my last piece in the jigsaw, everybody wants you, but I'd love to have you at Leeds.' So I agreed. He said: 'All you have to do is, whoever comes in for you, say no and refuse to talk to them.'

"This went on for a couple of months and then I got a phone call from Revie to ask me if Burnley had said anything to me about an offer. They hadn't, and he said: 'Well, we've made an offer and have asked for permission to talk to you.' It was well known that Bob Lord and Manny Cousins, the Leeds chairman, hated each other and didn't speak, so I went into Burnley and asked had Leeds made a bid for me. I got a swift answer of 'no'! This did not worry Revie, who told me all I had to do was wait and eventually they would have to cut their losses and sell me."

So that is what Willie did. The season started and he stayed away, spending most of his time playing golf at Bacup Golf Club. It was on this golf course in August, on a Friday night, that Willie noticed a figure coming across the course towards him: "I came down the ninth, as it is only a nine-hole golf course, and I saw this guy walking down the hill towards me. He said: 'Can I have a word with you?' I agreed, but told him to stay where he was. He said: 'I've been sent by Matt Busby, would you come to Old Trafford as Matt would like to meet with you and sign you for Manchester United.' So I went with this man, who was called Jeff Mitten, and who was a very good friend of Matt's.

"We came to Old Trafford and I met Jimmy Murphy, who took me up to Matt's office. Matt said to me: 'We've always wanted to sign you, and I think you're the greatest winger in the world. We've spoken to Burnley and we've agreed a fee with Mr Lord. Would you come here?' I said: 'Yes, it would be nice.' They were European champions, were going to be in Europe again that year and they were about to play Estudiantes in the Inter-Continental Cup final. So Matt invited me to come back the following day to sign the contract. He asked me if there was anything I wanted, so I told him I wanted the No. 7 shirt. He replied that there would be no problem, as he would give George Best the No. 11 shirt. 'Is there anything else?' he asked. I told him that I was not that keen on Nobby Stiles, as every time we had played against United he had given me a kicking. The players were arriving at that time as they were playing a game against Chelsea and so Matt sent for Nobby. It didn't take me long to realise that he is the loveliest guy in the world."

Willie signed the contract on 24th August 1968, and then went off to fulfil a prior engagement to play golf whilst Chelsea hammered his new team-mates 4-0. The following Wednesday he made his debut at his new home ground in a 3-1 victory over Tottenham. The line-up that day was:

Stepney, Brennan, Dunne, Fitzpatrick, Sadler, Stiles, Morgan, Kidd, Charlton, Law, Best.

Willie had joined a collection of world-class team-mates, some of whom were reaching the veteran stage, and it seemed reasonable to believe that Matt Busby was on the threshold of rebuilding with a new generation of top performers, including himself.

Some players can have all the ability in the world, but when they get to United and see the size of the club, and feel the weight of expectation that goes along with wearing the red shirt, it all becomes too much. They shrink and wither and end up skulking away to another side. Then there are players like Morgan, who are born to grace the pitch at Old Trafford and to whom the red shirt seems like a second skin. From his first game, when he set up two goals, the crowd took to Willie Morgan immediately. He was everything a Manchester United player should be, and played football in a way that Matt Busby had encouraged fans to expect. Willie didn't know the meaning of playing backwards. He would receive the ball and then attack whichever poor defender found himself guarding the right-wing. He played the game with a swashbuckling arrogance that immediately made him the darling of the Stretford End. Willie remembered how it felt to become a United player:

"It was amazing going out into that arena, in front of 63,000 playing against Spurs, who were a big team. I think Cyril Knowles was left-back that night and I destroyed him, and of course I never looked back. But then I realised it was like a travelling circus in the nicest possible way. Jesus, everybody loved us, there was bunting out everywhere we went. It was like travelling with royalty, it was a different world, completely different to Burnley. I didn't realise that before I went, I didn't realise how big they were. When I was at Burnley, we were never envious of United in any way, shape or form, because we always thought we were great anyway. It's only when you went there that you realise how big this thing is, but still a very United family. It was lovely."

Not only was he joining the United family, he was working with Sir Matt Busby – who left an indelible impression on the young Morgan: "The great thing about Matt, apart from the fact that he was arguably – and certainly in my opinion – the greatest manager that has ever lived, was that he didn't have any tactics. All Matt said was, 'You're the best players in the country, that's why you're here, just go out and play.' That was his philosophy, but he commanded incredible respect – he never demanded it. Footballers swear for the world, as you probably know, but no one ever swore in front of Matt and there were no rules saying you must not swear in front of him. You just didn't."

Willie soon realised the size of the club he had joined, when he found himself flying to Buenos Aires to take part in the Inter-Continental Cup final first leg against Estudiantes. It wasn't so much a football match as a blood bath. Nobby Stiles, who was described as "El Assassin" in the match programme by the Estudiantes manager, was head-butted, spat on, kicked and finally sent off. United lost the game 1-0, and Matt commented: "The shambles of a match almost defies description. We were subjected to a series of acts of intimidation, aggravation and provocation that prevented us from even approaching our best football against a team we would have beaten hands down for football skills." Things were no better in the return game at Old Trafford. The teams clashed, and this time George Best was sent off along with an Argentinean. The game ended in a 1-1 draw, with Willie scoring his first goal for United, while the father of Juan Sebastian Veron scored for Estudiantes.

United were progressing well in the European Cup, which Matt was determined to defend – and probably the reason he hadn't retired the year before. Willie managed to get on the scoresheet in the quarter-final against Rapid Vienna, and it seemed like nobody would stop United reaching the final again. The team were 2-0 down after the first leg of the semi-final against AC Milan, but were confident that they could turn the deficit around when they got the Italians back to Old Trafford.

The ground was like a cauldron for the second leg, as 63,000 United fans roared the team on – but they seemed to hit a steel wall of an Italian defence. Willie tried all his tricks on the wing, but received no protection from the referee – and plenty of kicks from the Italian defenders. Bobby Charlton eventually scored after 70 minutes, and a few minutes later Paddy Crerand delivered a beautiful ball into the Milan box. A scramble of bodies ensued, but it was Denis Law who got a touch that saw the ball rolling towards the Milan net for what appeared to be a perfectly good goal. Suddenly the Milan substitute Santin kicked the ball from what appeared to be a foot behind the line. The crowd and all the United players shouted "Goal" as one voice, but the referee, who had a perfectly good view, waved play on. Willie and the rest of his teammates couldn't believe it, and the crowd showed what they thought of the referee as howls and whistles could be heard all over Manchester.

United bowed out of the European Cup and ended up enduring their poorest season for a long time, finishing 11th in the league and failing to pick up any silverware. But the big news was not on the pitch but off it, as Sir Matt Busby announced his retirement and selected Wilf McGuinness as his successor. Wilf was a Collyhurst lad who was United through and through, but was in the unenviable position of managing a team that contained lads that he had grown up and played with. Now he had to establish himself as the man in charge, and some of his methods upset some of the senior players. Wilf dropped many of the big names from the first team, and the players he brought in to replace them weren't up to United's standards. What it did mean was that anyone going to watch the reserve team at that time could see Best, Charlton, Morgan or any number of first-team 'regulars' turning out.

This arrangement was never going to work long-term and Wilf was relieved of his post, with Busby again taking charge. Willie remembers how he found out: "We had been at The Cliff training, and I think it was Paddy who said: 'Have you heard, Wilf's gone.' I think I replied, 'Good'. We were playing Chelsea the next day, so Paddy said: 'You had better go and have a look at the teamsheet.' There were about five changes from the previous game and we were all back. So we went to Chelsea and beat them 2-1. It was like a big weight being lifted off the club."

Everyone knew Matt was only back for the short-term and the board appointed Frank O'Farrell as manager in the summer of 1971, bringing Malcolm Musgrove with him as assistant. A new boss brought new tactics and formations. O'Farrell didn't want wingers – he liked to pack his midfield, and expected Willie and George to fall back into midfield, rather than play their natural game. This did not affect the fans' appreciation of Willie, as for two seasons running he was voted their player of the season. Internationally Willie also impressed. He travelled with Scotland, managed by Tommy Docherty, to Brazil to compete in the 'mini' World Cup – with Brazil's manager claiming he was the best winger in the world.

O'Farrell's managerial career at United started well, and the team were 10 points clear at one stage at the top of the table. However, form plummeted and O'Farrell's impersonal approach, whereby every player had to schedule an appointment just to see him, didn't help morale. A poor start the following season culminated in a 5-0 thrashing at a Don Rogers-inspired Crystal Palace, which ultimately sealed his fate. In December 1972, O'Farrell was sacked with three-and-a-half years left on his contract. The next manager at the helm secured his job due to a chat that Willie had with Busby:

"I was playing golf with Matt at Mere Golf Club on a Thursday. I played a lot of golf with the gaffer and he never talked football. Then on that Thursday after golf, when we were having a cup of tea and a current cake, he said to me: 'Did you enjoy the Brazil trip?' I said: 'It was great gaffer.' He then asked what I thought of Docherty. So I told him that I thought he was really good with players, and that he had improvised to sort problems out and he was good to work with. Matt then asked me if I thought he would do a good job here. Now in all the time I had known Matt privately – and we were very close, our families went out for meals and on holiday together – he had never discussed football with me. I said I thought he would. He said nothing more about it, but on the Thursday night when I was at home I got a phone call from him asking if I had Docherty's number. I did, and I gave it to him – and Tommy got the job on the Saturday."

It seemed like a marriage made in heaven. Willie had played for Tommy when he was manager of Scotland, and he had enjoyed it. Tommy played entertaining, attacking football, and the supporters loved him. Willie also had one big advantage going for him: he was Scottish, and it seemed that Tommy was attempting to turn the team into "MacChester United," buying up numerous Scottish players. At first it seemed perfect for Willie, as he remembered: "The Doc took over and initially it was very good, a breath of fresh air after Frank O'Farrell and Wilf. I later ended up in the Old Bailey with him, but I still maintain if he had stayed on as the manager of Scotland we would have won the World Cup in 1974. We never got beaten don't forget, but were eliminated. If he had stayed on as manager I think we would have won it, or at least come very close. I think he was a great Scottish manager and the reason for that, of course, was that you only saw him in small doses."

Tommy made George Graham club captain after Bobby Charlton, but George was struggling in a team that was heading towards relegation – and this didn't suit George's laid-back style of football. The crowd didn't take to George and he was struggling to get into the team. Willie recalls how he found out that he was to be the new captain: "After training one day he called me upstairs and told me that he had a problem as George wanted to resign as captain. He said that he was struggling and that maybe without the pressure of being captain he could regain his form. He said that he had attended a meeting with the directors and that they'd like me to take over as club captain. I told him that it was not really my bag, as I was a winger, but he insisted that everyone wanted me as captain so I agreed to have a go and that's how it happened."

However, as with everything connected to Docherty, things weren't quite that simple – as Willie found out: "A couple of weeks later George had been brought back into the team and he picked the ball up and said: 'Come on lads, let's go.' The Doc then picked up the ball, threw it to me and said: 'Here Willie, take 'em out.'

"The following day I was having a bath and George was being funny with me so I said to him: 'What's up with you?' He replied: 'You and your pal have stitched me up.' I then explained to him what Docherty had said to me about him not wanting to be captain any more. He told me that he had never said a word to Docherty. I confronted Docherty and told him what George had said. He told me to forget about George as he was getting rid of him anyway."

Willie took the responsibility of being captain seriously. He loved Manchester United – and he loved the fans. The team were going through bad times and he did everything he could to try and help, but the team was on an irreversible slide towards relegation. Best, Law and Charlton had left – and not been replaced with quality. Martin Buchan was the only truly world-class player that had been brought in since Willie. The team's performances illustrated this point, as they now lost to sides who used to fear Old Trafford.

Manchester United were relegated not because of a back heel from Denis Law, but because of a poor season and with players not good enough to wear the red shirt. If the team had beaten Manchester City 6-0 they would still have been relegated, as other results went against them that day. Subsequently Willie did not once consider leaving United and moving to any one of the many clubs that would have gladly paid for his services. United was in his blood; he loved the club and was happy to sign a new six-year contract to show his commitment. Willie was looking forward to seeing out his football career playing for the club, but things don't always work out as you want them to. With the Machiavellian Docherty in charge, things would never run smoothly.

The 1974/75 season was a thrilling campaign for United and their supporters. They took Division Two by storm, and were only ever heading in one direction. Supporters clamoured for tickets to every game they played. 'Doc's Red Army' invaded towns like an occupying force, as every ground turned into a sea of red and white. Willie had played for Scotland in the 1974 World Cup, and picked up an eye injury. He had been hit in the eye with a tennis ball, which had caused a detached retina. So he started the season unfit, but still willing to play. He should have been rested, but Willie was committed to United and to the supporters. He was desperate to get the club back to the First Division.

Things couldn't have gone better for the team as they went undefeated until the end of September. Norwich defeated them 2-0, but that was only a minor blip as the team went on another long undefeated run. The Second Division was not seeing the best of Morgan, though, as he was playing with niggling injuries, and his eye problem was affecting his touch. But it was issues off the pitch that were to have a bigger effect on Willie, as he remembered:

"It was phenomenal, we were fantastic, we broke all the attendance records for the division, we brought all the glamour and everything that came with it. It was obviously a great season, but during it Doc and I were at loggerheads. We didn't know what he had done to Denis [Law], and the first thing I knew was what he did to George Graham. The final straw with me was Jim McCalliog, who was a very close friend of mine. Instead of telling Jim that he wanted to get rid of him, he went behind his back and spread rumours about him. What he did was to call me in and tell me that he planned to get rid of Jim. I went to see Jim and warned him what was happening, but told him not to say anything to The Doc, as he would know where he had found out about it. But Jim was so angry he went roaring in to see him, and that was the beginning of the end for me and The Doc."

The Doc was furious, taking the captaincy off Willie and handing it to Martin Buchan. Then on Saturday 1st March, playing against Cardiff City at Old Trafford, Willie was substituted for the first time in his professional career. His place was taken by new signing Steve Coppell, who The Doc had bought from Tranmere Rovers. Willie did not play for the first team again until Saturday 5th April at The Dell, when a 1-0 win against Southampton (with a goal by Lou Macari) secured promotion back to the First Division. The following Saturday, Willie played his last game for Manchester United in a 1-0 win against Fulham at Old Trafford. The final match of the season saw United brush Blackpool aside 4-0 and get presented with the Division Two championship trophy. It was Martin Buchan who led the team in a lap of honour, with Alex Stepney holding the trophy.

Willie was still very happy at the club and was over the moon with promotion. He was looking forward to getting himself fit over the summer and then returning to the team in the First Division. Unfortunately he was about to find out that he was no longer in The Doc's plans:

"At the end of the season he called me in and said: 'Look, I know things haven't been good between us, but I want to put all that to rest, I want to be friends.' He then added: 'We're going on a tour and I think it would be better if you had a complete rest for the summer, get yourself back to full fitness. The people who we are going to play want you there, but I will explain to them that I think it's better for you to rest, and then let's get you back next season.' So I agreed. He then asked me if I would like the club to pay for a holiday for my family and me, but I told him I was in a position where I could pay for my own holidays.

"I went off and the day after I switched on the radio, tuning into Piccadilly Radio – it was about four o'clock in the afternoon. They said that Willie Morgan had been placed on the transfer list. I drove straight to Old Trafford, went up to the office – but he wasn't there. I phoned him, but he wouldn't answer the phone. I went round to his house but he wasn't in. The *Manchester Evening News* that night had the headline 'Morgan refuses to go on tour.' Docherty was then quoted as saying, 'We have committed to taking players and he has refused to go.'"

Docherty sold Willie back to Burnley, but he didn't stay long at Turf Moor and moved on to Bolton, where he treated the Burnden Park crowd to some of the magic that had made him such a special player.

Manchester United has a tradition of having some great players who have worn the No. 7 shirt: Best, Cantona, Robson, Beckham, Coppell and Ronaldo. Willie sits comfortably in that company. He was a fantastically gifted footballer who joined the right club, but the wrong team. At his peak, he would have graced any United team, past or present. He was popular with the supporters at Old Trafford, winning their player of the season award two years running, and he is still a favourite of those lucky enough to have seen him play. I can still picture Willie, at his prime, receiving the ball wide, committing the full-back, going past him inside or outside, accelerating away and then putting in a cross.

He had all the qualities you expect of a winger – fleetness of foot, a range of tricks and feints. The ability to go both ways off either foot, pace, crossing ability and above all, the knack of producing the unexpected. Always spontaneous, he had that bit extra to unhinge the most organised of defences, and sink the tightest of markers. He was born to play for United, and grace Old Trafford.

Was he a natural captain? I don't think so. Did he take the job seriously? Incredibly so, always giving 100%, often playing injured, but never dull or predictable. He entertained the crowd every game he played. It was a love affair that has never ended, as the club and its supporters are still in his heart – and he remains fiercely loyal. The Stretford End will always remember when they used to tell the world: "We've got Willie Morgan on the wing."

Defender of the Faith

MARTIN BUCHAN

1975-1982

*'The Duchess of Kent shook hands with me and gave me
the cup...thinking back maybe I was a bit rude, as I couldn't
wait to take it and show the fans, so I didn't reallly say
"thank you very much" properly. I just wanted to get hold
of the trophy and show it to the fans'*

Few players can claim to dominate and define a decade at a club the size
of Manchester United, but as I sit in the plush offices of the PFA in
Manchester, I am about to interview a man who was head and shoulders
above any other player at United in the 1970s. As Martin Buchan walks
up to greet me, I am taken back all those years ago, when as a boy I
would watch him lead the team out. Always cool and always immaculate, Buchan was the first player I remember making me feel safer when
he was on the pitch. It was the same with Robson in the 80s and Keane
in the 90s. All three seem to have that special quality of unquestionable
leadership that supporters, as well as players, can sense and admire.

To Martin and Violet Buchan, a son, Martin McLean Buchan, was
born on 6th March 1949. The family were living with Martin's paternal
grandparents in Glenbervie Road, Torry, near the docks in Aberdeen.
His father worked in the shipyards as a riveter, as well as playing football for local sides. He started at Aberdeen, moved on to Dundee United
for a spell then ended up at Buckie Thistle, where as a "poacher" he was
the top scorer in the Highland League for 10 years.

When Martin was four years old, the family were given a council
house in Stewart Terrace, Northfield, on the outskirts of Aberdeen. The
family kept expanding and along came a brother, George, and three sis-

ters – Irene, Sheila and Sylvia. Martin attended Westerton Primary School briefly and then Cummings Park Primary School in Northfield, where he made his first appearance in a football team. Dressed in black shirts, black shorts and yellow and black socks, the school team, captained by Martin, managed to go through a season without conceding a goal. Starting off as an inside-forward, it wasn't long before Martin was moved to the wing-half position he found so comfortable. The highlight of the season was when the team got to play against a North of Scotland team at Victoria Park, home to his father's team, Buckie Thistle.

Martin was a bright boy who enjoyed the academic life and when it came to the 11+ exams, he came in the top seven in the North East of Scotland. He was offered a bursary to Robert Gordon's College, a private fee-paying school in Aberdeen. Martin's parents had to find the money for books and uniforms, though the school fees were paid for by the education department. Most of the boys were the sons of doctors and lawyers, but Martin never felt inferior, knowing he was a match for them academically, and an excellent sportsman. There was, however, one big problem – Robert Gordon's college was a rugby-playing school.

Martin was good enough to get picked for the school rugby team but when he did get selected, he refused to play. At the time, Martin was playing football for the Boys' Brigade, and he feared that if he played rugby on a Saturday morning, he would get injured and not be able to turn out in the afternoon for the Brigade's football team, of which he was captain. Martin was ordered to stand in front of the school and explain his reasons for not wishing to turn out for the rugby team; not for the last time, the strong-willed Buchan refused to bow to pressure.

Even at that young age, attending a good school and getting an excellent education, deep down he knew he wanted to be a footballer. When Martin was 12 he was invited, along with other promising footballers in the area, to join coaching classes at Aberdeen FC twice a week. They trained on the car park across from the ground, along with the part-timers at the club. When he was 15, he was signed as a probationary professional, earning £1 a week. Martin was also doing well at school at this point. He sat his exams, and obtained a university entrance.

During the holidays he went to Aberdeen for pre-season training. He was only back at school three days into sixth form when Eddie Turnbull, manager of Aberdeen, asked him to go full-time. This was a big decision. Martin and Violet had sacrificed much to put their son through school and now he was at a point where he could continue his academic path at university, or he could try and make it as a footballer. After hours of thrashing it out with his parents, the decision was left up to Martin. It was decided he would try and be a footballer, giving it until he was 21. If he hadn't made it by then, he would go to university.

Martin was called up by Turnbull at the beginning of the 1966/67 season, and made a great impression on the coaching staff. Weeks into the campaign, a 17-year-old Buchan was handed a league debut against Dunfermline at East End Park. Martin played at left-half and the cool and collected Buchan did his long-term prospects no harm with a near faultless display. Unfortunately for Martin, Turnbull had already agreed to sign Francis Munro from Dundee United to solve his right-half problem, and so Buchan had to continue his apprenticeship in the reserves.

During the summer of 1967 Aberdeen went to the USA to take part in the Presidents Cup, and here Martin staked his claim. His poise, style and all-round awareness gave him the look of an old head on young shoulders. Martin seemed tailor-made for the sweeper system Turnbull was trying to introduce. Turnbull thus began the 1967/68 season with Martin at inside-left, rather than leaving him in the reserves any longer.

In Bulgaria, playing against Slavia Sofia in the Inter-Cities Fairs Cup, Martin came off the bench to fill the sweeper role and from that point, he never really looked back. Soon after the Slavia game, Francis Munro was sold to Wolves and Martin looked set for a long stay as Aberdeen's regular No. 6. A close-season road accident kept Martin out until mid-November, but a season that had started badly picked up dramatically when Martin returned and in February 1970, a month short of his 21st birthday, Buchan was appointed club captain. Martin must have wondered what he had let himself in for as Aberdeen struggled to beat lowly Clydebank 2-1, and were roundly booed off the pitch by the home support. Incredibly, two months later, he was climbing the steps at Hampden Park as the youngest-ever captain to lift the Scottish Cup after beating Celtic 3-1.

When Celtic travelled to Hampden for that Scottish Cup final in 1970 they wore a mantle of near invincibility. They had captured their fifth successive title and were on their way to a second European Cup final in four seasons, the domestic showpiece coming between the two legs of the semi-final victory over Leeds. Only an Aberdeen side captained by the young Buchan stood between Jock Stein's side and a clean sweep of Scottish honours. Aberdeen's subsequent success was largely down to solid defending by a tight unit, superbly marshalled by Buchan. The following season, they came within a whisker of ending Celtic's stranglehold on the Scottish League title. The importance of Martin in that effort was emphasised by the fact that the defence conceded just 17 goals, and it was no surprise that Martin was named as the Scottish Player of the Year. On 13th October 1971 Martin made his full international debut, coming on as a substitute for the last nine minutes of a 2-1 win over Portugal in a meaningless European Championship game.

It was at Aberdeen that Martin got to work with his hero and, "the finest coach he ever worked with", Eddie Turnbull. During the 1950s, Turnbull was one of the "famous five", the noted Hibernian forward line along with Gordon Smith, Bobby Johnstone, Lawrie Reilly and Willie Ormond. Turnbull won three Scottish titles with Hibs, and in 1955 Turnbull was the first British player to score in European competition. There is still a sense of admiration when Buchan speaks of Turnbull:

"I wrote a foreword for Eddie's autobiography and in it I said that he took a group of young local hopefuls as boys, gave us a wonderful education in the game and in the process, made men of us. I'm also on record as saying that when I left Aberdeen I felt I could have gone and played in any system, anywhere in the world, as a result of what he taught me. He was light years ahead of any other coach I worked with in almost 20 years as a professional, at club or international level. He explained the game thoroughly and with great patience on the training pitch in 'shadow' sessions, walking the whole team through various scenarios without opposition. He was the best I've ever seen in that two-minute spell at half-time, when a manager or coach often has to change things by making tactical changes, substitutions, or even by applying the 'hairdryer'. He coached limited players at Aberdeen so well, mainly by simplifying the game and making them aware of their options in any given situation, that they won Scottish caps at Under-23 level."

Turnbull still lives in Edinburgh, and such is the admiration that Martin holds him in that whenever he goes back to Aberdeen, he tries to visit him and his wife, either on his way north, or on the journey home.

In 1971 Turnbull went back to his beloved Hibernian, leaving Aberdeen without a manager – and Martin without his mentor. Aberdeen promoted Turnbull's assistant, Jimmy Bonthrone, who was fair to Martin and in March 1972 he told him three clubs were interested in signing him – Liverpool, Leeds and Manchester United. United were the first team to come in with an offer, a figure of £125,000. They assured him he was being bought to replace David Sadler, who was suffering knee problems, so he had a guarantee of first-team football. When Martin looked at Liverpool, he saw Tommy Smith in his position and Phil Thompson champing at the bit for an opportunity to play. When he looked at Leeds, he saw Norman Hunter standing in his way.

Martin met with United officials at Bellshill, the village that Matt Busby hailed from. Martin went down with Aberdeen's manager while Matt, Frank O'Farrell, Les Olive and Johnny Aston represented United. They discussed terms; he was on £40 a week at Aberdeen and United offered him £110, plus 5% of the transfer fee. Martin excused himself. He went to find the nearest phone box and called Eddie Turnbull, to ask him what he should do. Eddie told him it was a good deal, and to go for it. That was all he needed to hear. Martin went back to the group and agreed terms, signing for a then club record fee. United were prepared to pay £150,000, but Aberdeen snapped their hands off at the lower fee – a fire at Pittodrie had left the club needing cash for repairs.

Martin travelled back south with the United contingent, as they had a cup game against Middlesbrough the following afternoon. He watched the game and then travelled back to Manchester with the team. The following Saturday, 4th March, he made his debut at Tottenham in a 2-0 defeat. On Wednesday 8th March, two days after his 23rd birthday, Martin made his home debut at Old Trafford against Everton. The game was played in the afternoon as the power strikes made it impossible to use floodlights. Bobby Charlton missed out due to injury, but Frank O'Farrell had every confidence in Buchan – and made him captain.

Old Trafford had a crowd of just over 38,000, and the United faithful were keen to see what United had paid the money for. They were not to be disappointed. The always-immaculate Buchan led the team out to a great roar, and he knew immediately he had found his spiritual home. The game ended goalless, but the watching fans had seen enough to know they had bought a cool character who always had time on the ball – and never looked flustered. Martin scored his first goal in his first derby at Old Trafford on 12th April 1972. He played a ball to George Best and ran on to the return pass, smashing the ball into the Stretford End net. The feeling of elation didn't last long though as Rodney Marsh came off the bench and scored as City won 3-1. Getting forward and supporting the attackers had been part of his game at Aberdeen, but he soon realised at United that his first priority was to defend.

Buchan was coming into a team in decline, one that he describes as "a curious mix of superstars and players that wouldn't have got a game in Aberdeen's reserves." It still had the "Holy Trinity" of Best, Law and Charlton, who were still worth the admission price of any ground they played at. Alongside them though were players who weren't up to Manchester United's standards. Many people said that Busby had allowed the team to grow old, and had not replaced like-for-like. Wilf McGuinness had been unlucky and not been allowed to buy the players he wanted. In Buchan, O'Farrell believed he was buying class and the type of player that would make United great again. Martin recalled:

"When I went there and when I joined them, I had a lot of faith in my ability because of the education I had from Eddie Turnbull. I could have gone and played anywhere in the world, in any system, because of the thorough grounding in the game he gave me. So I had no inferiority complex about going in and mixing with these players."

Initially, O'Farrell seemed to galvanize a United team that had a blend of youth and experience. Many publications have claimed that he inherited an ageing team, but that simply wasn't true. Of the squad who had won the European Cup in 1968 just three years earlier, Stepney, Burns, Dunne, Sadler, Kidd, Charlton, Law, Aston and Best were still around. Scottish international winger Willie Morgan had been purchased from Burnley, so the forward line was as potent as anything in the First Division at that time. Youngsters Tommy O'Neill (who sadly suffered a heart attack and died in 2006, aged just 53), Alan Gowling, Steve James and Sammy McIlroy were the other members of the first-team squad.

Bobby Charlton was club captain when Martin joined, and he believes that Bobby finished too early. "Bobby could have played a lot longer than he did, he was a very fit man and took a great pride in his fitness. He was very dedicated. When he was left out, rather than go and sulk he would go and do extra training on his own to keep his fitness up, and he took me under his wing. He took me up to Lymm and said that it was a nice place to live. At the time it seemed so far. As a captain he was ever the optimist. If we went in at half-time and we were trailing he always looked on the bright side, saying, 'If we get one we'll get back at them.'"

Everything started so well for O'Farrell. On 4th December 1971, after beating Nottingham Forest 3-2 at Old Trafford, United were five points clear at the top. Up until that point of the season they had played some scintillating football, and were favourites to win the title. However, after that victory, there followed a disastrous sequence of results that saw United fail to win another league game until mid-March. By this time they had fallen to eighth, nine points behind leaders Manchester City.

For a young player like Buchan, moving to a club like Manchester United was a dream come true. But the next few years were to show a rapid decline in fortunes, and Martin must have wondered if he had made the right move. There were strong personalities in the dressing room that weren't frightened to voice an opinion, and O'Farrell found it a difficult task to deal with. United would finish the season in eighth.

If the second half of the 1971/72 season was disappointing, then the first half of the 1972/73 season was disastrous. For Frank O'Farrell, it was the end of his tenure at United. It took United 10 league games to register their first win, and in the previous nine they had only mustered four points. Old Trafford wasn't a happy place to be. O'Farrell tried everything, signing Ian Storey-Moore from Nottingham Forest. He also paid in excess of £200,000 for Ted McDougall, who was scoring for fun in the Third Division for Bournemouth. In September 1972 O'Farrell also signed Wyn Davies, the big Welsh centre-forward, from Manchester City. No matter what O'Farrell tried it didn't work – and he'd lost the dressing room. In December 1972, with three-and-a-half years of his contract left, he was sacked. The team were annihilated 5-0 by Crystal Palace at Selhurst Park, and the club's directors acted quickly. Just a few days later, Tommy Docherty was appointed manager.

Throughout the turbulence, Martin Buchan kept a low profile. Despite having to play in several different positions, he kept his head down and got on with his job. Docherty breathed fresh air into Old Trafford, but he knew what a difficult task he had. Things would only get worse before they got better, and he had a relegation fight on his hands.

Buchan knew The Doc; he had picked him for Scotland, though he was not as close to him as the older Scottish players like Willie Morgan and Denis Law. It didn't take The Doc long to add to the Scottish contingent at United as he brought in Alex Forsyth from Partick, Lou

Macari from Celtic, George Graham from Arsenal and a centre-half from Shrewsbury Town named Jim Holton. The team was in trouble, ageing and heading for relegation, but Docherty kept them up, finishing in 18th. Buchan was an ever-present, shining in a poor team.

The new season saw a United team minus the Holy Trinity. Charlton had left to become player-boss of Preston, Best had walked out and Denis Law had been given a free to Manchester City. Not only did United lose these greats, but they also let Tony Dunne go on a free to Bolton which, in hindsight, was probably too early as he went on to play a further 200 games. Docherty made George Graham captain, but even with his class and Buchan in defence, the team was not good enough. The Doc attempted to bring players in, but how do you replace Charlton, Best and Law? Certainly not with the players Docherty had at his disposal. The season was at least memorable for the Buchan family, as in May 1973 Docherty bought Martin's brother, George, from Aberdeen. He was an inside-forward like his father, but unfortunately not of the standard of his brother. He only made four appearances as a sub.

Not only could the season have been the last for George – it could have been the final one for Martin, too. In September 1973 United were at Ipswich, and The Doc was playing Martin at left-back. He recalls: "Defensively I was fine against forwards on the left-hand side, but Ryan Giggs I was not and I said to him, 'if you are going to play me at full-back, then play me at right-back and I'll get forward and get some crosses in rather than having to check back on to my right foot all the time.' Docherty and Tommy Cavanagh came steaming into me at half-time and said that if I wasn't happy, then they'd get me a move. They then asked if I wanted a move. I said I did. I didn't really, but I wasn't having him speak to me like that. The next thing I know, The Doc tells me that Dave Sexton, the QPR manager, fancies signing me and did I want to go? Once again I said I did. He told me £160,000 and I said 'yes'. I never heard another word about it – wiser counsel might have prevailed."

The team struggled and found themselves staring down the barrel of relegation on Saturday 27th April 1974, when they faced Manchester City at Old Trafford. They had two games left; they needed to win both, and hope Birmingham lost theirs. Blues won their game and sealed United's fate, whatever the derby result. What happened will forever go down in Manchester folklore. The game was poor, with few chances until Francis Lee went on a diagonal run inside the United area in the 81st minute. Lee was surrounded by defenders but managed to find Denis Law. With his back to goal he back-heeled the ball into the United net. The City players raced to celebrate with Denis, but he just walked away with his head bowed, his heart broken that he had scored against his beloved United. The thing Martin remembers is Denis's face, and feeling that this was no way for a legend to end his career. As it was Martin saw relegation as a blessing in disguise, giving Docherty a chance to get rid of the dead wood and bring in new players.

United in the Second Division: the unthinkable had happened. It would go on to be a season that supporters of a certain age will always remember fondly. The Second Division loved United. Everywhere they went The Doc's 'Red Army' was there in force; they attracted record attendances, as locals turned out to see the home team take on a legend. At Old Trafford the average gate of 48,000 was the highest for a quarter of a century. Buchan remembers the season fondly:

"We started well and never looked back. The new signings bedded in like Stuart Pearson, who was a great player. That pairing of Pearson and Greenhoff was wonderful, you almost felt you could stand at the back, close your eyes, knock a ball upfield and one of them would get on the end of it. Lou Macari used to say it was a 'piece of cake that Second Division' – but not for me. I think it's because when you're a forward and you get a ball played up to you and it's not perfect you can leave it. When you're at the back, you've got to see every ball out, you cannot assume it's going to go to the goalkeeper, you have to be on your toes. So our Second Division campaign wasn't as easy as Lou said."

The season began well for United with three comfortable wins against

Leyton Orient, Millwall and Portsmouth. This instilled confidence, and from then on they never looked back. Docherty encouraged his team to play a free, swashbuckling style of football. His philosophy was, "We tried to play tight, to play defensively, and we were relegated. From now on we attack." They were thrilling crowds, and it was a style of football that suited the gifted Buchan. The captain at that time was Willie Morgan, but he and Docherty fell out. Without much fuss, Martin was told he was now club captain. Buchan's influence in the dressing room duly became enormous. He made sure that the players bonded, and that everybody pulled for each other. In many ways he was similar to Roger Byrne, a bridge to the management. Martin was never a 'yes' man and on several occasions let his feelings be known to management. He could be stubborn, and was never seen by players as being over generous.

Being the man he is, Buchan took it all in his stride. He was a natural captain, having skippered every team he played in – and he had already captained a cup-winning team. This was a natural progression, and he was a popular choice with supporters. Martin didn't know it at the time, but these next couple of years would be the best of his career. The players responded to Buchan's leadership both on and off the field. He had a precociously cool demeanour on the pitch, and was his own man off it. When all the players signed a contract worth £300 each to wear Gola boots and tracksuits, Martin decided to make his own deal with Adidas. But it was on the pitch that Buchan proved he was world class. He was such a great reader of the game that when teams would break and attack, he could spot them and snuff them out before their moves reached fruition. He was also quick and he used to test himself by leaving tackles to the very last moment, relieving the attacker of the ball and milking the Old Trafford applause for a wonderful interception.

As well as appointing Buchan as captain, Docherty made probably his finest United signing. Steve Coppell played for Tranmere, as well as taking a degree in Economic History at Liverpool University. Docherty offered £60,000 for Coppell, and offered to double his wages. Coppell signed and made his debut as a sub in a 4-0 win over Cardiff City on 1st March 1975. To this day Martin still believes that Coppell was the best player he played with at United. For anyone lucky enough, like myself, to see Coppell fly down that right-wing and whip the ball over, it would be hard to argue. The fact that Steve was studious appealed to Martin as well. On the coach travelling to games, Martin would rather read a book than play cards and so received a reputation as a loner – while Steve would have his head in his books and was known as a student.

Promotion was guaranteed at Southampton on 5th April, with Lou Macari scoring the only goal. Two games later a draw at Notts County was enough to clinch the title. The trophy was presented at Old Trafford on the final day of the season, with Martin and Alex Stepney running around the pitch with the trophy, accompanied by thousands of fans, who scrambled onto the pitch. Martin recalled his feelings that day:

"I knew when we got relegated that there were clubs who wanted me, but it never crossed my mind to leave. I thought I was one of the squad that took the club down and I owed it to them to get them back up. Fortunately that's how it worked out."

United's summer tour of 1975 would be unthinkable nowadays. They began in West Germany, went on to Iran and then Australia. After the German leg the team flew back into Manchester, where Martin departed, having been required for international duty. He rejoined the squad in Hong Kong, before heading to Australia. Before the tour began, the club decided that all players would hand their passports into the club to be held centrally. Buchan rebelled, telling the club that the passport was his own responsibility and that he would not be handing it in. There was a stand-off – but ultimately Martin won the day.

When it came to United returning to the top flight, experts believed that their attacking style would get found out. How wrong they were. When the new season began they started how they had finished the previous campaign, taking the First Division by storm. They played bright, open, attacking football, and their youth and innocence allowed them to play without fear. In November 1975, Docherty signed winger Gordon Hill from Millwall. It meant that United now had a potent threat on both flanks, with Coppell and Hill winning the hearts of the fans with their dashing wing play. United were playing the game in the top flight with a smile on their collective faces for the first time in years.

April 1976 saw United take on Derby in the semi-final of the FA Cup at Hillsborough. The crowd of around 55,000 was predominantly red and white, and after 12 minutes the majority were celebrating as Hill curled home a wonder goal. The second half saw Derby, with the rotund Francis Lee, throw everything at United to try and get an equaliser, but with six minutes remaining United got a free-kick just outside the area. Hill stepped up and scored again – and United were on their way to Wembley. This was 1976 – 'The Fonz was cool but Buchan was cooler.'

Whether reaching the FA Cup final affected the team's performance over the next month is open to debate, but Buchan is certain of it. Driven on by Buchan they were challenging for the title and when 1975 turned into 1976 they were joint-top of the league with Liverpool on 33 points. After the semi-final they lost three of the five league games before the final. When the last league game was over, even though United had beaten Manchester City 2-0 at Old Trafford, they had slipped to third in the table, four points behind the champions, Liverpool.

As was the fashion in those days, the cup final teams usually made a record to celebrate their achievement. United's was imaginatively titled 'Manchester United', with Martin penning – and singing – the B-side, the glorious 'Old Trafford Blues'. On the track, Martin takes us through his United team-mates. Make no mistake about it, Martin thought he was Elvis Presley, but the song didn't turn out as he had planned:

"I used to take the guitar away with us sometimes and we would have a sing-song, so I wrote a little song about the lads. Somebody had the bright idea of putting it on a record so I had to clean it up. We sent a tape down to Tony Hiller, who was a producer. We did the song at Strawberry studios in Stockport, and he came up with this backing track. It was all slowed down and he added some orchestra. I didn't have the balls to say, 'Sorry, that's not what I wrote,' because he had a No. 1 hit that week with 'Save Your Kisses for Me' by The Brotherhood of Man. I thought he must have known what he was talking about, and I went along with it. We're all allowed some mistakes."

The 1976 FA Cup final took place on 1st May between United and Southampton. United had finished third in the First Division, whilst the Saints had finished sixth in Division Two. As far as the press and media were concerned the Saints would be mere cannon fodder for The Doc's precocious young team. Southampton were a team of ageing players, who would struggle to live with United's pace. The score could get embarrassing – or so everybody thought. Martin was not so confident:

"I had misgivings because a lot of the lads got distracted by the glamour of the run, players' pool and everything. It went to their heads and they assumed they just had to turn up and collect their medals. Well they did get medals – loser's medals. The players alienated the press, asking for money for interviews, they thought they were going to be millionaires because of the players' pool, which was nonsense. If I had my way we wouldn't have had it, but you have to go with the majority.

"The cup run affected our league form and I think we would have come very close to winning the league if we hadn't done so well in the cup. Late on we lost to Ipswich, Stoke and Leicester, when five more points would have given us the title."

Martin Buchan led the United team out from the famous old Wembley tunnel into the bright sunshine that enveloped the stadium. United fans sat and waited for the massacre to begin – but it never happened. United started strongly, and missed several opportunities. Southampton then got into the game and started to create chances. With eight minutes to go Jim McCalliog lobbed a ball forward to the onrushing Bobby Stokes, who appeared to be in an offside position. He fired it first time with his left foot on the half volley, across Stepney and into the corner. Despite the controversy, the goal was given and Southampton won. Several of

United's young players had 'frozen' in the Wembley atmosphere.

There couldn't have been a bigger crowd in Albert Square outside the Town Hall waiting to meet the team if they had won the cup. An estimated 500,000 supporters cheered every one of the team, and when Tommy Docherty came out and promised that they would go back next year and win it, no one doubted him. "Standing at the Town Hall, as Tommy promised we would go back and win it next year," remembered Martin, "it just drove it home to me what Manchester United was all about. You couldn't see a square foot in the Town Hall square. I was just amazed by the turn-out. As I drove home, if I hadn't known already what it meant to play for Manchester United, I did after that day."

One thing was certain. Along with Docherty and Tommy Cavanagh, Martin Buchan was leading United into a bright new era; they were firmly back in the First Division frame as title challengers. The cream on the cake was that United were also back in European competition, having qualified for the UEFA Cup (United would reach the second round, going down 3-1 to Juventus on aggregate). The team was playing a brand of football that hadn't been seen since the glory years of the mid-to-late Sixties. Buchan had bonded the team into an exciting unit, and had forged a great defensive partnership with Brian Greenhoff. Everybody looked forward to the 1976/77 season with anticipation.

However, the campaign proved to be a disappointment in the league as the team only finished sixth, without threatening to win it. Things had started well with Docherty sticking with the same team that had played in the final. The consistency was having a positive effect – but that was about to change when Martin picked up a thigh strain against Leeds. Everyone at Old Trafford knew how important Martin was to the team, but his absence magnified it. He missed eight games, of which United lost five and drew three. Everyone thought that The Doc would go into the transfer market and buy a stand-in for the defence. He did make a move, but he bought himself a striker: Jimmy Greenhoff.

The FA Cup run took on a special meaning for Martin and his team-mates. After the turn out in Albert Square and the promise that Docherty had made, the cup had taken on a sense of destiny. The fact that they went and achieved it was nothing short of a football fairytale. Walsall were first-up at Old Trafford in the third round, and a goal by Gordon Hill put an end to any giant-killing hopes before QPR met the same fate in the fourth round, going out to a single goal from Lou Macari.

Both Hill and Macari got the goals in a 2-2 draw at Southampton in the fifth round, but two goals from new signing Jimmy Greenhoff saw United go through 2-1 at Old Trafford. Aston Villa found themselves on the wrong side of a 2-1 scoreline in the quarter-finals, which set up a semi-final against Leeds at Hillsborough. The game was a tense, physical affair, with United under the cosh for most of the second half. But they managed to hold on for a 2-1 win, and a return to the Twin Towers.

The opposition would be the all-conquering Liverpool, who were going for an unprecedented treble. They had already won the league and would be playing in the European Cup final, as well as the FA Cup final. Despite this Martin felt confident his side could raise their game on any given day, and match Liverpool. United's problem had always been going to play teams like Coventry on a Wednesday night and dropping points, whereas Liverpool were the masters at grinding out a victory.

The weekend before the final, United hosted Arsenal on the Saturday, beating them 3-2. Then on the Monday they went to West Ham in the last game of the season. The game ended in a 4-2 win for the Hammers, and nearly saw Buchan out of the final. Martin found himself stranded on the halfway line against three West Ham players. Trevor Brooking took Buchan on rather than play in a team-mate and as Martin stretched to stop him, Brooking fell over Buchan's leg and opened up his knee joint. There was discomfort after the game, but nothing too worrying. The team was staying in London that night so Martin took some of his team-mates out to a nightclub to see his friend, Bill Fredericks, once a singer with The Drifters, in cabaret. The next morning Martin woke and he knew he was in trouble, as he could hardly walk. He went for breakfast, saw Docherty and told him that he may as well give him a ticket back up to Manchester, as he had no chance of playing. Physio Laurie Brown worked tirelessly to get him ready for the final. By Thursday Buchan was moving a little easier, taking part in light training on Friday morning to see how he felt. In the afternoon Martin declared himself fit, even though he knew in his head that he was taking a big risk.

It was a roasting hot day on Saturday 21st May 1977. It was the year of the Queen's Silver Jubilee – and this was the Silver Jubilee final. United were resplendent in their deep red shirts, which seemed even redder in the sunshine, contrasting against the white shirts of Liverpool.

The game was less than 10 minutes old when Martin went for a 50-50 with Tommy Smith. Martin knew it was a make-or-break moment. He went in hard and came out feeling fine, and now knew he could banish any lingering fears of breaking down. Not only did he complete the match – he also gave a commanding display, snubbing out Kevin Keegan's threat. Liverpool had the better of the first half though, with a Ray Kennedy header hitting the post.

Three goals came in a five-minute period in the second half, with Stuart Pearson opening the scoring when he latched on to a header from Jimmy Greenhoff, and shot past Ray Clemence. Liverpool replied when Jimmy Case hooked a right-footed half volley into the top corner – but three minutes later United were back in front. Lou Macari's shot deflected off Jimmy Greenhoff's chest, looping past Clemence and Phil Neal. United now had to hold on for 35 minutes – and this is where Buchan came into his own. Winning every ball in the air, he rendered Keegan a virtual spectator in his final Liverpool game on English soil.

The final whistle blew and the fairytale had come true. Just as The Doc had promised 12 months previous, they had returned to Wembley and won the FA Cup. In doing so they had also stopped Liverpool winning the treble. John Motson, commentating on his first FA Cup final, came out with the statement: "How fitting that it should be Buchan climbing the 39 steps," though I wonder how many fans watching got the literary connection? Martin was the first, and still the only captain to lift the cup in Scotland and England. He recalled his emotions:

"The year before the Queen had presented the trophy, this year it was the Duchess of Kent. She shook hands with me and gave me the cup, someone else gives you the medal and maybe I was rude, as I couldn't wait to take it and show the fans, so I didn't say 'thank you very much' properly. I just wanted to get hold of the trophy and show it to the fans."

As Martin and the rest of the players ran around the pitch showing off the trophy, none of them were to know that this would be the last game with Tommy Docherty in charge. No one had a clue what was happening in his personal life, and it would come as a massive shock when he was sacked for having an affair with Mary Brown, the physiotherapist's wife. They had just beaten a team that would become European champions four days later. Who knows how far he could have taken his side?

Buchan remembers fondly the trip back with the trophy. "The team travelled to Manchester and changed into an open-top bus in Bowden. We drove through Altrincham, past the Wheatsheaf pub on the left-hand side opposite the George and Dragon. The manager there was on the balcony, I knew him and as we went past I showed him the cup, pointed at my watch and said 'half past seven.' I was in that pub on time with the FA Cup. They told me after we had been to the Town Hall, that I was to take the cup and look after it, being the captain. So it was with me in the pub that evening, not with four security guards, just me. I took it into the club the next morning. It wouldn't happen now."

Six weeks later Docherty was gone and in his place the board opted for safety following the tumultuous tenure of The Doc. Dave Sexton had taken QPR to within a point of the league title in 1975/76, and was well respected throughout the game. Martin was already aware that Sexton was a fan of his, as Docherty had told him of a previous offer from the manager. Martin looks back on his time under Docherty very fondly:

"Those were the two happiest years of my career. You felt like you could play anyone at Old Trafford, give them a two-goal start and you would still beat them. We used to train at the ground on a Friday morning, then go and have a cup of tea upstairs in the old directors' lounge and have a team talk. You could almost feel the sense of anticipation around the ground; it was a magic time. It would have been nice to know what we could have achieved, because we'd broken the barrier and won a major trophy. There was a good mix of players; I was 28 at the time. Jimmy Greenhoff was the old head, but he could still play. We would have needed a new goalkeeper eventually, but it was a fairly young team. If we could have carried on with the confidence that cup run had bred, you never know what players Doc might have brought in."

Clubs never stand still – and United had a new manager and a new regime: from the extrovert Docherty, to the introverted Sexton. The one consistent, though, was the choice of captain – and that was never in doubt. "Dave was the nicest guy I met in football, but totally different from The Doc," Martin recalled. "The press would come to the ground on a Friday and would roll out at four o'clock after The Doc had got the wine out for them. They had so much in that couple of hours with The Doc; they didn't know what to put in the papers the next day and what to leave out. With Dave, who didn't trust the press and wasn't comfortable dealing with them, they didn't have anything, because he told them nothing and kept his cards close to his chest."

Coach Tommy Cavanagh had always looked after the players when it came to training, so things were pretty much as they had always been when the players returned to The Cliff for pre-season training. The first real difference came on matchday when Sexton introduced tactics into his team talks; Docherty never even used the word.

Dave Sexton had only a couple of weeks and a quartet of friendlies to get to know his players before the season began. He wasn't impressed with his first game as he saw United throw away a 2-0 lead against Werder Bremen and more worryingly, a sign of things to come, crowd violence involving United supporters. The next three games they won easily and returned to England with confidence. Sexton's first competitive game was the FA Charity Shield at Wembley against the now champions of Europe, Liverpool. The game was even, ending in a goalless draw, with both teams sharing the silverware. Sexton gave the United supporters hope that there would be more success to follow, but the season was a mixture of highs and lows with no real consistency.

As FA Cup winners, United were to compete in the European Cup-Winners' Cup, and their first opponents were St Etienne in France. The game ended in a 1-1 draw, but was marred by crowd violence involving the United supporters. The home game was played at Plymouth's ground after UEFA ordered United to play their home leg at least 200 kilometres from Manchester. United won 2-0 at Home Park, but in the next round they suffered a 4-0 defeat at FC Porto. A valiant effort at Old Trafford ended in vain as United won 5-2 but lost 6-5 on aggregate.

Sexton knew he had to make changes, moving for striker Joe Jordan from Leeds for £325,000. A week later he bought his team-mate, Gordon McQueen. Sexton intended to give his side more of a physical presence than the one he had inherited. He also changed the style of play, expecting his wingers to get back and help the defenders. This was never going to be to Gordon Hill's liking, as he didn't like the word work, nor understand the word tackle. Despite being the leading goalscorer in Sexton's first season, the manager made it clear that Hill was not in his plans. Tommy Docherty, who had taken over at Derby, came in and re-signed Hill. A popular player at United with the fans and the players, Hill is also part of Buchan folklore, as Martin explained:

"Gordon was lazy picking a player up in a game against Coventry at Old Trafford. Tommy Docherty wasn't there because he was ill. I just gave Gordon a smack as I ran past him, and called him a lazy so and so. If Tommy Doc had been there, he would have said as we came off the pitch, 'zip it', but he wasn't and there was a lot made of it in the press."

Hill was not the only one to go as Alex Stepney played his last game in United's centenary match against Real Madrid. Paddy Roche came in but was never up to the job, being replaced by the more solid Gary

Bailey. Sexton had his plans and his tactics, but this was Old Trafford. This was United, where there is only one way to play and that is to attack – and do it with flair. Docherty, for all his faults, had always given the fans the type of football they wanted to see, but this was different – and the crowd didn't like it. The team finished 10th in his first season and were knocked out of the FA Cup in the fourth round by West Brom.

The 1978/79 season started as the last one had ended, with United uninspiring. It got so bad that in November 1978 the team were booed off after a lifeless draw with Southampton. These were difficult times for Buchan, who could easily have played for any team in Europe, but who was now in a struggling team playing the kind of football that fans don't appreciate. The pressure was on Sexton, but he got one slice of luck, in the FA Cup. The team defeated Chelsea, Fulham, Colchester and Tottenham before taking on Liverpool in the semi-final at Maine Road. Liverpool were champions and big favourites, and also looking for revenge for the defeat in '77. United had the better of the play but it ended in a 2-2 draw, so both teams had to replay at Goodison Park. Fortunately for Sexton, Jimmy Greenhoff was back after a lay-off with a groin problem, and it was his diving header that proved the winning goal; 'Sexton's Soldiers' were marching back to Wembley.

At the time of the final, Arsenal were not the footballing power they were to become. They had finished only three points ahead of United in the league, with both clubs a long way behind Liverpool. In the final though it looked like there were leagues between them. Arsenal dominated, with Liam Brady torturing United. Nobody on the United side seemed to have a good game and after Brian Talbot and Frank Stapleton had given Arsenal a 2-0 lead, it seemed like the game was over.

Forget about the first 85 minutes – this match will always be known as the "Five-Minute" final. The Arsenal fans were already celebrating as there was seemingly no way back for United, who had simply not turned up. Then Gordon McQueen gave up any intentions he had of being a centre-half and found himself in the centre-forwards' position. He stuck out a long leg, and United had a consolation. The celebrations from the fans were more a case of, 'well, at least we did one good thing' when the ball fell to Sammy McIlroy, who I swear beat the whole Arsenal team twice. I am assured he danced past three yellow-shirted defenders and scored an improbable equaliser. I was still jumping around, hugging everybody and celebrating that strike – only to turn around to see Alan Sunderland running away from the United goal celebrating what proved to be the winner. I will let Martin explain what happened:

"This was one of the worst games I had for United. I'll never know why – I just felt a yard off the pace. Sometimes the harder you try, the worse it gets. I was actually on the right-hand side trying to stop the cross. It went in over Gary Bailey's head and Alan Sunderland squeezed it in. I don't blame Gary, you win as a team and you lose as a team."

There would be no fairytale for Sexton, and he knew he was running out of time as the board wanted success. Sexton bought the then Chelsea captain Ray Wilkins for a club record £825,000. Ray, like Martin, had been a very young captain at Chelsea, and he brought some style and elegance to the United midfield. However, that didn't help United make a great start to the 1979/80 season as they failed to impress, and the leading goalscorer in the first two months was Gordon McQueen.

Things did improve and that season would prove to be United's best in the league under Sexton, the team finishing second to Liverpool. United lost the last game to Leeds whilst Liverpool thrashed Aston Villa 4-1 to take the title. The defence had been United's strongest asset, conceding only eight at Old Trafford in 21 games. The partnership of Martin and Gordon McQueen, supported by full-backs Arthur Albiston and Jimmy Nicholl was formidable, and gave fans hope that they might be about to mount a serious challenge on Liverpool's First Division stranglehold.

The defence is the bedrock of all great teams, but to win a league you must have a consistent goalscorer. Since George Best, United had not been able to find a player that could score more than 20 goals a season. Many, including Sir Matt Busby, believed that they had one coming through the youth team in the shape of Andy Ritchie. Ritchie was a natural goalscorer and during the 1978/79 season he made 17 appearances, scoring nine goals. However, Sexton decided to sell him to Brighton for £500,000, and then pay £1.25m to Nottingham Forest for Garry Birtles. It was a gamble that failed. In his first 25 league games for United that campaign he failed to score a single goal (he would finally score, the following season, in his 30th appearance). Sexton's fate was sealed, and even though when Wilkins and McQueen returned from injury United went on a good run, winning their last eight games, it wasn't enough to save him. The fans had spoken with their feet, the average crowd was down and there were no trophies in the cabinet. In the years of stability enjoyed during the Ferguson era it is easy to forget that United had six managers in a decade, each one being a reaction to his predecessor.

United's answer to the failings of the shy and retiring Sexton was to employ a larger-than-life character, someone with a big enough personality to handle the job – and they found one. On 2nd June 1981 Ron Atkinson, who was just as comfortable answering to the moniker of "Big Ron", held his first press conference as United manager, at the Millionaires' Club. He was photographed pouring himself champagne, with gold and jewellery dripping off his wrists and fingers. It was all show and smiles for the media, but Ron meant business – and soon had the squad in for a meeting. He made it clear that apart from Steve Coppell and Ray Wilkins, he thought the rest of the squad were either too old, or not up to it. Martin remembered Ron going through the teams' birth certificates at the first meeting.

"He went round us and it got to me, mine was '06.03.49' and I knew I was buggered, he wasn't going to build a team around an old man. I played two seasons under Ron, the first I was captain when I was playing. If you do your maths there were 42 league games, two central defenders, so 42 x 2 is 84. I played around 25 games, Kevin Moran may have played 26, Gordon McQueen might have played 27. In the other games people filled in like Mike Duxbury, and he never had a selection problem because one of us three would always be injured so I was never left out in that first season. I didn't agree with some of Ron's plans, I'd been brought up differently and had different ideas about the game."

Ron wanted his defence to push up onto the halfway line, which meant a lot of space behind them to cover. This might not have been a problem to Martin in his younger days, but he was getting on in footballing years and this style did not suit him. The way that Martin found out he was no longer captain does not cover Ron in any glory:

"In my last season I only played six games in the first team, and I read in the paper that he had appointed Ray Wilkins as club captain. He had not long signed Bryan Robson, I think he wanted to appoint him really but Ray was there and Bryan had just come. The back page said 'Buchan Axed', so my daughter asked my wife what axed meant, which wasn't really a nice way to find out you're no longer captain."

Age was catching up with Buchan and although United reached Wembley and won the FA Cup in 1983 after a replay with Brighton, Buchan played no part in either game. In August 1983, Martin left on a free transfer to Oldham. After he had finished playing he spent a brief spell managing Burnley, but soon realised that it wasn't the life for him. He now works for the PFA in Manchester as an executive.

Make no mistake; Martin Buchan was a world-class footballer, as good as any centre-back who has ever played for United. He was good enough to play in any United team from the Busby Babes to any of Fergie's title and cup-winning teams. He stands alone as the most influential player at the club during the Seventies. He captained a team that though they won only one FA Cup and a Second Division championship, they thrilled supporters up and down the land playing the game in a way that made United loved and famous all over the world. He understood exactly what it meant to wear the red shirt and play for the club. If United was a religion then he was defender of the faith. As for being captain, it was never work or pressure. In his own words:

"It was always an honour."

Diamond Geezer

RAY WILKINS

1982

'When Ray joined, he was criticised for his cautious, safety-first approach and frequent use of the lateral pass – Ron Atkinson gave him the nickname "The Crab" for always moving sideways. He did develop a more positive approach, with a style marked by his composure on the ball coupled with his superb distribution skills'

The date of 5th February 1982 was a usual busy day at Old Trafford. There was a game the next day against Aston Villa, which would mark the 24th anniversary of the Munich Air Disaster. Ray Wilkins had just finished training when he was called into Ron Atkinson's office. Ray had been acting as stand-in captain on the pitch whilst Martin Buchan was out injured, and assumed that as soon as Martin came back he would regain the captaincy of the team. So it came as quite a surprise when Ron asked Wilkins to continue the role on a permanent basis, even though Martin would be playing in the next game. Ray mumbled an automatic 'yes' in response, but it wasn't until driving home that it really sank in just how great an honour had been bestowed upon him.

He didn't sleep well that night, and was up with the larks for what was to be his first game as club captain of Manchester United. What a game – and a day – it turned out to be. As always, a solitary flag flew at half-mast on the roof of the Cantilever Stand at Old Trafford, on the anniversary of Munich. The crowd was highly charged, expecting the team to play in a way that would do credit to the memory of the Babes. That is exactly what they did as they put Aston Villa, the reigning league champions, to the sword 4-1. Villa actually scored first, but United hit back with an equaliser just before half-time. The second half belonged to

United and as if a prediction of the future, Bryan Robson scored his first goal for United at Old Trafford.

Raymond Colin Wilkins was born on 14th September 1956 in Hillingdon, Middlesex. His father, George, was a professional footballer who played for Brentford, Nottingham Forest and Leeds. Ray was one of four boys, who all went on to be footballers – though none were as successful as Ray. He picked up the nickname "Butch" as a youngster, which stuck with him well into his 20s.

A naturally gifted footballer, Ray stood out in his school team and at the age of 10 he started going down to Chelsea to play in their youth teams on a Tuesday and Thursday night. When he was 12, he joined a team in East London called Senrab. The side also contained John Sparrow, Ray Lewington and Tommy Langley, who all went on to become Chelsea regulars. Later on players such as Sol Campbell, Ledley King and John Terry would also play for the club. Ray loved Saturdays, as he would go and watch Chelsea play in the afternoon at Stamford Bridge, and then get on the Underground and go over to the East End to stay with his friend Tommy Westwood, who was the goalkeeper at Senrab. He would stay with Tommy's family and then play football on Sunday morning, before going home in the afternoon. It was perfect for Ray, just playing football with his mates, training and playing competitively on Sunday. It never seemed like hard work or an effort – it was just football. At that age, playing with your mates, having a bit of fun and hopefully winning were the only things on Ray's mind.

It didn't take Chelsea long to realise that they had uncovered a diamond and prodigious talent in Wilkins. His touch and vision far outweighed his tender age, and it was obvious that he was destined for great things. In 1973, aged 17, Ray signed as an apprentice, but it wasn't long before Dave Sexton gave him his first-team debut, against Tottenham. Unfortunately for Ray he was coming into a team in decline and at the end of the 1974/75 season they were relegated to the Second Division. Several senior players departed and Eddie McCreadie took over as manager. His first act was to hand the captaincy to the 18-year-old Wilkins. Ray took to the role immediately, and the team won many friends in the Second Division playing fast, attractive football, with Wilkins acting as 'puppet master', pulling the strings from midfield. The fans saw a bright future for Chelsea with Ray leading the way, and they idolised him. He was voted the fans' player of the season in 1975/76 and 1976/1977, the latter the campaign he led a triumphant Chelsea back to Division One.

Ray represented England at all levels: schoolboy, Under-19, Under-21 and in the summer of 1976 Don Revie picked Wilkins for his full England debut, in a mini-tournament game against Italy in the USA. It was the start of a decade's involvement with the national side. Not known for his speed but renowned for his finesse, control and accuracy, he would prove to be the perfect partner for Glenn Hoddle and Bryan Robson in England's midfield. He scored only three goals for England but his second, against Belgium at the 1980 European Championship, underlined his vision and skill. In order to spring the Belgian offside trap, he lobbed their defence and ran straight through as they streamed out of their area, before collecting the ball and coolly lobbing the keeper. Unfortunately the match ended in a draw and England, although they'd qualified strongly, could not progress from the group stage.

It was to prove a familiar story for most of Wilkins' England career. Next up was the World Cup of 1982 in Spain under Ron Greenwood, where an inability to score in the second league phase saw them go home early. Under new England manager Bobby Robson, Wilkins was appointed captain – but England failed to qualify for the 1984 European Championship. Despite only losing one match, they lost out to Denmark by one point at the top of the qualifying group table, with the lack of goalscoring talent up front a key factor.

In the 1986 World Cup the problem was resolved with the emergence of Gary Lineker and his partnership with Peter Beardsley. The tournament in Mexico ended for England when Argentina's Diego Maradona, first with guile and then with skill, defeated Robson's side 2-1. For

Wilkins, the tournament would have very different memories. In the second group game against Morocco, Bryan Robson was carried off with a recurrence of a shoulder injury and handed the captain's armband to Wilkins. Less than a minute later, having only just received a yellow card, Wilkins threw the ball away in disgust at a refereeing decision, and unfortunately it hit the official. The second yellow card meant instant dismissal and an automatic two-match ban, meaning that England were without him for the final group match against Poland and the second-round game against Paraguay. Due to the loss of Robson and Wilkins, Bobby Robson was forced to change formation and the 4-2-4 layout seemed to work better for Lineker and Beardsley – as reflected by the 3-0 wins in both matches, with Lineker scoring five of the six goals including a hat-trick against Poland – while Beardsley netted the other. It was no surprise when Wilkins was overlooked for the quarter-final.

Wilkins played only a couple more games for England after the tournament. Robson was rebuilding and Wilkins' last match proved to be a qualifier for the 1988 European Championship. The 2-0 home win over Yugoslavia was Wilkins' 84th cap, with 10 of them as captain.

The 1977/78 season saw Chelsea consolidating their position in the First Division, but the following season saw McCreadie leave the club and the team were once again relegated. With Dave Sexton now manager at United, he saw it as a perfect opportunity to go back to his former club to steal their jewel. Chelsea were in a financial crisis, and could not turn down the £825,000 that United offered for their England international. Sexton explained why there was no risk in buying Wilkins:

"I have known him since he was a young schoolboy coming along to Chelsea for training when I was the coach at Stamford Bridge. He joined us when he left school and was instantly a player far more mature than his years. He was a thoroughbred who captained the England youth team and by the time he was 17 I felt he was ready for first-team football. I was the manager by this time and had no hesitation in giving him his league debut. That was the kind of confidence I had in him and he didn't let me down. His first game was against Spurs, which of course meant a big London derby, but it didn't shake him. I played him in three or four more games that season and then he became a regular the following year after Alan Hudson had left. He became our captain at the age of 18 and by the time he was 19 he was playing for England."

Liverpool tried to buy Wilkins in 1975, as did Arsenal two years later. United were 'third club lucky' but they didn't get their man immediately. It took three months for United to clinch the transfer, Sexton having begun negotiations with Chelsea the week after the 1979 FA Cup final with an offer of £600,000. The Londoners rejected the bid, although United were convinced that their offer of hard cash would be impossible for financially-stricken Chelsea to turn down. United calculated that there would be pressure from the bank for Chelsea to reduce their £2m debt. No doubt with their eyes on the massive fees being paid throughout the summer for players less experienced – and older – than Wilkins, Danny Blanchflower, the now Chelsea manager, stuck it out. United chairman Louis Edwards stepped into the negotiations while the team was on their pre-season tour in West Germany. He pressed for a decision and authorised Sexton to increase their offer to £700,000. Again they were refused, but Edwards was just as determined. As soon as they got back to England he contacted all his directors by telephone to reach an agreement to go all the way to £825,000 to meet Chelsea's asking price.

Both Ipswich Town and Everton posed a threat to the deal, but they could only come up with down payments, with the rest of the fee paid over time compared to United's whole amount payment. The United chairman had backed his manager completely, and given him the player he wanted. Blanchflower accepted that Wilkins needed to move, saying: "Ray is too sophisticated for the Second Division, where he would have been playing had he stayed at Stamford Bridge. With Manchester United he is in the right setting. Dave Sexton will bring the best out of him and make him an even better player."

Ray quickly established himself at Old Trafford but unfortunately for

United, the fans found Sexton's style of play ill-suited to United. They found it boring, and were quick to vent their feelings. The season after he arrived, 1980/81, was a poor one for Wilkins as he suffered a serious injury and was ruled out for the rest of the season, having made only 15 appearances. It was also the campaign that saw the end of Sexton's tenure as manager. Despite the team winning their last seven league matches, new chairman Martin Edwards and his board bowed to the pressure of fan opinion, and Sexton was fired.

The new managerial appointment of Ron Atkinson was like a breath of fresh air for the club. Arriving from West Bromwich Albion having just led the Baggies to fourth in Division One, Atkinson was renowned for allowing his teams to play entertaining, attacking football. Although Atkinson was not the board's first choice, the appointment was popular with the fans that remembered several titanic games between Atkinson's previous club and United.

October 1981 saw Atkinson raid his former club to make one of the most significant signings in United's history, Bryan Robson, while Remi Moses also arrived as part of the deal. The buys augured well for Wilkins' style, as both he and Robson complimented each other. Initially, when Ray joined the club, he was criticised for his cautious, safety-first approach and frequent use of the lateral pass – Ron Atkinson even gave him the nickname "The Crab" for always moving sideways. He did though develop a more positive approach, with a style marked by his composure on the ball, coupled with his superb distribution skills.

The following year there was another more unexpected signing in the form of Holland international midfielder Arnold Muhren from Ipswich. The team soon began to gel and take shape. It was no coincidence that United's midfield was quite formidable, and Atkinson was seen to be doing a good job. Club captain Martin Buchan was still at the club but was seeing little or no first-team opportunities, with the central defensive positions now being occupied by Gordon McQueen and the emerging Kevin Moran. The club captaincy was handed to Wilkins, although it didn't sit too well with him, even though he'd had four years' experience as skipper at Chelsea. To most observers, it was clear that the driving force behind the team was Bryan Robson. United finished in third position in 1981/82, and Ray went away to the World Cup finals with England. On 16th June, the date of England's opening match against France, Ray was handed a personally delivered letter from the United supporters' club two hours before kick-off, informing him that he had won the player of the year award.

It was obvious to everyone that there was an outstanding player and personality in the dressing room at Old Trafford in the shape of Bryan Robson. Robson's style of play and personality was empowering, and he was Ron Atkinson's talisman. There was no doubt that there was a special affinity between the pair so it came as no surprise to any United fan when "Robbo" was appointed captain, and there was little argument from Ray when Ron told him of his decision. Robson was also to replace Ray as captain of the national side, first skippering his country in late 1982. In the wake of losing the captaincy, Ray suffered a loss of form, but managed to recover and play some of his best football, especially in his last season at United.

In the 1982/83 season, Ray suffered an injury in a League Cup tie at Bournemouth, and he struggled to win his place back when fit. However, he was recalled in time to take part in the season's two domestic cup finals. Bryan Robson was injured and missed the League Cup final that saw Ray lead a United team that went down 2-1 to Liverpool. Robson was back to skipper the team in the FA Cup final against Brighton & Hove Albion. No one will ever forget Wilkins' curling left-foot shot from 25 yards in the first game which beat Graham Moseley, the Seagulls' keeper, to put United 2-1 up in a match that ended 2-2. It was as good a goal as you will ever see in a final, though only one of 10 that he scored in his five-year United career. But Wilkins at least ended up with an FA Cup winner's medal following a 4-0 victory in the replay, the only honour he would take away from his time at Old Trafford.

When Ray was asked to name the best game he had ever played in, he cited Manchester United against Barcelona in the European Cup-Winners' Cup in March 1984. In the first leg at the Nou Camp Barca, containing Maradona and seven Spanish internationals, were clearly superior but did not overwhelm United. Winning 2-0 courtesy of Graeme Hogg's own goal and Rojo's brilliant strike from distance, they looked favourites to progress.

In the return, Bryan Robson's first-half diving header gave United the breakthrough. Robson netted a second early in the second half and with the momentum clearly with them, United completed a stunning turn-around as Frank Stapleton blasted home the winner with minutes to go. United went out to eventual winners Juventus, but both Wilkins and Robson had attracted the attention of clubs around Europe with their midfield performances. The summer of 1984 saw Italian giants AC Milan come in with a £1.5m bid for Wilkins, and Atkinson knew that for financial reasons, if he wanted to hold on to Robson, then he would have to let Wilkins go abroad.

There was talk in 1991 of Ray making a return to Old Trafford, when Alex Ferguson was desperately in need of a ball-playing midfielder. He was said to be on the verge of offering a role to Ray, who at the time was enjoying an Indian summer at QPR. As it was Ray stayed at Loftus Road (eventually taking over as player-boss), and Alex pursued other options.

Ray's period as club captain was short, and it's hard to judge just what his contribution was – especially off the field. Was he too nice? Maybe. He was certainly one of the most popular players around the club. Perhaps the captaincy weighed too heavily upon his shoulders? Being club captain at Manchester United is no easy position, and many a player who has accepted the role has found it a heavy burden to carry, affecting their playing form. Perhaps this was the case with Ray Wilkins. There was also another factor, in the form of Bryan Robson.

Captain Marvel

BRYAN ROBSON

1982-1994

'I can't think of anyone in the last 15 years at this club who's been a greater player than Bryan Robson...he just has this talent to time things and be there at the right place at the right time...Apart from the courage and his influence on our team it's been a great experience for me to have him as a player'

For anybody who, like me, watched Manchester United through the 1980s when English football was dominated by Liverpool, there was one compensation – we had Bryan Robson. As Martin Buchan did the decade before, Robson dominated the era for United. Regarded by many as the most complete English midfielder of the Eighties, he was a miracle of commitment who pushed himself beyond every imaginable limit on the field. Universally adored by United supporters, he was given the nickname "Captain Marvel" for his superhuman efforts. When Ron Atkinson smashed the British transfer record to sign him, he knew that he was bringing the best player in the country to United.

Bryan Robson was born on 11th January 1957 in Chester-le-Street, County Durham, at his grandmother's house. He was the second of four children to lorry driver Brian Robson and his wife, Maureen. Bryan's sister Susan was the oldest of the siblings and he had two younger brothers, Justin and Gary. The first six years of his life were spent in Witton Gilbert, near Chester-le-Street. As Bryan's father was away so much due to work, the family moved to South Pelaw in Chester-le-Street to be near Bryan's grandmother, so she could help with the children. Although it was a predominantly mining area, it wasn't just a place with pits and slag heaps – there were plenty of fields where Bryan and his brothers could play football. It was all they wanted to do.

Bryan was a Newcastle United fan, though the first game his father took him to was in 1964, an FA Cup tie between Sunderland and a United side containing Best, Law and Charlton. The atmosphere was electric and the experience captivated the young boy – little was he to know that one day he would wear the United shirt with distinction.

Captain of his school team and then of the Washington and district side, he even joined the Cub Scouts, as he knew they had a team. He hadn't thought about becoming a footballer until one Saturday, when he was watching *Grandstand* eating his lunch. A scout from Burnley visited the family home, and offered Bryan a trial. Soon other clubs followed suit, including Coventry City, Sheffield Wednesday and West Brom.

Then an offer came from his beloved Newcastle, where he trained for a couple of nights – but somehow it didn't feel right. This was in contrast to West Brom, where the atmosphere was friendlier and more encouraging, especially to those living away from home. Bryan had no doubt this was the club he wanted to join, but he also realised that if he was going to make it in the game, he would have to build himself up.

Bryan started training regularly with West Brom, spending the holidays there and being treated like an apprentice. Everybody told him he would get taken on, but he was still nervous as he walked into Don Howe's office in the summer of 1972. Howe had a reputation as a great coach, but was a hard taskmaster. Robson had nothing to worry about though and at the age of 15 he was offered a contract as an apprentice professional. He was to be paid £5 a week, rising to £8 in year two.

Robson's biggest worry was his height and weight. He was just over 5ft tall, and a little over six stone. West Brom put him on a diet consisting of raw eggs, boiled potatoes and a bottle of Guinness a day. The plan appeared to work, and Robson started to grow and gain weight. He played well in the youth team and was called up for a reserve debut at Everton. Playing at left-back he had a comfortable game until the second half, when the Everton centre-forward barged him into the cinder track that surrounded the pitch. The striker who was responsible for giving Robson this painful introduction was a certain Joe Royle. He had done enough to earn a professional contract though, and in the summer of 1974 signed a deal worth £28 a week plus a signing on fee of £250.

In April 1975, Don Howe was sacked and Brian Whitehouse became caretaker-boss. With three games left, Whitehouse handed 18-year-old Robson his debut at York City. Playing in midfield, Robson impressed in a 3-1 win. The following week was even better as he scored his first goal in a 2-0 victory against Cardiff, and he repeated the feat at Nottingham Forest in the final league game of Albion's season. It could not have been a more impressive start – two goals in three games from midfield. That summer, now standing 5ft 10ins tall, he played centre-half for England youth in the mini World Cup. It was a talented team, containing Ray Wilkins and Glenn Hoddle. They were undefeated, and beat Finland 1-0 in the final with Wilkins scoring the winner.

The former Leeds midfield general Johnny Giles took over as player-manager at West Brom and made a positive impression on Robson, as he could pass the ball well with either foot. He led the team back into the First Division, though Bryan did not get many chances as Giles had yet to decide what his best position was. Robson went to see Giles and told him about his wish to play central midfield, and he was duly given his chance in the 1976/77 season when Giles was injured. Robson impressed his manager and when he was back fit and ready to play, he put himself on the subs' bench rather than take Robson out of the team.

Things were going well for Bryan, but he was about to suffer the first of the many injuries that littered his career. He was playing left-back against Tottenham, when he challenged Chris Jones. As he nicked the ball, Jones' boot caught Robson on his left leg. He went down and was carried off, but went home thinking that it was just bruised. The pain got worse over the weekend and by Monday he was taken to casualty to get it X-rayed. The scan revealed that his left leg was broken.

Bryan was in no mood to let the injury get in the way of his career;

within five weeks he was back playing in a reserve match. It wasn't long before Robson found himself going into a 50-50 tackle. As Robson felt the pain in his leg he knew that it was broken – and that he had come back too soon. By Christmas he had made a full recovery though and was back in the first team. Things were looking up for Bryan, as he scored his first hat-trick, against Ipswich, and was then called up to the England Under-21 squad. However, West Brom pulled him out as they wanted him to play at Manchester United. The match ended in a 2-2 draw, with Robson scoring on his first appearance at Old Trafford.

In April 1977 Robson was selected for England Under-23s, but on the Saturday before the international, in a game with Manchester City, Bryan went into a tackle with Dennis Tueart – and his right ankle cracked. This run of misfortune came to epitomise Robson's career – he was an outstanding player and natural leader but, for a good proportion of each season, he struggled with injury. He was, however, fortunate that his injury record consisted almost exclusively of broken bones and dislocated joints, injuries that were straightforward in their healing process. He had also sustained a broken hand, and nose, at West Brom.

During summer 1977, when Bryan was pushing to get back to fitness, Johnny Giles headed back to Ireland to take a job with Shamrock Rovers. Ronnie Allen took over for a short spell but was soon off to coach in Saudi Arabia, leaving captain John Wile in temporary charge. Wile decided to change things, and Bryan found himself left out. This state of affairs did not last long though as the larger than life, ebullient Ron Atkinson was given a chance at managing at the top level. He'd come from relative obscurity, having started his managerial career with Kettering but had then moved on to Cambridge United, where he had guided them to the Fourth Division title in 1977. When Albion approached him, the club were riding high in the Third Division. The appointment brought Atkinson and Robson together, and it was a move – and relationship – that would have a big impact on their careers.

Atkinson took to the job with relish, and had the side playing attacking football. However, Atkinson was initially unimpressed with Robson. Years later, he told Ian Ladyman of the *Daily Mail*: "I didn't rate Robbo. All I could see was the permed hair that made him look like Kevin Keegan, and I thought that was all they had in common. But I was wrong. I had to play him as centre-half in an FA Cup replay in 1978 – ironically against Manchester United – and he obliterated Joe Jordan. He was 19, and he was magnificent. He never looked back after that."

That 1977/78 season was a campaign tinged with disappointment. Albion improved one place on their league position from the previous season, finishing sixth, and also reached the last four of the FA Cup. Atkinson chose to leave Robson out of the semi-final, and a slow first 20 minutes against Ipswich found Albion two-down. Despite pulling a goal back, Ipswich ran out 3-1 winners and they eventually lifted the FA Cup. Ron recalled Robson, and Albion qualified for the UEFA Cup – but it was scant reward for a season that could have delivered more.

Bryan made himself an integral part of the fabulous West Brom team that came to Old Trafford in December 1978, coming back from 3-2 down to win 5-3. It was a perfect display of powerful, attacking football that was too much for United. The team even led the First Division for a short period, and ended up finishing in third position in 1978/79.

It was whilst Bryan was at West Brom that he went out for a drink in a local pub and bumped into a young girl called Denise Brindley, who was out celebrating her 21st birthday. Soon they were going out together and in June 1979 Denise became Mrs Robson – though her honeymoon had to wait as he flew out after the wedding to join up with the England Under-21 squad. They did eventually get away to Ibiza for a short honeymoon, but Bryan had to be back for pre-season training.

The 1979/80 season turned into a nightmare for West Brom. The club were knocked out of the UEFA Cup in the first round and the FA Cup in the third and rather than pushing the teams at the top of the table, they found themselves scrambling at the bottom. Only a recovery in the second half of the season saw the team finish 10th, which seemed like a disappointment after the promise shown the previous campaign.

On 6th February 1980, a date that is always poignant to any United supporter, Bryan Robson made his full England debut in a European Championship qualifying match against Republic of Ireland. Robson would go on and play more significant games for his country, and contribute a lot more, but he still played well in a 2-0 victory – with Kevin Keegan scoring twice. The team were heading to Italy for the European Championship, and Bryan had done his cause no harm.

Back at West Brom the following season, the team seemed to find some of the form that had previously deserted them. Robson scored 10 in 40 games as they finished fourth, which again qualified them for a European place. Then, out of the blue, Bryan returned from an end-of-season tour with England to find that Ron Atkinson had left for Manchester United. Bryan was happy at Albion, but was concerned when he noticed that players like Len Cantello and Laurie Cunningham were being sold, and not replaced, with players of the same quality. It didn't take the media long to pick up on unrest and soon they began to link Robson with a move, to teams like Liverpool and United.

Ron Atkinson made no secret of his desire to see Robson wearing the red of United. He had attempted to buy Glenn Hoddle from Spurs, but had failed; now he was determined to get his man. One day Bill Shankly was sat in Ron's office at Old Trafford, and "Big Ron" asked him what he should pay for Robson. In his familiar Scottish growl, Shankly replied: "Every penny it takes Ron, every penny it takes."

Atkinson contacted his successor at Albion, Ronnie Allen, to ask about Robson and was told: "Robson will leave Albion over my dead body – unless the money is right." Atkinson persisted and was initially told it would cost United £1.5m to land him, only for Allen to phone him the following day adding a further £250,000 to the price.

Negotiations persisted, but seemed to be going nowhere and Big Ron started to believe that he wasn't going to get his man. But unexpectedly, he received a call telling him that if West Brom were knocked out of the UEFA Cup then Robson would become available. Luckily for every United supporter Grasshoppers of Zurich did the club the favour of beating Albion, and thus making the transfer of Bryan Robson to Manchester United possible.

On 1st October 1981 Ron got his man. Atkinson ended up paying around £2.4m for Robson and the combative Remi Moses. Robson was officially priced at £1.5m (although the *Daily Mirror* reported the figure as £1.75m plus add-ons), which made him the most expensive player in English football history. It is doubtful that the United board would have been willing to sanction any more for the transfer as they had just given Atkinson £900,000 to buy Frank Stapleton from Arsenal.

At the press conference to announce the signings, Ron was asked if he considered Robson to be worth the money. Atkinson was unequivocal in his reply: "He is the most complete midfield player in the game. He can defend, create and inspire. He is a great tackler, good in the air, he has a superb range of passing and he scores. He is like Duncan Edwards and Dave Mackay – a scruff-of-the-neck player. He can take over any game. He is the kind of player who makes a good team great. He will increase United's chances of winning the major prizes from day one."

One of the fallouts of Robson's signing was the resignation of Sir Matt Busby from the board. He did not believe Robson to be an inferior player or unnecessary in United's planning. He just couldn't accept the money that was being spent on one player. He believed that paying over a million pounds for a footballer, no matter how good, was madness and if this was the way football was heading, he wanted no part in it.

Everybody arrived early at Old Trafford on 3rd October, as the press claimed Robson would be signing on the pitch before the home game against Wolves. The ground was bristling with excitement, especially when a makeshift desk was placed on the pitch. The Stretford End was chanting his name before they caught sight of him. Then, just before kick-off, out he came with Ron Atkinson and Martin Edwards, to put pen-to-paper. He sported a bubble perm that Kevin Keegan had made fashionable. Ron was grinning like a Cheshire cat, milking the crowd. Edwards, in contrast, cut an uncomfortable figure; never popular, he hoped the deal would at least show the fans that he was determined to make United the best side in England.

It seemed like Old Trafford was lifted – especially the team. They brushed aside Wolves 5-0 with Sammy McIlroy, whose place was now under threat, scoring a hat-trick. The result and performance didn't stop Ron selecting Robson to face Tottenham in the League Cup at White Hart Lane four days later. The first-leg tie didn't go United's way as they lost 1-0 – but Robson was just relieved to get his debut over with.

Robson made his league debut for United in an uneventful goalless derby at Maine Road. Robson had always been superstitious, and the No. 7 was his lucky number. Steve Coppell was injured and so Robson asked if he could have the shirt, without realising that he was about to write his own chapter amongst the legends who have worn that number.

A fortnight later United went to Anfield, earning a 2-1 victory against Liverpool before travelling to Roker Park soon after, where they beat Sunderland 5-1 – with Robson grabbing his first goal. The team enjoyed some impressive results, and won seven of their last nine games. But a slow start, plus some inconsistent mid-season form, ensured only a third-placed finish, behind champions Liverpool and Ipswich Town.

Robson had made a big difference and was starting to exert his influence, but it was his England team-mate, Ray Wilkins, that Ron Atkinson decided should take over as captain. Both were about to head off to the World Cup in Spain, but they would not be the only United representatives. That season, a 16-year-old man-boy was introduced: Norman Whiteside. Whiteside represented Northern Ireland and broke Pele's record as the youngest player to appear in a finals when he made his debut aged 17 years, 41 days, against Yugoslavia. He started all five of his country's matches, including the historic 1-0 victory over the hosts.

As for Robson, the World Cup could not have started in a more dramatic fashion, in England's opener against France. As soon as the game kicked-off, England won a throw-in on the right and sent forward Terry Butcher, to add aerial presence to the attack. As Steve Coppell hurled in the long throw, France were completely disorganised and left a huge gap as they went to deal with Butcher. The defender flicked the ball on, and Robson was left free to rush in and hammer home. The goal was timed at 27 seconds and won Bryan a gold-inscribed Seiko watch, which he still occasionally wears, for scoring the fastest goal at the tournament. England went out in the second stage, even though they were undefeated, but with Robson a far better player for the experience.

United started 1982/83 by winning five out of six games, but they faded in October. The team had been knocked out of the UEFA Cup by Valencia, and the defeat seemed to hit confidence. United began their League Cup campaign against Bournemouth, winning 2-0, with Peter Beardsley making his only United first-team appearance. But in the second leg, Ray Wilkins was involved in a collision and broke his cheekbone. Wilkins was captain of England and United – and it was Robson who replaced him in both roles. Wilkins accepted the decision, and did not let it affect his attitude – or his relationship with Robson.

With Robson as captain, United saw off Bradford City, Southampton and Nottingham Forest before facing Arsenal in the semi-final. United came through 6-3 on aggregate, although Robson picked up an injury to his ankle ligaments that meant two months out, including the final against Liverpool. Ray Wilkins led the team at Wembley and United started confidently, having lost only once in 17 games. Norman Whiteside scored a superb opener, but some injuries and the rub of the green saw Liverpool level – and eventually go on to win.

On 9th April Robson made a goalscoring return against Southampton. A week later, at Villa Park, Bryan led the team out for an FA Cup semi-final, again against Arsenal. The tie did not start well for United, and they trailed to a Tony Woodcock goal after 37 minutes. Then Robson did what he would do game after game for United, getting hold of the game by the scruff of the neck, turning it in United's favour. Robson burst forward onto a through ball, held off Brian Talbot and slotted the ball past George Wood to level. Then Whiteside ran on to a pass from Arthur Albiston and lashed home a volley to give United the lead. The scenes at the end were as if United had won the FA Cup as fans streamed onto the pitch. Robson was so jubilant that he handed one young supporter his shirt – and a memory that he is probably still talking about today.

This is what Atkinson had paid the money for – and two cup finals in one season was a decent start. Robson was delivering, and the United fans loved him for it. The bookies made United favourites for the 1983 FA Cup final against Brighton & Hove Albion. The Seagulls had finished bottom of Division One, but had beaten Liverpool at Anfield.

United began confidently, knocking the ball around effortlessly. But like a prizefighter who gets caught by a surprise left hook, they suddenly found themselves on the ropes. The Seagulls took the lead through Gordon Smith, and United went in at half-time a goal down – before Frank Stapleton levelled early in the second half.

Ray Wilkins then scored one of the finest goals in FA Cup final history, when he curled a long-range effort into the top corner. But Gary Stevens levelled with three minutes left, to take the final into extra time. The destiny of the trophy was always in the balance in the added 30 minutes, but with the match entering the final seconds, Albion's Gordon Smith found himself 10 yards out, with just Gary Bailey to beat. Luckily for United, Smith hit the ball straight at Bailey, and the keeper smothered. Afterwards United realised that they had been let off the hook.

The following Thursday's replay took place on Sir Matt Busby's 74th birthday – and United put on a performance for him. Brighton had their captain, defender Steve Foster, back in the side, having missed the first game due to suspension. His return made no difference to their fortunes though as they were outclassed by a rampant United side.

The game set off at a frantic pace, with Brighton showing an attacking intent. Then after 25 minutes, winger Alan Davies received the ball inside the box; he laid it out for Robson, whose left-footed strike from outside the box found the corner. The goal seemed to rock Albion, and four minutes later Whiteside doubled the advantage. A minute before half-time Robson added his second – and United's third.

The second half saw United start as they had finished the first, with Robson dominant. He burst onto a pass from Frank Stapleton, only to be pulled back in the area to earn a penalty. Steve Coppell, United's normal taker, was injured so Arnold Muhren was down to take the kick. Some players encouraged Robson to step up to take it and score a cup final hat-trick, but he has always been about the team rather than personal glory, and was happy to see Muhren slot the penalty away to give United the biggest post-war winning margin in FA Cup final history.

For those, including Sir Matt Busby, who had doubts about Robson and the money paid for him, their questions had been answered by a near perfect performance. Robson had been dominant, seemingly covering every blade of grass. Wearing a United cap and a scarf, Robson climbed the famous steps to collect his first trophy as captain. Ironically, it was Sir Matt who had the biggest grin on his face as Robson held the trophy aloft. The celebrations continued into the early hours, and the train carrying the team home pulled into Piccadilly station at 4am on Friday morning – to be greeted by thousands of United supporters.

The FA Charity Shield provided the curtain raiser to the 1983/84 season, pitting United against champions Liverpool, who had also beaten United in the League Cup. This time though Robson was playing and he showed what a difference he would have made to that final by scoring the goals in a 2-0 victory. The result gave United real belief that this would be the season that they could put in a serious title challenge.

The cup success meant European football in the shape of the Cup-Winners' Cup. The early rounds saw United see off Dukla Prague and Spartak Varna, with Robson scoring in both rounds. In the quarter-final, United were paired with a Barcelona side containing Diego Maradona. They found themselves 2-0 down after the first leg, but United's performances, especially Robson's, had attracted many envious glances from Europe's top clubs – and Juventus had made their interest clear to the club. The supporters petitioned, begging United not to sell Robson.

In the meantime there was the second leg of the quarter-final to come. The memory of that Wednesday, 21st March 1984, will live forever with anyone fortunate to have been at Old Trafford that night. It was as if the crowd knew they were about to witness something special – and they were not let down. Inside the dressing room, Ray Wilkins was giving instructions and geeing up players whilst Robson did his own thing, leading by example. They were like silk and steel together: Ray controlling the ball, talking, pulling team-mates into position, whilst Bryan was dynamic, a driving force, tackling anything in front of him.

There is no doubt that the atmosphere got to the Barcelona players, as they looked nervous from the off. United had knocked four goals past Arsenal on the previous Saturday, and looked the more confident team. The media talk had been about who would have the biggest influence: Maradona or Robson. There would be a clear answer. Midway through the first half a United corner was flicked on by Graeme Hogg for Robson, who threw himself at the ball to head home.

United came out for the second half kicking into the Stretford End, with 15,000 fanatical fans sucking the ball towards the goal. United players were all over the Barca defence, forcing errors – one of which Norman Whiteside jumped upon. The ball broke to Remi Moses on the wing, who sent over a cross that was met by Wilkins on the volley. The goalkeeper could only parry, and Robson was there to follow up.

The noise that had greeted the goal had yet to die down as Frank Stapleton scored a third to give United the overall lead. The Barcelona players looked on in stunned amazement. United had done the impossible, coming back from a 2-0 deficit against one of Europe's top teams to lead 3-0 – yet at the end it could have all been so different. A shot from Bernd Schuster beat Gary Bailey, but just slid past the post.

When the final whistle went, the players made a mad dash for the tunnel as the crowd spilled onto the pitch. Robson was mobbed, and then hoisted onto their shoulders to take the adulation. Italian clubs may have shown admiration for Robson – but the Old Trafford faithful showed out-and-out worship. Robson had gone toe-to-toe against arguably the greatest player in the world in Maradona, and eclipsed him.

The semi-final saw United facing Juventus. This would have been a tough task with a fully-fit side, but with Muhren injured and Wilkins suspended the odds were stacked against United. Then, with the last kick of a training session before the game, Robson went down with a damaged hamstring. Robson did his best not to show watching journalists he was in pain, but it was a bad injury that would rule him out.

Though Robson did not play in the semi-final that United lost 3-2 on aggregate, he did travel to Turin for the second leg and was given permission to discuss a move. Ron Atkinson told Bryan that he didn't want him to go, but if an offer of £3m was made then United would have to accept. Bryan spent a week in Italy with his wife, staying with Sampdoria's Trevor Francis. The Robson's liked Italy, and the thought of teaming up with Michel Platini in the Juve midfield appealed. But the Italians were unable to match United's price, and he stayed in England.

One player who did make his way to Italy was United's player of the year Ray Wilkins, who joined AC Milan for £1.5m. United had been top of the table when Robson picked up his injury with 10 games left. But a loss of form, coupled with Robson's absence, saw United pick up only 10 points from 30 to finish fourth. During the period Nottingham Forest boss Brian Clough talked of his admiration for Robson:

"When Robson plays, he must expect to get hurt because that's him. When he sees a ball, irrespective of where it is, he automatically goes for it. Now afterwards he says, 'I don't really know why I went for it' and he'll be asking that when he is lying in the treatment room. But that is Robson. Now if Robson had known fear he wouldn't have got injured so much, but he doesn't know it, it's something that you can't put into them and something that you never want to knock out of them."

Robson found himself with a new midfield partner at the start of the

1984/85 season, as Atkinson used the money from the Wilkins sale to buy Gordon Strachan from Alex Ferguson's Aberdeen. Any lingering doubts about Robson's future were also put to bed when in October 1984 he signed a seven-year contract, the longest ever offered to a United player, which made the United captain financially secure for life.

United struggled for league consistency, but the team did reach Wembley again for the FA Cup final. They went through an epic semi-final against Liverpool, drawing the first game 2-2 at Goodison Park before coming from behind to win the replay 2-1 at Maine Road. Robson's goal in the replay was memorable; picking the ball up on halfway he drove forward, leaving players in his wake. As he approached the area, he let fly with a rocket that Bruce Grobbelaar got his fingertips to – but couldn't keep from flying into the top corner.

Now they were due to face Everton in the final, a Toffees side who had the chance of completing a treble of league and Cup-Winners' Cup, the latter of which they had won the Wednesday before in Rotterdam. The Merseysiders were favourites, having already hammered United 5-0 in the league and knocked them out of the League Cup.

The game itself was not a great spectacle, with both defences on top. However, with 12 minutes of the game left history was made as Kevin Moran became the first player to be sent off in an FA Cup final. It appeared a harsh decision by referee Peter Willis, with Moran guilty of no more than badly timing a tackle on Peter Reid in the middle of the pitch. The Everton midfielder did his best to get the referee to change his mind, but to no avail. United were down to 10 men, and hanging on.

They made it to full-time, and this gave Ron Atkinson a chance to reorganise. With 10 minutes of extra-time left, Mark Hughes knocked the ball out to the right wing where Norman Whiteside was waiting. Whiteside, who was covered by Pat Van Den Hauwe, moved inside, gave a little step over and without warning curled a shot around the defender and a helpless Neville Southall, whose view had been obscured, into the corner. The United bench went ballistic while Moran, who believed he had cost his team the cup, leapt up and down with joy.

The final 10 minutes seemed to last forever, but the referee finally blew his whistle and United had won their second FA Cup in three years. Bryan Robson made the same journey he had made two years earlier, up the Wembley steps to collect the trophy from the Duke of Kent. However, the closeness of those victories didn't subdue the massive crowds, who turned up in Albert Square to greet the victorious team.

Although Everton gained a semblance of revenge in the FA Charity Shield months later with a 2-0 victory, the 1985/86 league season began with United in imperious form and full of confidence. They won the first 10 games, conceding only three goals in the process. Mark Hughes scored 10 goals in the first 15 games, and it seemed as if United were certainties for a first top-flight championship in 19 years.

Unfortunately, as with previous seasons, injuries were to play a key role in United's season. Robson tore a hamstring playing for England that put him out for weeks, defender John Gidman broke his leg while Gordon Strachan suffered a dislocated shoulder. Robson made a couple of abortive comebacks, but suffered a dislocated shoulder against West Ham. He was advised to have an operation but it was only six weeks until England's 1986 World Cup preparations. Rather than missing the tournament and United's end-of-season run-in, Robson decided to wait.

At the same time as injuries were piling up, it was announced that Mark Hughes would join Barcelona at the end of the season. From then on his form slumped, and he only managed to score one goal in 17. It was obvious this was not a move requested by Hughes, who had only signed a five-year deal at the start of the season; he looked gutted to be leaving. United duly came up short again as Liverpool won the Double.

England's World Cup qualifying campaign had been pretty much flawless, with Robson missing only two matches. He celebrated his 50th cap against Israel in February 1986 by scoring both goals in a 2-1 win. England travelled to Mexico in good form and spirits. Robson, now dubbed "Captain Marvel" by his namesake England coach Bobby, was now seen as one of the world's finest all-round players.

There was lingering concern though over his injury, a problem that had recurred in a friendly a month before the competition. Sadly, after England lost the opening group game to Portugal, this is what happened during the second match with Morocco, which ended goalless. Robson stretched to keep a ball in play, fell awkwardly and had to be helped off, with his arm held tightly in a sling. Meanwhile, his deputy as skipper, Ray Wilkins, was sent off for throwing the ball at the referee and suddenly England seemed to have no leaders. Goalkeeper Peter Shilton took the captaincy, and England recovered to beat Poland 3-0 to go through to round two. Unfortunately, Robson's tournament was over.

England went out after a controversial quarter-final against eventual winners Argentina, which featured the the infamous "Hand of God" and the magnificent "Goal of the Century", both from the inspirational Diego Maradona. Robson meanwhile should have come home to have an operation on his shoulder, but stayed in Mexico to offer support.

When United's players returned for the 1986/87 season, five of the squad who had gone to the World Cup needed operations. This did little for United's cause, as they struggled from the off. Ron Atkinson had targeted England defender Terry Butcher to partner Paul McGrath, but the board turned down his request – it was clear they were beginning to lose faith in their manager. As well as poor form on the pitch, there were stories of unrest. In November 1986, after being knocked out of the League Cup by Southampton, Atkinson was sacked. It did not take the board long to name his replacement. On 7th November the squad got to meet their new boss: Alex Ferguson. The players had heard about Ferguson from Gordon Strachan, but not many were ready for the real thing.

Robson played hard on and off the pitch, gaining a hard drinking reputation along with players like Paul McGrath and Norman Whiteside. Robson was as fit as the proverbial butcher's dog, and had a metabolism and constitution that was beyond belief. Not all his team-mates were of the same mould, though. Robson was the main man in the dressing room, and the one whose lead was followed. He did part of Atkinson's job in that whenever there was a poor performance, Robson would not wait for the manager's input. He would call a meeting at a local Cheshire pub, believing that the team that drinks together, plays together. In some ways Atkinson contributed to his downfall; although he knew what was happening, he turned a blind eye. As long as the team was performing, his philosophy was – let them get on with it. Eventually it took its toll.

As club captain should Robson have been more responsible? Robson has always had strong ideas about team bonding, but maybe there were better ways of implementing it. Did it cause a clique within the club, as Gordon Strachan claimed in his autobiography? After leaving training each day, once the players arrived in Cheadle it was apparently a choice to either turn right to go home, or turn left for a session in the pub. It was not uncommon during the period to see a United player in the Four Seasons Hotel in Hale Barnes, at The Griffin in Bowdon or the Little 'B' in Sale. Leading the drinking would be Robson, oblivious to the damage it was causing, as he knew he could sweat it out at training. Others weren't as lucky, and the effects were apparent. Atkinson should also shoulder blame. He refused to believe the drinking had got out of hand – and ultimately paid the price.

This behaviour was never going to fit in with Ferguson's philosophy, and it was obvious that something would have to give. McGrath and Whiteside were moved on, maybe too early in McGrath's case. Ferguson knew what he was doing though, and the message it was sending to the younger players. He did however have no intention of letting Robson go – indeed, he was full of praise for his captain in later years.

"There was an aura about Bryan," Alex said, "and it was understandable that, when I arrived, there was a feeling that winning or losing depended on whether he was playing. I can't think of anyone in the last 15 years at this club who's been a greater player. People assessing him say what's his great strength? I think it's his courage, and his ability to score as a midfielder. He has a quality that you can't coach, and that is timing. When two lads go up for the ball, a red jersey and another team's jersey, Bryan always knows where the ball is going to land. When a ball is coming in to the back post, he knows he needs to be there. If it is going to the near post, he will attack it and he knows he has to be there; he has this talent to time things and be there in the right place at the right time. It's been a great experience for me to have him as a player."

Success didn't come immediately for Fergie's United but everyone, including Robson, could see that he was doing things the right way, trying to bring the right kind of player in. He did not get everyone he went after, with Paul Gascoigne being a notable 'miss'. He was though successful in bringing back Mark Hughes as well as signing Brian McClair from Celtic. After Robson mentioned to him an impressive defender from Norwich City, he also brought in Steve Bruce. Later on he added Gary Pallister, and the foundations of a good side began to show.

Many people will say that the FA Cup run in 1990 saved Alex Ferguson's job – but Sir Bobby Charlton will always tell you that for those who could see what he was doing behind the scenes, this was never an option. What it did achieve though was to open the floodgates for the many trophies that have flowed United's way under Ferguson.

The first FA Cup final of the '90s took place between United and Crystal Palace, and would prove to be one of the best of modern times. The underdogs took the lead through Gary O'Reilly after 18 minutes but Robson, just as he had done so many times before, came to United's rescue by heading the equaliser 10 minutes before the break. Hughes gave United a 2-1 advantage but then Palace brought on Ian Wright midway through the second half, and the game swung back in their favour. The striker, who was coming back from injury, levelled three minutes after coming on to take the game into extra time, and then struck in the 92nd minute to stun United. Fortunately Hughes netted an equaliser seven minutes from the end, meaning another United cup final replay.

The following Thursday saw Ferguson drop regular goalkeeper Jim Leighton for Les Sealey. This was a huge risk to take in a cup final, but

Ferguson was confident Sealey could do a solid job for him – and he was proved correct. The game was a far duller affair than the first match, and was eventually decided on the hour by a goal from the most unlikely of players. Left-back Lee Martin controlled Neil Webb's long pass on the run, and smashed the ball home to give United the FA Cup.

It was Ferguson's first trophy as manager of United, and it meant that Bryan Robson was the first – and only – player in the 20th century to captain three FA Cup-winning teams. Robson had faced his familiar fight against injury during the season, and been restricted to only 20 league appearances as United finished 13th, their lowest placing since relegation in 1974. But now there was a new confidence in the squad, and the belief that they could go on to win the league again.

Robson captained a confident England squad as they jetted off to the World Cup in Italy. His third finals would again prove eventful – and again for the wrong reasons. The 1990 finals saw Robson pick up an Achilles tendon injury, which forced him out of yet another World Cup early as England finished fourth, their best performance in the competition overseas. The injury would keep him out until December 1990, with fellow England midfielder Neil Webb captaining the side in his absence. Webb, signed from Nottingham Forest in July 1989, was a talented player who was unlucky at Old Trafford. He received a bad injury playing for England, and never returned to his best. It would have been impossible for anyone to step into Robson's boots during this time and not suffer from comparisons. When away supporters came to Old Trafford they would always chant "Robson, Robson, man of the match" in a tongue-in-cheek reference to the fact that when United were on TV, the award was always given to Robson, no matter who the opposition.

It wasn't just Robson's skills that were missed when he wasn't playing; it was the steel he brought to the side. Robson could mix it with the best of them – and often did. Robson considered it his duty to protect his team-mates and if they were playing against a team like Wimbledon, whose style of play was to intimidate and bully, Robson would search out the main protagonists like Vinnie Jones or John Fashanu, and let them know he was there with a few bone-crunching tackles. No opposition player ever took liberties when Robson was on the pitch, and this was something that supporters could identify with, and loved him for.

When he returned, against Coventry City, he noticed that David Speedie was going around fouling the younger members of the team such as Lee Sharpe, and he then slyly went down the Achilles of Lee Martin. In the second half he hit Gary Pallister in the head with his elbow, splitting it open and leaving the defender needing stitches. That was enough for Robson, and the next chance he got he hit Speedie hard in a tackle that sent him flying. The City players came over to remonstrate with Robson, especially captain Trevor Peake. Robson looked him in the eye and told him that if he came any closer, he would be next.

Team-mates knew he would run through brick walls for them – and they would do the same for him. Robson was a player who, as a supporter, you always looked for first on the teamsheet; when you saw his name, you felt safe knowing he was on your side. They are few and far between, and United have been lucky in having some of them – and been captained by a few. The ability to lead your team, perform on the pitch and be universally adored by the fans.

The 1990/91 season once again saw United fall short in the league, with Robson restricted to 17 league games. He did get back to lead the team out in the League Cup final against Ron Atkinson's Sheffield Wednesday. At the time the Owls were riding high in the Second Division, but were not fancied to cause an upset. However, a goal by boyhood United fan John Sheridan gave Wednesday a 1-0 victory.

There was a feeling that perhaps United had their thoughts on a higher prize. The club had progressed to the European Cup-Winners' Cup final, where they were to meet Barcelona. Robson had been struggling with a hernia problem and needed an operation, but put it off as he was determined not to miss out. He tried to rest as much as he could the week prior to the final, only taking part in light training, but had done no shooting – and had only kicked the ball with his weaker right foot.

The final had a 'home' feel to it. Along with the rain, it seemed that all of Manchester had made it over to Holland to witness United's first European final since 1968, filling two thirds of the ground. United dominated the first half, although the sides went in goalless. But midway through the second half the opener came. Robson chipped a ball into the area and Steve Bruce was there to meet it, sending a header goalwards. The ball was about to go in when Mark Hughes made sure by putting his foot behind it. There was some debate about who should be credited, but there could be no doubt about the second. Robson made an interception before playing in Hughes, who had just the keeper to beat. He pushed the ball to the right, past the keeper, and everybody in the ground – and on the pitch – thought he had pushed it too far. But Hughes, ever the one for the spectacular goal, unleashed a rocket of a right-footed shot that flew into the net from the tightest of angles.

Barcelona got themselves back into the game soon after when a free-kick from Ronald Koeman slipped under Les Sealey. Although Clayton Blackmore had to clear off the line at the death, United held on to win their first European trophy for 23 years. As the crowd chanted, "We're the pride of Manchester", Robson made his way onto the makeshift podium to collect the trophy. It had been a superb captain's performance, and he and United were deserving of a European trophy.

The team didn't fly straight back to Manchester, but instead took over a whole hotel for players, their families and friends. It was a party that lasted all night especially for Robson and Brian McClair, who were still sat at the bar in the morning when the rest of the squad were coming down for breakfast. Later that day they flew home and toured Manchester in an open-topped bus, with Robson eventually retiring to bed at 10pm that night – spending the next 24 hours in bed recovering.

During the summer Fergie made one of his best ever signings when he paid £600,000 for goalkeeper Peter Schmeichel. With the purchase, Ferguson now felt he had the team that would finally win the league.

They did continue the by now annual collection of silverware, as the League Cup was won. United edged out Nottingham Forest 1-0, who fielded a young Roy Keane, but Robson missed out due to injury. They also won the European Super Cup by beating Red Star Belgrade 1-0 at Old Trafford, with Steve Bruce captain in the absence of Robson.

However, the season ended in huge disappointment as a fixture pile-up saw United get pipped to the championship by Leeds United. They finished runners-up in a title race that for most of the season they'd looked dead certs to win. It was the biggest setback of Robson's career, and he was starting to wonder if he would ever get his hands on that elusive championship medal. But things were about to change – and that change would be influenced by a Frenchman called Eric.

Robson only made 14 appearances during the 1992/93 season, the first of the new Premier League era. United started sluggishly, suffering a hangover from the devastating way they missed out on the title the previous campaign. Then, at the end of November, United announced the signing of Eric Cantona, a snip at £1.2m. One of the greatest showmen ever to grace the pitch at Old Trafford, he walked out for his debut as if he owned the place – and from that moment United never looked back.

The club's regular central midfielders that season were Paul Ince and Brian McClair, with Mike Phelan or the wider-lying Andrei Kanchelskis and Lee Sharpe occupying Robson's other favoured position on the right. The side was flying, and led by four points with two games to go. Aston Villa were United's closest rivals and realistically needed to beat relegation-threatened Oldham to stay in the title race. United were playing the day after so Bryan decided to watch at home on TV. Everyone expected a Villa win, which would have left United needing a victory on the following day to clinch the title. However, the Latics earned a priceless 1-0 win to hand the title to United for the first time in 26 years.

Robson's phone was soon ringing, and Steve Bruce invited him to his house in Bramhall to celebrate. Bramhall is a small village in Cheshire that was once home to George Best, when he lived in his famous goldfish bowl house. Even when George lived there, I doubt it had seen a party like this. The whole team were there, and in the mood to celebrate. Robson and his wife Denise failed to make it home after the party. When Bruce finally woke and came downstairs, he was greeted by the sight of Robson and his wife tidying up and making breakfast.

Anybody who was at Old Trafford on 3rd May 1993 will remember the rejoiceful atmosphere before, during and after the game. The opponents were Blackburn Rovers, but they never really stood a chance – even though most of the United team was suffering from the previous nights' festivities. The visitors did open the scoring, and for a couple of minutes they looked like they might be party poopers – but luckily that was not going to happen. Ryan Giggs hit a glorious free-kick to equalise, Paul Ince put United in the lead and then the ever-present Gary Pallister rounded the evening off by scoring a free-kick in the last minute – his only goal of the campaign.

Prior to the match the team had discussed going up for the trophy. Robson, though he was club captain, believed that Steve Bruce, who had skippered the team for most of the season, should pick it up. Ferguson and Bruce were having none of it, and it was finally agreed that Bruce and Robson would go up together. With Sir Matt Busby in the stands watching on with tears in his eyes, Bruce was first up the steps, followed closely by Robson. Bruce had become a leader in his own right but it was only fair that Robson be there to lift the trophy with him. When Bruce reached the trophy, he paused and waited for Robson to catch up. Then together they lifted the trophy – and the roof was nearly blown off Old Trafford by the cheer they received. Robson had done what he had set out to achieve when he left West Brom – he had brought the championship back to United. Days later Robson rounded off the season with his only goal of the campaign as Wimbledon were defeated 2-1.

Robson's first-team chances weren't now just restricted by injuries, as they had been before. With Eric Cantona now partnering Mark Hughes in attack, Hughes's former strike-partner Brian McClair had been converted into a midfielder to play alongside Paul Ince. This limited Robson's opportunities, but the biggest blow to his claim for a midfield berth came in the summer of 1993 when Alex Ferguson broke the British transfer record by paying Nottingham Forest £3.75m for Roy Keane, who in everyone's opinion was his natural successor.

The 1993/94 season saw the introduction of squad numbers, with Robson given the No. 12 shirt – with the No. 7 he had become synonymous with given to Cantona. This was another sign that Robson's time was coming to a close. If only Robson had been five years younger, we can only imagine what a midfield that might have been – and how many more medals he would have won. Robson still made enough appearances to qualify for another title-winning medal, and he also scored one of the goals in the 4-0 FA Cup semi-final replay victory over Oldham at Maine Road. But the fact that he was left out for the final tells you everything you need to know about Alex Ferguson, and what makes him the most successful football manager of his generation. With Ferguson there is no room for sentiment – the selection has to be for the good of the team. Ferguson later admitted that it was one of the hardest decisions of his career. Anyone who knows Bryan would agree that he would hate to be picked on sentiment. He never needed charity through his career – and he wasn't going to end it by being picked as a token gesture.

Robson's last appearance in a United shirt came on the final day of the league season on 8th May 1994 when United drew 0-0 with Coventry City at Old Trafford. In the summer Robson was given a free, and took up the offer of becoming player-manager of First Division Middlesbrough. He had played 461 times for United in all competitions, and was one short of 100 goals. He will always be regarded as one of the club's greatest players, who never gave less than his all when he wore the red shirt. Only Bobby Moore and Billy Wright have captained England more than the 65 times that Robson led his country.

Was he a good club captain? No – he was a great club captain, a "club captain marvel" whose contribution to the club is immeasurable.

Double-Winning Captain

STEVE BRUCE

1994-1996

'It was fitting that Bruce scored the goals. He was a warrior, a player who did not know the meaning of defeat. His face pays testament to somebody who was prepared to put his head anywhere if it meant scoring a goal or, more often than not, saving a goal'

In the last century, two Englishmen captained Double-winning teams. One was Tony Adams, for Arsenal in 1998. The other – and first – was Steve Bruce, who captained Manchester United in 1994. For Bruce, who eventually found his way to the top of the professional game, the journey could never be described as easy. He was born on New Year's Eve 1960 in Corbridge, Northumberland to a Geordie father and Irish mother. Sheenagh, his mother, met Joe when she was over in Newcastle, and he was doing National Service in the army. Joe was a mad Newcastle fan, and made sure that his sons Steve and [younger brother] Ian were brought up the same way. Whenever Steve wasn't playing football on a Saturday he could be found at St James's Park. Steve claims he never paid to watch his heroes, as he could sneak in under the gates.

The Bruce family lived in Daisy Hill near the shipyards in Wallsend, Newcastle. Fortunately for Steve, the house backed onto playing fields and so it only took a hop over the back fence and Steve was free to kick a ball around. He attended Walker Gate Primary School, and it was there that he won his first trophy, captaining the team to victory in the Bagnall Cup. The side played in green and Steve's mum would often find herself washing the strip. Mr Bell, who ran the school team, sent a prophetic note home to Mrs Bruce thanking her for washing the teams' kit, adding that 'when Steve is playing for Manchester United, someone else will do the washing'. It was also whilst at Walker Gate that he started playing for Newcastle Boys, from Under-11 level through to Under-16s.

Outside of school, like many good players before him, he found himself playing for the famous Wallsend Boys' Club, whose impressive roll of honour includes Eric Steele, Steve Watson, Tony Sealey, Alan Thompson, Lee Clark, Robbie Elliott, Peter Beardsley, Alan Shearer and Michael Carrick. It was Pete Kirkley who spotted Bruce's potential at an early age, and he ran the club. Kirkley had contacts at Burnley and he took Bruce down for a trial on his 12th birthday. Whereas others before him were quickly snapped up by watching scouts, it didn't happen for Steve. He was turned down by a number of clubs, including his beloved Newcastle and their arch-rivals, Sunderland. They all felt he was too small to cope with the physical rigours of the professional game and even if he did have positives in the skill department, that aspect wouldn't matter if he couldn't look after himself in a tough game.

It seemed that Bruce was not destined for a life in football – and he had not shone academically at school, either. Fortunately his cousin got him a job as a trainee plumber at the Swan Hunter shipyard. It wasn't what Steve wanted to do, but he was in no position to turn down gainful employment. This appeared to be Bruce's future, as all football doors seemed to be closing. Even his time at Wallsend was finishing, as most of the players he had grown up with were going their separate ways.

The team were invited to take part in a tournament at Charterhouse Public School in Surrey, and saw it as a perfect way to celebrate their time together. What Steve was unaware of was that Pete Kirkley had arranged for Gillingham boss Gerry Summers to come and have a look at some of the players. The team lost, but Steve had done enough to impress and was invited to Gillingham for a trial. This was to change his life. Together with Peter Beardsley (who'd also been offered a chance), he made his way south to Kent. Talking in later years about Wallsend Boys' Club, and of his early years at Gillingham, Steve was to say:

"It's got a wonderful tradition, and the number of professional players to come out of that boys' club is incredible. I think there's even a rule to this day that you have to live in a five-mile radius of the club. I spent the best part of my youth in that club. In my opinion, more kids should be doing exactly the same; it's how I started on the journey to where I am.

"The two of us came to Gillingham. Unfortunately, they turned Peter away and he went on to Cambridge, who were in the Fourth Division then, and he didn't make it at Cambridge either. The pair of us were small – undernourished might be the best word for it!"

Steve was offered an apprenticeship, and while Summers looked after the first team, Bruce came under the watchful eye of mentor Bill "Buster" Collins, who was in charge of the Gills' youth scheme. Collins was of the old school, and would help shape Steve's life. Born in Belfast in 1920, he'd come up through the lower ranks of professional football, playing for Irish League clubs Distillery and Belfast Celtic before moving across the Irish Sea to join Luton and then finally Gillingham, where he finished playing in 1956. Collins worked in various positions in non-League before Freddie Cox, the Gills manager, asked Collins to take over the reserve-team manager's role as well as putting him in charge of the club's newly-formed youth set-up. Having taken the post in 1965, it was a position that he would oversee for 20 years. Bruce reveres him.

"He has been one of the biggest influences on my life. Without him and his family, I could easily have gone home. In the end, I became part of his family. I still call them today, and go and see them whenever I have the opportunity. He was an influence not just on my football career, but also the way I wanted to be as an adult. He taught me so many things and for that I'll always be extremely grateful."

Steve started on £12 a week, plus an extra £2 if the youth team won. It was an ideal club for Steve as he got to play regularly. Not only did he play for the youth team on a Saturday, he also got the opportunity to play for the reserves against the top London teams including Arsenal, Tottenham, Chelsea and West Ham. Being Gillingham, the team were always up against it, but it helped instil a pride, hunger and passion to do well. It was an attitude Collins drilled into his young players, and was something that Bruce carried with him throughout his career. What it did give him was a good grounding for as well as playing football, he would clean the changing rooms, the kit and the boots for the pros.

In the early years, Bruce played in midfield, but he wasn't making the progress he should have been. When he was 18, Collins moved him to centre-back. He told Steve: "You're decent in the air, and you like to tackle. Why don't you try it?" It turned out to be a masterstroke. From the minute Bruce moved to defence, his performances improved significantly. He admitted that looking back on his early years, playing initially as a midfielder, he didn't have quick enough feet, nor speed of thought, to make it in that position at the top level. Bruce still has vivid recollections of his early days as a youth player and his introduction into the professional game. He will tell you that his time at Gillingham was paramount as to how his career was to shape up and develop. It was a terrific grounding as far as he was concerned. Whilst at the club he was also selected for the England youth team, winning eight caps.

Steve's Football League debut was against Blackpool at the start of the 1979/80 season. The late Alan Ball was then Blackpool player-boss, and Steve was in the Gillingham midfield. He recalled: "I was a young whippersnapper of a boy and I was thinking, 'Here's my chance, I'm going to nail him and put him into the stands if I can.' I never got near him, never got a kick. That was my introduction to League football. He was absolutely fantastic. Great days, and a huge learning experience."

Steve's career blossomed at Gillingham, and he picked up player of the year, young player of the year and players' player of the year awards. He went on to make over 200 first-team appearances, and despite suffering a broken leg during his time at Priestfield, he was to earn a move into the big time. In 1984, shortly after his recovery, the Gills were drawn against Everton in the FA Cup fourth round. The tie went to three games and although the Toffees won through in a second replay, the

Third Division side had earned two 0-0 draws against the eventual cup winners. It was these games that persuaded Norwich to move. They obtained his services, but the actual £135,000 transfer fee was set by a tribunal. Gillingham thought that they had been short-changed – and as things turned out, they were. On arrival at Carrow Road Sir Arthur South, who was then the Canaries' chairman, was to ask Steve if he really thought that he was worth the money!

Bruce joined a club bristling with talent; Dave Watson (the two would be opposing captains in an FA Cup final just over 10 years later), John Deehan, Asa Hartford, Mick Channon and Chris Woods were on the books. However, the City coaching staff which included boss Ken Brown and his assistant Mel Machin, made it clear to Steve that he was overweight and not fit enough for top-level football. Steve duly spent the pre-season running and running; he was also introduced to a healthier diet. The benefits became obvious to Steve when the season began, and he felt as good as he ever had whilst playing.

Steve's debut was one he will never forget. The Canaries were at home to Liverpool on a humid August day. Carrow Road was packed, and there was a great atmosphere for the visit of a Reds team who had won a treble of league, European Cup and League Cup months earlier. With barely a minute gone the visitors attacked down the wing, with debutant Paul Walsh whipping in a cross. Steve, eager to impress, went for the ball and threw himself head-first – only to see the ball flash past goalkeeper Chris Woods. For a few seconds the ground fell into silence, as a stunned home crowd couldn't quite believe what they had just seen. This was no deflection or ricochet – this was a full-on powerful diving header that gave Woods no chance, and would have been proudly claimed by any centre-forward. It was a baptism of fire, and Bruce could have crumbled – but he was determined to show the Norwich fans that he was worth the money their chairman had spent. He recovered well, and helped the team come from two goals down to earn a 3-3 draw.

Barely six months after joining the club, Steve was playing at

Wembley in a League Cup final against Sunderland. City came out 1-0 winners, giving him his first senior winner's medal, as well as a silver salver for man of the match. This wasn't Steve's first appearance at a Wembley Cup final. In 1974 Newcastle United played Manchester City in the same competition, and Steve had been chosen as one of the six lads from the Newcastle Boys' side to provide the ball boys.

Just a year after their Wembley triumph, Norwich allowed Dave Watson to return to his home city of Liverpool to join Everton, who had just finished as runners-up in league and cup. Bruce was duly named as Norwich's new club captain. Steve was also recognised internationally, called up for the England 'B' squad to play Malta. England boss Bobby Robson had just appointed Graham Taylor to take over the 'B' team from Howard Wilkinson, and when Taylor announced the side, he made Bruce's heart swell with pride when he noted that he would be captain. As quickly as Steve rose to dizzy heights, he fell crashing to earth as Taylor followed his announcement by adding that this was not his decision – it had been decided before he had anything to do with the squad.

Why Taylor chose to make such a remark has never been answered, nor what he had against Steve Bruce as a player. Even though Steve did not let the comments affect his performance, captaining the side to a 4-0 victory, Taylor did not consider him good enough for his next squad. Later in life Bobby Robson apologised for not giving him a full cap, but as soon as Taylor took over the running of the national side Steve knew his chances of making the full international side had all but evaporated.

Another Englishman who was managing an international side did ask about his availability. Jack Charlton, who was managing the Republic of Ireland, found out that Steve's mum was Irish and offered him the chance to pull on the green shirt. Steve would have jumped at the opportunity but, unfortunately for him, he had already played for England in a UEFA youth tournament, and was therefore ineligible to represent any other country at senior level. History has gone on to show what a great player Bruce was, and what an addition he would have been to England.

It has also shown us what kind of international manager Taylor was.

Things started to change dramatically for Bruce's club career in November 1987. Norwich were struggling for top-flight survival and the board had lost patience with manager Ken Brown, relieving him of his duties. Dave Stringer was appointed as the new manager, but he soon found out that Alex Ferguson was casting admiring glances in Bruce's direction. Steve had negotiated a clause in his contract that meant he had to be informed if any big clubs showed interest. Norwich told him that United had tabled a bid of £700,000, but the club was holding out for £1m. Steve was then informed that Chelsea were also interested in him, as well as Tottenham. However, Steve's mind was made up – he wasn't interested in going anywhere other than Old Trafford.

Alex Ferguson had not long taken the United job. The team was in transition, and was not performing. Ron Atkinson had taken his eye off the ball, and become too close to his players. Ferguson arrived in November 1986, and it was something of a culture shock to them. One of the problems he encountered was in central defence. It shouldn't have been the case because the two incumbents, Kevin Moran and Paul McGrath, were as good a pairing as you could find in the First Division. However, both were injury prone, and McGrath also had off-field problems. In reserve, there was only young Scotsman Graeme Hogg and Salfordian Billy Garton. Ferguson tried combinations of all four over an 18-month period, but he wasn't getting what he wanted from them.

There was a lot of Brinksmanship between United and Norwich over a deal for Bruce, and at one point Ferguson phoned the defender to tell him he was pulling out as he felt that he was being messed around. Chelsea and Tottenham were offering Bruce more money, but his heart was set on a move north and he finally got his wish. Ferguson brought Steve Bruce for a fee of £800,000. In just four years, Bruce had moved from tiny Gillingham to the biggest club in the country, while Norwich City had made a tidy profit on their initial outlay.

What ultimately attracted Ferguson to Bruce? There's no doubt that in addition to being a terrific defender who could also weigh in with his fair share of goals, a capacity for hard work and determination to succeed, Ferguson saw that he was also a leader. At the time, Bruce was almost 27 – and approaching his footballing prime.

When Bruce arrived, it must have been difficult to adapt. There were strong characters in the dressing room. Bryan Robson was skipper, while there was also goalkeeper Chris Turner, Gordon Strachan, Norman Whiteside, Paul McGrath, Kevin Moran, Viv Anderson and Brian McClair. He'd arrived in December 1987, and by the end of the season had played alongside all four of the other centre-backs – Moran, Hogg, McGrath and Garton. With the talent available at the club, it was evident to him that the team had been underperforming.

Ferguson had begun to rebuild. He reorganised the club's scouting structure, and began to analyse the senior players. There was a drinking culture, and it took Ferguson time to rid the club of the issue. Some of the players he inherited were also past their best. Towards the end of his first season in charge he sold Peter Barnes, Mark Higgins, John Sivebaek, Terry Gibson and Frank Stapleton, whilst Gary Bailey had his contract cancelled due to injury. In came Anderson, McClair and then Steve Bruce. The following season, 1988/89, Remi Moses was forced to retire due to injury, while the following players were allowed to leave: Arthur Albiston, Graeme Hogg, Kevin Moran, Chris Turner, Jesper Olsen, Peter Davenport and Liam O'Brien. In came Jim Leighton, Mark Hughes, Lee Sharpe, Mal Donaghy and the infamous Ralph Milne.

Steve's move went through on 17th December 1987, and he travelled with the team to play against Portsmouth. The side that day was:

Turner, Duxbury, Gibson, Bruce, Moran, Moses, Robson, Strachan, McClair, Whiteside, Olsen.

It was a debut that he will never forget. Not only did he give away a penalty, he also broke his nose. United won 2-1, and that is when Steve got his first taste of his new manager's standards. Having reached the changing room, he was expecting everyone to be happy – but when

Ferguson got in he was fuming. The team had been sloppy, they had not passed the ball well and they had not played "The Manchester United way". This was a culture shock for Steve, coming from a team who were just happy to win to a team who had to win with style. The next away game was at Newcastle, so Steve's family didn't have far to travel to watch him. They were probably very happy with the 1-0 home win.

Steve made his home debut against champions Everton in what was always a highly competitive game. Things went well for Steve – United won 2-1, and at the end of the game he made a last-ditch tackle to prevent Graeme Sharp from scoring a certain equaliser. The Old Trafford faithful had come to see their new signing, and they liked what they saw.

Ferguson was searching for a blend, but he knew that it would take time and that he would have to offload the driftwood that wasn't performing. The fans were restless because, as they saw it, no progress was being made. The team seemed to be treading water. In 1988/89 gates fell steadily until towards the end of the season, the club was struggling to attract 30,000. Gordon Strachan was allowed to join Leeds, and before the following season began both Norman Whiteside and Paul McGrath left, for Everton and Aston Villa respectively. Ferguson's patience with the players' off-the-field indiscretions had disintegrated.

Mike Phelan, Neil Webb, Paul Ince, Danny Wallace and a gangly centre-half from Middlesbrough named Gary Pallister were brought in. The signing of Pallister was to prove perfect for Bruce. Initially, Pallister had a rough time adjusting to the rigours of the First Division, but once he had settled he blossomed. The central pairing of Bruce and Pallister was as good as anything that has ever played at the club.

Steve also came out of his shell. Gone were the dressing room personalities from when he had arrived, and he was now one of the more senior players. Bryan Robson was still club captain, and Steve watched and learned from him. The club now had a better feel to it, and the players bonded more easily. Despite the improvement in camaraderie, United's league form in 1989/90 was indifferent – and the fans were not happy.

By the turn of the year there were more than a few, supporters and media critics alike, calling for Ferguson's head. However, in the FA Cup, their form was a different matter. After winning every tie away from home, they met Second Division Oldham in the semi-final at Maine Road.

The first game was a classic, an end-to-end clash which finished in a 3-3 draw. The replay saw United edge through 2-1, booking a clash with Crystal Palace in the final. The Wembley showpiece was memorable for a number of things – a 3-3 draw after extra time being one of them. Jim Leighton endured an uncertain performance in goal, while centre-forward Ian Wright came off the Palace bench to lead United a merry dance – Bruce and Pallister in particular – scoring twice.

For the replay at Wembley, Ferguson dropped a bombshell by leaving Leighton out and in came the effervescent Les Sealey. United ended up lifting the trophy with a 1-0 win, and it was a happy Steve Bruce who jogged around the old stadium with a winner's medal clutched in his hand. It was the start of a fabulous five-year period for the Geordie.

The following season proved another successful one for United in the cups, culminating with the club winning the European Cup-Winners' Cup. United were underdogs when matched with Barcelona. However, a superb team performance saw them triumph 2-1, with two goals from Mark Hughes. The game had been goalless for 66 minutes when Bryan Robson chipped a free-kick into the area. Steve saw the Barcelona keeper Busquets coming towards the ball, and managed to get his head to it first. His header lobbed over the goalkeeper and towards goal, and to this day Steve maintains that the ball was over the line when Hughes did what all good strikers do, following the ball in and smashing it home.

There was no doubt about Hughes's second though, as he rounded the keeper and blasted home from a tight angle. Ronald Koeman pulled one back with 11 minutes to go and United started to feel the pressure. Steve nearly gave a goal away as his dreadful back pass only found Michael Laudrup. The Dane beat goalkeeper Les Sealey and he darted towards goal – only to see Clayton Blackmore clear the ball off the line.

The final whistle went and United had won, inspired by a defensive performance in which Bruce and Pallister were major contributors. The team had finally come together, and the 1991/92 season was eagerly awaited. It should not be forgotten that in that 1990/91 campaign Steve scored 19 goals, a post-war record for a defender that still stands today.

In the summer of 1991, Alex Ferguson made one of the most astute signings of his managerial career. He paid £600,000 to Danish club Brondby for the services of 27-year-old goalkeeper Peter Schmeichel. It was another piece in the jigsaw of finding the team that would bring back the much-coveted First Division title, and throughout the 1991/92 season it looked as though United would end their 25-year drought.

Though the team had endured disappointing results in the European Cup-Winners' Cup and the FA Cup, they did reach Wembley again, triumphing 1-0 in the League Cup final against Nottingham Forest. This was a memorable occasion for Bruce, as he stood in as skipper in place of the injured Bryan Robson, and lifted his first trophy at Wembley.

However, there was bitter disappointment as far as the league title was concerned, as United lost three of their last four games to virtually hand the title to Leeds United. The final away game of the season was at Anfield, and the 2-0 defeat to Liverpool was a bitter pill to swallow, the final nail in United's coffin. It was a painful experience for the players – and one they would learn from.

The inaugural Premier League season began poorly, as United lost 2-1 at Sheffield United and then 3-0 at home to Everton. However, that 1992/93 season was memorable for a number of reasons. The team kept 17 clean sheets in their 42 league games, with the "golden triangle" of Schmeichel, Bruce, and Pallister key factors. It was also the season that saw Steve take over the team captaincy from the legendary Bryan Robson. Robson had been club captain for almost 10 years and he had been inspirational for both United and England. He was the most respected player in the United dressing room, but age (he was then 35) and the effects of numerous injuries had finally caught up with him.

Bruce had become the elder statesman of the dressing room and his leadership qualities shone through – he was Robson's natural successor, and Ferguson had recognised this.

In November 1992 Ferguson surprised everybody by signing the enigmatic Eric Cantona from Leeds United. It was the final piece in the jigsaw, and the catalyst that was needed to push the United team on to greater achievements, more than fans or the sporting press could ever have imagined. In later years, Bruce was to say of Cantona: "In my entire life, I've never seen anyone with a presence like his. When he walked into a room, it went a deathly quiet. But the lads loved him because of his humility. He was different to the rest of us."

The title run-in became a two-horse race between United and Aston Villa. One of the pivotal moments came on 10th April 1993 in a home game against Sheffield Wednesday. Trailing 1-0 and with time running out, six minutes of stoppage time was added on due to an injury to referee Mike Peck. He pulled a calf muscle and could not carry on, so linesman John Hilditch replaced him halfway through the match.

Within a minute of taking over, the official awarded Sheffield Wednesday a penalty as Paul Ince challenged Chris Waddle. John Sheridan, who scored the winner that beat United in the 1991 League Cup final and who was a United supporter himself, stepped up and scored, leaving Old Trafford shell-shocked. A year previous United had lost the league to Leeds by 'bottling it', starting with a home defeat to Nottingham Forest – now it appeared it could be happening again.

The score remained the same until the second minute of added time when Bruce headed home Denis Irwin's corner from beyond the penalty spot. Most teams would have settled for a point – but not United. They pushed on in search of a winner and minutes later Gary Pallister found himself on the wing. His attempted cross took a deflection off Nigel Worthington and looped into the box. The ball was met by a charging Bruce, determined to get to it first. His header flew like a rocket beyond Chris Woods to give United a vital victory.

The scenes that followed will forever be part of United folklore, as Alex Ferguson and his assistant, Brian Kidd, took to the pitch. Kidd fell to his knees and beat the ground with his fists as they celebrated as if they had just won the league. It was fitting that Bruce scored the goals. He was a warrior, a player who did not know the meaning of defeat. His face pays testament to somebody who was prepared to put his head anywhere if it meant scoring a goal or, more often than not, saving a goal.

On Sunday 2nd May 1993, Aston Villa needed a point to at least stay in the title race when they hosted lowly Oldham Athletic at Villa Park. The players were under strict instructions not to watch the game, but to go home and rest, as they would be playing Blackburn Rovers at Old Trafford the following day. In Bruce's mock Tudor mansion in Bramhall, he sat nervously, watching and hoping. Then at around 5.45pm it was all over. Joe Royle's Latics side had surprisingly beaten Villa with an early Nick Henry goal, and United were champions.

Bruce's house became the focus for the team's celebrations, as they made their way from all corners of Manchester to his house. Peter Schmeichel, who lived in the same purpose-built cul-de-sac, was the first to arrive, but he was soon followed by team-mates Paul Parker and Paul Ince, who lived just around the corner. The party lasted all night, and those players who didn't get home were greeted in the morning by the sight of "Captain Marvel" Bryan Robson and his wife tidying the house and organising breakfast.

It was a carnival atmosphere that evening inside the stadium, with one wonderful white-haired old man sitting in the stands with a huge smile on his face. He had built a football empire, seen his boys strewn across a runway in Munich, rebuilt a team, won the European Cup and now he was witnessing his beloved United back as English champions. It was no wonder that tears filled Sir Matt Busby's eyes as the teams walked out. It was a proud Steve Bruce who led his team – and an even prouder man when he went up to receive the first Premier League trophy after United had triumphed 3-1. It said a lot for the man that he also called on Bryan Robson to be alongside him, and they jointly took hold of the trophy, to the delight of the crowd.

It was a happy club to be around and through sheer grit, determination and persistence, he drove his team-mates to greater heights. In the 1993/94 season, although United failed in the Champions League, going out to Turkish side Galatasaray on the away goals rule, Bruce became the first Englishman to lead his team to a league and FA Cup Double. United also reached the League Cup final, only to be beaten 3-1 by Aston Villa. The Manchester United team of that season was, according to the big Geordie, the finest during his time at Old Trafford, and he rattles off the names to support his argument:

"Schmeichel, Parker, Pallister, Bruce, Irwin, Kanchelskis, Keane, Ince, Giggs, Cantona, Hughes. That team could have taken on any side. If we wanted to play football, we could do that. If we wanted a fight, we were okay with that, too. With those guys, it wouldn't have mattered, they were born to win."

A few years later, in an interview with sports journalist David Walsh, he was asked to imagine that if he was shipwrecked on a desert island, which three United players would he like to have with him. "Jesus, I don't think I'd like to spend time on an island with any of them," he joked. "If I had to pick three, [Gary] Pallister would have to be one, although we'd never get off the island because he would just find a palm tree, lie under it and be happy.

"I was close to Roy Keane at United. He was young, I was a senior lad and the Premier League was just getting going, with live matches on Sunday afternoon. There were a number of times when we'd end up in each other's company in those days. I would have to have him on the island and, of course, Bryan Robson. He was always a big pal and as the elder statesman at United in my time, he would be one of the three. Robson, Pallister, Keane – yeah, I like that." You could imagine that the beach football, played with a coconut, wouldn't have been bad either!

The following season Robson was gone, to pursue a management career with Middlesbrough, and Bruce was named club captain. He led by example, and had a tremendous relationship with the manager. Bruce was a natural captain on and off the field; a friendly face for new arrivals, an old head for the younger players and a good listener for anyone with problems. That is not to say he was a soft touch: if you messed up on the pitch, you could guarantee it would not be long before you would hear Bruce's Geordie tones rollicking you. Never was this truer than with Peter Schmeichel, who was a daunting figure when he came charging out with a face bright red with anger. You could guarantee that at least once a game he and Bruce would have a disagreement. Steve was never afraid to let the great Dane know what he thought.

It was obvious to anyone who met Steve that he knew just how lucky he was to be playing for United, let alone captaining them. He always felt he had a sense of responsibility to the supporters, to always fight to the very end for the cause. It is an ethos that the club has become famous for, and no player was a better example of this than Bruce.

The 1994/95 season was seen by many as a massive disappointment. United failed to win a third consecutive Premier League crown after being held at West Ham United on the final day of the season, while six days later they also lost the FA Cup to Joe Royle's "Dogs of War" Everton side. In Europe, the team had also again been hampered by UEFA's rule concerning foreign players.

Just before the start of the season, the English transfer record had been broken when Blackburn paid £5m for 21-year-old Norwich striker Chris Sutton. It was a mark that was to last until the following January as United paid £6m for Newcastle's Andy Cole, in a deal which also saw £1m-rated Keith Gillespie move the other way. United had also bought David May from Blackburn in the summer, to offer some competition – and back-up – for the centre-half position. But it was not a new signing that shaped United's season, or the destination of the Premier League trophy. It was a cold, wet night on 25th January 1995 at Selhurst Park.

United were playing Crystal Palace, when Eric Cantona was sent off for a vengeful kick at defender Richard Shaw after Shaw had pulled the striker's shirt. As Cantona walked towards the tunnel, Crystal Palace supporter Matthew Simmons ran down the steps of the stand to get close and abuse Eric. What happened next was every United supporters' Kennedy assassination moment. They can all tell you where they were when they saw the incident – and every one of them has a theory about it. Cantona flew into the crowd and directed a kung fu-style kick into Simmons's chest. He then followed this up with a few punches.

The club consulted with the Football Association and, in accordance with their wishes, suspended Cantona for the remaining four months of the season. They were given the impression that this would be sufficient, but the FA and particularly the chief executive, Graham Kelly, appeared to succumb to media pressure and increased the ban to eight months. It is a testament to the strength of the United squad that the loss didn't completely throw them off the quest for honours, and they maintained a league and FA Cup challenge. Unfortunately the title slipped away at Upton Park, when a win would have given them the title as table-topping Blackburn lost 2-1 at Liverpool. There was even more frustration a week later in the FA Cup final when they lost 1-0 to Everton.

There was controversy over the close season as the sales of Mark Hughes, Paul Ince and Andrei Kanchelskis were announced, yielding £14m. The fans' frustration was compounded when the new season approached without a major signing being made and increasing uncertainty over the future of Eric Cantona, who was linked with a move to join Ince at Inter Milan. What neither Alan Hansen or any United supporter had any idea about was the quality of the youngsters Ferguson was putting his faith in. What he had in Bruce was a captain who would help guide them to success.

Unfortunately, Bruce was not fit for the opening game of the season at Villa Park. The team that day lined up as:

Schmeichel, Parker, Irwin, Gary Neville, Pallister (O'Kane, 59), Sharpe, Butt, Keane, McClair, Scholes, Phil Neville (Beckham, 45).

United were soundly beaten 3-1 by Aston Villa, prompting *Match of the Day* pundit Hansen to make a comment that will haunt him to his grave: "You'll win nothing with kids." Obviously Ferguson knew more about them than Hansen and with Bruce back in the side, United were unbeaten in their next 10 league fixtures, the run only ended with a 1-0 defeat at Arsenal thanks to an early Dennis Bergkamp strike. From then until Christmas, United's patchy away form prevented them making the running, while an exuberant, attacking Newcastle side, managed by Kevin Keegan, was leading the way. The sides met on 27th December, with the Magpies 10 points ahead in the league. A 2-0 win for United reduced the gap to seven points, and two days later they beat QPR 2-1 to close to four points. It seemed that the wheels had come off when United lost 4-1 at Tottenham on New Year's Day, and then drew 0-0 with Aston Villa, allowing Newcastle to establish a 12-point lead in January.

A run of 13 wins from their remaining 16 league fixtures saw United storm to the title. Alex Ferguson's side had travelled to Newcastle in early March, and a goal by Eric Cantona – and inspired goalkeeping by Schmeichel – helped United to a 1-0 win, cutting the Magpies' advantage to a point. The pressure was beginnng to tell on Keegan. In the run-in Ferguson suggested that teams were making less of an effort to beat Newcastle, to ensure United didn't win the league. The claims prompted Keegan's famous "I'd love it if we beat them. Love it!" outburst in a live post-match interview with *Sky Sports*. However, as the season was closing, Bruce was becoming a peripheral figure.

With one game left of the league season, United led by two points. For Newcastle to win their first title since 1927, they had to beat Tottenham and hope Middlesbrough defeated their Mancunian rivals. The momentum was with United though, and they easily defeated Boro 3-0 whilst the Magpies could only manage a 1-1 draw with Spurs. Although not selected for the team or named on the bench, it was Bruce who went up to collect his third Premier League trophy – and third winner's medal. It was to be the last time that fans would see him as a United player.

Six days later United faced Liverpool in the FA Cup final without Bruce in the starting line-up, or on the bench. Roy Evans's side had walked out for a pre-match walkabout wearing ludicrous cream designer suits, and were desperate not to allow United a second league and FA Cup Double since the start of the Premier League era. They would have loved nothing more than to inflict United's second consecutive FA Cup final defeat at Merseyside hands. Luckily for United, Liverpool goalkeeper David James chose the occasion to live up to his billing as "Calamity James" by weakly punching a late United corner towards a lurking Eric Cantona on the edge of the area. Cantona did what Cantona did best, striking the ball off-balance but with technical perfection – on the half volley through a crowd of players – into the back of the net. The striker was captaining the side that day and tried to persuade Bruce to go up and collect the trophy, but Bruce gently – but firmly – refused.

David May had been brought in as Bruce's long-term replacement – and his pay packet reflected this plan. He was earning considerably more than Bruce and when United's club captain attempted to have his contract renewed on favourable terms, he did not get the response he was looking for. Knowing that first-team chances were now limited, he was allowed to drop down a league to join Birmingham on a free. The deal was reportedly worth £2m over two years – a contract that would have made him one of the highest-paid players in the First Division.

Was he a good club captain? He was the perfect man for the clubs' transition of introducing the youngsters and as with so many captains, he was a reflection of his manager on the pitch. His never-say-die attitude spread through the club, a mentality evident in the 1995/96 season when United clawed back a 12-point deficit to catch Newcastle. Bruce may have been born a Geordie and Newcastle may have been his boyhood club, but there is no doubt which club is in his heart – Manchester United. He is now carving out a managerial career at the top level and you can guarantee that if the chance ever came to manage his old club, he would crawl over broken glass to get there.

Collars, Seagulls and Gallic Genius. The French King

ERIC CANTONA
1996-1997

*'It was a testament to the faith shown in the Frenchman
by Alex Ferguson and everybody at United that he had
single-handedly gone about dragging his team back into
the title race with his goals in tight games'*

In 2000, the official Manchester United magazine invited its readers to vote on their top Reds player of all time. *Manchester United's 100 Greatest Players* was published the following year. The list contained all the greats who have graced United's history, but the fans voted the number one player of the last century as Eric Daniel Pierre Cantona. Of course, there will be older supporters who would say he was no Edwards, and that he couldn't hold a candle to Best – but what he was, was Cantona! And that brought a special magic to the club, lifting them from being "almost-rans" to champions. He did it with a style and arrogance that made him a hero from the minute he walked out onto the pitch, with his collar high, looking around as if to say: 'I am big enough for Manchester United – is Manchester United big enough for me?'

There are some United fans who believe that Eric Cantona was born in a stable with three wise men present, but the truth is a little different, if a tad strange. Cantona was born on 24th May 1966 in a cave in one of the hills in the Caillols area of Marseille. It was Eric's paternal grandmother who, during the summer of 1955, discovered the cave up in the hills and decided to buy it. By the time Eric was born the cave was only one room in the house, with the rest of the building above it. It was a home that contained all the Cantona family – grandparents Lucienne and Joseph, parents Albert and Eleonore and children Jean-Marie, who is four years older than Eric, and Joël, who is 17 months younger. They were not wealthy, but they had the sunshine, the sea and each other.

The three brothers were close and played football everyday. At the infant school of Caillols and at the Grande Bastide Secondary School in Mazargue, they made an effective trio. Eric also played for SO Caillolais, who had produced French superstar Jean Tigana. The club was based in the Marseille suburbs, 10 minutes from the centre. It provided training and games for boys aged five to 15. Eric would later say that he learnt just as much from playing in the streets with his peers.

Eric started playing as a goalkeeper, just like his father before him. This arrangement did not last long though as Eric was given the opportunity to play up field at an Under-12s tournament in Cannes. Caillolais won, and Cantona was voted player of the tournament. He played over 200 games in the blue and yellow of his childhood club, and was only on the losing side a handful of times. Eric scored hundreds of goals for his club, mostly against boys a lot older than himself. There are those who believe Eric may have benefited more if he had played for a lesser team. Defeats were rare for Caillolais and Eric never got used to the taste of failure, or how to handle it. That, along with his parents' indulgence, led to an individual who believed he was going to win every time he played. When things did not go his way, he struggled to deal with it.

When Cantona was 14 professional clubs began to show an interest, and it seemed that Nice would win his signature. He went for a trial and at the end of it asked if he could have a pennant and a shirt for himself. He came home disappointed, as the club insisted that if he wanted the souvenirs, he would have to pay for them. Things could not have been more different when he went to Auxerre, 400 miles from his family home, as he returned loaded down with gifts and shirts. A small gesture perhaps, and maybe Nice arrogantly thought the same – after all, they were a successful club while Auxerre were mere newcomers. But, as it would prove in Cantona's career, he needed to feel wanted and loved –

and that is what Auxerre had done. Eric's family tried their hardest to get him to sign for Nice, as it was based not far from the family house, but his mind was made up and he would not budge: he was joining Auxerre.

The 15-year-old Cantona made the long trip up to Auxerre, and quickly settled in. Several weeks earlier Cantona had been selected to play for the French schoolboy team, and Auxerre were aware that they had found someone special. Eric made swift progress and in the spring of 1982 manager Guy Roux decided to play the reserves – including Cantona – against the first team. Still only 15, he tortured the first-team defenders and left everyone in no doubt that here was a player for the future.

Prior to the 1982 World Cup, France played a friendly against Bulgaria. The game was preceded by a curtain raiser between France's Under-17s and their Switzerland counterparts, which saw Eric score the winner. People were now realising that Auxerre had uncovered a star, and it was only a matter of time as to when he would make his debut. They would not have to wait long. Eric made his bow against Nancy on 5th November 1983. The team eased to a 4-0 victory and though Eric failed to score, he could not have been happier with his performance.

In France, young men were still required to complete National Service – and it was no different for Eric. Those of you picturing a young Cantona square bashing or going on long marches are going to be disappointed. Eric joined the Joinville Battalion, made up of the country's top sportsmen. Based at Fontainebleau near Paris, Eric enjoyed a year playing football for the Army team, as well as Auxerre, and also spent a lot of time sleeping in the day – and partying at night. They were allowed to do pretty much whatever they liked, often displaying acts of indiscipline that would get a normal soldier a couple of nights behind bars. This was not healthy living; they saw no need for recuperation, or preparation, no need for healthy diet and plenty of rest. Fortunately for Auxerre – and for Eric – National Service only lasted 12 months.

The 1985/86 season did not start well for Cantona. It should have been his breakthrough, as an opportunity came for him to be the club's centre-forward, but a viral infection sidelined him and gave Roger Boli, brother of French international Basile, the chance to shine. The striker helped the side defeat AC Milan 3-1 in a UEFA Cup game also notable for being Paolo Maldini's European debut. Eric returned for the second leg, but it was a disappointing display that saw his team lose 3-0. Several days after the defeat boss Guy Roux approached Eric, and suggested that a loan to Second Division side Martigues might help him develop quicker. This may seem like a strange thing to do with a club's brightest hope, but Roux always took an interest in his players. He knew Eric had fallen for a girl named Isabelle, who lived near Martigues, and it was obvious his thoughts were with her. Eric spent the season with Isabelle and when he returned to Auxerre, she came with him.

Happy with his life off the field, Eric made a huge impact on his return, repaying the faith that had been shown in him. He was also recognised nationally, making a scoring debut for France's Under-21s in a 4-1 thrashing of Hungary, and he also helped them to success in the 1988 European U21 Championship. He was becoming France's first celebrity footballer, and began to appear in the country's weekly news magazine *Paris Match*. His selection for the senior side soon followed, and it seemed that his footballing dreams were coming true.

Inevitably Cantona was outgrowing Auxerre, and bigger French clubs lined up to win his signature. But who could afford him? The answer was Olympique Marseille, with Eric returning to his boyhood team for a French record fee of around £2.2m in the summer of 1988.

It was at the Stade Velodrome that the demons that have followed Eric throughout his career began to surface. Cantona had already shown signs of a short fuse, and in January 1989 he lapsed again. During a friendly with Torpedo Moscow, he kicked the ball at the crowd, ripped off and then threw his jersey after being substituted. His club duly banned him for a month. Just months earlier, he'd also been suspended from the national side for a year after insulting the France coach on TV: "I will never play for France again as long as Henri Michel is manager. It's a choice between Michel and myself. I would like it to be known that I think he is one of the most incompetent managers in world football. I am not far from thinking that he is a s***bag." These were the thoughts of a 22-year-old Cantona, at odds with the national team boss.

It was too much for Marseille and they sent him to Bordeaux on a six-month loan, and then to Montpellier on a year-long agreement for the 1989/90 season. At Montpellier he was involved in a fight with team-mate Jean-Claude Lemoult, and threw his boots in Lemoult's face. The incident led to six players demanding that Cantona be sacked. However, with the support of team-mates such as Laurent Blanc and Carlos Valderrama, the club retained him – though banned him for 10 days.

On the field Cantona was at least able to inspire the club to success, being instrumental in his side's French Cup victory, and his form persuaded Marseille to take him back. Having been welcomed back, Cantona initially played well under coach Gerard Gili and his successor, Franz Beckenbauer. However, chairman Bernard Tapie was hard to please, and replaced Beckenbauer with Raymond Goethals, with whom Cantona did not see eye-to-eye. Cantona was also at odds with Tapie and despite helping the team win their third successive league title, he was transferred to Nimes the following season for around £1m.

In December 1991, during a match for his new club he threw the ball at the referee, having been angered by one of his decisions. He was subsequently summoned to a disciplinary hearing by the French Football Federation, and banned for one month. Cantona responded by walking up to each member of the hearing committee and, in turn, called each of them an "idiot." His ban was duly increased to three months. For Cantona, this was the final straw and he announced his retirement.

Fortunately for Eric and for English football, national manager and French football legend Michel Platini was a keen fan of Cantona, and persuaded him to make a comeback. Platini knew Trevor Francis, the then Sheffield Wednesday manager, and recommended Cantona to him. So negotiations began to bring Eric to England, with a potential loan deal mooted. Eric came for a week's trial, with Francis seeing it as an opportunity to get to know the player, as well as assessing his talents. Having enjoyed two indoor sessions, Francis had still to make up his mind. He asked Cantona to extend the trial for another week, an offer that was declined, and he duly returned to his homeland. He was not there for long, though. Howard Wilkinson, manager of Leeds, was on the phone and keen to sign Eric – and the adventure was about to begin.

Eric joined for a £100,000 loan fee at the end of January 1992, with the figure due to rise to £1m should they choose to make the move permanent. The club, who had returned to the top flight the previous season, were challenging United for the title. Eric played only 15 games for Leeds that season, completing 90 minutes only five times, but his impact was immeasurable. Eric made his debut on 8th February at Oldham, a game Leeds lost 2-0. But by the end of that month, Eric had scored his first goal and the supporters had a new hero as the chants of "Ooh Aah Cantona" rang out around Elland Road.

Cantona, who had insisted upon signing that his aim was to be "champion of England in May", duly achieved his ambition a few days shy of his target, as United faltered. Eric then went off with favourites France for the 1992 European Championship in Sweden, although he was to suffer disappointment as they bowed out at the group phase.

It wasn't long before he was back with Leeds, preparing for the first Premier League season having completed a permanent move. The preseason FA Charity Shield curtain-raiser at Wembley saw Leeds collect further silverware as they saw off FA Cup winners Liverpool 4-3, with Eric scoring a hat-trick. It seemed that Leeds were continuing to improve and in Cantona, they had a genuine world-class player. Things could not look better for the Yorkshire club – but it wouldn't last.

Wilkinson had the nickname "Sergeant Major", and liked things to be done his way. He did not care for stars, believing in the collective team ethic. He was uncomfortable with the adulation that Cantona received, and thought that he should contribute more to team play rather than show touches of individual brilliance. Wilkinson was determined to show Cantona that things had to be done his way, and decided to leave him out for some games to prove his point. The final straw came when Cantona wasn't selected against Arsenal, a game which Leeds won 3-0. Wilkinson believed the result vindicated his decision, but all it did was push Eric over the edge. Eric refused to turn up for training the following Tuesday, and a transfer request was faxed to the club in which Eric stated that he wished to move to either Liverpool, United or Arsenal.

In 1990, United had won the FA Cup, the first trophy of Alex Ferguson's tenure, a near four-year period that had been turbulent to say the least. The job of rebuilding the squad was the mammoth task he faced upon his appointment in 1986, and the fans were of the opinion that four years was more than enough time to accomplish this. They had begun to show a restlessness and frustration with what they perceived to be a lack of significant progress. Certain sections of the crowd were calling for him to be fired in that 1989/90 season. However, the United board, knowing what was happening behind the scenes, gave him the thing that he needed most – time. Winning that FA Cup was the event which proved the igniter for the success that was to follow.

Ferguson built his team based on some astute transfer dealings, combining a mixture of youth and experience. In 1991 the European Cup-Winners' Cup was won in Rotterdam against favourites Barcelona. The following season, United had triumphed in the European Super Cup against Red Star Belgrade, and in the League Cup against Nottingham Forest. However, after seemingly having the First Division title sown up, they slipped up in the run-in and allowed Leeds to pip them over the last few games. It was a bitter pill to swallow, having been so near, yet so far.

The squad that Ferguson had built was impressive. Added to skipper Bryan Robson and youth products Clayton Blackmore, Ryan Giggs and son Darren Ferguson, he had brought in goalkeeper Peter Schmeichel, defenders Denis Irwin, Mal Donaghy, Steve Bruce and Gary Pallister; midfielders Paul Ince, Neil Webb, Mike Phelan, Andrei Kanchelskis and Lee Sharpe; and strikers Mark Hughes (for a second spell) and Brian McClair. During the summer of 1992, Ferguson had further strengthened his forward line by acquiring Dion Dublin from Cambridge after missing out on Southampton's rising star, Alan Shearer.

On the opening day of the inaugural Premier League season, 15th August 1992, United faced Sheffield United at Bramall Lane – and lost 2-1. They also lost 3-0 at home to Everton the following Wednesday evening. The third game, at home to Ipswich, was drawn 1-1 and there then followed five consecutive league victories against Southampton, Nottingham Forest, Crystal Palace, Leeds United and Everton.

Sadly, in the game against Crystal Palace at Old Trafford, Dublin broke a leg and it would be six months before he played again. The striking department was left wanting again, and this could be seen from the results that followed their victory at Everton in mid-September. In the UEFA Cup they drew both games against Torpedo Moscow 0-0, and went out by losing on penalty-kicks. In the League Cup United were paired with Brighton and drew 1-1 at the Goldstone Ground, edging through 1-0 at Old Trafford in the second leg. Five consecutive league draws followed, against Tottenham (1-1), QPR (0-0), Middlesbrough (1-1), Liverpool (2-2) and Blackburn (0-0). Following this there was a 1-0 loss to Aston Villa in the League Cup, and two more consecutive defeats in the league to Wimbledon and Aston Villa – both 1-0 score-lines. By mid-November and after the Villa game, United were down in 10th position in the league, eight points behind leaders Arsenal.

United were not scoring enough, an issue that had hindered them in the second half of the previous season, costing them the title. The final two games of November 1992 were at home to Oldham and away to leaders Arsenal. Two wins – 3-0 and 1-0 respectively – were recorded, with the result at Highbury propelling United into fifth although they were now nine points behind the new shock leaders, Norwich City. At that point in the season United had played 17 games but had only scored 18 goals, conceding 12 in the process. League titles were not going to be won with such a goal ratio: Ferguson was pondering his next move.

It was a wet Wednesday afternoon in Manchester, November 1992. Alex Ferguson and Martin Edwards were sat in the chairman's office discussing players they would like to sign. A £3.5m bid for Sheffield Wednesday's David Hirst had been turned down, and the club were also considering Peter Beardsley, who was at Everton. One name that did crop up was that of Eric Cantona. Gerard Houllier was a good friend of Ferguson. When he was manager of Paris St Germain, he had mentioned Cantona and had sung his praises. In early September, United had beaten Leeds 2-0 at Old Trafford but both central defenders, Steve Bruce and Gary Pallister, had raved about the qualities of the Frenchman. He'd apparently pulled them all over the place, and in Bruce's own words: "We couldn't get close to him."

As Edwards and Ferguson continued to talk over potential targets, the telephone rang. Uncannily it was Bill Fotherby, the Leeds chairman, who was enquiring as to whether United would be willing to sell Denis Irwin to them. Irwin had initially started as a pro at Leeds, before moving on to Oldham. After playing against United in the FA Cup semi-final in 1990, Ferguson had signed him and the Irish full-back had blossomed. Of course, Fotherby's enquiry was rebuffed but in the course of the conversation, Edwards probed him about some of the Leeds players that they would be willing to allow to leave. Ferguson took a piece of paper off Edwards' desk and scribbled something on it, before passing it over to his chairman. When Edwards looked at it the name 'Eric Cantona' was written. Looking at Ferguson, he saw the manager mouth the words "ask about him". Surprisingly, they were given an encouraging response, as it seemed that it only needed Wilkinson's agreement for the deal to happen. Half-an-hour later Fotherby was on the phone and Cantona was sold to United for £1.2m. Ferguson contacted his assistant Brian Kidd, and told him the news. When Kidd found out the price, he asked in astonishment: "For that money? Has he lost a leg?"

Word spread like wildfire as supporters rang their friends to ask them if they had heard the news. Equal to the joy felt on the west side of the Pennines was the anger felt in Yorkshire, as Leeds supporters couldn't believe the news. The pain of selling him was bad enough, but to one of the club's fiercest rivals as well, was a double whammy. Not everyone was convinced, though. Former England captain Emlyn Hughes wrote in his *Daily Mirror* column that, 'he's a flashy foreigner who will score for United when they are two-up', while Leeds legend Johnny Giles, who billed himself as the man the players read, said: 'He is a great entertainer. But there has never been any mention of Cantona as a great player. And I don't think he is.' Hughes, Giles and other detractors would be forced to eat their words as he proved them wrong almost instantly.

When Eric joined United they were in sixth place, nine points off the top. In Cantona, Ferguson believed he had bought a solution to the club's goalscoring problems. As soon as he saw him on the training pitch at The Cliff he knew he was on to a winner. As the training session ended and the players made their way to the showers, Eric asked for a couple of young players so that he could do some extra practice. Eric obviously believed that he was naturally gifted as a footballer, and the more he practiced the more naturally gifted he became. For youngsters like Beckham, Scholes, Butt and the Nevilles this was ideal schooling. Ferguson talked about Eric in training, and praised him for his attitude:

"He's the best prepared footballer I've ever had. He's first at the training ground, he does his own warm-up and then he does our warm-up. He trains brilliantly, and then he practices after training and he's the last to leave the car park, signing autographs. He's happy to do hospital visits whenever you ask him. He's a model pro, a dream footballer."

It was obvious that Ferguson, a master at man-management, knew how to handle Eric. The fact that neither was English was seen as a positive by Ferguson, who at the first press conference confirming the signing, mentioned the "Auld Alliance" – and promised a new one. The rules that he set and applied to other players, did not apply to Eric. Fergie knew what Eric wanted. "If there was ever a player who was made for

Manchester United it was Cantona," he said. "He had been searching all his life for somebody who looked at him and made him feel at home. He travelled around so many countries; there is a wee bit of gypsy about some people. But when he came here he knew: this is my place."

The Old Trafford crowd got its first sight of Eric in a red shirt on 6th December 1992 in the 117th Manchester derby. In years to come Eric would shine against United's fiercest rivals like City and Liverpool, but this was not one of those occasions. Eric sported No. 12, as he came on as substitute for the injured Ryan Giggs. United won 2-1, but Eric's contribution was minimal, save for a few nice passes. What was there from the beginning though was an acceptance from the crowd that they were witnessing someone special, someone who was born to play for United. There he stood on the touchline in front of the dugout, chest puffed out, shirt collar turned up, standing straight, surveying the scene. It was a sight that would thrill United followers regularly for the next five years. He ran onto the pitch in that glorious red shirt – and it just looked right. The turned-up collar was not a gimmick. Cantona explained: "I put my shirt on. It was a cold day. The collar stayed up so I kept it like that. We won, so it became a habit to play with my collar up."

Eric didn't have to wait long for his first goal. Six days before Christmas, United visited Chelsea. On a dreadful, muddy pitch Eric seemed to glide over the surface, and he scored the equaliser to earn a valuable point. When on Boxing Day the team came from 3-0 down with 20 minutes to go at Sheffield Wednesday, it was Cantona who scored the late equaliser. Not only was Eric scoring – so was the whole team. In the seven games before Eric made his debut United scored six goals; in the seven after his bow they found the net 18 times. Soon a team that looked like it was running out of steam in the title chase was finding fresh legs but, more importantly, it now had a brain. Everything the team did seemed to flow through the Frenchman, and the team was charging forward. Only Ron Atkinson's Aston Villa could stop them.

Eric brought a calmness that had been missing the previous season as nerves had got the better of them. It was as if the team felt like the fans, that now Cantona was a United player, it was their destiny to be champions. When it happened Eric was in the same position he had been in at Leeds, sat on a sofa watching his nearest rivals being beaten to hand his team the title. As he watched in his hotel the phone rang and he recognised the voice of Steve Bruce on the other end, demanding that he got himself over to his house in Bramhall for a celebration party.

The following evening, as the team defeated Blackburn, Eric played with a broken wrist in plaster. As the players paraded the trophy, Eric took the silverware and placed it on his head as if it was a giant, gleaming crown. It was the closest he ever got to a coronation at Old Trafford. But one thing is for sure; no King has ever been loved as much as Eric was in those heady days. It didn't just stop with the supporters – it seemed that he could get away with anything. At a civic dinner organised in the club's honour, his team-mates turned up in club-crested blazers and matching trousers. Eric made an entrance dressed in a designer silk jacket over a T-shirt. As his team-mates jokingly shouted for him to be fined, his manager just shrugged his shoulders and smiled. In his time in management, has Ferguson been so accommodating to a player? Maybe that is just as much a sign of the brilliance of Ferguson's man-management as his genuine affection for the Frenchman.

The time to strengthen is always when you are on top – and Ferguson did just that by smashing the British transfer record to prize Roy Keane from Nottingham Forest. Kenny Dalglish had also come in for the midfielder, and Blackburn had been convinced the 21-year-old was signing for them. Keane went straight into the team for the new season, that began with an FA Charity Shield win over Arsenal. It was only a half-fit Cantona who played, as he had picked up an injury for France during the summer. He should really have been left out, as he aggravated the injury and missed the first five league games. Not that United suffered without him, though. This was a different team than the nervous one Eric had joined. Here now was a side strong and confident. They were probably the most powerful United team there has ever been with a spine of Schmeichel, Bruce, Pallister, Keane, Ince, Robson, Hughes and Cantona. They would play breathtaking football, but if teams wanted to get rough and mix it, they could accomodate their style accordingly.

United started the season in all-conquering fashion, brushing aside most teams. They tasted defeat in their seventh game, 1-0 at Chelsea, but not before Eric nearly scored one of the greatest goals ever seen at Stamford Bridge. Gary Pallister hit a long ball, with Roy Keane in hot pursuit beyond the Blues' defence. Goalkeeper Dmitri Kharine rushed out of his area and bravely headed the ball back towards the halfway line and out of danger – or so he thought. The ball fell to Eric who, with his back to goal, swivelled and volleyed the ball from 40 yards, whilst the keeper scrambled towards goal. The ball dropped a couple of feet short of the goal, bounced up, hit the bar and rebounded into the arms of the relieved goalkeeper. Could any other player have done it? Would any other player even have considered trying something so audacious?

As a result of winning the championship United were now back in the European Cup – now rebranded as the UEFA Champions League. English sides were hindered on their return to European competition with UEFA's ruling that any one team could field no more than three foreign players and two 'assimilated' players (i.e. players who had lived in the country for five years and been part of the club's youth squad). What was worse for United was that Scottish, Welsh and Irish players were regarded as foreigners, which meant United's first team in domestic games sometimes contained eight 'foreigners' by UEFA's reckoning.

Having been introduced the season before, the new cup format meant two rounds of two-legged knockout games before the make up of the group phase could be decided. United were drawn with Hungarian champions Kispest Honved in round one, with the first game being played at the Bozsik Stadium on 15th September 1993. United earned a 3-2 win, with two goals from an inspired Roy Keane while Eric Cantona added a tap-in – all in the first half. The home tie a fortnight later saw

United beat the Hungarians 2-1, with Steve Bruce scoring twice.

Turkish champions Galatasaray were next up, a tie United went into full of confidence. Having enjoyed some impressive league results, it appeared they would enjoy an easy night against notoriously poor European travellers – particularly when they took a 2-0 lead through Bryan Robson and a Hakan own goal inside 15 minutes. However, the Turks hit back to level before the break, and a second Kubilay Turkyilmaz goal just after the hour put them 3-2 up, leaving United's proud unbeaten European home record in jeopardy. Then, with nine minutes left, Roy Keane lifted a hopeful ball forward – which Cantona met on the volley, to level. The 3-3 draw kept the unbeaten record intact – although realistically, a win would now be needed in the away leg.

Nothing the Manchester United players had ever been through before would prepare them for the reception they received when they touched down at Istanbul airport for the return leg. A baying mob making throat-slashing motions was waiting in the airport, and surrounded the team and the team bus. Even when they got to their hotel, employees made it clear that they would be lucky to get out alive.

The game at the Ali Sami Yen Stadium was played in an atmosphere of hate and intimidation, and Cantona missed some easy chances. The 0-0 draw saw United bow out, and as the players made their way off with missiles raining down, Cantona approached the referee and made it clear he thought the Turks had bribed him. This earned the Frenchman a red card and as he made his way down the tunnel, a policeman man-handled Eric. When he retaliated he was struck on his head by a truncheon. Bryan Robson jumped in to help, and was struck with a shield that left him needing stitches. It had been a frustrating, painful lesson.

Manchester City must have been Eric Cantona's favourite opposition as he scored in the seven Manchester derbies he started – and he never finished on the losing side. That was almost not the case as United went to Maine Road days after being knocked out. The team seemed to be suffering from a European hangover and found themselves 2-0 down at half-time, looking like they could be on the end of a hammering.

As the teams came out for the second half it was as if Eric knew that it was now time for him to step up. A mistake by Michel Vonk presented Eric with the chance to score his first – and from then on he dominated the City defence. When Ryan Giggs knocked the ball into the box Cantona was again there where it mattered to make it two for him and two for United. City were now holding on – but this United team could smell blood. Irwin and Sharpe combined on the left and Keane arrived late to slide the ball home and win the game in the last minute. This was United at their majestic best – and Eric was the fulcrum of the side.

The 1993/94 season saw a United team so dominant in the league that they looked as if they may win it by Easter, leading Ron Atkinson to comment: "The only way anyone will catch them is if we all get six points for a win and they got none." But this would not be Cantona if everything went to plan. There is a demon that lives inside him, and the only way he can deal with it is to let it out sometimes. For all the breathtaking performances he gave that season, which saw him come third in the Ballon D'or and win the PFA Player of the Year, there was also the petulant Cantona. He had been sent off in Turkey, and was then dismissed in successive league games at Swindon and Arsenal in March. The red cards saw him banned for five matches – including the FA Cup semi-final with Oldham, which United drew 1-1 to force a replay for which Cantona was available, duly helping them win 4-1.

This team was so good that it should have won every domestic trophy – but they missed out on the League Cup, losing 3-1 in the final to Aston Villa. Blackburn managed to hold on to United's coat tales in the league, but Kenny Dalglish's side could not prevent them from winning a second successive title. Now they faced Chelsea in the FA Cup final, and the chance to go down in history as a Double-winning team.

The final took place on a rainy May afternoon, and in the first half Chelsea had the better of the chances. Gavin Peacock's half volley hit the crossbar and it seemed that, as in the League Cup final, the real

Manchester United had not turned up. However, the Londoners had not taken their chances – and would pay for it.

The second half saw United take over with three goals in the space of nine minutes. On the hour Eddie Newton brought down Irwin in front of referee Mike Riley, who did not hesitate in pointing to the spot. The Chelsea players protested and as Cantona was setting himself to take the kick, Dennis Wise asked him if he fancied a £100 bet. Eric accepted the wager, and then waved Wise away with a dismissive gesture. As if on the training ground he casually stepped up and side-footed home.

Barely five minutes later Cantona repeated the feat, after United were awarded a second penalty. Mark Hughes then scored a third following a slip by Frank Sinclair, and Brian McClair scored a late fourth following an unselfish pass from Paul Ince. It was the icing on the cake – and it seemed that nothing could stop Cantona and this tremendous United side. But dark clouds and dark days lay ahead for the Frenchman.

The 1994/95 season will always be remembered for one evening at Selhurst Park. On 25th January United were playing Crystal Palace. The game was a niggly affair and Palace players were taking it in turns to try and wind Eric up. Finally he was shown a red card for a kick on Richard Shaw, after Shaw had pulled his shirt. As Eric walked towards the tunnel Matthew Simmons, a Palace supporter, ran to the bottom of the seating area of the Main Stand to shout abuse at Cantona. However, neither he, nor anybody else, could have predicted what would happen next. Eric launched a kung fu-style kick into the chest of his abuser, followed by a series of punches. Simmons was later tried for threatening language and behaviour, receiving a seven-day prison sentence – although he was released the following day. It was later revealed that Simmons had previous criminal convictions, including an attempted violent robbery. His conviction and sentence also resulted in a £500 fine, as well as a one-year ban from all football grounds in England and Wales.

Ferguson came out immediately and supported Cantona but in accordance with the FA's wishes, United fined Eric £10,800 and suspended him for the remaining months of the season. They had been led to believe that this punishment would be sufficient, but that was seemingly not taken into account when the final outcome was revealed. There was frenzied media hysteria during this period, as newspapers outdid each other in calling for Cantona to be banned from football. The FA decided to increase the ban to eight months, and fined him a further £10,000. The FA chief executive Graham Kelly described his attack as "a stain on our game", that had brought shame on football. FIFA then confirmed the suspension as worldwide, meaning that Cantona couldn't escape the ban by transferring to a foreign club.

Eric was sentenced to 120 hours of community service after an appeal court overturned a two-week prison sentence for assault. At a press conference called later, Cantona gave what is perhaps his most famous quotation. Perhaps referring to how journalists would constantly monitor his behaviour, Cantona commented, in a slow and deliberate manner: "When the seagulls follow the trawler, it is because they think sardines will be thrown into the sea. Thank you very much."

Cantona was frustrated by the terms of his ban, which even prevented him from playing in friendlies, and on 8th August he handed in a request for his contract to be terminated as he no longer wanted to play football in England. Inter Milan were said to be interested, with speculation suggesting they were prepared to quadruple his wages. But the request was quickly turned down and two days later, following a meeting in Paris with Alex Ferguson, he declared that he would remain at the club. Without Eric, United had lost the league on the final day to Blackburn and the FA Cup to Joe Royle's Everton. The absence of Cantona only highlighted his importance. Most people agree that with Eric in the side, it is likely to have been another Double-winning season for United.

If any other player's actions had caused such chaos around the club, then Ferguson would have taken the earliest opportunity to move him on – and most supporters would have backed their manager. But this was Cantona. Not only was he the team's talisman, he also had a unique relationship with the fans. He was the player they felt closest to, the player they wanted to be, their representative on the pitch. Supporters had been known to find themselves playing table football against him in the Peveril Of The Peak pub in Manchester. Cantona understood the love the supporters had for him, and he respected it – he never abused that emotion. He would always stay as long as it took to sign every autograph that was requested from him, and shake every hand that was offered to him.

The return of Cantona was an occasion that had to be seen to be believed. The build-up to the game against Liverpool was hyped and heightened by the press and television. Early that Sunday morning crowds were already congregating around Old Trafford. Black market tickets were changing hands for ridiculous prices. Thousands of tricolours were being waved and to the tune of "La Marseillaise", "Ooh Aah Cantona" reverberated around the adjoining streets.

As kick-off time approached, the tension heightened. Being the showman that he was, Cantona had not appeared during the warm-up. The stadium was buzzing, and hordes of photographers and TV cameras crowded around the tunnel, awaiting the arrival of the teams. The noise built up, Old Trafford was awash with red, white and blue colours – and suddenly there was movement down in front of the tunnel.

The teams began to appear and suddenly there he was, the last United man out. Collar turned up, chest puffed out, striding and then running out onto the pitch. Focused, embracing the atmosphere and finally standing, surveying the scene. His stare seemed to say it all: 'I am Cantona...and this is my stage!' For the United fans who were present that day, it was a moment they will never forget. The United supporters had not forgotten him for one second: they had sang his name at every game, and backed him completely. Now it was time for their faith, as well as the manager's, to be repaid.

The game started at a furious pace, and most players making their way back from a long absence would have taken time to find their touch – but not Cantona. He received the ball on the left and picked out Nicky

Butt, who controlled the ball on the run before smashing the ball home.

Liverpool had not come to be extras in the Cantona show though, and in Robbie Fowler they had a player who was at the top of his game. He scored two impressive goals that gave the visitors the lead, and it looked as if Roy Evans's side would give their fans the pleasure of spoiling Cantona's day. But with time running out Eric played in Ryan Giggs, who was brought down in the area by Jamie Redknapp – and United were awarded a penalty. There was only ever one man who was going to take it, and Eric duly sent David James the wrong way to make it 2-2. For a second he looked unsure of what to do, and then ran towards the fans and swung from one of the poles that held the netting up. He had served eight months for a moment of madness – and now he was back.

Eight months out had inevitably taken its toll, and Cantona struggled prior to Christmas. The gap behind leaders Newcastle had increased to 10 points by Christmas Eve. Things changed in mid-January: a goal by Cantona at Upton Park gave United a 1-0 win against West Ham, which then triggered a run of 10 wins from 11 in the league. Over the second half of the season, several more United games were tight affairs that ended in 1-0 wins – with Cantona scoring the only goal in victories over Newcastle, Arsenal, Tottenham and Coventry. It was actually a draw at QPR (with Eric scoring the last-minute equaliser) on 16th March that saw United finally overtake the Magpies on goal difference.

In the run-in Alex Ferguson, being the master of mind games, cranked up the pressure by saying that teams wouldn't try as hard against Newcastle. With the title slipping away and United only needing victory against Middlesbrough to secure the championship, Newcastle manager Kevin Keegan finally 'lost it' and let rip live on television in a post-match interview following a 1-1 draw at Leeds. Keegan ranted on how he would "love it" if his Newcastle side beat United to the title, but it was not meant to be. The destiny of the Premier League trophy was in United's hands – and they weren't about to let it slip.

Captain Steve Bruce was out injured so it was Eric Cantona that led the side out at the Riverside Stadium. Any sign of nerves were quickly banished as from the kick-off, there was only ever one side in it. David May scored off a Ryan Giggs corner after 15 minutes, then Andy Cole, who had come on as a sub for Paul Scholes, scored immediately from another Giggs corner nine minutes into the second half. Giggs then turned goalscorer as he let fly from outside the box to seal the win.

Cantona, like a Phoenix, rose from the flames of a disastrous year that saw him almost leave English football, to raise the league trophy above his head. It was a testament to the faith shown by Alex Ferguson and everybody at United that he had almost single-handedly gone about dragging his team back into the title battle with his goals in tight games. That Ferguson had made him captain that day, was a message to the so-called experts, who had demanded that Cantona be thrown out of football forever. Now all that stood between the team and a historic second Double was an FA Cup final against their biggest rivals – Liverpool.

Once again Alex Ferguson took the tough decision to leave Bruce out due to doubts about his fitness, and he had no hesitation in passing the captain's armband to Cantona. Liverpool grabbed the attention pre-match for the white suits they turned up in, looking as if they were attending a celebrity wedding in *OK* magazine. The game itself was a let down as both teams were cautious and cancelled each other out. Early in the second half Eric nearly broke the deadlock with a volley that was saved at the near post by David James, but chances were sparse.

With five minutes left and extra time looming United got a corner, which David Beckham whipped over. James could only weakly punch out to the edge of the area, where Eric was waiting. Adjusting his body, he volleyed the ball on the up, into the Liverpool goal. The final whistle signalled that United had made history, becoming the first team to complete the 'Double Double'. Eric took it all in his stride. Interviewed on the pitch, he said: "It was important for us, two years ago we won the Double and this season we have done it again. Now we can go and have a nice holiday." Nobody could have predicted, when Eric returned, that in May he would be walking up the Wembley steps to collect the FA Cup as captain of a Double-winning United team. In doing so Eric was also the first foreign player to captain an FA Cup-winning side.

Following the departure of Steve Bruce to Birmingham in the summer of 1996, Eric Cantona was named as club captain. Years before him, Sir Matt Busby had made his King, Denis Law, skipper – and now Ferguson was doing the same. Both players were not obviously captain material, but both were unanimously adored by fans and players alike. Cantona's influence on the young players had already been far reaching, and was now coming to fruition. Both players had a certain amount of devilment about them, and would never be bullied by the opposition. How would Sir Matt have dealt with one of his players striking a supporter?

In April 1960 United were playing at Luton. Throughout the match the home fans had been volatile and increasingly belligerent, unsurprising given their team's rapidly worsening plight. There was incessant bar-racking of goalkeeper Harry Gregg from behind him in the compact, noisy stand, which maybe rattled him, perhaps contributing to his errors. At the end – a 3-2 United win – a supporter made a beeline for Harry. To the crowds' amazement the big Irishman, having failed to take evasive action, felled his potential assailant with a right-hander. The man went down as if taken out by the proverbial sniper. Those spectators, who hadn't already rushed disconsolately for the exits after Luton's defeat, were in uproar. Gregg was bundled off by the police, and ushered away by his skipper, Maurice Setters. In a flash the players were gone, leaving astonished fans to make what they could of the incident.

In contrast to the media firestorm that greeted Eric Cantona's martial arts moment 35 years later, the considerable newspaper interest in the Gregg punch was neither disproportionate, nor especially slanted against him or United. There were no editors supporting rival teams taking the opportunity to demand life-long bans. The reports were balanced and fair, and nobody could deny that the media interest was legitimate, given the explosive nature of the incident and the 'national hero' status of the assailant. Although the pole-axed victim had been badly bruised, Gregg could plead provocation and self-defence, justifying his pre-emptive punch by stressing that he feared he was about to be attacked.

We now know that there were police moves to prosecute Gregg for assault but when Busby stood by him, albeit with the biggest telling-off of his career, the authorities backed off and no charges were pressed – again, unlike the Cantona affair. It was generally accepted that the man had approached in a threatening manner, obstructing Harry as he repeatedly tried to side-step him in order to shake hands with his friend and Luton midfielder, Billy Bingham. The clincher was probably when it was forcefully pointed out that the police had signally failed to protect Harry from an aggressive intruder, who had no right to be on the pitch.

The 1996/97 season began with the FA Charity Shield, with United playing league runners-up Newcastle. Eric gave a man-of-the-match display as the team obliterated Kevin Keegan's side 4-0, sending out a message to the rest of the league that United would be in the hunt for honours again. The big prize for Alex Ferguson would be the Champions League, the competition that would mark United's place in world football history as a great team – and Eric wanted to be part of it.

The new United skipper seemed weighty, and struggled with his early-season form. It was as if he had given everything the season before to win the Double – and now he was paying for it. He wasn't the influence that he had been, though he did show flashes of genius. What was noticeable was the way the team coped with his absence whenever he was suspended or injured. Youngsters like Giggs, Beckham and Scholes, who had learned so much from watching him in training and playing with him, were now turning into match-winners themselves. Not that the season wasn't without breathtaking moments of beauty from Cantona. There was one such incident, which caused Alex Ferguson to marvel at his star's audacity: "I will always remember when we played Sunderland at Old Trafford. We had a great little piece of play. Eric played a one-two with Brian McClair, and then chipped the goalkeeper inside the box. He turned to the crowd as if to say: 'The Emperor is here.' It was an unbelievable moment no-one will ever forget."

In February 1997 Wimbledon knocked United out of the FA Cup, the only defeat Eric ever suffered in the competition. There was no such problem in the quarter-final of the Champions League though, where United brushed FC Porto aside to set up a semi-final with Borussia Dortmund. Luck was not with United in the first leg as they wasted chances and lost 1-0, but they were still confident of progress at Old Trafford. Unfortunately, they would have to do so without Roy Keane, suspended after picking up a yellow card in Germany.

The return could not have got off to a worse side as the Germans scored after eight minutes. From then on United peppered the goal, but it was a night when nothing would go in. You could see the players' frustration, including Cantona. The morning after Eric went into the manager's office and told him he had decided to retire at the end of the season. Believing this to be a knee-jerk reaction to the disappointment, Fergie said he would leave until the end of the season to make the announcement. There were plenty of reasons for Eric finishing when he did: he was not happy with the way his image was being used by United, and was not seeing the rewards. He was also not seeing the kind of players brought in that he thought could take the team to another level. When United won the league and were presented with the trophy at Old Trafford, there was no kiss for the trophy from the Frenchman, no joyous grin, just a faint smile as he stood at the back for the team photo.

On the morning of Sunday 18th May 1997 United called a press conference – but nobody was aware of the bombshell that would be dropped. Chairman Martin Edwards made the announcement that Eric was retiring from football. Immediately, hundreds of United supporters, some of them in tears, converged on the forecourt at Old Trafford, somehow hoping the news wasn't true. But it was true – Eric was gone, he had gone out at the top and was not interested in dragging out his career.

The one season that Eric Cantona was captain was probably his poorest at the club. No matter how much he was adored and deified, closer scrutiny has to be paid as to his time at United. Was he a great player? Without doubt he was one of the greatest to wear the red shirt, and he was the final link to Ferguson's successful United team. Was he a big influence on the team? Massively so, especially the younger players, who learnt so much about combining hard work with natural ability.

Was he a great captain? That is harder to answer, as it was a role that did not come naturally. His term as skipper was short, and he was very much the father figure in the team. The younger players revered him and it was a masterstroke of Ferguson's to give him that responsibility – but in that last season, did that burden also weigh heavily upon him, and affect his performances? I happen to think that it did. He will always have the criticism that he never really did it in big European games, but that was probably due to the fact that he was constantly man-marked, and never allowed the space he received in the Premier League.

The one season he was club captain he was putting on weight and seemingly falling out of love with the game, not necessarily great attributes in a captain. But during his time at United, he won four Premier League titles, two FA Cups and three FA Charity Shields – plus his peers recognised him as PFA Player of the Year in 1996. In his last seven seasons as a professional, he'd finished a champion on no less than six occasions. There is also no doubt that Ferguson handled Cantona expertly, and got far more out of him than any other manager.

Cantona's arrival at Manchester United provided him with the stage he had always yearned for. The love United supporters hold in their hearts for Cantona has never diminished, and only will when those privileged enough to have seen him play stop going to the game and singing his name. Eric Cantona is written into United's folklore – and rightly so – and he did contribute so much. I will leave the last word with Eric, who summed it up better than anyone when he said: "Till the last minute of my life I will have this club in my heart."

Celtic Tiger

ROY KEANE

1997-2005

*'It was the most emphatic display of selflessness I have
seen on a football field. Pounding over every blade of grass,
competing as if he would rather die of exhaustion than
lose, he inspired all around him. I felt it was an honour to
be associated with such a player'*

If you wanted to provoke heated debate amongst football fans, just ask
one question: "What do you think of Roy Keane?" Prepare to stand back
and watch the lively response. The devil incarnate, a single-minded
brute or a genius, depending on your point of view. Even though his
playing career finished some years ago, he still stirs up emotive
responses. Keane has been called many things, and some would apply
the term 'flawed genius' to him. Although there was never any doubting
his wonderful ability to play the game, there was a temperamental brit-
tleness which led him into so many scrapes both on – and off – the field.

At the end of the 1996/97 season, when Eric Cantona surprisingly
announced his retirement, Ferguson had no hesitation in naming Keane
as his successor as club captain. Keane would go on to lead United to
nine major honours, making him the most successful captain in the
club's history. He was the manager's mouthpiece on the pitch, and he set
the standards, insisting players got to training half-an-hour early. They
were his instructions then, and they continue to this day. There can be
no higher compliment than that paid by Bobby Charlton: "As a player
and competitor, the nearest thing I've seen to Duncan Edwards."

Roy Maurice Keane was born at 88 Ballinderry Park to Maurice
(Mossie) and Marie Keane, in the north suburb of Mayfield, Cork,

Ireland on 10th August 1971. His father took work wherever he could find it due to the economic hardships of the time, which included jobs at a local knitwear company and at the Murphy's Irish Stout factory. Roy's first sport was boxing and he excelled, winning his only four novice fights by knockout – perhaps no surprise to those who've seen his dominant and aggressive nature when playing football.

As a young boy Roy was small for his age and even in his teens he always seemed the smallest on the pitch. But as he showed throughout his professional career, he had a giant will, a determination and resilience that would drive him on to eventually succeed in anything he attempted. Following a family tradition, Roy joined Rockmount AFC's Academy at nine years old, staying for nearly 10 years. His skill and determination saw him voted player of the year in his first season at Rockmount, which ended with him playing for the Academy's Under-11s team – two years ahead of his age group. He wasn't frightened of a reputation, or phased by any of the older players. Speaking to a reporter in later years about those early days at Rockmount, and of him eye-balling other players, he was to recall: "I have done it since I was eight or nine. I did it at Rockmount. I fell out with people when I was 10, 11. Mainly it was with people who didn't train properly."

His nickname at Rockmount was the "Boiler Man", given to him by his manager Timmy Murphy as he was the fiery one who got things heated up – and kept it that way. Even at 11 years old he was the leader of the team who were one of the best in the area, attracting attention from scouts in England and Scotland. None were coming to see Roy as he was deemed too small and even though he was gritty, he wasn't too gifted. But Murphy believed Keane was special – and would make it.

Despite Roy's promise, a future career in football began to look uncertain. He was turned down for Ireland schoolboys after a trial in Dublin; one explanation from former coach and scout Ronan Scally was that the 14-year-old Keane was "just too small" to make it at the required level. Roy decided to write to English clubs applying for a trial. Aston Villa,

Chelsea, Sheffield Wednesday and Brighton must all now regret turning down the young Keane. The rejections disappointed Keane and also angered him, fuelling his burning desire to succeed.

In 1989 Cobh Ramblers persuaded Keane to join them. Keane was desperate to get on to the FAI Academy scheme and Eddie O'Rourke, the club's youth-team manager, said he would nominate Keane for the course. Cork City were also in the hunt for Keane's signature and he had signed for them when O'Rourke talked to him about joining Cobh. It is a mystery as to how Cobh's forms arrived at the League's headquarters before Cork's, but it is a good job they did. If they hadn't, Keane would never have had a place on the FAI course. Cork City had already nominated their youngster, a player named Len Downey. Downey recalled how driven Keane was, even when he was at the Academy in Dublin: "He would never have a go if you missed a goal, but would tear into anyone for missing a tackle or not tracking back. He was forever having a go at me because I could be a bit lazy. Players were afraid of him, even those who were much older. Even though he was small he had no hesitation in telling the bigger lads what to do, and what he thought of them. He actually stood out because he was so small, but he tackled players twice his size, won the ball and sent them flying. He was tiny when he got into the Ireland youth squad and people told him that he was not going to make it. That just made him more determined."

Noel McCabe was an Irish football scout for Nottingham Forest. He cycled all over Dublin watching junior football, hoping that one day he would find Brian Clough a gem. He was a methodical man who watched Keane for months, to get a good idea of what kind of player he was. The game that finally clinched it for him was an FAI Youth Cup quarter-final replay at Fairview Park in North Dublin where the Cobh youth team were playing Belvedere. Roy's team lost 4-0, but McCabe saw enough to know that he had found a star. Forest were impressed, and paid Cobh £47,000 for his signature in summer 1990. Roy's dream of joining a top English club was finally realised – all before he was 20 years old.

"The Irishman", as Cloughie affectionately referred to Roy, found life away from home difficult, and would regularly look for a few days off to visit his family. There was seldom any difficulty meeting this request from his manager, though. Quiet and withdrawn in these early months, it didn't take long for the midfielder to establish himself. His performances were eye catching and he soon displaced England international Steve Hodge. As soon as a game finished on a Saturday Roy would be on the plane to Cork, arriving in time for last orders. Cork was a rough place, and there were always people looking for a rumble – but Roy would have mates with him, backing him up. It was the price he was prepared to pay in order to go home and be with his friends.

Back in Nottingham, pride prevented him from making the first move to initiate friendships and he would seem aloof, when really he was just lonely. His drinking became problematic, and was almost certainly borne on the back of loneliness, boredom and being away from home.

He was making a big impression on the field though and at the end of his first season, Keane played in the FA Cup final against Tottenham. In the third round Keane had made an error against Crystal Palace, gifting them a goal that allowed them to earn a replay. Afterwards Clough charged into the dressing room and punched Roy in the face, knocking him to the ground. This was a passion that Roy understood and he bore no hard feelings for the man who had given him a start in England.

Roy finished a loser in the final in '91. He had appeased Clough by agreeing to play, even though he was carrying an ankle injury. But with the season over, Roy went 'on the lash' and when he reported back for pre-season he was over a stone overweight. Clough was far from happy.

The 1991/92 season saw Roy and Forest back at Wembley, and again he was on the losing team – this time against Manchester United. Even before this final Alex Ferguson was starting to take notice. In his first game against United he had gone into tackles against Bryan Robson like a bull charging a gate. Robson was no wallflower when it came to putting his foot in, and he knew he had been in a game against the young man from Cork. Keane was becoming a wanted man and in the autumn of 1992 he negotiated a new, improved contract with Forest. Clough was far from happy with Keane, who he described as "a greedy child", believing him to be asking for too much money. In the end both sides compromised and a new deal was signed, including a clause that stipulated that in the event of Forest being relegated, Keane could demand a move. This did not prevent the Forest supporters from voting Keane as their player of the year due to his battling performances.

Ferguson became more determined to get his man. He would phone Clough every week trying to talk about Keane, but Clough would ignore his calls. Clough had his own problems – the main one being his battle with alcoholism. Several key players from what had been a very good Forest team had already left the club and, despite his best efforts, Keane could not save Forest. Just before the season ended, after a 2-0 home defeat by Sheffield United doomed them to relegation, Clough announced his retirement after 18 years at the City Ground.

The relegation opened the door for Keane's departure. There was speculation that he would join Arsenal, but Blackburn manager Kenny Dalglish acted first. Dalglish had been installed as Rovers' new manager in October 1991, and was assembling a formidable team with the help of steel magnate Jack Walker's millions. Once Forest's relegation had been confirmed, a £4m transfer was agreed between the clubs. Keane shook hands on the deal with Dalglish but as it was late on a Friday, they could not get all the forms processed, so the agreement was that this would be done the following Monday. However, when the story broke in the Saturday dailies, Ferguson immediately got in touch with Keane; he was destined for United: "Once I knew of United's interest, there was only one place that I was going to go to – and that was Old Trafford."

Keane signed in August 1993, a little over three years after leaving Cobh Ramblers. He moved into a dressing room full of strong characters – Bryan Robson, who had been a boyhood hero of Keane's, was club captain, but was now 36 years old. The drinking culture was still in evidence at Old Trafford, despite Ferguson's attempts to put an end to it, and Roy embraced it – in fact, he flew headlong into it!

On the field his performances were impressive and Keane looked as if he had been born to play for United. He scored twice on his home debut against Sheffield United, and grabbed the winner in his first Manchester derby when United overturned a 2-0 deficit to win 3-2. In his first season United won the Double under the stand-in captaincy of Steve Bruce, a success that was repeated in 1996, but at the end of that 1995/96 season Bruce moved on, with Eric Cantona taking over as club captain.

The title was retained in 1997, but then Cantona surprisingly announced his retirement. Ferguson had no hesitation in naming Keane as his successor as club captain. He was a fantastic player, who was maturing into probably the most prolific midfield player in Europe.

Keane's first season as captain, 1997/98, did not get off to the best of starts. In the ninth league game of the season, against Leeds, he went into a tackle with Alf-Inge Haaland and collapsed. As Keane lay prone on the pitch Haaland stood over Keane, accusing the injured United captain of trying to hurt him and of feigning injury to escape punishment; an allegation, which would lead to an infamous dispute between the pair four years later. Keane missed the rest of the season, initially expressing doubts as to whether he would play again.

Keane saw his team-mates squander an 11-point lead over Arsenal to miss out on the title. The long lay-off caused by his cruciate injury was a bleak time for a man whose life, as he realised, was defined by the regular 90-minute bouts of combat on the pitch. He felt lost and frustrated, without the purpose and adrenalin of football. His drinking escalated. He had a row with a barman at a United reserves' party; he had another with his manager after he was subsequently banned from attending the first-team party. Most experts pointed to Keane's absence as the reason United had surrendered the league, and it was a relief for fans when he recovered and began pre-season training for the new campaign, for what would become Manchester United's most famous season.

Much has been written about the "Treble Season" of 1998/99 and the never-say-die attitude of the squad. The season didn't start that well as they were beaten 3-0 by Arsenal 3-0 in the FA Charity Shield, with new defensive signing Jaap Stam being given the run around by Nicolas Anelka. The first two league games ended in draws, followed by a couple of wins, only for the team to be brought crashing back down to earth by Arsenal at Highbury as they were again well beaten 3-0. However, this was the last defeat they suffered in the league until December, when they were surprisingly beaten by Middlesbrough at Old Trafford.

In the Champions League United qualified from a group containing Barcelona, Bayern Munich and Brondby. After getting through a tricky quarter-final against Inter Milan, they found themselves with a semi-final against Juventus. The first leg at Old Trafford ended 1-1, with United lucky to come away with the draw as Ryan Giggs scored a late equaliser. In the second leg on 29th April, in the Stadio Delle Alpi, Keane gave arguably the greatest performance by a captain in United's history. He single-handedly dragged United back from the brink to ensure their place in a European Cup final for the first time in 31 years.

United had conceded two soft goals within the first 12 minutes, meaning they were 3-1 down on aggregate. United looked dead and buried, but Keane drove his team on, urging them, cajoling them to greater effort. He was booked for a trip on Zinedine Zidane that meant he would play no part in the final should United get there. There were no Gascoigne-type tears though. Keane rolled up his sleeves and dragged United back into the game, scoring with a delightful header from a corner-kick. It breathed fresh energy and impetus into the team, and they responded. By half-time they had equalised with a Dwight Yorke header and as things stood they were going through.

Twice United hit the post as Keane drove the side on in search of a goal that would guarantee a place in the final. Then, with a few minutes of the game remaining, Peter Schmeichel launched a huge kick into the Juventus half that the Italians failed to deal with. The ball fell to Dwight

Yorke, who drove at the heart of the Juventus defence. He went through, rounded the keeper and was then brought down – but the ball fell to Andy Cole, and it was "full speed ahead Barcelona". United would now have the chance to become European champions and Alex Ferguson would get the opportunity to emulate Sir Matt Busby. Ferguson was in no doubt who was responsible for his team being in the final:

"It was an emphatic display of selflessness. Pounding over every blade of grass, competing as if he would rather die of exhaustion than lose, he inspired the side. It was an honour to be associated with such a player."

It must have been the bitterest sweet of feelings for Keane; he had played the game of his life and got his team to a Champions League final, yet he would be sat watching like any other supporter, unable to affect the game. It was no consolation that United had also reached the final of the FA Cup; those occasions had become common to this team. This was the pinnacle of any career, and Keane would not be playing.

On Sunday 16th May 1999 the first of the historic treble games was played at Old Trafford, against Tottenham. A win would be the first step in achieving something no other team in English football history had done. As Alex Ferguson has always said, "Manchester United never do things the easy way" – and so it was on this day. Even though Tottenham were hardly flying into tackles, they led through a Les Ferdinand goal.

A piece of magic from David Beckham produced an equaliser and then two minutes into the second half, substitute Andy Cole put United ahead. It gave United 43 minutes to hang on to their lead and although they and the crowd did get a little nervous in the last 10 minutes, the final whistle went and United had nailed the first leg of the treble.

Roy and the team decided they would go out and celebrate. It was a night that would change Keane's attitude to drink when he spent a night in the cells after a brawl in a club. The incident had all the trademarks of a tabloid set-up – it made *The Sun* the following morning – but it meant that Alex Ferguson was summoned to a Manchester police station in the early hours, just days before the FA Cup final. It was a familiar pattern for Roy, drink and cities: Cork, Nottingham and Manchester, it all added up to aggravation. It was a long night for Keane, and the humiliation of his manager having to come and get him hit home. Ferguson's reading of the situation was, as always, spot on. He could see that Keane was disgusted with himself and not looking for sympathy, so he just checked that he was okay and took him home.

Saturday 22nd May 1999 and the second game in the historic treble, the FA Cup final against Newcastle. This would be Roy's final game of the season, due to his European ban. Some speculated that Ferguson would leave him out as a punishment for the night in the cells – but the thought never crossed the manager's mind. As it was he only lasted eight minutes, having picked up an ankle injury courtesy of a Gary Speed challenge. Fortunately Roy was not missed in a one-sided final that was more like a stroll in the sunshine for United. Newcastle offered little resistance, and the 2-0 scoreline flattered them. Teddy Sheringham, who came on for Keane, scored one and set up Paul Scholes for the other. Roy went up the Wembley steps as a Double-winning captain to collect the famous trophy from Prince Charles, knowing that he could do no more to help the club obtain the treble.

Wednesday 26th May 1999: Roy Keane and Paul Scholes stood in their club suits in the dressing room at the Nou Camp and wished their team-mates well. Both would have been thinking about the silly yellow cards they had picked up in earlier games, that now meant that on the biggest day in United's modern history, arguably the two best players would not be taking part. The opposition, Bayern Munich, were surely given a boost by the absence of two such influential players – and they took full advantage, scoring after six minutes from a scrappy free-kick.

To every United fan, it is only the final three minutes of that game that matter. They will be forever woven into the tapestry of the club and its supporters; no club has ever won the competition, be it the European Cup or in its latter-day Champions League guise, in such dramatic fashion. It was almost as if Keane's spirit, drive and determination had found its way onto the pitch for those moments, and had driven his team on.

Though he had played 12 of the 13 European games that season, Keane was reluctant to collect his medal, feeling that he had not been part of it as he had missed out in the final. When he looks back he will realise that not one player on the pitch that night deserved a medal more than their inspirational captain, whose single-minded determination was the reason they stood on the winner's podium.

After the triumph, there was a sense of déjà-vu. George Best had recalled years earlier that after the win at Wembley against Benfica in 1968, several players were heard to be saying that there was nothing else to win – that they had done it all. In Barcelona Keane, as he sat in the dressing room, was hearing similar things. The player, who had innocently said on the night that he didn't care if they never won another match, foretold the stagnation that would follow. Roy knew that the great teams didn't just win the competition once; they went back and won again and again. What Keane saw were some players who had reached their zenith. This feeling of achievement is fine for some players – but not for Keane. It was with this in mind that he took the summer to decide if his future lay at United. Top Italian teams were interested in signing him, and he made no secret of his admiration for them.

The 1999/2000 season began amidst uncertainty over Roy's future. He knew his worth, but United were not prepared to pay the money he expected. This was potentially United's biggest ever season as they would be in seven competitions – FIFA Club World Championships, World Club Cup, European Super Cup, Champions League, Premier League, FA Cup and League Cup. However, one of those trophies was taken out of the team's options. It was made clear to the club by certain politicians that for England to have any chance of winning the right to stage the 2006 World Cup, they needed United to go to Brazil and take part in the Club World Championships. However, they could not do this and also take part in the FA Cup without fielding a reserve or even youth side, so they relinquished their hold on the trophy without competing.

In November 1999 the team flew to Japan to play South American champions Palmeiras, aiming to be the first British side to be called world champions. The game was played at the Olympic Stadium in Tokyo, and fittingly it was Keane who wrote United's name in history by scoring the only goal in the 35th minute. It was a great night for Roy and his team-mates – but a greater night for the club's merchandisers as they saw 'their brand' beamed around the globe as world champions.

Any fears of Roy leaving the club were put to bed when ITV made the announcement prior to a European game against Valencia that Roy had signed a new four-year deal. Roy was angry when the club sent a letter out to season-ticket holders, blaming the rise in prices on his higher wage, although a swift apology from the club eased the situation.

The season was going well for United, having already secured one trophy, and they were looking good for further honours. However, Peter Schmeichel had left in the summer and been replaced by Mark Bosnich from Aston Villa, who had not got off to the best of starts with Roy by turning up an hour late on his first day. Keane did not take long to let him know that this was not the way things were done at his club.

When United went to Brazil in January 2000 to take part in the first FIFA Club World Championships, it all ended in disappointment as they failed to make the final stages. However, they at least returned to league action rested and not much worse off points wise than when they left. By the time they were due to play Real Madrid in the quarter-finals of the Champions League, the team was odds-on to win the title. They claimed a fortunate 0-0 draw at the Bernabeu, which set up one of those special European nights that Old Trafford is famous for.

As it was, United received a master class and lost 3-2, with Roy contributing an unfortunate own goal. The team did at least retain the league with games to spare, but Roy's dream of defending the Champions League had failed. On a personal level, there was individual success for Roy, who was voted PFA Players' Player of the Year and Football Writers' Player of the Year, having led United to their sixth

Premier League trophy in eight years.

Roy's desire and hunger showed no sign of waning at the start of the 2000/01 season when he was sent off in the FA Charity Shield game against Chelsea. Roy received a nasty tackle from Jimmy Floyd Hasselbaink close to the hour mark, which went unpunished – but he found himself looking at a red card soon after when he committed a bad tackle on Gus Poyet. The 10 men of United lost 2-0 but despite this setback, in the league United started strongly and had opened up an eight-point gap at the top of the table by November, having lost just once.

United hosted Dynamo Kiev in a Champions League group game needing to win to progress but they struggled, even though Teddy Sheringham had given them an early lead. The Old Trafford crowd had been spoilt by the riches they had tasted over the past couple of seasons and they did not really get behind the team. United did hold on to win 1-0, but Keane did not hold back on his opinion of the support:

"A lot of people come here expecting three or four goals, but it's not always the case. Our fans away from home are as good as any, but at home sometimes you wonder if they understand the game. Some come to Old Trafford and I don't think they can even spell the word football, never mind understand it. You have to get behind the team. Away from home our fans are fantastic, what I call the hardcore fans, but at home they've had a few drinks and probably their prawn sandwiches and don't realise what is going on out on the pitch. It's right out of order."

The 'prawn sandwich' comment was manna from heaven for the press and the fans of other clubs, who used it as a stick to beat United's support with. The comment held some truth, as there was now an element of support who were there because they had money; it was the place to be seen, a way of being linked with success. People failed to realise that it wasn't really the fans that were getting to Roy – he was making a general comment on the attitude around Old Trafford including some of the players, who had started to take success for granted, and had lost some of their hunger. The treble had been a wonderful thing, but for Roy it was in the past – yet some of his team-mates were acting as if it was yesterday and there was nothing left to achieve. They were starting to slacken in their attitude to training and the game. Maybe the manager should have anticipated this, and freshened the squad. They could have gone out and bought big, and really sent a message to the rest of Europe as well as certain players in the team, who were resting on their laurels.

Having gone through a second group phase unbeaten, United were drawn against Bayern Munich in the quarter-finals of the Champions League. The German side arrived like a team hungry to put right what they felt had been the injustice of the final two years previous. They were the only team that looked like winning and it was no surprise when four minutes from the end Paulo Sergio scored a winner. The second leg in Munich wasn't much better. United scored through Ryan Giggs, but the Germans hit two and were comfortable winners. To Keane, the result had been inevitable, even though they were breezing through Premier League opponents. But when they played in Europe against world-class players, they were flat and uninspired. Keane counted himself amongst players who had failed in the quarter-finals and that made him angry – not the best mood to be going into a Manchester derby!

United were still suffering a hangover from the Champions League defeat and late in the second half, with the score 1-1, Keane's anger found its victim. Alf-Inge Haaland had moved to City and had been vocal about Roy's lucrative new contract. Then there was the past history between the pair, where Haaland had accused Keane of feigning injury to avoid punishment. Keane had waited for his opportunity – and with five minutes of the game left it came to him.

There was a 50-50 ball that fell between Haaland and Keane, which the Norwegian got his toe to. Keane though went over the top of the ball and hit Haaland high on the knee. Keane didn't wait for the referee to brandish the red card. Before he left the pitch he crouched over the injured midfielder and reminded him to never accuse him of feigning injury again. It was the last game that Keane played that season, though

United were so far ahead of the chasing pack that Keane's absence made little difference. A 2-0 victory in the next game at Middlesbrough ensured another Premier League title.

They subsequently lost their final three games, but that still didn't stop United from finishing 10 points clear of nearest rivals Arsenal. The trophy was presented after a 1-0 defeat to Derby, with United becoming the first team to win the Premier League three times in a row. However, the concerns that had been niggling Roy were about to come true. Teams must progress – they can't just stand still and admire past achievements.

United finished the 2001/02 season trophyless for the first time in four years, despite the acquisition of three world-class players in the form of record signing Juan Sebastian Veron, Ruud van Nistlerooy and Laurent Blanc. The 2002 Champions League final was due to be held at Hampden Park in Glasgow, Alex Ferguson's home city, and the manager made it the top priority for his team. Ferguson also made the decision to announce that he would be retiring at the end of the season, hoping that his last game would be the final in his homeland. Maybe this had a distracting effect on the players – and maybe some of them believed that he had taken his eye off the ball? Whatever the truth, domestically they finished third, their lowest final position in the league since 1991 – perhaps a reflection of the high standards Ferguson had set.

Having been beaten 2-1 by Liverpool in the FA Charity Shield curtain-raiser to the season, United also suffered early disappointment in the FA Cup, losing 2-0 at Middlesbrough in round four and in the League Cup, going down 4-0 in round three at eventual Double winners Arsenal.

United did reach the semi-finals of the Champions League, keeping Ferguson's Hampden dream in sight. Unfortunately they were beaten on away goals by Bayer Leverkusen – a 2-2 home draw in the first leg proving costly. Keane had scored in the second leg 1-1 draw, and as he looked around the dressing room afterwards he could see the players who were gutted – and the others who had lost their hunger and replaced it with Rolex watches, garages full of cars and mansions. Still, Roy had one consolation to look forward to: he would be captain for the Republic of Ireland's 2002 World Cup campaign in Japan and South Korea.

The Irish had always been looked upon as a bit of a joke when it came to international football, everyone's second team, always good for a laugh. This was a major finals though and Roy was serious about any game he played in. As a United player he was used to the best facilities available. During the course of the first training session in Saipan, South Korea, Keane expressed misgivings about the adequacy of the training facilities and the standard of preparation for the squad. He was angered by the late arrival of their training equipment, which had disrupted the first training session on a pitch that he described as "like a car park."

The second day got no better and after a row with Packie Bonner, the goalkeeping coach, over the lack of any goalkeepers for a training game, Keane announced that he was quitting the squad and that he wished to return home due to his dissatisfaction with Ireland's preparation. The FAI were unable to get Keane an immediate flight home at such short notice, meaning that he remained in Saipan for another night – although they decided to call up Colin Healy as a replacement. The following day manager Mick McCarthy approached Keane and asked him to return to the training camp, and he was eventually persuaded to stay.

Despite a temporary cooling of tensions after Keane's change of heart, things soon took a turn for the worse. Roy gave an interview to journalist Tom Humphries of the *Irish Times*, in which he expressed his unhappiness with the facilities in Saipan and listed the events and concerns which had led him to leave the team temporarily. McCarthy was furious and decided to confront Keane over the article, in front of the entire squad and coaching staff. Keane refused to relent, saying that he had told the newspaper what he considered to be the truth, and that the Irish fans deserved to know what was going on. He then unleashed a string of personal insults in a tirade against McCarthy, that left those present speechless. None of Keane's team-mates voiced support for him during the meeting, although some backed him in private afterwards.

McCarthy subsequently held a press conference, sitting alongside veterans Niall Quinn and Steve Staunton. He announced that he had dismissed Keane from the squad and sent him home. One or two players knocked on Keane's door to wish him luck, telling him how gutted they were he was leaving. This was a row that would split a country – you were either in the McCarthy camp, or the Keane camp.

Back with United, Keane still had some anger issues left from the World Cup fallout. He was sent off against Sunderland at the end of August for elbowing international team-mate Jason McAteer. The midfielder had made comments about a recently published autobiography that Roy had released in which he criticised his World Cup team-mates, and also went into detail about how he intended to hurt Haaland with that infamous tackle. Keane was duly fined £150,000 by Ferguson and suspended for three matches, a ban that was compounded by an added five-match suspension for the controversial comments about Haaland.

Keane used the break to undergo an operation on his hip, which had caused him to take painkillers for the previous 12 months. Despite fears that the injury was career threatening, and suggestions of a future hip-replacement from his surgeon, Roy was back by December. During his recuperation, Roy reflected on the cause of his frequent injuries and suspensions. He decided that the cause of these problems was his reckless challenges and angry outbursts, which had increasingly blighted his career. As a result, Keane became more restrained on the field. Some observers felt that the "new" Roy Keane had become less influential in midfield as a consequence of the change in his style of play. However, after his return, Keane displayed the tenacity of old, leading the team to another league title in May 2003 and this time on Merseyside as he received the trophy at Goodison Park, after beating Everton 2-1.

The 2003 Champions League final was held at Old Trafford, but once again the players got sucked into the hype of people telling them that it was their destiny to play in the final. They were beaten 6-5 on aggregate in the quarter-finals again, this time by Real Madrid, although the 4-3 second-leg victory for the Spanish side remains one of the finest European games ever witnessed at Old Trafford.

People assume that Roy's injuries and his withdrawal from the Republic of Ireland squad at the World Cup were the biggest disappointments in his career – but in reality it was the games they lost in Europe that frustrated him most. He wanted to get back to the Champions League final again to prove what a good team they really were.

For all his disappointments in previous seasons, Keane needed to look at himself when United were knocked out of the Champions League by Jose Mourinho's Porto the following season, 2003/04. The first leg of the first knockout phase tie in Portugal started well for United as they took the lead through Quinton Fortune, but Porto dragged themselves back into the game and eventually took a 2-1 lead. With only minutes remaining Keane chased a ball into the area, which was collected by Porto goalkeeper Vitor Baia. Keane leapt over the keeper, but then stamped hard on Baia's backside with his studs. Keane received his matching orders, the 11th red card of his United career, and it ruled him out of three potential Champions League games. It was a moment of madness that left United without one of their most influential players.

For the home leg two weeks later, Ferguson brought in Eric Djemba-Djemba to shore up the midfield and to protect a defence that was now short of record signing, centre-half Rio Ferdinand, who was banned for eight months due to a missed drugs test. Despite fielding a patched up team United scored the goal they needed through Paul Scholes, and were seconds away from progressing through on the away goals rule.

Late on Phil Neville pushed sub Edgaras Jankauskas close to the penalty area. Tim Howard strained to reach Benni McCarthy's free-kick and could only push the ball down into the danger area, where Costinha, quick to pounce, bundled home the goal that put Porto in the last eight and saw Mourinho sprint down the touchline with his coat flapping. The outcome might have been different had a linesman's flag not denied Scholes, onside by a yard, a second goal on the verge of half-time.

United rarely impressed all season, with their failings illuminated by an Arsenal team who would eventually ease to the Premier League and create history by going the whole season unbeaten. Only the FA Cup could spare Ferguson and the team their second trophyless season in three years – and they had to get past the Gunners in the semi-final. Villa Park has always been a lucky venue for United in these matches and for this one it was packed with United supporters, desperate to get something out of a disappointing season. The team rose to the occasion, claiming a 1-0 victory thanks to Paul Scholes' strike.

The final against Championship side Millwall was one of the most one-sided that Cardiff's Millennium Stadium has ever witnessed. The game plan for Dennis Wise's side was to get men behind the ball, defending deep and attempt to hit United on the break. They were rarely able to put this tactic into practice though as United dominated. A goal from Cristiano Ronaldo and two from Ruud van Nistlerooy made the result 3-0 – though the margin could have been a lot bigger. Roy lifted the cup for the second time as captain, his fourth time as winner.

Roy Keane had always maintained a healthy rivalry with Arsenal's Patrick Vieira. There was bad blood between the teams, supporters and managers. But when battle reached the pitch it was war between the pair. The most noticeable incident took place at Highbury on 1st February 2005. This was the final time the two would cross swords in the league, but perhaps that lends an air of greater nostalgia to the event.

United were still smarting from Arsenal's unbeaten season in 2003/04, and Arsenal were still raw from United ending that 49-game unbeaten league run in acrimonious circumstances the previous October. There was a three-month media whirlwind stoking the fires for the return fixture, and the dangerous fuse didn't take long to ignite – we didn't even have to wait until the first whistle. During the warm-up Vieira approached Gary Neville and gave out some verbals, and then had another go at him in the tunnel as the teams were lining up.

Roy heard the commotion and took umbrage at the six-foot plus Vieira finding the smallest player on the United team and singling him out for intimidation. Sky TV cameras caught the action live as Vieira walked hurriedly and sheepishly to the front of the Arsenal players in the tunnel, with an angry Keane being restrained by referee Graham Poll – but getting louder and louder. You could visibly see Vieira and the rest of the Arsenal players wilt in the presence of Keane's anger. Phrases like "I'll see you out there", and "[He] thinks he's a nice guy" were uttered and became part of United folklore. If ever a team were beaten before they took to the field it was Arsenal that day and by one man: Roy Keane.

What happened next was a breathtaking display of football – word of the incident had obviously reached the terraces as the atmosphere was at fever pitch, almost boiling over when Ashley Cole dived in the box early on in an attempt to 'win' a penalty. This was soon forgotten though when Vieira headed the opener for Arsenal. It was to be his last real meaningful contribution, as Keane set the tempo for a resurgent and stunning comeback. After a breathless 90 minutes that saw six goals and a red card for Mikael Silvestre, United were deserved 4-2 winners, giving Arsenal a footballing masterclass. Unlike Keane, Vieira had shrivelled and wilted under the psychological battle that he had created.

The pre-match incident was a microcosm of Keane and Vieira's approaches to the game – Vieira's attempt to bully Neville, and Keane's absolute loyalty to his team-mates and the shirt they wore. Where people had previously tried to claim that Arsenal were the superior footballing side, Roy Keane and Manchester United left no spectator in doubt, after the game they had witnessed, that the claim was fraudulent.

Keane and Vieira had one more showdown, in that season's FA Cup final, with Vieira and his Arsenal team-mates overrun for 120 minutes as United threw wave after wave of fruitless attacks at them. Fortunate for the score to be 0-0 after 120 minutes, the Gunners became the first team to win the famous old trophy on penalties and, predictably, it was Vieira who scored the winning penalty with what turned out to be his last kick for the club. This was Keane's seventh appearance in an FA

Cup final – and the last final he appeared in for Manchester United.

Maybe the fact that he cared too much brought to an end Keane's 12 years at United. If things weren't going well, if new signings weren't working out, if the reserves or youth team were having a bad time, he took it personally. It was a 4-1 defeat at Middlesbrough on 29th October 2005 that brought it to a climax. It was a game that Roy didn't play in, or even attend. Due to an injury he had gone to Dubai to get some rest and had watched on TV, walking out at 3-1 in disgust. It was the manner in which United had been defeated that hurt him most. The following Monday Keane appeared on MUTV analysing the game – and was critical of the players. The club decided not to broadcast his comments, but an inaccurate account was leaked and by Tuesday the content was splashed all over the tabloids. At a meeting involving players and coaches following the airing of Keane's criticism of some team-mates, there was some sharp swordplay between the club captain and assistant-boss, Carlos Queiroz. Queiroz's subsequent ultimatum put Ferguson in a tricky situation   keep Queiroz or Keane. Since Keane's time was almost up, Ferguson chose his trusted Portuguese coach. It was agreed between player and manager that Keane be allowed to leave immediately, but would still be given a testimonial to mark his time at the club.

On 15th December 2005 Roy Keane was unveiled as a Celtic player. The closest relationship between any manager and player in United's history was over. Ferguson cut Keane slack for his various misdemeanors, and supported him when he walked out of the World Cup. Keane gave Ferguson his most influential figurehead, and played as though he would walk through a brick wall for him.

Overall, Keane led United to nine major honours, making him the most successful captain in the club's history. His departure is a void that Manchester United has never filled. If ever they find another midfield general who has half the skill, tenacity, courage, determination and who has anywhere near the indomitable and indefatigable spirit that Roy Keane had, they will be a very lucky outfit.

Red Nev

GARY NEVILLE
2005-2011

*'Medals are great, but the real miracle is that I shared a
dressing room with six of my best mates and my brother
for more than 10 years'*

No player polarises opinion amongst fans as much as Gary Neville. He
has lived the dream of every United supporter, given the opportunity to
play and wear the red shirt. To opposition supporters, Neville is the devil
in red that celebrates United goals at the Liverpool end and runs on a
non-defined anger. To United fans, "Red Nev" is a folk hero. The finest
right-back of his generation; dedicated to the club, he always gave
100%. Gary Neville has been one of the finest servants in the club's history. Never one to shrink from confrontation, Neville sees self-assertion
as an expression of his club's identity. The grasping of the United badge
on his shirt comes naturally. Unlike the majority of players, who grab
their shirt badge and then kiss it as they run towards their own fans –
only for them to later show that the badge, or the club which they play
for, means nothing at all – Neville's commitment to both means everything to him. Shortly before his retirement in 2011, he commented:

"I always tell the young players, if you look down at your shirt and see
a Manchester United badge, you're not having a bad day. You're doing
all right. The day I don't have the United badge on my chest will be a
sad one for me. I don't think I can ever have the same feeling playing
for another football club. That is no criticism of anyone else, but I am
so ingrained in United and it is such a big part of my life."

On 18th February 1975 Neville and Jill had their first child, a boy they named Gary Alexander Neville. Next to join the Neville household in Bury, Lancashire were the twins, Philip and Tracey. Father Neville had been on the playing staff at Lancashire County Cricket Club. There was a strong sporting ethos in the family, and as the children grew they were encouraged not only to pursue their academic studies, but their sporting abilities, too. Gary was a natural sportsman who played for an Under-11s football team whilst still only seven years old. As a United fan he was overjoyed when one of his teachers put his name forward for a trial with United's School of Excellence. Despite kids coming from all over the North West for trials, many a lot bigger than Gary, he was one of the 16 who were selected for the Under-11s at the School of Excellence. He was also picked for Bury and Greater Manchester schoolboy teams.

Training at the School of Excellence was held every Thursday and it was the first time Neville came under the influence of Eric Harrison, the coach who would be so influential in his development. As a youngster, the coaches concentrated on technical aspects: passing drills, building up touch and four and five-a-side games. For the youngsters, it made the hours spent training a lot of fun, and it produced an end product. Though technically nowhere near as good as some of the lads attending the sessions, what Gary did have as well as the basic skills was a brilliant attitude to hard work. If training started at 5pm, he would be there at 4.15 knocking a ball against a wall to practice his passing.

Gary had to work hard to progress, especially in those formative years at United. The level of competition that he faced from other youngsters was immense. He looked at local lads Paul Scholes and Nicky Butt, who were later joined by out-of-town kids like David Beckham, Keith Gillespie and Robbie Savage, and he knew he was never going to stand out technically. His progression in those early years came from his sheer determination, desire and will to make it as a professional footballer.

It was those early years at the School of Excellence, the fear that it could all end in tears, that helped shape Gary Neville's character. He put hours of extra training and fitness work in as he was never going to be the most skilful of players – but he was determined to keep up with them if they went past him. At the age of 16 Neville made the decision to alienate himself from his young friends and their social life. He knew they would be doing what teenage boys do, including having a few drinks. Neville knew he had a small chance, an opportunity nonetheless of making it as a pro, and he was never going to look back and think, 'if only I had worked harder or gone to bed earlier.' I am sure there are lads reading this who think, 'I played with Gary Neville and I was a better player than him.' The truth is they probably were – but they didn't have his dedication and didn't apply themselves to the task in the way he did.

Gary was taken on as an apprentice after Eric Harrison saw significant improvement in his abilities, mainly down to his work ethic. Harrison was so impressed with the young Neville's attitude and drive that he made the 16-year-old captain of the Manchester United youth team ahead of 17 and 18-year-olds in the team. It was a great relationship, Neville and Harrison, a coach and his most eager student. Harrison would point out a failing in Neville's play, and the youngster would go away and practice for hours until he improved. There can be no doubt that without Harrison's guidance, Neville would never have made it in the professional game. It was Harrison who converted him from a mid-field player to a defender, and it was Harrison and his coaches who put in the hours of work teaching him the art of defending.

The exploits and achievements of the famous "Class of '92" are well chronicled. But for the staff at the United School of Excellence, it must have been a pure joy working with, and watching, so many gifted and talented young players blossom. That crop of youngsters that emerged in the early 1990s are now deeply entrenched into Manchester United's rich history, and quite rightly stand alongside the famous Busby Babes who came through in the early-to-mid 1950s.

The period of 1991-1995 produced such a rich vein of talent. Not only young Gary, but other future professionals Ryan Giggs, Paul Scholes,

Nicky Butt, David Beckham, Robbie Savage, Keith Gillespie, Chris Casper, John O'Kane, Kevin Pilkington, Ben Thornley, Phil Neville, Ronnie Wallwork, David Johnson, Philip Mulryne, Terry Cooke and John Curtis. There was a bond between them, similar to the way that the Babes had grown up together. Even outside of the club, they were inseparable, hanging out together, very obviously a unit, a band of brothers. Harrison never needed to go into the dressing room on training days, as it was their second home – he could do his talking out on the pitch. They trained with the first team and never looked out of place. Sometimes Ferguson would put them against the first team to sharpen things up. Both sides would have something to prove: the youngsters showing they were ready to step up, with the first team telling them they weren't. They were competitive games as the kids were often technically better than the opposition the first team would face on a Saturday afternoon.

Even before United won the FA Youth Cup in 1992, rumours were circulating that this was a crop of players to compare to the famous Busby Babes who had first won the competition in 1953. It is incredible that the side Neville captained to victory over Crystal Palace contained no fewer than seven future internationals: Gary Neville, Nicky Butt, David Beckham, Ryan Giggs, Robbie Savage, Keith Gillespie and Simon Davies, who made a single appearance for Wales. Giggs was actually named as a sub, having already broken into the United first team.

Paul Scholes and Phil Neville are often cited as being part of this group, but Salford's "Ginger Prince" and the younger Neville only made the team for the 1993 final, which United lost to Leeds. Phil Neville was able to make up for the defeat, as he was young enough to captain the lesser-known 1995 side to victory. The 1992 line-up was:

Kevin Pilkington; John O'Kane, George Switzer, Chris Casper, Gary Neville (c); David Beckham, Nicky Butt, Simon Davies, Ben Thornley; Colin McKee, Robbie Savage.

Gary Neville's first-team debut came out of the blue for him when he was named as a substitute in a UEFA Cup first-round tie against the

Russian club, Torpedo Moscow, on 16th September 1992. It was a rather subdued Old Trafford that was to witness his first appearance as only 19,998 turned out to see a dour 0-0 draw. Nevertheless, it did not dampen the experience for the 17-year-old Neville when he entered the field of play as a second-half substitute. Although that experience whetted his appetite, it was going to be a long time before he would get a taste again.

Just one month before Gary's 18th birthday in January 1993, he signed his first professional contract as a United player. All the hard work, the extra time spent in training, the sacrifices he had made, all contributed to him achieving his dream of becoming a United player. His ambitions didn't end there though – he now had to try and cement a place in the first team. United's back four at that time was firmly established, with full-backs Paul Parker and Denis Irwin flanking Steve Bruce and Gary Pallister. Breaking into that line-up was going to be extremely difficult.

However, as Eric Harrison and Alex Ferguson were to find out, if you put an obstacle in Neville's way, he just works harder. The education Gary received from age 16 to 20 was vital. Eric and Brian Kidd instilled into him what it took to be a United player. The most important lesson was the message that 'you've never made it.' With a young player, sometimes you hear people say – 'he's made it.' Harrison and Kidd taught Neville that the opposite was true. There's always someone who has done better, although Gary did develop the winning habit early on. From the minute he joined the club – FA Youth Cup in the first year, Lancashire League Division One, then the reserve league: he continually wanted to win trophies.

On 8th May 1994, in the last Premier League game of a triumphant Double-winning 1993/94 season, Alex Ferguson decided to give Neville his first league run-out. It was a meaningless game against Coventry City that ended 0-0. The title was already won, and there was an FA Cup final to look forward to, but for Gary it was the biggest day of his life. The manager was sending him a message that he saw him as part of his future plans for United – and this was just a taster.

The 1994/95 season was Neville's breakthrough, when he became a regular member of the first-team squad. Not that it was easy for Gary, as he now had to leave the comfort and friendship of the youth team set-up and make it with the established stars. They were a group of winners, and they looked at new members and thought, 'is this kid going to keep me winning medals?' You could not afford to show weakness as players like Steve Bruce, Roy Keane and Paul Ince snarled and shouted at you for the slightest mistake. You just had to take it on board, and make sure it didn't happen again. They demanded high standards, the standards they set themselves and if you could not live up to them, there was no place for you in the team. Ferguson was always shrewd at knowing when to introduce young players, and when to take them out and rest them. Not everyone could make it, and many failed to adapt.

During the summer of 1994, Ferguson bought central defender David May from Blackburn Rovers. Paul Parker picked up an injury in pre-season, and May slotted into the right-back position. When May picked up an injury, Roy Keane was moved into the back four.

In September, United played a League Cup second-round tie at Port Vale. For the first time Ferguson decided to use the competition as an opportunity to give some of his youngsters experience. In came Gary Neville, Nicky Butt, Keith Gillespie, David Beckham, Paul Scholes, Simon Davies and, on the bench, was John O'Kane. United played well in a 2-1 victory, with the young Scholes scoring both goals. Neville would go on to make a further 23 appearances in the first team that season, but he found it a difficult experience and a very steep learning curve. The season was not a memorable one for United. There were certainly highlights, such as the 9-0 thrashing of Ipswich. But United failed where it really counted, losing out on the league to a faltering Blackburn Rovers side on the final day (who lost to a late goal in a 2-1 defeat at Liverpool), having only drawn with West Ham at Upton Park. Six days later, Gary played in his first FA Cup final at Wembley, but it was to be a bittersweet experience for him as Everton defeated United 1-0.

There was one personal landmark to look back on with pride. The summer of 1995 saw Gary win his first cap for England when manager Terry Venables selected him to play against Japan in the Umbro Trophy tournament. It was quite a landmark, as well as another of his dreams fulfilled, as he set a new record for the fewest club appearances before earning an England cap since World War II.

A lot of people talk about the 1994 side as one of the greatest ever United teams, and it is certainly one of the most powerful. But it was an ageing side and the manager felt that it was never going to win the European Cup with their British style. He needed to introduce a more fluid European approach, but what people didn't know was that before the 1995/96 season three established first-team internationals would leave in Paul Ince, Mark Hughes, and Andrei Kanchelskis. There were elements of the '94 team still in place like Roy Keane and Peter Schmeichel, but now was the time to bring in the youngsters.

The first game of the 1995/96 season saw United field a team against Aston Villa that included Gary Neville, Nicky Butt, Paul Scholes and Phil Neville, with David Beckham and John O'Kane on the bench. An experienced Villa side eased to a 3-1 victory, leading a smug Alan Hansen to make his famous "You'll win nothing with kids" comment on *Match Of The Day*, a phrase that will haunt him for the rest of his days.

For Neville, it was the beginning of a glorious period in his playing career. After that Villa Park defeat, the team went on to win the Premier League and FA Cup Double. In the cup final at Wembley, United met Liverpool and again it was another learning curve for the young Neville. He had to cope with the disappointment of being named as one of the substitutes, his own place in the team being taken by brother Phil. However, he did come on and witness first-hand the feeling of winning the cup as Eric Cantona's late winner secured United's second Double.

There was no rest that summer. Gary was now an integral part of Venables's England set-up as the hosts prepared for the European Championship. For the Neville family it was a proud time as Phil had also broken into the England team, earning his first cap against China in May 1996. The tournament went well for hosts England as they reached the semi-final against Germany. Unfortunately, Gary was ruled out having received a second booking of the tournament in the quarter-final against Spain. Gary could only sit and watch as England were defeated on penalties, following a dramatic 1-1 draw after extra time.

On Gary's return to United for the start of the 1996/97 season he was rewarded with a five-year deal, his first long-term contract at the club. He celebrated as United retained the title, with Gary cementing the right-back position at the club and soon after, he was captaining the side for the first time. Having suffered a number of injuries to more established stars in a March 1998 Champions League quarter-final clash at Monaco, United were due to host Sheffield Wednesday the following Saturday. A day before at training, assistant-manager Brian Kidd informed Gary that he would be skipper. It was not a game that will live long with United fans as the side went down 2-0.

The rest of the season petered out as United threw away a substantial lead to allow Arsenal to win their first Premier League trophy. It was the first time that Gary and his team-mates had finished the season empty-handed since 1995, and the critics believed that the team needed breaking up like the previous trophyless team. Not for the first time, United's players answered their critics in a most spectacular fashion.

When the 1998/99 season kicked off, nobody at United could have imagined what lay in store. In the space of two weeks at the end of the campaign they secured the Premier League title, the FA Cup and became European champions in dramatic style. The league was not settled until the final day against Tottenham Hotspur at Old Trafford – and they had to come from behind to do it. Les Ferdinand had lobbed Spurs ahead, but goals from David Beckham and Andy Cole wrenched the title back from Arsenal.

In the FA Cup there was a thrilling third-round tie at Old Trafford against arch-rivals Liverpool. Michael Owen had put the Merseysiders in front after only three minutes, and it was a lead they held until the dying seconds. Dwight Yorke equalised and then with almost the last kick of the game, Ole Gunnar Solskjaer scored to win the tie.

There was more drama in the semi-final against Arsenal at Villa Park. With the scores level and United down to 10 men following Roy Keane's sending off, Arsene Wenger's side were awarded a last-minute penalty. Dutchman Dennis Bergkamp, already a scorer in the match, strode forward and drove the ball towards the right-hand corner. However, Peter Schmeichel had read the kick and pushed the ball away to safety.

Extra time had to be played, and Ryan Giggs stamped his name on the competition by scoring one of the most brilliant individual goals ever seen. It secured United a place in the final – and at Wembley the match was more straightforward as Newcastle were defeated 2-0.

The "Holy Grail" was now a distinct possibility and it was on to Barcelona for the Champions League final against Bayern Munich. It was to be another never-to-be-forgotten night of high drama. Again, trailing 1-0 going into three minutes of time added on, United drew on their incredible reserves of nerve and strength to turn the situation around. First Teddy Sheringham equalised, and then in the final seconds he flicked on a David Beckham corner and Solskjaer stole in at the back post to divert the ball high into the net.

The United end at the Nou Camp went absolutely crazy. All those boys that Gary had grown up with and come through the United ranks with were now treble winners. But such is Gary's hunger for the game that the achievement was never going to be enough – he has always wanted to win everything for Manchester United every season. After that night in Barcelona, Gary Neville was to pick up another five Premier League winner's medals, as well as an FA Cup winner's medal.

Some say it is how you handle defeat that shows how you can judge a man – and Ferguson saw all he needed to on 10th March 2004 when United were knocked out of the Champions League by a last-minute Porto goal. What happened afterwards in the Porto dressing room left an enduring memory with the self-styled "Special One" Jose Mourinho, who had celebrated his side's late strike with a dash down the touchline.

"You would have thought we had won the World Cup," said Mourinho. "Then there was a knock on the door. It was Alex [Ferguson], with Gary Neville. As they came in, everybody fell silent, respectful. The party stopped. The party was over. As Gary Neville went around shaking hands with my players, Alex shook hands with me and said that, after the press conference, I was invited to come to his office for a drink."

This gesture can't have been easy for Neville, whose will-to-win is as fierce as any player in the club's history. But when his manager needed a representative from the players to accompany him, he knew who he could rely on. It was just another sign that Gary was being looked up to more as a leader and, in 2005, when club captain Roy Keane suddenly left, Neville was named as the new skipper.

For Neville himself, it was a dream come true. He'd been at the club for 20 years and had seen captains come and go – Robson, Bruce, Cantona, Keane – and now he would carry the mantle. The red of Manchester United courses through his body. He is steeped in everything that the club stands for. It had been a long journey since those first formative days at Old Trafford. From the unsure but dedicated youngster he had made it to the top of his profession, both domestically and internationally. Outspoken at times, sometimes brash but always one to put the club – and the players – first. Ferguson had no hesitation in handing over the torch to Neville for he knew that encoded in his new club captain's head were the secrets of United's recent success, and the culture of insatiability that renders each triumph a fleeting moment. Does that mean that Neville curbed his personality?

Saturday 21st January 2006 – United were playing Liverpool in a Premier League fixture at Old Trafford. There were seconds to go, the score stood at 0-0. Then Ryan Giggs was fouled and awarded a free-kick midway between the touchline and the visitors' 18-yard box. Giggs stood on the ball, awaiting the arrival of United's big defenders John

O'Shea, Rio Ferdinand and Wes Brown. Liverpool had 10 men back inside their penalty area, marking man-for-man. Giggs took three paces back, looked up and then strode towards the ball, striking it perfectly. It floated towards the gathering masses inside the area. It seemed to take an age...but then there was a blur of red as Ferdinand ran forward and out-jumped the static Liverpool defenders. He met it squarely with his forehead and thumped the ball towards the goal. Jerzy Dudek, the Liverpool goalkeeper, got a hand to it...but couldn't prevent it from hitting the back of the net. Old Trafford erupted as the game was won.

Captain Gary Neville leapt into the air, then turned and ran towards the area set aside for Liverpool supporters. Standing immediately in front of them, pumping both arms in celebration, Neville grasped the United badge on his shirt and pulled it outward towards the opposition fans. His face was contorted with joy and passion. The Liverpool fans went ballistic with rage at this act of what they saw as incitement. Neville didn't care, living the moment – and it did not come better than beating United's rivals from down the East Lancashire Road in the final moments of what was a tough, and sometimes bitterly-fought game.

United fans, seeing him in his moment of triumph, responded in unison: "Gary Neville is a Red, is a Red, is a Red. Gary Neville is a Red, he hates Scousers." Forthright, indomitable and unafraid of conflict with Liverpool fans, Neville was later fined £5,000 by the FA for his actions. This behaviour played into the hands of the anti-United brigade, who accused Neville of acting like a stroppy teenager. Neville has never been one to hide his feelings, wearing his heart on his sleeve.

Like the United captains before him, he enjoyed an influential presence and was the figurehead in the dressing room. Over the years there had been many pretenders to his position, and it says much that not one was able to keep him out, injury permitting. Neville comes from an era where a player could be approached in a car park for an autograph, and would stand for hours taking pictures and signing things. A link to when footballers were at least in touch with the game's "working-class roots".

Gary's first trophy as club captain came in the League Cup final against Wigan on 26th February 2006 at the Millennium Stadium in Cardiff. The game was a comfortable 4-0 win as Wayne Rooney scored two, with Cristiano Ronaldo and Louis Saha also on target. As Gary led the team for the trophy presentation the players all wore special shirts that read "For You Smudge", referring to Alan Smith, who had broken his leg in an FA Cup tie at Liverpool the previous week. United were in the spotlight again and the United fanatic, who became captain of the team that he loves, had taken them back on to the winner's rostrum.

For players such as Wayne Rooney, it was their first medal as a United player; for Gary, it was just another to add to his growing collection but, as he said on the pitch when interviewed: "We have to win trophies at this club, it's the expectation level and rightly so. Hopefully this is the start of winning more." Typical of Neville, who'd not yet taken the winner's medal from around his neck. He was already looking to the future and more trophies, showing the hunger that Alex Ferguson looks for in his players. Unfortunately the rest of the season did not go so well, as Chelsea beat them to the title for a second successive season.

The team could not have sent out a clearer message to their supporters or title rivals that they wanted the league title back as they thrashed Fulham 5-1 at Old Trafford on the opening day of the 2006/07 campaign. In fact, it seemed at one point that they were going for every trophy available to them. For Gary, the season ended after a collision with Bolton's Gary Speed during a Premier League clash in March 2007, which left him with a combination of ankle and groin problems.

United and Chelsea were both chasing the treble. The teams met in the FA Cup final, and were knocked out at the semi-final stage of the Champions League. The Blues' draw with Arsenal handed the title to United, their first since 2003, and although Gary hadn't played since the Bolton game, he and Ryan Giggs were presented with the Premier League trophy in front of a packed Old Trafford.

It was Giggs that led the team out for the FA Cup final as both teams looked to complete a Double, Chelsea having already won the League Cup. It was the first final to be played at the new Wembley Stadium, and expectations were high for a memorable game between the two best teams in the country. Unfortunately, it was widely considered to be a disappointment as both sides were cautious, cancelling each other out.

With neither side doing enough to score in normal time, the match went into extra time for the third consecutive FA Cup final. United's best chance fell to the stand-in skipper, who was denied by Petr Cech from close range. Giggs appealed for a goal, claiming the ball had crossed the line in Cech's arms, but the linesman didn't flag – and referee Steve Bennett waved play on. Television replays appeared to show that the ball had just crossed the line, but only after Giggs's momentum had pushed the goalkeeper backwards into his own goal.

The deadlock was finally broken after 116 minutes when Didier Drogba prodded the ball past the onrushing Edwin van der Sar. It was the final, decisive act of the final and a sad end for Ole Gunnar Solskjaer, who had endured an injury-plagued final few years of his United career. The Norwegian striker made his final appearance for United before retiring three months later.

Manchester United's start to the 2007/08 season began with a whimper. At one point they even found themselves in the bottom three, though many experts were quick to point out that the last time United were in the relegation zone after three games, in 1992, they went on to win their first title in 26 years. The team played the full season without their club captain, who was fighting to recover from his injury. He did make one appearance that season on 9th April 2008, coming on as an 81st-minute substitute against Roma in the quarter-finals of the Champions League. He was welcomed back onto the pitch with a standing ovation, and was promptly given the captain's armband.

United went on to win the Premier League again on the last day of the season and it was Ryan Giggs who went up and collected the trophy. The team also met Chelsea in the Champions League final in Moscow. The final marked the 50th anniversary year of the Munich Air Disaster, and the 40th of their first European Cup victory at Wembley. There was a poetic inevitability that United would reach the final of the competition.

The match took place on Wednesday 21st May at the Luzhniki Stadium in Moscow. For the first time in the competition's history, it was an all-English affair. Neville was ruled out by injury, which must have cut him to his very core on this night of all nights.

It just felt like destiny was on United's side that evening, as if they were playing for the memory of the Babes. Neville would have given anything to be on the pitch, captaining the side on such a historic night. One consolation was that Paul Scholes, who had so unjustly missed out on the '99 final, got to play in a European final nine years later.

United started much the brighter and Cristiano Ronaldo opened the scoring with a header. They could have scored more, but let Chelsea back into the game just before half-time when Frank Lampard levelled. There would be no more goals and the game went to penalties. Rio Ferdinand, who was captaining the side that night, won the toss and chose for United to go first in the shoot-out. The penalties were all scored until it came to Ronaldo, who missed and handed the advantage to Chelsea. The remaining United players did their job and scored their penalties and so it fell to captain and self-styled "Mr Chelsea" John Terry to score the final penalty and win the Champions League.

We shall never know what happened that night, if it was the rain or the ghosts of the Busby Babes, but Terry lost his footing when planting his standing foot by the ball and, even though Edwin van der Sar was sent the wrong way, Terry's miss-hit effort hit the outside of the right post and went wide. When Giggs slotted home his penalty the Dutchman pulled off the crucial save. Distracting Nicolas Anelka, he pointed to his left but correctly dived to his right to deny Anelka, securing United European football's top prize for the third time. The United squad and staff ran onto the pitch including Gary Neville but, unlike his team-mates who celebrated with each other, he went over to the distraught

Chelsea captain to offer words of consolation before going to celebrate.

Gary did get himself back in the team for the start of the 2008/09 season, and was captain for the FA Community Shield against Portsmouth at Wembley. The match marked the shield's 100th year, which was also won by United in 1908. It was his first start in 17 months, and he was substituted halfway through the second half. He was though on hand to go up and collect the shield as United won the game on penalties.

On 21st September 2008 Neville started his first league game in almost 18 months when he played against Chelsea. It was obvious for everyone to see that Neville was no longer the force that he had been on the pitch, and that he had lost some pace. He did at least offer experience and leadership, and he was obviously in Ferguson's plans.

United competed in the 2008 FIFA Club World Cup, which had been revamped to include the club champions from each of FIFA's six continental confederations. Having overcome Gamba Osaka 5-3 in the semifinal, United faced South American champions LDU Quito at the Yokohama International Stadium in Japan on 21st December. The Quito goalkeeper Jose Cevallos made a series of stops to deny Wayne Rooney, Carlos Tevez and Park Ji Sung in the first half, as United dominated.

United's hopes were hit when Nemanja Vidic was sent off after 49 minutes for lashing out with an elbow, but Rooney won it with a neat finish into the bottom corner on 73 minutes. Gary was disappointed to only be a substitute for the game as Rio Ferdinand led the team out, but he did get onto the pitch on 85 minutes. Neville and his United teammates duly celebrated, collecting the world crown to go with their Premier League and European titles secured earlier in 2008 – becoming the first English club to win the global event in its current format.

It was a stop-start season for Neville, as he never got a run in the side. He missed the League Cup victory over Tottenham and was only making fleeting league appearances. Meanwhile United's main title contenders were Liverpool, who were determined to stop their rivals from equalling their 18 top-flight titles record. It was a close-run thing, but on 16th May United were confirmed as champions courtesy of a 0–0 draw at home to Arsenal. Gary Neville held the trophy above his head and celebrated as if it were his first – but disappointment was to follow.

United reached the Champions League final for the second year running and it was the showpiece everybody wanted, against Barcelona. For Gary, as with the previous year, he played no part and wasn't even a sub. It was a cruel twist of fate as once again, like Denis Law and Roy Keane before him, Neville as club captain missed the final of Europe's premier competition. There must have been mixed emotions as he watched United concede early, and then look on as his team-mates spent the rest of the game chasing the ball – only to concede another late goal. There was the sense of 'what could have been', with Gary knowing that the Champions League is not just won or lost by the players on duty on the final day, but by the 20 players who took part in the earlier games.

What the game and team selection did do was tell you everything you need to know about the United boss. Some managers would have let sentiment get in the way and found a place on the bench for Neville – but not so Ferguson. With him it is all about what is best for the team and Neville, more than anyone, knows that to be the case. He had seen great captains like Robson and Bruce miss out on finals in the past, knowing that Ferguson was always looking to the future.

The 2009/10 season was a disappointment for United as they lost out to Chelsea by a single point in the league and were stopped from reaching a third consecutive Champions League final by Bayern Munich, having been in a commanding position. The one consolation was the League Cup, where United met Manchester City in an epic two-legged semi-final. The matches were the first time in nearly six years the two sides had met in a cup tie, and the first time in over 40 years that they had played in a semi-final. The first leg was played at the City of Manchester Stadium and saw City take a 2-1 lead into the second leg.

United set the pace at the start of the home leg, but it was City who made the better chances. Nevertheless, the first half passed without a goal – and United soon took the lead seven minutes into the second half when Paul Scholes' low shot found the corner of the net. Michael Carrick doubled United's lead with 20 minutes left, but former Red Carlos Tevez drew City level on aggregate five minutes later. With the scores level going into added time, the tie was set for a further 30 minutes of play before Ryan Giggs' cross into the six-yard box was headed home by Wayne Rooney to secure another trip to Wembley.

United's opponents in the final were Aston Villa, and Gary Neville found himself on the bench. The game started perfectly for the Midlands side as James Milner put them ahead from the penalty spot after five minutes following Nemanja Vidic's foul on Gabriel Agbonlahor. Villa felt referee Phil Dowd should have sent Vidic off after he hauled down the striker as he closed in on goal – and their burning sense of injustice was fuelled even further when United quickly restored equality. Richard Dunne lost possession to Dimitar Berbatov, and when he attempted to repair his error he could only find Michael Owen, who slipped a perfect finish past Villa keeper Brad Friedel.

Neville came on to make an appearance, as did Wayne Rooney, who scored the winner for United. It was another winner's medal for Gary Neville though and he would have qualified for a Premier League winner's medal as well, if Chelsea hadn't pipped the club by a point.

The start of the 2010/11 season saw the United boss announce that although Gary would remain as club captain, he would no longer be captain on the pitch. Ferguson said of Neville:

"Gary is still club captain but I have been looking for someone who is going to be playing consistently every week. Over the last two or three years we have had to pass the baton along the line a few times. We have not had a consistent captain because Gary's injuries have prevented him playing all the time. If he were available all the time he would be the captain. But I have to look at the overall picture. With all due respect to Gary's time at United, he knows and I know, we don't play him every week and I am looking for someone who does [play]."

Time and injuries had caught up with Gary. He struggled to get into the team as young Brazilian Rafael Da Silva made the position his own. When Gary did play, his lack of pace got him into trouble, forcing him to lunge into tackles. On 1st January 2011 Gary played his last game against West Brom at The Hawthorns. United won 2-1, but Neville was lucky not to be dismissed for a professional foul on Graham Dorrans. It was Gary's 602nd appearance for the Red Devils, the only club he ever played for, but it was obvious he had fallen below the standard required to wear the red shirt. On 2nd February he announced that he was retiring with immediate effect. Typical of the man, he knew when the time was right to call it a day, always putting the club before personal glory.

On 24th May 2011, the class of '92 were reunited for Gary's testimonial against Juventus at Old Trafford. Gary played in a United team that included Ryan Giggs, Nicky Butt, David Beckham, Paul Scholes and his brother, Phil. It was a trip down memory lane, and a reminder of the illustrious company he held his own with for the best part of 20 years. The smile on his face, as he was substituted near the end of the game to take the applause from the 42,000 supporters, showed he was still a fan at heart – just living the dream.

Some would say that Gary Neville was born to be club captain of Manchester United. He has worked harder and sacrificed more than any other player at the club to get to his position. His is not a story of natural talent and skill. His is a story of grit and determination, and an unerring will to succeed and win with Manchester United. He was terribly unlucky as club captain, missing two European finals due to injury. But his heart was always worn on his shirt, right next to the badge he loves.

He never had the presence of Keane or Robson, players never looked up to him as they did with Law or Cantona and he never had to carry a team like Buchan. But what can't be denied is that he has given everything for the club every time he has pulled on the red shirt and crossed the white line. When Gary dies, I can guarantee the one thing he would want writing on his gravestone: Captain Manchester United FC.

Other publications produced by Sport Media:

An amusing look at the
best of the worst
clothing crimes from
some of the biggest
names in football
£9.99

Fascinating account
of the legendary
football genius
between
1971-1973
£9.99